George J. Annas is a professor of Health Law, Bioethics, and Human Rights at Boston University School of Public Health, the chair of the Health Law Department, and a professor in the Boston University School of Law and the Boston University School of Medicine. He has taught in all three of these schools for the past thirty years. He is also cofounder of Global Lawyers and Physicians, a transnational association of lawyers, physicians, and others working together to promote human rights and health. He holds degrees in law, public health, and economics from Harvard University.

Annas is a member of the Institute of Medicine (National Academy of Sciences); a fellow of the American Association for the Advancement of Science; cochair of the American Bar Association's Committee on Health and Bioethics (Individual Rights and Responsibilities Section); an honorary fellow of the American College of Legal Medicine. In 2003 he was ranked as the nation's most cited law professor in the field of health law. He has held a variety of government regulatory posts, including vice-chair of the Massachusetts Board of Registration in Medicine, chair of the Massachusetts Health Facilities Appeals Board, and chair of the Massachusetts Organ Transplant Task Force.

Since 1991, he has written the regular feature "Legal Issues in Medicine" in the *New England Journal of Medicine,* and he previously wrote the legal feature for the *Hastings Center Report* and the *American Journal of Public Health.* His other books include *Judging Medicine* (1987); *Standard of Care: The Law of American Bioethics* (1993); and *Some Choice: Law, Medicine, and the Market* (1998).

D0048508

THE RIGHTS OF
PATIENTS

The Authoritative ACLU Guide to
the Rights of Patients

Third Edition

§

George J. Annas

General Editor of the Handbook Series
Eve Cary

NEW YORK UNIVERSITY PRESS
New York and London

NEW YORK UNIVERSITY PRESS
New York and London
www.nyupress.org

Library of Congress Cataloging-in-Publication Data
Annas, George J.
The rights of patients:
the authoritative ACLU guide to the rights of patients /
George J. Annas.—3rd ed.
p. cm.—(An American Civil Liberties Union handbook)
Includes bibliographical references and index.
1. Hospital patients—Legal status, laws, etc.—United States.
2. Hospitals—Law and legislations—United States.   I. Title.   II. Series
KF3823.A96   2003
344.73'03211—dc21
ISBN 0–8147–0503–0 (pbk. : alk. paper)   2003004765

New York University Press books are printed on acid-free paper,
and their binding materials are chosen for strength and durability.

Manufactured in the United States of America

p 10 9 8 7 6 5 4 3 2 1

To Jay Katz and Jay Healey

Contents

Introduction to the ACLU Handbook Series
Eve Cary, General Editor

This book is one of a series published in cooperation with the American Civil Liberties Union (ACLU), which are designed to inform individuals about their rights in particular areas of law. A guiding principle of the ACLU is that an informed citizenry is the best guarantee that the government will respect individual civil liberties. These publications carry the hope that individuals informed of their rights will be encouraged to exercise them. In this way, rights are given life. If rights are rarely used, however, they may be forgotten and violations may become routine.

In order to understand and exercise individual rights, it is important to know something about how our legal system works. The basic document that sets up our legal system is the United States Constitution. The Constitution explains how we elect the government of the United States and provides the government with the specific powers it needs to run the country. These include the power to pass laws that are "necessary and proper" for carrying out the other powers. The government does not have the authority to do anything that the Constitution does not permit it to do. Therefore, a better question to ask than "Do I have the right to do this?" is "Does the government have the right to stop me from doing this?"

Although the government may not deny a citizen the right to do something unless the Constitution gives it the power to do so, the framers of the Constitution thought certain rights are so critical they should be specifically guaranteed. Therefore, the framers added ten amendments, known as the Bill of Rights, that are among the most important rights the government may never deny to its citizens. Four of the amendments to the Constitution are particularly important for individuals seeking to understand their rights in relation to the government.

The First Amendment contains two important statements. The first is that "Congress shall make no law . . . abridging freedom of speech, or of the press; or the right of the people peaceably to assemble, and to petition the government for a redress of grievances." This means that a person cannot be forbidden from or punished for expressing opinions out loud or in print, either individually or with a group of people, as long as he or she does it at a reasonable time and in a reasonable place and manner.

The second statement of the First Amendment is that "Congress shall make no law respecting an establishment of religion, or prohibiting the free exercise thereof." This means that the government may neither prohibit nor encourage the practice of a particular religion; indeed, government may not encourage the practice of religion at all. In short, religion is none of the government's business.

The Fourth Amendment says, "The right of the people to be secure in their persons, houses, papers, and effects, against unreasonable searches and seizures, shall not be violated, and no Warrants shall issue, but upon probable cause, supported by Oath or affirmation, and particularly describing the place to be searched, and the persons or things to be seized." This means that the police may neither search a person nor anything he or she is carrying, nor may they make an arrest, unless they have a very good reason for believing that the person has committed a crime. Moreover, they may not search a house or other private place without a warrant signed by a judge who has decided it is reasonable to believe that the person involved has committed a crime. (Note that the police have more leeway in searching automobiles.)

The Fifth Amendment says, "No person shall . . . be deprived of life, liberty, or property without due process of law." This means that the government may not punish individuals without giving them a fair chance to defend themselves.

In addition to the rights guaranteed by the Bill of Rights, the Fourteenth Amendment says, "No State shall deprive any person of life, liberty or property without due process of law; nor deny to any person within its jurisdiction the equal protection of the laws." This amendment means that, just as the federal government may not punish individuals without giving them a fair chance to defend themselves, the government of a state may not do so either. Moreover, all laws must apply equally to all citizens who are in the same situation as one another. For example, the government may not pass a law saying that people of one race or sex or religion are allowed to do something that people of another race or sex or religion are not allowed to do. (It may, however, pass laws that apply to children but not to adults, since children are not always in the same situation as adults. For example, laws requiring children but not adults to go to school are constitutional, as are laws prohibiting children from buying alcohol and cigarettes.)

Before going any further, it is important to understand two things. First, when we talk about "the government" in this book, we mean not only elected officials but also the people who are hired to work for the government, such as police officers and public school principals. All of these people must obey the Constitution when they are performing their jobs.

Second, the Constitution applies *only* to the people who work for the government. It does not apply to private individuals or people who work in the private sector. This means, for example, that while the principal of a public school may not make students say prayers in class because that would violate the First Amendment guarantee of freedom of religion, students in parochial or other private schools may be required to pray.

In addition to the United States Constitution, each state also has its own constitution. Many of the provisions of these state constitutions are the same as those in the United States Constitution, but they apply only to the actions of state officials. Thus, a public school principal in New York is prohibited from holding religious services in school, not just by the federal Constitution but also by the New York State Constitution. While a state may not deny its citizens rights guaranteed by the United States Constitution, it may, and often does, provide more rights. For example, while the Supreme Court has held that the death penalty does not violate the federal constitution, the Massachusetts Supreme Court has held that it does violate the Massachusetts Constitution.

Although federal and state constitutions do not oversee the actions of the private sector, limitations on personal behavior do exist. Both Congress and all of the state legislatures pass laws that apply to the private sector. The laws enacted by Congress are for the entire country. Those passed by the state legislatures are just for the people of that state. Thus, for example, people in New York may have more or fewer or different rights and obligations than do the people in Louisiana. In fact, in Louisiana anyone over the age of eighteen can buy alcohol, while in other states the legal drinking age is twenty-one.

Just as we have separate federal and state governments, we also have separate systems of federal courts and state courts. The job of the federal courts is to interpret laws passed by Congress; the job of the state courts is to interpret laws passed by their own state legislatures. Both courts have the power to interpret the United States Constitution. State courts may, in addition, interpret their own state constitutions.

In this book, you will read about lawsuits that individuals have brought in both federal and state courts asking the courts to declare that certain actions by state officials are illegal or unconstitutional. In the federal system, these suits are filed in a district court, which is a trial court that decides cases in a particular district. The district court hears the evidence and reaches a decision. The losing party may then appeal to one of the thirteen circuit courts of appeals, which hear appeals from several districts. The loser in the Circuit court may ask the Supreme Court of the United States to decide the case. Because the Supreme Court agrees to hear only a small fraction of the cases that litigants wish to bring before it, as a practical matter, the circuit court is usually the court of last resort. Each state also has its own court system. All are a little different from one another, but each works in basically the same way as the federal court system, beginning with a trial court, which hears evidence, followed by two levels of appellate courts.

In such a complicated system, it is inevitable that courts may disagree about how to interpret a particular law. When this occurs, the answer to the question "What are my rights?" may be "It depends where you live." Moreover, the law may change; in some areas of law, it is changing very rapidly. An effort has been made in this book to indicate areas of the law in which movement is taking place, but it is not always possible to predict precisely when this will happen or what the changes will be.

If you believe that your rights have been violated, you should, of course, seek legal assistance. The ACLU affiliate office in your state may be able to guide you to the available legal resources. If you consult a lawyer, take this book with you as he or she may not be familiar with the law applicable to your particular situation. You should be aware, however, that litigation is usually expensive, takes a long time, and carries with it no guarantee of success. Fortunately, litigation is not always necessary to vindicate legal rights. On occasion, government officials themselves are not aware of their legal obligations to respect the rights of individuals and may change their practices or policies when confronted by an individual who is well informed about the law. We hope that this book will help provide the basic information about the legal principles applicable to this area of law and will, as well, suggest arguments that you might make on your own behalf to secure your rights.

This introduction is being written in the aftermath of the terrorist attacks on the World Trade Center and on the Pentagon. It is precisely at times of national stress like these that civil liberties come under attack. It is therefore crucial in such times that Americans rededicate themselves to protecting the precious liberties that our Constitution and laws guarantee us. This book is part of that effort.

The principle purpose of this handbook, as well as the others in this series, is to inform individuals of their legal rights. The authors from time to time suggest what the law should be, but their personal views are not necessarily those of the ACLU. For the ACLU's position on the issues discussed in this handbook, the reader should write to Public Education Department, ACLU, 125 Broad Street, 18th Floor, New York, NY 10004-2400 or access <http://aclu.org/>.

PREFACE

It has been almost thirty years since the first edition of this book was published, and fourteen years since the second edition appeared. In the second edition, I decided to change the title of the book to *The Rights of Patients* (it was originally published as *The Rights of Hospital Patients*). This was because although almost all major surgery, much high technology medicine, most teaching, and most serious injuries to patients occur in hospitals, there is much more to health care than hospital care. Moreover, patient rights center on the individual patient, and the rights of the patient as person, not the setting in which the patient is treated. People have rights because they are human beings with dignity not because of where they are treated. Although much of *The Rights of Patients* deals directly with hospital-based care, most of the specific patient rights discussed apply in all health care settings, such as physician offices and clinics, and in other in-patient settings, such as long-term care facilities as well. This book, nonetheless, does concentrate on legal rights in the acute-care setting, and it is not the reference you should use for an understanding of patient rights in either mental health care or long-term care.

Thirty years ago, patient rights was in its infancy and the term itself was contested. It was not uncommon for physicians to assert that patients had needs, not rights, and that asserting rights brought unnecessary conflict and discord into the doctor-patient relationship. This attitude has almost entirely disappeared—so much so that the term "patient rights" is now taken for granted and is used in a variety of contexts to promote a variety of agendas, not all necessarily good for patients. The major change in American health care in the past decade, for example, has been the rise of managed care and for-profit medicine, coupled with the almost religious belief that the market can effectively and efficiently deliver health care (at least to those who can afford to pay for it). Reaction to overzealous cost-containment has produced a major negative public reaction to managed care, sometimes termed the managed care backlash.

The proposed solution was misleadingly labeled a "patient bill of rights" by both President Bill Clinton and President George W. Bush and by others as varied as Families USA and the American Medical Association. It seems that no one can publicly oppose patient rights any more, although getting bills out of conference committee has been incredibly difficult for Congress (the major issue being whether to "federalize" managed care lawsuits or let them be brought in state court). This particular type of "patient bill of rights," however, has little to do with what might be categorized as "hard-core" patient rights: the right to informed choice, to dignity, to emergency care, to privacy and confidentiality, and to have an advocate help you exercise your rights. Instead, the congressional bill of rights concerns managed care reform only and should be more properly labeled simply "managed care reform."

Managed care reform rights, of course, are severely limited both in terms of coverage and content. In terms of content, they apply only to people in managed care plans. And in terms of coverage, the "rights" are narrow ones (although important), such as the right to a copy of your contract with the health plan, the removal of any "gag" rules that would prevent physicians from talking with patients about certain things such as treatment options, payment for emergency care if a "prudent layperson" would have thought seeking it necessary, direct access to obstetrician/ gynecologists for women, and an internal appeals mechanism that can be used to challenge denials of benefits. The most contested right is the right of patients to sue their health plans for negligence, something all people have a right to do when harmed by, for example, their physicians or hospital. This is remarkable, because the only two entities that cannot now be sued for their own negligence in the United States are managed care plans and diplomats.

I strongly favor reforming managed care. Nonetheless, managed care reform is no substitute for taking seriously core patient rights, and no one should be confused into thinking it is. The phrase *patient rights* has been used in other strange contexts as well. As medical historian David Rothman has pointed out, the power of the concept of patient rights can also have unintended consequences by being expropriated for purposes that can actually be dangerous or excessively expensive for patients. Examples include direct television advertising of expensive prescription medications under the guise that the public has a "right to know" and the dangerous movement promoting physician-assisted suicide under the misleading rubric that patients have a "right to die."

On the positive side of the ledger, with globalization and the increasing attention to universal human rights, patient rights have increasingly come to be recognized as a particularly important component of human rights. In this regard, although this third edition continues to focus on U.S. law, many of the basic patient rights, including informed consent and dignity, are universal and apply in every country of the world. No country in the world, however, spends as much money as the United States does on medical care (almost $1.3 trillion annually, $4,500 per capita, or more than $1 of every $30 that is spent in the entire world on everything). The extraordinarily high cost of American medicine means that economic considerations will often take precedence over medical ethics and sometimes even over legal requirements. Economics and technology often seem to dictate choices. Human rights is the only force powerful enough to prevent medicine from becoming a profit-motivated, impersonal, and dehumanizing industry.

Unlike rights in many other areas of life, most of us prefer not to think about patient rights, because we don't like to think of ourselves as sick or dying. We are masters of denial. Nonetheless, we will all likely be seriously ill many times in our lives, and we will all die. In addition, we will have many other opportunities to help our family and friends when they are ill. It is important that we all be active decision makers in medical treatment, because medical decisions will have a powerful influence on our bodies and our lives. That is why medical decisions are fundamentally personal decisions: different people place different values on longevity, functioning, risk, and appearance.

The Rights of Patients is built on three premises: (1) patients have rights that are not automatically forfeited by becoming sick or by entering a care facility or a doctor-patient relationship; (2) many physicians and care facilities fail to recognize the existence of these rights, fail to preserve, protect, and promote them, and limit their exercise without effective recourse for the patient; and (3) a doctor-patient partnership in which the rights and personhood of the patient are respected is the most beneficial model for medical decision making for both patients and physicians.

As I will note often in this book, when patients are sick they are "not themselves" and are often incapable of exercising their rights on their own. Accordingly, patients need someone I term a *patient rights advocate* to help them. For almost two decades, I have hoped that health care institutions (or an agency of state government) would routinely make such an advocate available to sick people. This hasn't happened, and it is now apparent that each of us will have to take on the responsibility of identifying our own advocate. This will usually be a family member or close friend, someone who can help us make important medical decisions and protect us from medical mistakes.

In order to be an effective advocate, it is necessary to know what rights patients have and to have some idea of how to assert them effectively. The goal is primarily to prevent problems and secondarily to solve problems that do occur as close to the bedside as possible, with the focus always on the patient. The foremost purpose of this book is cataloging and explaining the rights of patients and detailing how those rights can be exercised. Knowledge of rights can increase the likelihood that they will be respected; and knowledge also provides a critical tool for self-protection.

Most of the legal rights discussed in *The Rights of Patients* have been enunciated by the courts, often in the context of malpractice suits brought against physicians and hospitals by injured patients. Successful suits demonstrate that the physician or hospital not only injured the patient but also did so as a result of substandard care, termed *negligence*. Collecting these cases, as is necessary to explore and explain the legal rights of patients, present health care institutions and physicians in a less-than-favorable light. Knowledge of these cases, nonetheless, is essential to an understanding of patient rights. In addition, I emphasize throughout the need to be vigilant in protecting yourself from harm in the health care system.

This may seem like an indictment of the system and to some extent it is; change is needed. It is not, however, meant to be an indictment of physicians as a whole or the doctor-patient relationship, which I believe warrants strengthening, not weakening. This is because in almost every situation the physician and patient should be natural allies who seek the same goal and who are most often threatened not by each other but by external forces, such as the hospital and risk managers, the health plan and its benefit rules, and the government and its rules. Mostly, however, identifying injuries that routinely befall patients is a recognition that the health care system is extremely complex and that even a small mistake by inattention or simple exhaustion can have permanent negative consequences for the patient.

It seems best to think of this type of vigilance as analogous to defensive driving: it is not enough to simply follow the rules of the road and hope for the best. To survive driving in America, we must anticipate that some other drivers will make foolish mistakes, driving carelessly, driving drunk, or just talking energetically on a cell phone. Safety has not been "job one" in American medicine, but it is for the patient rights advocate. Promulgating and promoting a bill of patient rights is neither antimedicine nor antidoctor, any more than promoting the Bill of Rights of the U.S. Constitution can be considered antigovernment. The purpose is to promote the rights of patients and thereby to make the American health care system better for everyone.

This edition has been completely rewritten and updated to September 2003. Like the last edition, it contains fifteen chapters—some new ones and many reorganized ones. The notes contain references to legal source materials, as well as to other articles and books on the subjects under discussion. The most important change has been to emphasize the role and importance of having a patient rights advocate. This has been done by moving the chapter on the advocate from the last one in the book to chapter 2 and by adding to almost every chapter a section, "Tips for Advocates," in which the major points of the chapter are summarized in bullet form for people who are acting as patient advocates.

Much of this book is written in the third person; but when the material is personal, the pronoun *you* is used, which always refers to the reader as patient or potential patient. *Your advocate,* on the other hand, refers to the person you choose to help you during an illness, and the sections called "Tips for Advocates" are addressed directly to advocates. In this edition, three chapters on the hospital have been consolidated into one, and new chapters—"Reforming American Medicine" and "Pain, Suffering, and Suicide"—have been added. When I began this revision more than five years ago, I had planned to also write new chapters on genetics and on the Internet. Neither topic, however, turned out to warrant its own chapter. Relevant material on genetics appears in the chapter on medical records (DNA can be seen as a type of medical record), and material on using the Internet to obtain health information appears in appendix A.

The Rights of Patients is primarily a reference book for patients and their advocates, friends, family, and care providers. It has also been used as a textbook for medical students, public health students, and nursing students, and I believe it should be required reading for medical house staff. I also believe it should be available in every hospital gift shop. Even if you don't read any more than this introduction, it may benefit you to have the book visible during hospitalization for an illness. Many people have reported that they believe their care in the hospital was improved simply by placing this book on their bedside table. If so, this is an example of how rights safeguard us all, sometimes even if we are unaware of their existence. But I hope you do read more. My purpose in writing this book is to encourage patients to exercise their rights, especially by having a knowledgeable patient rights advocate, and to help health professionals recognize, understand, and respect patient rights. The goal is to resist the dehumanizing effect of cost-containment and medical technology by re-asserting the primacy of the patient as person.

The last two editions of *The Rights of Patients* were dedicated "to the sick, and the healers who treat them as persons." I obviously like that dedication; but at the beginning of a new century, I have decided to dedicate this edition to the two people who have had perhaps the most profound effect on promoting patient rights in the twentieth century: my friends and colleagues psychiatrist and professor Jay Katz of Yale University Law School and lawyer and professor Jay Healey of the University of Connecticut Medical School.

ACKNOWLEDGMENTS

This now thirty-year ongoing project to protect and promote patient rights was not (and could not have been) done alone. The book has been greatly enhanced by the comments, criticisms, and debates with my colleagues at the Health Law Department of the Boston University School of Public Health over the past quarter century. Leonard Glantz (who is also the school's associate dean) has been especially generous and insightful in his critiques of the entire work; Wendy Mariner (who is also the director of the department's Patient Rights Program) has been especially helpful in placing patient rights in the context of the American health care "system"; and Michael Grodin (with me, the cofounder of Global Lawyers and Physicians and an expert on medical ethics) has made me always try to see the issues from the clinician's point of view as well. In addition, I am pleased to acknowledge the insights of my law, medicine, and public health students over the past three decades, many of whom will find their questions reflected in this book.

Special thanks are also due to other health law colleagues, especially Ken Wing, Barbara Katz, Lori Andrews, and Frances Miller, and most of all to my mentor Jay Katz and my star student, the late Joseph (Jay) M. Healey. Comments by Gail Douglas and John Tobias Nagurney were also invaluable, as were those of Ann Blattner. All of the physicians, lawyers, and judges I have had the privilege to address on the issues discussed in this book have contributed to my thinking on patient rights through their questions and comments. Dozens of law students and public health students have researched various parts of the book over the years, and I thank them all, with special thanks to A. B. Maloy. Manuscript preparation was expertly done by Emily Bajcsi, and administrative support was expertly supplied by Marilyn Ricciardelli and Sarah Linville. Mary Annas also gets special thanks for preparing the index. The consistent support of my work on patient rights over the past three decades by the Boston University School of Public Health, especially of Deans Norman Scotch and Robert Meenan, as well as the Rubin Family Fund, made this third edition possible.

THE RIGHTS OF
PATIENTS

1

Patient Rights

B oston *Globe* medical reporter Betsy Lehman undergoes a stem cell transplant to treat her breast cancer. A young physician misreads the protocol, and she is given four times the proper dose over a period of days. Desperately ill, she calls a friend to say "something's wrong"; a little more than an hour later she is found dead in her room. She was thirty-nine years old and one of forty-four thousand to ninety-eight thousand patients who die each year in the United States from medical errors.

Dawnelle Barris brings her eighteen-month-old daughter Mychelle to an emergency department because she is vomiting, lethargic, has trouble breathing, and has a temperature of 106.6 degrees. The examining physician does not order blood work but instead has Mychelle transferred to a facility run by her mother's health plan. Mychelle dies almost immediately after admission. An autopsy finds a massive infection that could have easily been treated with antibiotics. Mychelle is just one of the many victims of "patient dumping," transferring patients to other hospitals not to improve their treatment but to save money.

Eighteen-year-old Jesse Gelsinger travels across the country to participate in a gene transfer research project he thinks could help cure his condition, OTC deficiency. The research, however, is a Phase 1 trial, designed not to try to cure but simply to test the safety of the intervention. Gelsinger has a catastrophic reaction to the gene transfer and dies. His family, which saw the research as a possible treatment, is shocked, as is most of America. Nonetheless, Gelsinger is just one of thousands of U.S. patients who see even Phase 1 research studies as treatments and join them without knowing their real purpose or dangers.

1

Teenager Jesica Santillán is smuggled into the United States from Mexico in the hope that she can be treated for her serious heart condition. She is ultimately put on the waiting list for a heart-lung transplant. Tragically, an inexplicable error is made when the organs used for the transplant do not match her blood type: the potentially life-saving transplant, which is unsuccessfully followed by a second one, kills her. She is pronounced "brain dead," and her ventilator is removed even though her parents object and ask for a second opinion. The incredible medical mistake is rare, but families frequently are faced with questions regarding organ donation and determination of death on brain criteria, and the actions and explanations of physicians can make a tragedy even worse.

Catherine Shine, twenty-nine years old, comes to a major emergency department seeking care for a severe asthma attack. She soon learns that the physicians want to intubate her, a procedure she refuses. When she attempts to leave the hospital, she is forcibly restrained, her arms and legs are tied to the bed, and she is intubated against her will. No one ever questions her competence, but instead the physicians and nurses seem to assume they can do whatever they want to this competent adult patient. No one knows how many patients are restrained and treated against their will; but this is a fundamental violation of patient rights.

Each of these cases, and many more, will be used to illustrate legal principles in this book. These are extreme cases, but they all illustrate the potentially lethal consequences of ignoring basic patient rights. Patient rights are not just abstractly important: they can literally save your life.

Like a glacier, the patient rights movement has slowly but relentlessly changed the landscape of medical and health care. The idea that patients have rights was strange and even quixotic as recently as the early 1970s. And even during the 1980s and 1990s, patients and their families often had to fight for their rights in court. Today, however, the conviction that patients have rights is so ingrained that it is no longer questioned but simply asserted.[1]

There is no longer any doubt that patients have the fundamental right to make important decisions about what will (or will not) be done to their bodies by physicians and others, to obtain all relevant information needed to make those decisions intelligently, to refuse undesired medical treatment, to be treated with dignity and respect, to have their privacy respected and their medical information kept confidential, and to have a friend or family member who takes the role of patient advocate to help them assert these and other rights when they are sick. What quibbling there has been about patient rights, and about the content of various proposals for a national "patient bill of rights" (a more politically attractive term than "managed care reform"), involves primarily the circumstances under which injured patients can sue their managed care plans. Of course, as I will discuss later in this book, this is a critical issue, since lawsuits remain the primary way in which patients can hold health care providers accountable for their actions, but it is only one of the rights that patients have.

It is also a strange and uniquely American phenomenon that although we take rights in health care seriously and try to design more effective ways of promoting and enforcing them, we resist the most central patient right of all: the right to health care. There is no excuse for this. Very few sick people are in any way responsible for their illness. Illness and injury can change and diminish a person's life dramatically. Society has an obligation to provide basic medical care to the sick and injured not only because of the tremendous suffering people experience without it but also as a matter of human solidarity and decency. That the United States has not yet found a way to make health care accessible to all remains an international scandal.

Should patients be called consumers?

I use *patient* in the title of this book and believe that this word, even with its baggage of paternalism in the doctor-patient relationship ("the doctor knows best"), is the best term to describe an individual who is sick or injured and in need of medical care. That the term carries historical notions of long-suffering (from the Latin *patiens,* to suffer) and complaining behavior, however, does mean that *patient* needs some refining. There is, for example, a strong argument that the term *consumer* (or *client*) is more empowering (since, among other things, "the customer is always right").[2] Nonetheless, the truth is that only in rare settings, when someone is healthy and contemplating a choice of health plans or is undergoing some elective (often cosmetic) procedure, is it accurate to consider a person in the health care setting a consumer.

The fact that there have never been any sustained or effective consumer movements in health care, comparable to other consumer or civil rights movements, can be explained by the difference between the sick (patients) and the well (consumers). When we are sick or injured, our first priority is personal: to regain our health and identity. As F. Scott Fitzgerald observed in his masterpiece of American fiction *The Great Gatsby:* "[There is] no difference between men, in intelligence or race, so profound as the difference between the sick and the well."[3] And Susan Sontag drives the distinction home in *Illness as Metaphor,* "Everyone who is born holds dual citizenship, in the kingdom of the well and in the kingdom of the sick."[4] As sick people, we often voluntarily relinquish rights we would otherwise vigorously assert in the hope that this compromise will aid our recovery. In the words of Dr. Oliver Wendell Holmes, "There is nothing men will not do, there is nothing they have not done, to recover their health and save their lives."[5] Some of the extremes he describes include being half drowned, half cooked, seared with hot irons, and crimped with knives. We are literally "not ourselves" when we are sick.

There are other reasons why no organized patient groups exist. First, when people are very sick they are not physically or psychologically capable of either exercising their own rights or organizing to help protect and assert the rights of others. Second, most diseases are time limited; they don't last long enough for people to try to build any type of patient organization. Moreover, when we recover our health, we quickly forget what it is like to be sick. As Lorrie Moore has described it:

The healthy, the feeling well, when they felt that way couldn't remember feeling any other, couldn't imagine it. They were niftily in their bodies. Whereas the sick could only think of being otherwise. They were not in charge. They had lost their place at the top of the food chain. The feeling well were running the show, which was why the world was such a savage place.[6]

Finally, when well, most Americans prefer not to think about being sick, just as we prefer not to think about death, and so do not plan for it.

Local consumer-patient rights organizations have been built around some neighborhood health centers, and by individuals interested in specific populations (such as children and mentally ill and disabled people), specific occurrences (such as childbirth and end-of-life care), and specific diseases (such as kidney disease, breast cancer, and HIV/AIDS). There is only one national patient rights organization, the People's Medical Society; one major advocacy group, Public Citizen's Health Research Group; and one major academic group, Boston University's Patient Rights Program.[7] On the whole, patient rights as a consumer movement in health care is diffuse and unstructured. This also seems to be true around the world.[8]

The attention of the American people, nonetheless, is focused on patient rights and the increasing power of medicine to cure disease and delay death. Other important concerns are access to medical care, its quality, and its relentlessly rising cost. Access concerns have prompted greater enthusiasm for some form of comprehensive national health insurance, such as expanding the Medicare program to include everyone. Medical advances in the areas of life-prolonging technology, prenatal diagnosis, organ transplantation, and genetics have all tended to increase the technological and to decrease the human aspects of medical care. This is why the most common complaints of patients about physicians are that physicians don't listen, don't take time, and don't explain. To maintain a balance in which decision making is shared and the patient retains the right and responsibility to make the ultimate decisions regarding personal care and medical treatment, explicit recognition and protection of the legal rights of patients, especially informed consent, are essential.

What are rights?

A right to something is an *enforceable claim* to it.[9] When you are arrested, for example, you are *entitled* to be warned that you have a right to remain silent; that anything you say may be used against you; and that you have a right to a lawyer, at government expense if you can't afford one. This right is backed by law. If there were no laws concerning your rights upon arrest, you might have to appeal to some secular or religious moral rule. Some rights are unequivocal and certain, having been interpreted and applied by courts. Others are less clear because they have not been specifically ruled on by the courts or clearly articulated in statutes by legislatures. These rights have presumptive or "probable" legal status if it is probable that they would be upheld if tested in court.

Three kinds of rights are discussed in this book: *legal rights,* or claims that would certainly be enforced by law if a case went to court; *probable legal rights,* which would likely be enforced by law if a case went to court; and *human rights* (some of which have the status of legal rights themselves), which are critical to maintaining human dignity but may not yet have attained sufficient legal recognition to be enforceable in court.

As these examples demonstrate, there is no single or absolute definition of rights. To understand any definition, we must know the purpose for the definition, the audience for which it is intended, and the identity of the definer. In regard to the concept of a right, it is most helpful to think of a continuum. At one end is all the rights that are recognized as legal rights. These include the rights of citizenship arising under the U.S. Constitution and its amendments, the laws of the fifty states, and court decisions.

Somewhere near the middle of the continuum are those rights that with a high degree of probability would be recognized and enforced as legal rights by a court of law. In most situations, all that is needed is the appropriate case to present the court with the opportunity to recognize a new legal right. This type of right is the expression of a reasonable expectation of what a court would do if called on to deal with the issue. This is a *probable legal right.* It approximates Oliver Wendell Holmes's predictive theory of the law: "The prophecies of what the courts will do in fact, and nothing more pretentious, is what I mean by law."[10]

At the other end of the continuum are statements of what the law ought to be, based on a political or philosophical conception of the nature and needs of humans. In making a declaration of what we believe should be, we are making a political statement. Such rights may be considered of fundamental importance and preexist recognition by positive law. The civil rights movement in the United States provides numerous examples, as do many of the provisions in the United Nations Universal Declaration of Human Rights, adopted in 1948. Article 25 of the declaration, for example, states: "Everyone has the right to a standard of living adequate for the health and well-being of himself and of his family, including food, clothing, housing and medical care and necessary social services, and the right to security in the event of unemployment, sickness, disability, widowhood, old age or other lack of livelihood in circumstances beyond his control." This may be termed a *human right,* one intended to apply to all human beings.

This book is primarily concerned with legal rights and probable legal rights. But at times, the formal recognition of human rights (those not currently recognized by positive law) will be advocated when their existence is important to patients, since legal rights are often based on human rights. Rights are based on human dignity and protect us. If we have a right to something, we can insist on it without embarrassment or fear: We do not, for example, feel embarrassed in demanding our right to vote or exercising our right to practice our religion. Nor do we depend on our neighbor's kindness in not peeking through our window or going through our mail. Patients need not request but should insist, even demand, to be treated as persons with rights.

Is there a right to health care in the United States?

The right to health care appears neither in the U.S. Constitution nor in our Declaration of Independence (although "life, liberty and the pursuit of happiness" are all made much more difficult without proper health care). Almost every U.S. president since Harry Truman has supported universal health care. The strongest congressional expression on the subject is found in the preamble to the 1966 Comprehensive Health Planning Act, which states that "the fulfillment of our national purpose depends on promoting and assuring the highest level of health [not medical care] attainable for every person." Persons who qualify for Medicare and Medicaid enjoy a statutory right to have some of their medical bills paid, but there is no general legal right to demand medical services except in an emergency or when in state custody.

The adoption of a program of national health insurance would, by itself, serve only to expand access to payment sources without necessarily addressing the problems of access and quality. Nonetheless, since access is most often determined by the ability to pay, a comprehensive program of national health insurance would certainly be critical to the more than forty million Americans (most under the age of twenty-four) who have *no* health insurance.[11] Universal access to decent health care should be our primary health care policy goal. Nonetheless, rights *in* health care are critical, since without them, we may ultimately attain access to a system that is indifferent to both our suffering and our rights.

The right to health care is specifically recognized in proclamations of both the United Nations and the World Health Organization. It is also explicitly recognized in the International Covenant on Economic, Social and Cultural Rights (Article 12d: States shall take steps to create conditions "which would assure to all medical service and medical attention in the event of sickness"). The covenant binds individual governments that sign the treaty to work for the fulfillment of its provisions. The United States, however, has never ratified the economic covenant, having committed itself only to the rights spelled out in the companion Covenant on

Civil and Political Rights. Nonetheless, the language of the economic covenant is powerful, and the language of human rights is properly broad and challenging: in the health care field, it must include efforts to make basic health care available to all, to take action to prevent disease and injury, and to promote health worldwide.[12]

Are patient rights more important in hospitals than in other settings?

Patient rights are important everywhere. Rights protect our person-hood and our value system. Rights insist that we be treated as unique persons, and they help prevent us from being treated as interchangeable, inanimate objects. But rights have special importance in hospitals, as they do in other institutional settings, such as long-term care facilities, where individual identity is often replaced by feelings of anonymity and isolation. Patients do not check their rights at the hospital door along with their other valuables.

Patients seldom want to come to the hospital. Some uncontrollable or unexpected event, illness, or injury usually makes hospital admission necessary. Unless the patient enters through the emergency department, a physician is likely to have urged the admission and chosen the hospital. Upon arriving, the patient is required to sign a variety of forms that are generally explained only with the assurance that they are "routine." The patient may then be separated from accompanying friends or relatives and escorted to an assigned room. The patient's clothes may be replaced with a hospital gown, a one-piece garment designed for the convenience of hospital staff to make testing and treating the patient easier, but which helps strip the patient of a personal identity. The patient is given a plastic wristband with a number that may become more important than the patient's name. The patient is often confined to a bed and may even have to await permission to use the toilet.

Medication and food may be prescribed without consulting the patient. Nurses, students, aides, and physicians may regularly enter the patient's room without knocking and submit the patient to all manner of examination and treatment without explanation. Moreover, all this is carefully recorded in a written record that the patient is allowed to see, but that is available to almost anyone on the hospital staff and may be seen as well by medical researchers and insurance companies. Attempts may be made to restrict visiting hours. Finally, the most invasive and risky medical procedures will be performed only in hospitals.[13]

The hospital is a strange, alien environment to most people, and the hospital experience tends to intimidate and disorient and to discourage any assertion of individual rights. Medical care in the hospital is not a one-to-one relationship involving only the patient and physician. The patient is treated by a team of physicians, nurses, and technicians in a complex, unfamiliar, and sometimes frightening setting. Because of this, the institution-patient relationship can be more important than the doctor-patient relationship. Only a commitment to patient rights can prevent the dehumanizing influence of the institutional experience from becoming its dominant characteristic.

Is patient welfare more important than patient rights in health care?

They are both important, but rights ultimately trump welfare for individual patients in the unusual cases in which they conflict. Many health care providers seem to believe that patients should concentrate on getting better and not worry about asserting their rights. There is also a belief that physicians should attend to the patient's welfare, which is represented in a commonly heard phrase, "Patients have needs, not rights." In fact they have both. Improving health and prolonging life are the primary values espoused by health care professionals. But liberty, including the right to make one's own choice about treatment options, sometimes called autonomy or self-determination, is even more important to most people. It is, after all, the patient's body that is the site of the treatment, and it is the patient who will live with the results. Nor are these views of health providers and their patients uniquely American.

Literature from around the world informs us that many physicians cannot understand why patients seem to take personal decision making so seriously, when the physicians *know* that fighting death and teaching others to fight death are so much more important. In Aleksandr Solzhenitsyn's *Cancer Ward*, for example, a patient, Oleg Kostoglotov, discovers he has been receiving hormone therapy for cancer without his knowledge: "By some right—it doesn't occur to them to question the right—they are deciding for me, without me, on a terrible treatment, hormone therapy. This is like a red-hot iron, which, once it touches you, leaves you maimed for life. But it appears so ordinary in the ordinary life of the hospital!"[14]

Oleg fully understands that his physicians believe the treatment is absolutely necessary if he is to survive, but he also understands much more fully than they that there are fates worse than death: "What, after all, is the highest price one should pay for life? How much should one pay, how much is too much? . . . —to save one's life at the cost of surrendering everything that gives it color, flavor and sparkle. To get a life of digestion, breathing, muscular and mental activity, and nothing more? To become a walking husk of a man—isn't that an exorbitant price?"[15]

Most Americans believe we should be actively involved in medical treatment decisions and always retain the right to refuse *any* medical intervention. Nonetheless, most of us are concerned that our rights may not be honored in the hospital. Larry McMurtry's description of Emma's feelings on being hospitalized for cancer in *Terms of Endearment* conveys an almost universal resignation: "From that day, that moment almost, she felt her life pass from her own hands and the erring but personal hands of those who loved her into the hands of strangers—and not even doctors, really, but technicians: nurses, attendants, laboratories, chemicals, machines."[16]

This is powerful imagery, powerful primarily because of its accuracy. But it does not have to be like this. We do not have to choose between expert technicians and humane caretakers. We should expect better when we deliver ourselves "into the hands of strangers," and the articulation and assertion of patient rights, reinforced by a patient advocate (discussed in detail in the next chapter) can help make a humanized hospital experience a reality.[17]

But if we want to be treated like individuals while in hospitals, we will have to demand humane treatment. Even physicians dedicated to humanizing the hospital experience tend to blame the public, not the medical profession, for the current state of affairs. Dr. Melvin Konner's argument, which echoes Oliver Wendell Holmes's observations, is typical:

Most Americans are, so far, unwilling to sacrifice scientific and technical perfection even in these limited realms, believing, perhaps mistakenly, they will fare better by sticking it out in the great hospital-palaces, however cold and forbidding. For the treatment of most illnesses, for which technical knowledge and prowess make a difference, we seem to prefer a cold or even disturbed physician with full command of current medical sciences, to the most sensitive and compassionate bumbler. *Psychologically, we seem to tolerate anything, so long as the doctors make the pain go away, so long as we leave the hospital alive.*[18]

This dichotomy is a false one—there should be no need for *anyone* to have to choose between a "cold" and "disturbed" technician and a "sensitive and compassionate bumbler." Patients want and deserve physicians who are both knowledgeable *and* compassionate.

Are patient rights really important in the broader context of health care?

Patient rights are central to all humane and responsive health care systems. But there certainly are other important factors that affect patients. Another way to increase the power of the patient in health care delivery is to concentrate on wider questions, such as our economic and governmental system. Some critics believe that fundamental change in the doctor-patient relationship (to make it more responsive and equitable) is possible only after basic changes occur in our social structure. The argument is that the health system mirrors the larger social, political, and economic system of which it is a part, and that changes in health care policy and practices will come only from changes in that larger system. Problems of equity and access are thus seen not as problems of physician discrimination or hospital policy but as problems of poverty, social class, race, and geographic location.

There is merit in this argument. Not every problem can be resolved within the doctor-patient relationship because this relationship does not exist in isolation. Physicians not only have formal relationships with their patients but also have relationships with managed care plans, other health care providers, health care institutions, and numerous governmental agencies. These relationships strongly influence physician behavior. A physician's relationship with these institutions and individuals is often a very complex one, and providers themselves are often confused and therefore submissive in cases in which they do not understand their own rights.

Whether surgery is covered by insurance or by a managed care plan may depend on an interpretation of a contractual term by a clerk or on the review of its "necessity" by other health care professionals; whether medical research may be done may depend on a determination of the hospital's Institutional Review Board and the federal government's Food and Drug Administration; whether a medical student may practice medicine in a certain setting may depend on state statutes and licensing regulations; and how well a patient advocate can function may depend on the hospital policy.

In all these cases, both the physician *and* the patient will be better off if the law regarding patient and physician rights is understood and the means of change or challenge well delineated. The law informs physicians of such things as when they have the authority to treat children and emergency patients, and when a decision made by an informed patient to accept or reject treatment can be acted on without fear of criminal or civil liability. That is why *an understanding of the law and legal rights can be as important to the proper care of patients as an understanding of emergency medical procedures or proper drug dosages.*[19]

Whether our social, political, and economic system is changed in the future or not, we must all live in the real world today. In this world, knowing and asserting your rights will often be the only way to accomplish your specific care objectives.

What are patient bills of rights?

Patient bills of rights come in a variety of forms and serve a variety of functions, from educational and empowering to political and disarming. They did not become a topic of conversation until the early 1970s. Before that time, when medicine had far less to offer than it has today, people relied on the good will of health care providers to do their best to help them.

Simple statements, like the Boy Scout law, seemed to be all the guidance people needed. The Boy Scout law (which was easier to refer to before the Boy Scout organization tarnished the scouting tradition by adopting an overtly discriminatory stance against gays), states simply: A scout is "trustworthy, loyal, helpful, friendly, courteous, kind, obedient, cheerful, thrifty, brave, clean, and reverent." As I have told physician audiences (only half in jest) for the past decade: the first six of these attributes are what we patients want from our physicians, the last six what physicians want from us. Mathematician and engineer Solomon Golumb devised a code of ethical behavior for patients (tongue firmly in cheek) that advised, among other things: do not expect your doctor to share your discomfort; be cheerful at all times; try to suffer from the disease for which you are being treated; and never die while in your doctor's presence or under his direct care.

Whether or not anyone believes a simpler "golden" age of medicine ever existed, in which patients did not have to concern themselves with the qualifications of their physician and hospital or the available treatment alternatives and their risks and benefits, that era was over by the early 1970s.

In 1973, the American Hospital Association issued its patient bill of rights.[20] Although the twelve-point bill is vague and general, it was the first such document by a national organization and included many basic concepts of patient rights, such as the rights to receive respectful care, to be given complete information about diagnosis and prognosis, to refuse treatment, to refuse to take part in experiments, to have privacy and confidentiality maintained, and to receive a reasonable response to a request for services.

Informed consent, the most important of all patient rights, was articulated by U.S. judges at Nuremberg in 1947 and in U.S. courts in 1972. U.S. courts have been continually and consistently called on to enhance the power of patients ever since. For example, in a series of cases, beginning in 1976 with the case of Karen Ann Quinlan and culminating in 1997 with cases concerning physician-assisted suicide, the courts affirmed that competent patients have the legal right to refuse *any* medical treatment, including life-sustaining treatment. Moreover, patients, while competent, may legally designate another person (a health care agent or proxy) to make treatment decisions for them should they become incompetent, and patients may make their wishes known in advance through a living will. Other important rights were recognized in the 1970s by federal regulations to protect research subjects, and in state laws and court decisions to protect medical privacy and confidentiality. Patients were also granted access to their medical records, and the right to basic emergency care was protected.

The following basic patient bill of rights lists the primary rights that should be accorded all patients both as policy by health care facilities and as law by state legislatures. I developed it with Jay Healey in 1974, and I think it remains (with modifications that recognize legal developments in the past thirty years) the most complete statement of patient rights that exists. Most of the rights we advocated then have since been adopted by the courts. The term *rights* is used in the three senses described earlier in this chapter. Where the phrase *legal right* is used, the reference is to a legal right. The term *right* refers to a probable legal right, and "we recognize the right" refers to a human right. Once these rights are recognized, some mechanism for handling complaints and assigning and enforcing responsibility for upholding patient rights must also be established. If enacted into law or accepted as hospital or health care facility policy, all of these rights would then become legal rights.

The basic bill of patient rights is set out as it would apply to a patient in a hospital or other inpatient facility. The specific rights mentioned are all discussed in this book.

A PATIENT BILL OF RIGHTS

1. The patient has a right to all relevant information about proposed care and treatment.

2. The patient has a legal right to a clear, concise explanation in layperson's terms of all proposed procedures, including the possibilities of any risk of mortality or serious side effects, problems related to recuperation, and probability of success, and the patient will not be subjected to any procedure without the patient's voluntary, competent, and understanding consent. The specifics of such consent shall be set out in a written consent form and signed by the patient before the procedure is done, and the patient shall be given a copy.

3. The patient has a legal right to a clear, complete, and accurate evaluation of the patient's condition and prognosis without treatment before being asked to consent to any test or procedure.

4. The patient has a legal right to designate another person to make health care and treatment decisions for the patient, and based on the patient's own directions and values, in the event the patient is unable to participate in decision making.

5. The patient has a right to know the identity, professional status, and experience of all those providing service. All personnel have been instructed to introduce themselves, state their status, and explain their role in the health care of the patient. Part of this right is the right of the patient to know the identity of the physician responsible for the patient's care.

6. The patient has a legal right to prompt attention and treatment in an emergency situation.

7. The patient has a legal right not to be discriminated against in the provision of medical and nursing services on the basis of race, religion, national origin, gender, sexual orientation, or disability.

8. Any patient who does not speak English or who is hearing impaired has a legal right to have access to an interpreter.

9. The patient has a right to all the information contained in the patient's medical record while in the health care facility, and a legal right to examine and copy the record on request, and to have their private medical information kept confidential from those not directly involved in their care, payment of their bills, or quality control.

10. The patient has a legal right to access to a consultant specialist at the patient's request and expense.

11. The patient has a legal right to refuse any drug, test, procedure, or treatment, and to refuse to participate in educational programs.

12. The patient has a legal right to be treated with dignity.

13. We recognize the patient's right of access to people outside the health care facility by means of visitors and the telephone. Parents may stay with their children, and relatives with patients, twenty-four hours a day, and may act as the patient advocate to help the patient exercise the rights set out in this document.

14. The patient has a legal right to leave the health care facility regardless of the patient's physical condition or financial status, although the patient may be requested to sign a release stating that the patient is leaving against the medical judgment of the patient's doctor or the staff.

15. The patient has a right not to be transferred to another facility unless the patient had received a complete explanation of the desirability and need for the transfer, the other facility has accepted the patient for transfer, and the patient has agreed to the transfer. The patient has the right to a consultant's opinion of the desirability and necessity of the transfer.

16. The patient has a right to be notified of impending discharge at least one day before it is accomplished, to a consultation by an expert on the desirability and necessity of discharge, and to have a person of the patient's choice notified in advance.

17. The patient has a right, regardless of the source of payment, to examine and receive an itemized and detailed explanation of the total bill for services rendered in the health care facility. We also recognize the right of a patient to competent counseling from the facility staff to help in obtaining financial assistance from public or private

sources to meet the expense of services received in the health care facility.

18. The patient has a right to timely prior notice of the termination of eligibility for payment by any third-party payer for the expense of care.

19. We recognize the right of all patients to have twenty-four-hour-a-day access to a patient rights advocate who may act on behalf of the patient to assert or protect the rights set out in this document.

The most complete international document on patient rights, and a good place to start for anyone wishing to legally promulgate a bill of patient rights, is Europe's Convention on Human Rights and Biomedicine. It is reprinted in appendix B of this book. Bills of rights are important generally because compilations of rights make them more accessible and thus, like the American colonists, "the people might be better able to restrain the arbitrary acts of governors, courts and legislatures."[21] And, of course, patients might be better able to restrain the arbitrary acts of physicians, nurses, hospitals, and health plans. In the words of the 1841 slogan of the Rhode Island Suffrage Association: "We know our rights, and knowing, dare maintain them."

Has managed care changed patient rights?
    Managed care has certainly influenced how the term *patient rights* is used. With the rise of managed care and the consumer/patient backlash against its seemingly arbitrary denials of payment for medical services, patient rights has been used as shorthand for managed care reform. In common political discourse, patient rights in managed care refer not to the types of rights outlined in the basic bill of patient rights but to what may be more accurately termed *consumer rights:* rights consumers have to know about their health plan and its policies. These include, for example, coverage provisions, emergency care rules, the ability to see a specialist, and appeals mechanisms. President Bill Clinton unsuccessfully pressed Congress for a national "patient bill of rights," more accurately termed managed care reform, during the last three years of his presidency.
    In 1997, in response to proposals to limit "drive-through mastectomy" (modeled on the "drive-through delivery" legislation), the American Association of Health Plans (AAHP) offered *Putting Patients First,* also known as the "Nine Commandments." *New England Journal of Medicine* editor

Jerome Kassirer characterized this plan as "a thinly veiled attempt to ward off state and federal legislative actions to curb the abuses of managed care," and it may have been.[22] Nonetheless, the content of the plan is instructive. None of the nine provisions echo traditional patient rights. Instead, they all concern areas in which health plans have been widely criticized for restricting care and areas in which medical decisions seem to be made by nonphysicians.

The AAHP proposal, for example, would require members to be informed about how the health plan works (e.g., how utilization review is performed, drug formularies are set up, doctors are paid, and treatments are designated as experimental); put decisions about hospitalization for mastectomy in the hands of physicians and their patients; remove any "gag rules" restricting physicians' conversations with their patients about treatment options; describe rights of appeal; and promise "physician involvement" in quality-improvement programs, practice guidelines, and the development of drug formularies.

The AAHP proposal is similar in spirit to the National Committee for Quality Assurance's (NCQA) document *Members' Rights and Responsibilities*, which focuses on informing members of health plans about their contract with the plan, especially the rules the plan has adopted to make decisions about coverage and the procedures for addressing complaints and resolving disputes. These documents do not qualify as statements of patient rights in any meaningful sense because they concentrate only on contractual provisions.

Principles for Consumer Protection, which has eighteen provisions and was promoted by Kaiser Permanente, Group Health of Puget Sound, the Health Insurance Plan (HIP), the American Association of Retired Persons, and Families USA in September 1997, seemed to go one step further, but it was a very small step. The main thrust of the provisions, other than those that duplicate provisions in the AAHP and NCQA versions, is to require that all health plans provide certain benefits and services, such as coverage for out-of-area emergency care, availability of medical services at all times, and continuity of care through a primary care physician; to disclose specific information, such as the percentage of revenues actually spent on health care (the medical-loss ratio); and to restrict financial incentives that create conflicts of interest for physicians, including financial incentives to limit care. As the authors concede, these eighteen principles are not intended chiefly as an aid for patients or consumers but more as a marketing strategy to help nonprofit health plans compete on an equal basis.

The fact that these contract-centered consumer protection proposals are relevant primarily to payment issues makes comprehensive federal legislation to enforce patient rights seem both necessary and desirable. Enacting federal legislation is also the only way to protect all patients (not only those who are members of health plans) and to level the playing field for all health plans in the United States. What rights should be included in national legislation?

President Clinton took the first step toward a national bill of rights for patients by appointing the Advisory Commission on Consumer Protection and Quality in the Health Care Industry. In late 1997, the commission issued its proposal. Although flawed and incomplete, it recommended some of the basic elements of a national bill of rights for patients. The proposal enumerates four categories of traditional patient rights (the right to make medical decisions based on full information, the right to confidentiality, the right to emergency care, and the right to be treated with respect), as well as certain contract-based consumer protections (governing contract information, choice of a physician within a plan, and access to an independent appeals mechanism).

The core patient right is the right to receive care from an accountable physician who is required to share all relevant medical information with the patient and who guarantees the patient the right to make the final decision about treatment. The patient must be able to trust the physician to act honestly and in the patient's best interests. Loyalty to the patient also requires that the physician act as an advocate for the patient when the treatment the physician believes is most appropriate is not covered by the patient's health plan or insurer. Only provisions that honor and reinforce a physician-patient relationship based on trust deserve to be designated patient rights.

Consumer protection is also important but, as previously noted, pales in comparison with the rights of sick people in dealing with physicians and other care givers. Thus, the commission was on target to stipulate that any bill of patient rights include the following: the right to complete information about treatment, the right to emergency care based on what a prudent layperson would regard as an emergency, the right to confidentiality in the handling of medical information, and the right to respectful and nondiscriminatory treatment. As for the rights of persons enrolled in managed care plans, it is pretty thin gruel to guarantee access to the contracts they or their employers signed. Nonetheless, the call for an external, independent grievance mechanism to address denials of benefits is welcome. The grievance mechanisms available to patients are woefully inadequate in all health plans. Even though few Americans had any understanding of this proposal, in 1998, 83 percent believed a patient bill of rights should be "a binding agreement that specifies basic guidelines for patient care."[23]

Many of our rights as patients have already been articulated by the courts. Nonetheless, they often remain difficult for patients and providers alike to enforce and are especially difficult for sick people to exercise. Thus, enumerating all the essential rights in one document would facilitate an understanding of these rights and make it easier for patients to exercise them in their dealings with physicians, hospitals, and health plans. To this end, I believe any national bill of patient rights must include five core provisions.[24] These are explained in the following questions and answers.

CORE PATIENT RIGHTS

- The right to make informed decisions
- The right to privacy and dignity
- The right to refuse treatment
- The right to emergency care
- The right to an advocate

What is the right to make an informed decision?

The patient right to make an informed decision involving his or her health care includes a clear, concise explanation, in lay terms, of all proposed treatments; all reasonable medical alternatives (whether or not they are covered by the patient's health plan); the risks of death and serious complications associated with each proposed treatment and alternative (including no treatment); likely problems of recuperation; and the probability of a successful outcome (including the physician's own experiences with the treatments, risks, benefits, and outcomes). The patient has a right to know the diagnosis and prognosis in as much detail as the patient desires, as well as the existence of any research protocols that are relevant to the patient's condition and their availability. A competent patient will not be subjected to any procedures or tests without first providing informed consent. For procedures that entail a risk of death or serious disability, all aspects of informed consent will be explained on a written form (which the patient keeps and has time to think about in a nonemergency) that requires the signature of the patient or the person authorized to make treatment decisions for the patient if the patient is incompetent.

The patient has a right to know the identity, professional or student status, and clinical experience (including success rates) of all persons responsible for the patient's care. The patient has a right to know about all financial arrangements and incentives that might affect his or her care. Any patient who does not speak English has a right to an interpreter.

What is the right to privacy and dignity?

The patient has a right to privacy of both his or her body and information with respect to all medical and nursing personnel, allied health care professionals, health plan and facility staff members, and other patients. All patients must be treated with dignity and without regard to race, culture and ethnicity, religion, sex, sexual orientation, national origin, disability, age, socioeconomic status, or source of payment. The patient has a right to all the information contained in the patient's medical record and has a right to examine the record on request, to correct mistakes, and to receive a copy of it. No one not directly involved in a patient's care or in quality assurance should have access to the patient's medical records without a written authorization by the patient that is dated and limited in time and that specifies the medical information enclosed. Further disclosure of medical information without specific authorization is prohibited. The patient has a right not to be touched or treated by any particular physician or health care provider, including medical and nursing students.

What is the right to refuse treatment?

The patient has the right to refuse any drug, test, procedure, or treatment, whether the purpose is therapy, research, or education. A patient may not be discriminated against or denied any benefit by a health plan or health care professional because of a refusal to be touched or treated by a particular provider, or for refusing a particular medical treatment. A patient has the right to execute a health care proxy or a living will to direct treatment or nontreatment when the patient is no longer capable of making health care decisions, and health care professionals are obligated to honor an advance directive.

What is the right to emergency care?

The patient has a right to prompt and competent attention and treatment in an emergency. The patient may not be transferred to another facility without the patient's consent and not before the patient's condition has been stabilized and a qualified physician has determined that the transfer is in the patient's best interests because superior medical care is available at another institution and transfer is safe. If the patient does not agree to the transfer, the patient may not be transferred.

Does a patient have the right to an advocate?

The patient has the right to designate someone to act as his or her personal patient rights advocate with the authority to help the patient assert all the rights specified in the bill of rights. This includes the right of the patient to designate one or more friends or relatives to be his or her advocate. In addition, a patient in a hospital or other health care facility has the right to reasonable visitation. Parents have the right to stay with their child, and the patient's personal advocate has the right to stay with the patient twenty-four hours a day. The patient has the right to have an advocate, including a friend or relative, present during all consultations, examinations, and procedures, including the induction of anesthesia.

Why are patients so often blamed if something goes wrong?

As discussed in more detail in the last chapter of this book, acknowledging mistakes that harm patients is especially difficult for physicians, and even more so for physicians in training. Blaming the patient is easier but only adds insult to injury. Martha Lear chronicles her physician-husband Harold Lear's experience with four heart attacks and more than a dozen hospitalizations in her book *Heartsounds*. In the hospital, depersonalization is vividly portrayed and devastatingly destructive. Residents (physicians in training) were routinely uncaring and authoritarian. One resident refused Lear's request for a milder pain medication, saying, "If you want what I ordered, you can have it. If not, you'll get nothing."[25] Another resident gave him a huge dose of potassium before he had any food or water; the incident produced a stomach ulcer. And whenever he got worse or had a problem, health care professionals blamed him for it. The Lears call this response the "it's your fault" ploy:

Why did the operation take so long?
Because you lost so much blood.
Not: Because the surgeon blew it.

Why do you keep taking these tests?
Because you have a very stubborn infection.
Not: Because I can't diagnose your case.

Why did I get sick again?
Because you were very weak.
Not: Because I did not treat you competently the first time.[26]

Dr. Lear constantly asks himself if he treated patients this way and usually admits that he did. He suggests that every physician be required to spend at least a week a year in the hospital bed: "That would change some things in a hurry." And most observers agree that although physicians make terrible patients, physicians who have been patients are almost always better physicians because of the experience. When Lear views the hospital from a patient's perspective, he sees it as a vast slaughterhouse:

He thought with awe of the tension between this hushed hospital atmosphere and the things that were happening here: in this polite, muted, ordered way, people were being torn open, ripped apart, bones cracked, holes made and tubes stuck into holes, and they moved passive as cattle along the conveyor belt—oh, yes, passive, not even breathing for themselves; the tube that has been in his throat was like the slaughterhouse hook, embedded in the animal's throat, by which it, he, was hung.[27]

The "it's your fault" ploy is played out constantly in hospitals, and patients and their advocates need to be alert to it. It is not meant callously; it is almost done by rote, as if blaming the victim is actually part of the medical procedure. We all know the response to the question, "Why are you having so much trouble drawing blood?" "Because your veins are so small." (*Not:* Because I'm not very good at it.) *Saturday Night Live*'s Dana Carvey ran into an extreme case of the "it's your fault" syndrome after he underwent unsuccessful double-bypass surgery that left him with a dangerous blockage that required an emergency angioplasty. All he really wanted was an apology, but his surgeon, Dr. Elias Hanna, contended that bypassing the wrong artery was Carvey's fault, not his, because Carvey had an "unusual anatomy."[28] Carvey's malpractice case against Hanna was settled during trial. There is no excuse for physicians not to take responsibility for mistakes that harm patients. Advice to physicians is virtually unanimous: it is not only the ethically required action but also the medically and legally indicated action to inform patients immediately of mistakes that have harmed them and offer to do whatever you can to help the patient. It has been noted that medical injuries differ from most other injuries in two important aspects: first, patients are harmed by people in whom they have placed their trust to help them, and second, they continue to be cared for by members of the same profession—sometimes the same people—who have injured them. This makes the patient's reaction complex. An expert in the field, Charles Vincent, explains:

Many people harmed by treatment suffer further trauma if the incident is handled insensitively or inadequately. . . . A patient's initial reactions to a medical injury are most likely to be fear, loss of trust, and a feeling of isolation. Anxiety, intrusive memories, emotional numbness, and flashbacks are all common sequelae and are important components of posttraumatic stress disorder. The full effect of most incidents becomes apparent only in the long term.[29]

Patients have a right to expect that physicians and nurses who injure them will be open and honest about the injuries and not compound the injuries by attempting to cover them up.

Can sick patients effectively assert their rights?

Sick patients cannot assert their rights by themselves, and a statement of rights is necessary but not sufficient.[30] Patients need someone, whom I call an advocate, to assist them in asserting their rights. Parents are the natural advocates for their children. A spouse is usually a natural advocate; and children, in the case of the elderly, may also be the natural advocates for their parents. Family relationship alone, however, should not determine who a patient's advocate is. The patient, if able, should be the one to designate an advocate, who may be a best friend, personal physician, attorney, or other person in whom the patient has trust and confidence.

The main point is that when a person is sick or injured, the person (now a patient) is not in a realistic position to assert rights and runs the risk of being treated as a nonperson.

Doctors, nurses, and social workers all like to think of themselves as the primary advocate for their patients and may actually perform this role well. But only you can decide who you trust enough to help you exercise your rights. If you have no one who you believe can act effectively as your advocate, health care facilities should employ individuals capable of fulfilling this role for you (although many do not). The concept and role of the advocate is dealt with in detail in the next chapter.

NOTES

1. As medical historian David Rothman noted at a National Conference on Patient Rights, sponsored by the Health Law Department of Boston University School of Public Health in April 2000, the success of the patient rights movement has also had unintended consequences. Patient rights has become a slogan used to push a variety of agendas that can actually hurt patients, including direct drug advertising on television and the physician-assisted suicide movement, which seeks to grant physicians legal immunity for encouraging their patients to kill themselves with drug overdoses (a topic dealt with in detail in chapter 13). *See also* David Rothman, *Medical Professionalism: Focusing on the Real Issues,* 342 New Eng. J. Med. 1284 (2000).

2. *See, e.g.,* Julia Neuberger, *Let's Do Away with "Patients,"* 318 Brit. Med. J. 1756 (1999); Raymond Tallis, *Leave Well Enough Alone,* 318 Brit. Med. J. 1757 (1999); and Hazel Thorton, *Today's Patient: Passive or Involved?* 354 Lancet 48 (1999).

3. F. Scott Fitzgerald, The Great Gatsby, New York: Simon & Schuster, 1995, 131.

4. Susan Sontag, Illness as Metaphor, New York: Farrar, Straus & Giroux, 1978, 3.

5. Oliver W. Holmes, The Young Practitioner (in) W. H. Davenport, ed., The Good Physician, New York: MacMillan, 1962, 176.

6. Lorrie Moore, *Real Estate,* New Yorker, August 17, 1998, 66, 70.

7. Information on each can be found on their Web sites: People's Medical Society (www.peoplesmed.org); Health Research Group of Public Citizen (www.citizen.org); and Patient Rights Program of the Health Law Department, Boston University School of Public Health (patient-rights.org).

8. *See, e.g.,* Hilda Bastion, *Australia's Consumer Champion,* 319 Brit. Med. J. 730 (1999), and Maya Anaokar, *Patients' Rights a Charter Does Not Make,* 5 Patient's Network 5 (2000).

9. Joel Feinberg, Social Philosophy, New York: Prentice-Hall, 1973.

10. Oliver W. Holmes, *The Path of the Law,* 10 Harv. L. Rev. 457 (1897); *and see* Lon Fuller, The Morality of Law, New Haven: Yale U. Press, 1964, 106–7.

11. *See, e.g.,* John Z. Ayanian et al., *Unmet Health Needs of Uninsured Adults in the United States,* 284 JAMA 2061 (2000).

12. George J. Annas, *Human Rights and Health: The Universal Declaration of Human Rights at 50,* 339 New Eng. J. Med. 1778 (1998); *and see* Boston University School of Public Health, Health Law Dept., *Global Lawyers and Physicians* (available at www.glphr.org).

13. George J. Annas, *The Hospital: A Human Rights Wasteland,* 1(4) Civil Liberties Rev. 9 (1974). *See also* Charles B. Inlander, L. S. Levin & E. Weiner, Medicine on Trial, New York: Prentice-Hall, 1988, and Christine Hogg, Patients, Power & Politics: From Patients to Citizens, London: Sage, 1999.

14. Alcksandr I. Solzhenitsyn, The Cancer Ward, New York: Dell Pub., 1968, 346.

15. *Id.*

16. Larry McMurtry, Terms of Endearment, New York: Simon & Schuster, 1975, 356.

17. George J. Annas, Judging Medicine, Clifton, N.J.: Humana Press, 1988, 2–3.

18. Melvin Konner, Becoming a Doctor, New York: Penguin, 1988, 371.

19. George J. Annas, Leonard H. Glantz & Barbara F. Katz, The Rights of Doctors, Nurses and Allied Health Professionals, Cambridge: Ballinger, 1981, xiv–xvi.

20. The text of the American Hospital Association's original Bill of Rights:

1. The patient has the right to considerate and respectful care.

2. The patient has the right to obtain from his physician complete current information concerning his diagnosis, treatment, and prognosis in terms the patient can be reasonably expected to understand. When it is not medically advisable to give such information to the patient, the information should be available to an appropriate person acting in his behalf. He has the right to know, by name, the physician responsible for his care.

3. The patient has the right to receive from his physician information necessary to give informed consent prior to the start of any procedure and/or treatment. Except in emergencies, such information for informed consent should include but not necessarily be limited to the specific procedure and/or treatment, the medically significant risks involved, and the probable duration of incapacitation. Where medically significant alternatives for care or treatment exist, or when the patient requires information concerning medical alternatives, the patient has the right to such information. The patient also has the right to know the name of the person responsible for the procedures and/or treatment.

4. The patient has the right to refuse treatment to the extent permitted by law and to be informed of the medical consequences of his action.

5. The patient has the right to every consideration of his privacy concerning his own medical care program. Case discussion, consultation, examination, and treatment are confidential and should be conducted discreetly. Those not directly involved in his care must have the permission of the patient to be present.

6. The patient has the right to expect that all communications and records pertaining to his care should be treated as confidential.

7. The patient has the right to expect that within its capacity a hospital must make reasonable response to the request of a patient for services. The hospital must provide evaluation, services, and/or referral as indicated by the urgency of the case.

When medically permissible, a patient may be transferred to another facility only after he has received complete information and explanation concerning the needs for and alternatives to such a transfer. The institution to which the patient is to be transferred must first have accepted the patient for transfer.

8. The patient has the right to obtain information as to any relationship of his hospital to other health care and educational institutions insofar as his care is concerned. The patient has the right to obtain information as to the existence of any professional relationships among individuals, by name, who are treating him.

9. The patient has the right to be advised if the hospital proposes to engage in or perform human experimentation affecting his care or treatment. The patient has the right to refuse to participate in such research projects.

10. The patient has the right to expect reasonable continuity of care. He has the right to know in advance what appointment times and physicians are available and where. The patient has the right to expect that the hospital will provide a mechanism whereby he is informed by his physician of the patient's continuing health care requirements following discharge.

11. The patient has the right to examine and receive an explanation of his bill regardless of source of payment.

12. The patient has the right to know what hospital rules and regulations apply to his conduct as a patient.

Today, even the American Medical Association supports patient rights, although caps on medical malpractice awards remains their number one issue. Sheryl Gay Stolberg, *Lobbyists on Both Sides Duel in Medical Malpractice Debate,* New York Times, March 12, 2003, A19.

21. Patrick Conley & John Kaminski, eds., The Bill of Rights and the States, Madison, Wis.: Madison House, 1992, xiii.

22. Jerome Kassirer, *Managing Managed Care's Tarnished Image,* 337 New Eng. J. Med. 338 (1996). AAHP was planning to merge with the Health Insurance Association of America in late 2000 so the organizations could present a united front on federal patient rights legislation. Robert Pear, *Insurance Groups Seek to Merge in Battle over Patients' Rights,* New York Times, December 1, 2000, A21.

23. Louis Harris Poll conducted for Universal Health Services, January 20, 1998 (available at www.uhsinc.com/releases/release10.htm).

24. George J. Annas, *A National Patient Bill of Rights,* 338 New Eng. J. Med. 695 (1998). *See also* Wendy Mariner, *Standards of Care and Standard Form Contracts: Distinguishing Patient Rights and Consumer Rights in Managed Care,* 15 J. Contemporary Health Law & Policy 1 (1998).

25. Martha Lear, Heartsounds, New York: Simon & Schuster, 1980, 41.

26. *Id.,* at 47.

27. *Id.,* at 142–43.

28. Susan Schindehette, *The Heart of the Matter,* People, June 5, 2000, 96; *No More Heartache: Comedian Dana Carvey Settles His $7.5 Million Suit Against the Surgeon Who Blew His Heart Bypass Operation,* Time, June 12, 2000, 66.

29. Charles Vincent, *Understanding and Responding to Adverse Events,* 348 New Eng. J. Med. 1051, 1054 (2003).

30. *See* George J. Annas & Jay Healey, *The Patient Rights Advocate: Redefining the Doctor-Patient Relationship in the Hospital Context,* 27 Vand. L. Rev. 243 (1974); *and see* Jerome Kassirer, *supra* note 22, and Marcia Angell, *Patients' Rights Bills and Other Futile Gestures,* 342 New Eng. J. Med. 1663 (2000).

11

The Patient Rights Advocate

When people are sick, they are not themselves and often cannot effectively exercise their rights. Patients need help to exercise their rights; they need an advocate. The case for a patient advocate is the case for prevention: like defensive driving. It is not that we cannot trust specific drivers to drive well, to be alert, not to use drugs or alcohol; it is rather that we cannot trust *all* drivers to always pay attention and follow the rules. That is why every driver is urged to drive defensively. Likewise, every patient needs an advocate, someone to look out only for the patient's rights and welfare and to try to prevent death and harm from occurring because of sloppiness, negligence, or just inattention. In each of the cases mentioned at the beginning of chapter 1, for example, an advocate could have prevented disaster. Betsy Lehman might still have had one or more overdoses, but her condition would have been much more closely monitored, and the mistake could have been discovered before it was fatal. Mychelle would likely have gotten antibiotics in a timely manner, and transfer to another facility could have been stopped, at least until the antibiotic treatment was started. Jesse Gelsinger might still have died; but an advocate who understood the difference between treatment and research and understood the nature of a Phase 1 trial might have helped persuade him not to become involved in a phase one trial in the first place. An advocate might not have checked to make sure of the blood type of the heart and lungs to be transplanted and so saved Jesica's life. But an English-speaking advocate would have greatly facilitated discussions between the family and the transplant surgeons and would have understood the concept of "brain death" and helped ensure that her family would have been able to say good-bye to Jesica before she was pronounced dead and removed from the ventilator.

28

And Catherine Shine would less likely have had her body involuntarily invaded had her sister not been removed from her room before she was restrained.

We all need help when we are sick. Recognition of patient rights in the form of a patient bill of rights is necessary but not sufficient to protect and promote patient rights. Rights are not self-actualizing. We can look forward to the day when all hospitals and health plans and all physicians, nurses, and allied health professionals accord patients their basic human rights as a matter of course, but this day has not yet come. Until this goal is attained, mechanisms that help to ensure that patient rights are protected and honored are necessities. I continue to favor the protective mechanism Jay Healey and I first proposed in 1974: the patient rights advocate.[1] This and other approaches to protecting the rights of patients are discussed in this chapter.

As discussed in the first chapter, the idea of patient rights was novel in the early 1970s. Historians have, however, already put it in context. Paul Starr, a leading historian of American medicine, for example, discusses the patient rights movement as part of the "generalization of rights" in the United States. In addition to the movement (still scandalously unfulfilled) to recognize health care as a basic human right, he writes, there was the more attainable movement to work for: rights *in* health care,

such as the right to informed consent, the right to refuse treatment, the right to see one's own medical records, the right to participate in therapeutic decisions. . . . For every right there are always correlative obligations. . . . Recognized rights in health care, such as informed consent, obligate doctors and hospitals to share more information and authority with their parents. Thus the new health rights movement went beyond traditional demands for more medical care and challenged the distribution of power and expertise.[2]

As Starr goes on to note, increasing skepticism of the assumption that health providers always know best and always act out of concern for their patients led to the emergence of "a variety of legal safeguards aimed at limiting professional autonomy and power" and an attempt to "demedicalize critical life events, such as childbirth and dying." Courts contributed mightily to this trend, as is demonstrated throughout this book. *But patients should not need to go to court to have their rights validated or vindicated. When court intervention is needed, the system has already failed the patient.* To help protect patients from harm and to prevent system failure, the patient needs an advocate. Just as the decades before the turn of the millennium were a time of defining patient rights, the beginning of the new millennium is a time to make patient rights a reality in medical care by respecting, protecting, and fulfilling the rights of patients.

What is a patient rights advocate?

As physician-lawyer William Sage has noted, the term *advocate* "means different things to different people."[3] I use the term *patient rights advocate* to mean a person whose job is to help patients exercise the rights provided by law or in a patient bill of rights. Your advocate may be your spouse, child, parent, or other relative, or a close friend, preferably a physician, nurse, health professional, health lawyer or social worker. This individual can be termed your *personal advocate.* If you are hospitalized, you will need two or more advocates, since one of them should be with you in the hospital at all times, twenty-four hours a day. If this is not possible, your advocate should be there during all important conversations with physicians and nurses and should know their names and how to reach them.

Your advocate may also be employed by the health care facility, a health plan, an insurance company, a government agency, a consumer group, or by you, although this is unusual. The critical characteristic is loyalty: the patient rights advocate must represent only you, the patient. This is essential because the goal is to protect the patient and enhance the patient's position in making decisions, not to encourage the patient to follow hospital routine or to "behave."

A patient rights advocate is an individual whose primary responsibility is to assist the patient in learning about, protecting, and asserting his or her rights within the health care context. The specific rights of patients should be spelled out in a prominently displayed bill of rights that the hospital adopts as policy and that the advocate has the power to enforce. The word *advocate* is used in its classical sense, *advocare,* "to summon to one's assistance, to defend, to call to one's aid." Connotations of adversariness, contentiousness, and deliberate antagonism are unfortunate and unnecessary. The goals of all patient rights advocate systems are the following:

- To protect patients, especially those at a disadvantage within the health care context (for example, the young, the severely disabled, the

poor, racial and ethnic minorities, those without relatives, and those unable to speak English)
• To fulfill the right of the patient to make informed decisions about health and medical care
• To restore medical technology and pharmaceutical advances to their proper perspective by confronting the exaggerated expectations of many patients
• To reflect the reality of the health-sickness continuum, and assert the humanness of death as natural and inevitable

Most hospitals and health plans employ individuals with the job title "patient representative." This title can be misleading, since their real job may be not to represent the patient but, rather, to represent the institution that employs them.[4] I have been harsh on these individuals in the past, probably too harsh, calling them "hospital representatives." There certainly are some who do an excellent job of helping patients in spite of their potential conflict-of-interest position. I think you and your family-member advocate should give the hospital's "patient representative" a fair chance to help; but if it becomes apparent that the patient representative is unable to help you or is more concerned with protecting the hospital or health plan than looking out for you, other avenues to get results must be explored.[5]

Patients need real advocates, and whether or not the health care institution or health plan supplies one, patients will almost always do best to bring their own: either a friend or relative. In theory, anyone is qualified to perform the job, because anyone can help the patient exercise the rights specified in law and in the institution's patient bill of rights. Ideally, your personal advocate can work with the institution's formal advocate system. This will help make your advocate much more powerful because the institution's advocate is likely to have direct access to other members of the staff, administration, and relevant committees in the institution's structure and may have credibility in problem solving with the staff. No matter who you decide can properly act as your advocate, it is crucial to have one.

Isn't the physician a patient's advocate?

Ideally, the physician should be the patient's natural advocate. This is especially true when physician and patient are in agreement about the best way to proceed in treatment. But physicians are not professional advocates, as lawyers are, and even when there is no disagreement between physician and patient, the patient may need an independent advocate to, among other things, make sure that the physician has told the patient about all medically reasonable treatment options. The advent of managed care has created a "new adversarial relationship: between the health care system and the patient."[6] It also means that treatment decisions are no longer made just between the physician and patient but may be constrained by insurance rules about eligibility and coverage for specific procedures. Under managed care fee arrangements, physicians may also get paid more if they do not order tests or recommend expensive medical procedures than if they do.

In one case heard by the U.S. Supreme Court in 2000, for example, a physician recommended that his patient, Cindy Herdrich, wait eight days for an ultrasound test for abdominal pain at a facility sixty miles away, although a local facility could have done the test that same day. In the meantime, she suffered a ruptured appendix and had to undergo extensive emergency surgery. She later found out that her physician got a cash bonus at the end of the year for saving the health plan money by reducing diagnostic tests.[7] The Supreme Court determined that financial incentives like this are not illegal. Nonetheless, this case illustrates that patients may no longer be able to trust physicians to act in their best interests. Patients rightly worry that physicians do not recommend tests or procedures simply to make more money, rather than because of their medical judgment about what is best for patients, just as under the fee-for-service system the worry was that too many tests would be ordered.

As health law expert Max Mehlman puts it, "Clearly, patients need help coping with the threat of underservice from managed care providers."[8] If Cindy Herdrich had an advocate accompany her to her physician's office, for example, she would have been less likely to have simply waited eight days for a diagnostic test because she would have known this wait was a financial, not a medical, decision by her physician. Her ruptured appendix would then have been avoided, along with her emergency appendectomy operation. One way patients can act, of course, is to switch physicians—but this option is increasingly difficult to exercise if the patient is in a managed care health plan. Mehlman argues that, especially in managed care, patients need advocates. To distinguish patient advocates who work for health care organizations from advocates who work for patients,

Mehlman uses the term *medical advocate,* by which he means someone whose "job would be to make the health care system work as well as possible for the individual patient."[9]

Neither Mehlman nor I think that your physician alone can serve as your advocate. There are simply too many real and potential conflicts of interest in the contemporary health care system. Moreover, as William Sage argues so well, the advocate's role is much more in tune with the lawyer's role than the physician's, and "the medical profession's reputation for objective competence might not withstand the adversarial partisanship that accompanies lawyerly advocacy."[10] Sage also notes, tellingly, that "doctors think of themselves not as lawyers, but as judges." Physicians must be more than advocates for their patients; they must also act in ways consistent with good and accepted medical practice and be stewards of the medical commons for the sake of the community. For all these reasons, your physician cannot be your only advocate. On the other hand, physician-friends, as well as retired physicians, can function extremely effectively as patient advocates.

What about hiring an advocate?

Only wealthy individuals can afford to hire their own advocates. That's one reason there is no formalized advocacy system in place today. Financing and supervising an advocate system is a complex problem. Like most money problems, however, it is primarily a question of priorities. The rights of patients have not been treated as high priority in many health care facilities. Probably, the only way to ensure that advocates are not transformed from patient to management representatives or risk managers is to have them hired by someone outside the facility (or possibly by the board of trustees) and for them to be primarily accountable to the patients they serve.

In the future, an advocate program might be built into health maintenance organizations (HMO) and other managed care contracts (in which case the advocate could work for the consumer-dominated board of directors), be required as a condition of accreditation by the Joint Commission on Accreditation of Healthcare Organizations or participation in Medicare (or any future program of national health insurance), or be funded by a statewide consumer agency. Advocates could also open their own advocacy offices and could work for public agencies, such as consumer protection agencies and departments of health, as well. For now, health care plans and hospitals are likely to be the advocate's primary employer. As long as advocates see their primary loyalty to the patient, they can be helpful to the patients no matter who pays them. Indeed, in any "enlightened" health care facility, the administration will recognize that serving patients and respecting their rights are primary goals. Everyone is better served, communication is improved, injuries and litigation are prevented, and everyone is more legally secure in an environment that prizes and promotes patient rights. Suspected criminals have a right to a lawyer regardless of ability to pay; sick people should have a right not only to a physician but to an advocate as well.

What is an ombudsman?

The ombudsman is an alternative approach to direct patient advocacy, although both an advocate program and an ombudsman could function in the same facility. The ombudsman's role is to seek out broad problem areas, to research facts, to publicize grievances to appropriate audiences, and to make suggestions about resolving those problems. An ombudsman does not participate in the actual dispute resolution. The result is active problem identification without direct personal influence on the solution to the problem. Such an approach eliminates the potential problems created by an adversary system. The disadvantage, however, is that the ombudsman would have no influence on immediate decisions that affect real patients.

Another suggestion is to combine the best aspects of both approaches while discarding those aspects that would have a detrimental effect on functioning. Part of the hospital's (or health plan's) patient rights advocate's function could, for example, be as an ombudsman with respect to protecting and promoting the rights of patients. While remaining available to respond to all patients who desire services, the advocate could also review incident reports, compile lists of recurring situations in which patient rights are affected, classify them according to seriousness, and take action by publication and by making suggestions for changes when warranted. Prevention of problems is a primary goal.

What powers should an institution's ombudsman or patient advocate have?

The hospital or health plan advocate should be able to exercise, at the direction of the patient and the patient's personal advocate, rights and powers that belong to the patient. Patient rights that the institution's advocate should be able to enforce include

- Complete access to medical records and the authority to make notes in the medical record regarding patient complaints and demands
- Active and ongoing participation in the hospital committees responsible for monitoring the quality of care within the hospital context, especially utilization review, patient care, risk management, ethics, research (Institutional Review Board), and quality assurance
- Access to support services for all patients who request them
- Participation at the patient's request and direction in discussion of the patient's case
- Ability to delay discharges
- Ability to call in medical consultants to aid or advise the patient
- Ability to consult with the hospital's legal counsel and to lodge complaints directly with the attending physician, medical director, hospital director, and hospital executive committee

An advocate hired by a hospital or health plan need not be a physician but *should* have some basic knowledge of medicine—know the language and how to read medical records—and law. Patient advocates must also be able to communicate with patients, nurses, doctors, the hospital lawyer, and the hospital administration. Persons chosen should be overqualified rather than underqualified in terms of both knowledge and community acceptance. *Advocates need to know what questions to ask to get the information patients need to make decisions.* Often, just by asking the right question, a more candid and truthful dialogue can be facilitated. There is no data available to judge which background produces the most effective patient rights advocate.

Most of the criticism directed against the patient rights advocate has involved the alleged introduction of conflict. The criticism is not really a reaction to the concept itself but to one way of carrying out the responsibilities of an advocate. The empowered patient and the advocate both confront the hospital and resist the exercise of arbitrary authority. The relegation of all serious decision making to adversary proceedings would raise serious questions. But this is neither the goal nor the likely outcome of the advocate model (the goals are listed above). Even when adversariness does develop, the advocate should improve the doctor-patient relationship by promoting openness and honesty and by identifying real problems so they can be prevented or dealt with effectively.

Fifteen years ago, I used childbirth as an example of how an advocate with these powers can regularly help patients. Under intense pressure from insurance companies, the "standard" length of stay for maternity was continuing to shrink in the United States, down to twenty-four to forty-eight hours in many hospitals for an "uncomplicated delivery." It was not uncommon for women who had just given birth and were suffering from continuing and excessive postpartum bleeding to be severely pressured by the hospital to leave. In one case, nurses "hassled" a woman, continually asking her when she was going, saying that utilization review was "bothering them." Even though the patient felt very sick, the nurses told her she was "ready to leave." With no one to turn to, she felt obliged to leave the hospital and just go home. In her words: "Because I was so exhausted, I just could not advocate for myself. So I went home. I had no help. I could barely walk. My husband got sick immediately, and it took me literally months to recover [from childbirth]."[11]

I noted then that no excuse existed for "this type of shoddy treatment on either legal or medical grounds" and argued that the existence of an effective advocacy system in which the advocate could review medical records, call in a consultant, and delay discharge could put a quick stop to it. By the mid-1990s, insurance companies and health plans had increased the pressure so much that Congress acted. In the *only* federal anti-managed care measure so far, Congress required all insurance companies and health plans to provide coverage for a minimum of forty-eight hours following a vaginal delivery and ninety-six hours following a cesarean section.[12] Federal legislation is no real solution to a problem that should be dealt with reasonably by the physician and patient together, and it is ridiculous that this problem was the subject of congressional action at that level of detail.

What are hospital risk management programs?

Most hospitals have "risk management" programs to help control and limit their exposure to financial losses, especially through medical malpractice claims. These programs, if well run, help educate all hospital personnel about issues of patient rights and patient safety, and they benefit patients generally.[13] Many of these managers, however, view the job of protecting the institution as somehow separate and distinct from the job of protecting patients. And when risk managers withhold records from patients or conceal information about injuries caused by the hospital staff, they are engaged in active deception of patients and deserve nothing but contempt.

Responsible risk managers, on the other hand, can help patients by informing them of any medical mishap that may have injured them or compromised their care, and by taking steps to minimize its long-term impact on the patient's health. They also serve a valuable educational function when they help to raise the awareness level of patient rights in the hospital. Like patient representatives, risk managers should initially be given the benefit of the doubt. If the patient or the patient's family thinks a potentially dangerous or harmful situation exists and that harm can be avoided by taking action, the risk manager may be able to help—such as by calling in consultants if no one else will. Also, after an injury has occurred, the risk manager may be a useful source of information, at least if the risk manager understands that protecting individual patients and honoring their rights are the most effective and constructive ways to protect the hospital's integrity and reputation.

What are ethics committees and ethics consultants?

All hospitals have a mechanism for dealing with ethical issues. The ethics committee is a group of physicians and others (often including the chaplain, a lawyer, a nurse, an administrator, and an ethicist). Ethics committees help develop hospital policy in "ethical" areas (many of which are also legal), such as "do not resuscitate" or "do not attempt resuscitation" policies and policies on withholding or withdrawing treatment from newborns with serious disabilities and other incompetent patients. They may consult on specific cases and often run educational programs on ethics in the hospital and for the community. Some ethics committees also make recommendations on how individual cases should be resolved.[14] A functioning advocate system could, by improving communications, improve the consulting functions of these committees.

If the patient or the patient's family is having difficulty implementing a care decision because the doctors or nurses think the decision is "wrong," "unethical," or "illegal," the patient or advocate may find it useful to ask that the case be reviewed by the hospital's ethics committee. If the committee agrees with the patient, the patient's wishes will likely be carried out. If the committee disagrees, the patient is no worse off than when the exercise began, and the advocate can still resort to other mechanisms, including the courts, if necessary. One major problem is that the committees meet very infrequently, usually once a month, and so cannot really be helpful with decisions at the bedside.

An *ethics consultant* is a person, not a committee. The consultant may be an ethicist, philosopher, chaplain, or nurse but is often a physician with training in medical ethics. If the hospital has such a person, the ethics consultant can often be very helpful in resolving conflicts between patients and medical staff. Patients, their advocates, and their families should not hesitate to call on the ethics consultant for help when conflicts cannot be resolved by simply getting everyone involved in the care of the patient to sit down and talk to each other. It should be stressed, however, as my colleague Dr. Michael Grodin, a twenty-year veteran of ethics consultations at Boston Medical Center has observed, that more than 90 percent of all treatment conflicts involve misunderstanding and miscommunication. These conflicts are resolvable (and often resolved) by a "team meeting" in which all the caregivers (including physicians and nurses) and all family members (including the patient, if competent) meet to discuss the facts of the case, to clarify the goals of treatment, and to present their reasons for their differing recommendations on treatment. Such a meeting should be tried first. An advocate's presence during all crucial conversations, including such a meeting, is vital to clarify the questions (and answers) and to witness how the ultimate decision is made. The institution's patient advocate can convene such a meeting proactively.

What steps should hospitals take now to enhance patient rights?
Fifteen years ago, I called for immediate adoption of the following five points to enhance patient rights and help humanize the hospital environment:

1. Eliminate "routine" procedures.
2. Provide patients routine access to their medical records.
3. Permit twenty-four-hour-a-day visitation.
4. Require full experience disclosure before procedures are performed.

5. Implement an effective patient rights advocate program, which includes a patient-centered bill of rights.

Progress has been made on all points, except for the last, the subject of this chapter.

No routine procedures. It had been common for nurses and others to respond to the question "Why is this being done?" with "Don't worry, it's routine." This is not an acceptable response. Procedures should not be performed on patients simply because they are routine; they should be performed only because they are *specifically* indicated for a patient. Thus, routine admission tests, routine lab tests, routine use of uniform gowns, routine use of wheelchairs for in-hospital and discharge transportation, routine use of sleeping pills, to name a few notable examples, should be abolished. Use of these procedures treats patients like interchangeable robots rather than persons; and "routine" procedures are often demeaning and unnecessary. *Update:* Managed care has actually been instrumental in greatly reducing the use of "routine procedures" primarily as a cost-containment measure.

Routine access to medical records. Although currently required by federal law and many state statutes and regulations, routine access to medical records by patients remains difficult, and a patient often asserts the right to see the record at the peril of being labeled "distrustful" or a "troublemaker." The information in the hospital chart is about the patient and properly belongs to the patient. The patient must have access to it, both to enhance his or her own decision-making ability and to make it clear that the hospital is an "open" institution that is not trying to hide things from the patient. Surely, if facility personnel make decisions about the patient based on information in the chart, the patient also deserves access to the information, even in the absence of a specific law or health care facility policy on this subject. *Update:* Routine access to medical records is now both legally mandated and much more accepted.

Twenty-four-hour-a-day visitation rights. One of the most important ways to humanize hospitals and enhance patient autonomy is to assure the patient that at least one person of the patient's choice has unlimited access to the patient's room at any time of the day or night. This person should also be permitted to stay with the patient during any procedure (for example, during childbirth or induction of anesthesia), so long as the person does not interfere with the medical care of other patients. *Update:* Visiting hours have been greatly expanded. And with extreme cuts in nursing staff, family members are often welcomed not just as visitors but as caregivers. Family members can offer not only comfort but can also ensure that the patient gets proper medical attention.[15] Your advocate is not just a social visitor but is there to help you exercise your rights: visiting hours should therefore not apply to your advocate.

Full experience disclosure. The most important gain of the 1980s was the almost universal acknowledgment of the need for (and desirability of) the patient's informed consent prior to treatment. Nevertheless, information that is important to the patient's decision may still be routinely withheld: the experience of the person doing the procedure. Patients have a right to know if the person asking permission to draw blood, to do blood gases, or to do a bone marrow aspiration or a spinal tap (to list just a few examples) has performed the procedure before, and if so, how often, and what is the person's rate of adverse effects. This applies not only to medical students, student nurses, and residents but also to board certified surgeons. We all do things for the first time, but not every patient wants to take an active role in medical education. *Update:* Although patients frequently must ask, physicians and medical students are much less reluctant to discuss their own experience than they were a decade ago.

How can individuals promote patient rights?

Perhaps the most important step you can take is to educate yourself about your rights. Second, you can exercise your rights regularly, so health care professionals get used to the idea that citizens in the United States take their rights seriously and are not willing to abdicate them simply because they are sick. Third, you can support legislation that codifies and strengthens patient rights, including the right to health care, making rights easier to understand and easier to exercise. Fourth, you can be a patient rights monitor. In the human rights movement, there is a concept that everyone should be a human rights monitor: documenting abuses when they occur and bringing them to public attention. This is one of the most effective ways of preventing abuses in the future. When you act as an advocate, your primary responsibility is to the patient. Nonetheless, if you see other patients in the hospital or other facility being abused or neglected, you should do what you can to help. If such help becomes routine, patient care in hospitals will improve.

Patient rights are important to everyone. Insist that your rights be respected and take steps to ensure that the physicians you trust with your body treat you as a full partner in treatment decisions. And when you are hospitalized or very sick, and therefore "not yourself," make sure you have a patient rights advocate to help you navigate the health care system.

NOTES

1. George J. Annas & Joseph H. Healey, *The Patient Rights Advocate: Redefining the Doctor-Patient Relationship in the Hospital Context,* 27 Vand. L. Rev. 243 (1974). *See also* John Regan, *When Nursing Home Patients Complain: The Ombudsman or the Patient Advocate,* 65 Georgetown L. J. 691 (1977), and Marc A. Rodwin, *Patient Accountability and Quality of Care: Lessons from Medical Consumerism and the Patients' Rights, Women's Health and Disability Rights Movements,* 20 Am. J. Law & Med. 147 (1994).

2. Paul Starr, The Social Transformation of American Medicine, New York: Basic Books, 1982, 389.

3. William Sage, *Physicians as Advocates,* 35 Houston L. Rev. 1529, (1999); *see also* Bernard Dickens, *Patient's Interests and Client's Wishes: Physicians and Lawyers in Discord,* 15 Law, Med. & Health Care 110 (1987).

4. Studs Terkel, Working, New York: Avon, 1972, 647. The problem of misleading labels is well illustrated in Studs Terkel's classic book *Working.* One of the workers he interviewed was Betsy Delacy, a "patients' representative" in a 540-bed hospital. Delacy described her job as admitting the patient to the hospital, following the patient throughout the stay, and afterward making sure the bill is paid. In her words:

I don't feel I represent the patient. I represent the hospital. I represent the cashiers. I'm the buffer between the patient and the collection department. . . . We visit our patients as often as we can, so they get to know us as their representative. "Are you comfortable?" "Are you satisfied with your food?" Then when he gets to know me—"I know your account is going to be a problem. . . . " I'm not looking for money, but if the patient doesn't ask such questions, I mention it. I sort of joke with 'em and then lay it out and sock it to 'em.

It seems reasonable to ask why such a person is called a "patients' representative" in the first place. Delacy explains, "It seems strange that you should have a collection department in a hospital. Patient representative has a better sound. Nobody knows what it's all about. It's like any organized business. They give people such titles that nobody knows what it's all about." Unfortunately, Delacy seems to be correct. Few people seem to know what being a real patient representative or patient advocate is all about. This is unacceptable. Hospitals are not like "any organized business," and patients are not like any other consumer—they are sick and extremely vulnerable. They need advocates who can help them with their medically related problems, not an expert in housekeeping functions (that should be supplied, along with clean linen, as a matter of course). Without scrupulous attention to their rights as human beings, their personhood will be stripped from them, and they will be treated as if they were pets.

5. *See, e.g.,* A. W. Bird, *Enhancing Patient Well-Being: Advocacy or Negotiation?* 20(3) J. Med. Ethics 152 (1994); P. Allmark & R. Klarzynski, *The Case Against Nurse Advocacy,* 2 Brit. J. Nursing 33 (1992); and Laura Cohn, *Need Help with the Health Care Maze?* Business Week, May 6, 2002, 102.

6. Max Mehlman, *Medical Advocates: A Call for a New Profession,* 1 Wiedner Law Symposium J. 299 (1996).

7. *Pegram v. Herdrich,* 530 U.S. 211 (2000); Wendy K. Mariner, *What Recourse? Liability for Managed Care Decisions and ERISA,* 343 New Eng. J. Med. 592 (2000).

8. Mehlman, *supra* note 6, at 306.

9. Mehlman describes the job of the medical advocate:

They would serve as adjuncts to providers in supplying patients with the information necessary to make informed decisions. They would help the patient determine what benefits were provided under the patient's health plan. If requested, they would accompany the patient to the hospital, clinic, or physician's office; review treatment plans and related paperwork; and if necessary, intercede on the patient's behalf to obtain the maximum available benefits. If the patient were unable to travel, the medical advocate would be given authority to intercede without the patient being present. During and after episodes of care, the advocate would review medical records to assure that complete and accurate information was recorded, to detect and notify the patient of any evidence of malpractice or underservice. If disputes arose between the patient and the patient's providers, health plan, or third-party payers, the advocate would represent the patient's interests. The advocate would be familiar with administrative remedies available through the federal and state governments, including departments of health and insurance, Medicare peer review organizations, state medical boards, the Joint Commission of Accreditation of Healthcare Organizations (JCAHO), and the Office of the Inspector General in the Department of Health and Human Services (DHHS). If the dispute proceeded to mediation, arbitration, or litigation, the advocate would be available to represent the patient or would recommend an attorney.

The role of the medical advocate would be tailored to the needs of individual patients. Some patients would require little more than information or advice. Others would need informal or formal intervention by the advocate. Advocates would acquaint the patient with the range of services offered and allow the patient to decide how extensively he or she wished to take advantage of them. (*Id.,* at 321)

10. Sage, *supra* note 3. *See also* Kenneth Ludmerer, *Instilling Professionalism in Medical Education,* 282 JAMA 881 (1999).

11. Suzanne Gordon, *Insurers' Limits on Hospital Stay Cause Concern for New Mothers,* Boston Globe, July 4, 1988, 21–23.

12. George J. Annas, *Women and Children First,* 333 New Eng. J. Med. 1647 (1995).

13. Some states require hospitals to have a risk-management system as a way to improve the quality of care delivered in the hospital.

14. Raymond Devettere, Practical Decision Making in Health Care Ethics: Cases and Concepts, 2d ed., Washington, D.C., Georgetown U. Press, 2000.

15. Jane Allan, *More Patients and Their Advocates Check in Hospitals: Staffing Shortages and a Sicker Population Make Family Members and Friends Stand Guard Over Care*, Los Angeles Times, November 29, 1999, S1. Although the advice to stay with a patient "24/7" is now common, and I think necessary, even constant vigilance cannot guarantee that nothing will go wrong. As Rosemary Gibson and Janardan Singh write in their book, *Wall of Silence: The Untold Story of Medical Mistakes That Kill and Injure Millions of Americans*, Washington, D.C.: LifeLine Press, 2003:

For some families, their watchfulness and advocacy made all the difference between life and death. Yet for many others, the best advice on how to avoid harm rings hollow. They watched like hawks at the bedside of their loved one, spoke up repeatedly when things didn't seem right, and did their research. They did everything the experts say you should do, and it still didn't prevent harm. All their love and devotion wasn't enough. Devastating errors still occurred. They ask themselves over and over again whether there was anything else they could have done, and those questions may haunt them for a very long time, if not forever. One family member puts the advice on how people can protect themselves into perspective. "Patients can't fix this problem [of medical errors]. If, as a nurse at the bedside of my mother virtually the entire time in the hospital, I couldn't prevent something terrible from happening, we are fooling ourselves to think that patients and their families can do it. . . . It might matter in some circumstances, but it's not the answer. It's worth doing that, but I am afraid that people will be under the illusion that they will be safe. Errors in health care are going to be prevented only if the system does its job." (at 245–246)

The nurse is, of course, correct. Patients and their advocates alone cannot "fix" all the problems of medical care in the hospital, and you should not blame yourself if in spite of your best efforts as an advocate a tragedy befalls the patient.

III

Reforming American Medicine

T he most important point to understand about American medicine is that there is no medical care system: U.S. medicine is fragmented, uncoordinated, uncertain, and unconscionably expensive. Americans spend more than $1.5 trillion a year on health care, 14 percent of our gross domestic product (GDP), more than $5,000 per person per year, almost 4 percent of the GDP of all the countries of the world combined. We have tried government regulation, managed care, and market competition, and none of these strategies has had a permanent impact on rising health care costs.[1] As the entire nation learned in the aftermath of the September 11 terrorist attack on the United States, the metaphors we adopt to describe reality have a powerful effect on how we think and, thus, on what reactions we see as reasonable and responsible.[2] America's medical care is often described as a train wreck or a shipwreck. Julian Barnes describes his reaction to studying Gericault's disturbing painting, *The Raft of Medusa* (which portrays fifteen survivors of a shipwreck on their thirteenth day at sea as they spot a ship), as transporting us "through currents of hope and despair, elation, panic and resignation."[3] All of these emotions are appropriate responses to our continuing health care cost, quality, and access crisis; but how we ultimately act will be determined in large measure by the metaphors we adopt.

Does America's medical care "system" really need reform?

Yes, it does. Not only are large numbers of Americans uninsured (consistently more than 40 million) but also those that are insured are often uncertain of their benefits and are in public and private health plans that vary so widely as to be all but incomprehensible to most Americans. Citizens who are sixty-five years or older, for example, are covered by a federally funded health plan called Medicare. The plan is extremely well regarded by seniors (although most think a prescription drug benefit must be added to it), and the most politically attractive plan for universal health insurance is a "Medicare for all" plan. Nonetheless, Medicare itself must be modernized to cover prescription drugs and to better cover chronic care.[4] Medicaid, a state plan that is about 50 percent supported by federal funds, provides coverage for those with low incomes and, unlike Medicare, also covers residential long-term care. Together these two governmental programs pay almost half of all U.S. health care bills.

Almost all Americans who have private insurance obtain it through their employers, and it is employers who decide which health plans will be offered to their employees. In the 1990s, there was a tremendous shift in the private health care insurance market away from indemnity insurance (in which your insurance company simply pays the bills physicians and hospitals submit as long as they are "reasonable") to capitated plans in which health care providers are given a standard fee per patient per year regardless of how much care is provided. The indemnity system was said to encourage "overtreatment," whereas the capitated system is said to encourage "undertreatment." There are problems with both methods of paying health care providers, and most patients properly think it is better if their physicians make decisions about their medical treatment based on what the physician and patient think is best, rather than what treatment or nontreatment will provide the physician with the most money. Health maintenance organizations (HMOs) combine the insurance and health care delivery mechanisms into one: they both collect premiums and contract with physicians and hospitals to render care to plan members.

The theory behind a capitated system, sometimes called "managed care," is that if a health plan can save money in the long run by keeping its members healthy, it will have a financial incentive to encourage preventive care and patient education. In practice, however, many Americans have become increasingly disenchanted by what they see as a system that puts profits before patients; has much more concern with short-term financial gains than long-term health gains; and skimps on care, for example, by arbitrarily denying payment for expensive care and discharging patients from hospitals "quicker and sicker."[5]

Public disenchantment with managed care was well expressed by Helen Hunt's character in the movie *As Good as It Gets*. Hunt plays a waitress whose son has severe asthma. One of her wealthy customers, played by Jack Nicholson, arranges for a physician to see her son at her home. Both the Hunt character and her mother are amazed that any physician would make a house call, order specific tests, and especially give a patient his home phone number for follow-up. At one point, the physician asks her if her son has had a standard scratch test for allergies. She replies that her health plan told her the scratch test was not necessary. The doctor indicates that this is not true, and she angrily replies, "Fucking HMO bastard pieces of shit. I'm sorry." To which the physician replies, "No, actually I think that's their technical name." Audiences tended to identify with Hunt's character.[6]

This was terrific theater, but it is also mirrored in real life. Dr. Paul Ellwood, known as the "father of the HMO movement," himself became disenchanted with the American health care "system" when he experienced it firsthand as a patient. As he told a Harvard University conference, "[U]neven health care in the United States is a national disgrace. It's unacceptable and it can't be allowed to continue."[7] Ellwood called for increased government regulation of health care quality, including disclosure of mortality rates, treatment complications, and success rates. His own experience with the health care system, which he encountered after he was thrown from a horse and almost paralyzed, taught him how inexperienced virtually all of the technicians, nurses, and physicians were and how lucky he was not to have been permanently paralyzed. In his words, "Patients can get just atrocious care and can do very little about it. I've increasingly felt that we've got to shift the power to the patient." Ellwood is correct, and most of the people who support or are satisfied with the present system have not had to spend any time in the hospital or have not had a serious illness recently. Patients must take steps to protect themselves, because they cannot count on the health care system to protect them when they are sick or injured. In 2002, Ellwood announced that he and his Jackson Hole Group of health reformers would focus on "advocacy for immediate steps to give patients more power in the health care system."[8]

We live in a country founded on the proposition that we are all endowed with certain inalienable rights, including rights to life, liberty, and the pursuit of happiness. Any government-sponsored health care plan must account for the reality that many Americans assume these rights support entitlement to whatever medical treatments exist and to whatever might make them healthy. Perhaps as importantly, we live in a wasteful, technologically driven, individualistic, and death-denying culture. Every health plan, government-sponsored or not, must also take these postmodern American characteristics into account. How is it even possible to think seriously about reforming a health care system that reflects these basic and pervasive American values and characteristics? I believe the first necessary step, which will require us to look deeper than money and means to goals and ends, is to engage a new metaphor to frame our public policy discussion to help us develop a new conception of health care. We have tried the military metaphor and the market metaphor; both narrow our field of vision, and neither can take us where we need to go.

How does the military metaphor influence American medicine?

The military metaphor has had the most pervasive influence over both the practice and financing of medicine in the United States.[9] Examples are legion. Medicine is a battle against death. Diseases attack the body; uniformed physicians intervene. We are almost constantly engaged in wars on various diseases, such as cancer and AIDS. Physicians, who are mostly specialists backed by allied health professionals and are trained to be aggressive, fight these invading diseases with weapons designed to knock them out. Physicians give orders in the trenches and on the front lines, and use their armamentaria in search of breakthroughs. Treatments are conventional or heroic, and brave patients soldier it out as gallant fighters who hope to conquer their diseases. Physicians engage in triage in the emergency department, invasive procedures in the operating theater, and even in defensive medicine when a legal enemy is suspected.

The military metaphor leads us to overmobilize and think of medicine in terms that have become dysfunctional. It encourages us to ignore costs and leads hospitals and physicians to engage in medical arms races. It tempts us to believe that all problems can be solved with more sophisticated technology. It leads us to accept as inevitable organizations that are hierarchical and male-dominated. It suggests that seeing the patient's body as a battlefield is appropriate, as are short-term, single-minded, tactical goals. Military thinking concentrates on the physical, sees control as central, and willingly expends massive resources to achieve dominance.

Notably, we have not applied the military metaphor to assert that, like war, medical care should be financed and controlled by the government.

How does the market metaphor influence American medicine?

The market metaphor has transformed the way we describe and think about fundamental relationships in medical care, but it is just as dysfunctional as the military metaphor. In the language of the market, health plans and hospitals market products to consumers who purchase them based on price. Medical care is a business that necessarily involves marketing through advertising and competition among suppliers who see profit making as their primary motivation. Health care becomes managed care or, at least, managed cost. Mergers and acquisitions become core activities. Chains are developed, vertical integration pursued, and antitrust concerns proliferate. Patients are transformed into consumers. Consumer choice becomes the central mantra of the market metaphor. In the language of insurance, consumers become "covered lives." Economists become health-financing gurus. The role of physicians is radically altered, as physicians are instructed by managers that they can no longer be patient advocates but rather must advocate for the entire group of covered lives in the health plan. The percentage of insurance premiums a health plan spends on the delivery of health care to its members is referred to as the medical loss ratio, or simply as the loss ratio. The goal of medicine becomes a healthy bottom line instead of a healthy patient.

The market metaphor leads us to think about medicine in already familiar ways: emphasis is placed on efficiency, profit maximization, customer satisfaction, ability to pay, planning, entrepreneurship, and competitive models. The ideology of medicine is displaced by the ideology of the marketplace. Trust is replaced by caveat emptor (buyer beware). There is no place for the poor and uninsured in the market model. The market is designed for people who can pay for medical care, not for poor people who need medical care. Business ethics supplants medical ethics, and the practice of medicine becomes corporatized. Hospitals become cost centers. Nonprofit medical organizations tend to abandon their missions by adopting the values of their for-profit competitors. A management degree becomes as important, if not more important, than a medical degree. Public institutions, which serve people with needs and no money, cannot compete in the for-profit arena and risk closure, second-class status, or privatization.

Like the military metaphor, the market metaphor is also a myth. Consumer-patients are supposed to make choices, but the most important ones, such as choice of health plan, are actually made by employers. The market metaphor also conceals inherent market imperfections, ignores the medical commons, and disregards the inability of the market to distribute goods and services whose supply and demand is weakly related to price. The reality is that American markets are highly regulated; major industries enjoy large public subsidies; industrial organizations tend toward oligopoly; and strong consumer protection laws and consumer access to the courts to pursue product liability suits are essential to prevent profits from being too ruthlessly pursued. Reliance on the market metaphor has turned us away from facing reality.

How do metaphors affect health care reform?

American medicine's military and market metaphors help explain why the Clintons were never able to articulate a coherent view of their goals for a reformed health care financing system in President Clinton's first term. The Clinton plan, the last serious attempt at reform, was said by the president and first lady to rest on six pillars (or to be guided by six "shining stars"): security, savings, choice, simplicity, responsibility, and quality. These six characteristics mix the military and market metaphors in impossible and inconsistent ways and add new, unrelated concepts as well. The predominant metaphor of the Clintons seems to have been the military one: security was goal number one ("Health care that will always be there"). But in the post–Cold War pre-9/11 era, security as a reason to make major change was a tough sell. Even harder was selling the health care alliances that were the centerpiece of the new security arrangement. The military metaphor (undercut by words such as *savings* and *choice*) simply could not provide a coherent vision of the Clinton plan.

Nor could the market metaphor. The key concept of the market is, of course, consumer choice, and this was promised. The Clinton plan was founded on choice, but choice of health care plan, not choice of physician or treatment. Americans seemed to favor choice of physician over choice of health plan, and when this choice was seen as central (by characters Harry and Louise in advertisements against the Clinton plan, for example, who said of government health care, "They choose, we lose"), the plan itself collapsed, and the alliances with it. Choice, quality, and even savings can be generated by a market plan; but such an approach has little room for either responsibility or simplicity—ecology-related goals that have generated little enthusiasm among contemporary Americans. In retrospect, the Clinton vision seems to have been doomed from the day its six inconsistent foundational principles, goals, or guides were articulated. The Clintons also failed to engage the four deep-seated negative characteristics of American culture that dominate medical care (wasteful, technologically driven, death-denying, and individualistic).

Could a new metaphor, such as the ecology metaphor, help?

It seems reasonable to conclude that if Congress is ever to make meaningful progress on reforming our fast-changing medical care finance and delivery system, a new way must be found to think about health itself. This will require at least a new metaphorical framework that permits us to re-envision and thus to reconstruct America's medical care system into a health care system. I believe that the leading candidate for this metaphorical replacement is the ecology metaphor.

Ecologists use words such as *integrity, balance, natural, limited* (resources), *quality* (of life), *diversity, renewable, sustainable, responsibility* (for future generations), *community,* and *conservation.*[10] The concepts embedded in these words and others common to the ecology movement could, if applied to health care, have a profound impact on the way the debate about it is conducted and on plans for change that are seen as reasonable.

The ecology metaphor could, for example, help us to confront and accept limits (both on the expected length of our lives and the amount of resources we think reasonable to spend to increase longevity), to value nature, and to emphasize quality of life. It could lead us to worry about our grandchildren and thus to plan long-term, to favor sustainable technologies over ones that we cannot afford to provide to all who could benefit from them, to emphasize prevention and public health measures, to debate the merits of rationing, and to accept the function of responsible gatekeepers who act as stewards of the medical commons.

Drawing on the attempts of the "deep ecologists" to ask more fundamental questions than their "shallow" environmental counterparts (who concentrate on pollution abatement), psychiatrist Willard Gaylin fruitfully suggests that the Clinton approach to health care reform was itself shallow. He suggests that what was needed was a "wide-open far-ranging public debate about the deeper issues of health care—our attitudes toward life and death, the goals of medicine, the meaning of health, suffering versus survival, who shall live and who shall die (and who shall decide)."[11]

Without addressing these deeper questions, Gaylin rightly argues that we can never solve our health care crisis.

An ecological metaphor also naturally leads to considerations of population health rather than to sole concentration on the health of individuals. It leads away from concentration on individual risk factors, for example, "toward the social structures and processes within which ill-health originates, and which will often be more amenable to modification."[12] The ecological metaphor encourages us to look "upstream" to see what is causing downstream illnesses and injuries. It leads us to put much more emphasis on prevention and public health interventions and less on wasteful end-of-life interventions.

Unlike the military and market metaphors, which only reinforce our counterproductive American characteristics of wastefulness, technology obsession, fear of death, and individualism, the ecological metaphor could help us to confront them. The ecological metaphor in medicine can encourage an alternative vision of resource conservation, sustainable technologies, acceptance of death as natural and necessary, responsibility for others, and at least some degree of communitarianism. It can also help move us from predominately law-based practice standards that are an integral part of the market to a greater role for ethics and ethical behavior in the practice of medicine.

We need a new vision of health care in America, not just rearrangement of medical care. The ecology metaphor provides one that can directly address the major problems with our current culture, as well as the "deep" issues in health care: a way to energize the stagnating and depressing health care reform debate and reshape it.[13] We need a new metaphorical construct that can in turn lead society to think and act about health care in a new way. Adoption of the ecological metaphor could also help us confront what Vaclav Havel has called the end of the modern age and move us to something new: a state of human affairs that values universal human rights but also has space for an appreciation of "the miracle of Being, the miracle of the universe, the miracle of nature, the miracle of our own existence."[14]

For at least the short-term, the market metaphor will be challenged only by what may be termed the "rights metaphor," which is the primary focus of this book. This metaphor is founded on the concept that patients have rights, and that these rights must be protected by putting patients at the center of the health care system. But the rights metaphor does not demand that everyone have access to everything medicine can deliver. As long as the rules for access are equitable and democratically set, rationing health care is consistent with the rights metaphor.

How can patients effectively complain about their health care now?

It's not easy. In his book *Exit, Voice, and Loyalty,* economist Albert O. Hirschman argues that the ability to take one's business elsewhere may not be enough to empower consumers in markets in which all providers act similarly. Instead of simply going elsewhere by exiting, Hirschman argues that consumers must be able to effectively voice their complaints to give producers and service providers an incentive to be responsive to consumers' interests.[15] Health lawyer Marc Rodwin has suggested that the Hirschman analysis is particularly relevant to members of managed care plans and "individuals with on-going relations with providers such as nursing homes."[16]

Providing patients, who depend on their physicians for expert advice, with an effective voice is a long-standing problem that has been highlighted, but not caused, by managed care. The backlash against managed care, nonetheless, provides an opportunity to develop meaningful voice options for patients.[17] Because of this backlash, the questions of dispute resolution, grievance mechanisms, and appeals procedures have taken on urgency in the courtroom, as well as in legislative reform proposals at the state and federal levels.

What dispute-resolution mechanisms have health plans developed?

Managed care is in deep decline in that at least since the turn of the century, the vast majority of physicians report that they have sufficient control over medical care decisions to meet their patients' needs.[18] Health expert Michael Millenson argues that the real problem in American medicine is not care that is denied but the quality of care that is given. In Millenson's words, "The biggest threat to life and limb comes from what happens to you once you reach the doctor's office or hospital."[19]

This is certainly true. Nonetheless, if you are one of the individuals whose benefits have been denied, knowledge of your rights regarding an appeal of this decision is critical. Until we get meaningful health reform, patients will have to rely on their health plans to pay their medical bills. When care or coverage is denied, a user-friendly dispute-resolution system is needed. All health insurers have problems with dispute-resolution mechanisms. Managed care organizations are under special scrutiny because they deny treatment more often, physicians may be restricted in their role as advocates for their patients, and patients may have little opportunity to leave the plan. Federal law specifically requires that HMOs enrolling Medicare patients (so-called Medicare HMOs) provide "meaningful procedures for hearing and resolving grievances." Dissatisfied enrollees have a right to a hearing before an administrative law judge, if the dispute involves $100 or more, or a judicial review, if the amount exceeds $1,000. HMOs must have procedures for appealing the denial of payment for emergency treatment, the denial of payment for services rendered by a non-HMO provider, and the refusal to provide services.[20] The essence of the complaint in a class action suit against Health and Human Services (HHS) was that HMOs were not following these appeals requirements and that HHS was not enforcing them, thus violating both the statutory and constitutional due process rights of Medicare recipients.[21] Some details are useful, because the problems with these appeals are likely to be systemic until more fundamental reform is adopted.

A review of 570 denial of benefit notices to HMO members disclosed three problems. First, 52 percent of the notices were illegible, primarily because most were printed in type that was smaller than twelve points, the recognized minimal print size for readability by elderly persons. Second, 74 percent of the notices provided vague or ambiguous reasons for denial of services. Third, only 41 percent of the notices contained an explanation of personal responsibility for paying for care obtained after the denial.

The judge also found that the notices tended to "hide the ball" by obscuring the eligibility requirements, thus making it very difficult for a claimant to "fathom what additional evidence to present to rebut the denial." He was also concerned about the general lack of any face-to-face setting, such as an informal hearing, and noted, "Due process requires a meaningful opportunity to present one's case at a meaningful time." The judge also pointedly observed that denial of treatment can result in "unnecessary pain and suffering or death," and thus the ability to appeal an adverse decision quickly is essential to due process in these circumstances.

The judge concluded that HHS violated federal law by continuing to contract with an HMO that failed to meet the following constitutional due process notice and hearings:

Notice: 1. Shall always be given for any and all denials of service;
2. Shall be timely;
3. Shall be readable: at least 12-point type;
4. Shall state the reason for denial clearly and in such terms as to enable the enrollee to argue his or her case;
5. Shall inform the enrollee of all appeal rights, including PRO [peer review organization] review;
6. Shall inform the enrollee of the right to a hearing on reconsideration and that additional evidence may be presented, in person, and shall explain the procedure for securing an informal hearing; and
7. Shall provide instruction on how to obtain supporting evidence, including medical records and supporting affidavits from the attending physician. The HMO must abolish any policy or procedure which would impede such advocacy.

Hearing: 1. Shall be informal, in-person communication with the decision maker;
2. Shall be available upon request for all service denials; and
3. Shall be timely according to the seriousness of the medical condition implicated by the denied service: Immediate hearing shall be available for acute care service denials, specifically where delivery of the service is prevented by the denial . . . All other hearings can be within the normal course of the HMOs 60-day time frame for reconsideration.

The American Association of Health Plans, a trade association that represents managed care plans, pledged to streamline appeals processes and make them more "patient-friendly." The association said that its member plans "recognize that accessible, fair, and timely grievance and appeals procedures must be in place and understood by both enrollees and all providers and health plan personnel."[22]

This case highlights the tension in the doctor-patient relationship created by capitation and the limits of even the best-designed dispute-resolution mechanism to address this tension. A user-friendly appeals mechanism that protects the physician from retaliation by the HMO can help the patient obtain a recommended treatment. But if the physician does not recommend a treatment, or even suggest it as a reasonable option, the patient may not have sufficient knowledge to realize that a decision has been made not to offer further treatment. The possibility of appealing the decision may never enter the patient's mind. Of course, the equivalent of a warning label for all doctor-patient conversations, stating that the physician is being paid to minimize referrals and treatments could be provided, but this would simply serve to erode patients' trust in their physicians. Although user-friendly appeals mechanisms are helpful, even essential, they cannot address the fundamental issue of trust in the doctor-patient relationship. And to the extent that managed care plans are undermining this trust by recasting the doctor-patient relationship, confronting that problem will require much more than simply providing more accessible dispute-resolution mechanisms.

Wall Street Journal health columnist Marilyn Chase advises her well-heeled readers that if they are really convinced they need a specialist and their plans balk, they should go to the specialists anyway, pay out of pocket, and "fight later about who [ultimately] pays."[23] But such a response puts all of the burden on patients and none on the managed care plan and its physicians. This is unfair. Managed care plans and their physicians are certainly not incapable of error in making decisions about coverage. As administrative law expert Eleanor Kinney has properly emphasized, "It should never be forgotten that procedures are an important mechanism to confer power and adjust the balance of power among the parties to the process."[24] How should such a system be designed?

How should dispute-resolution mechanisms be structured?

Mechanisms for resolving disputes about medical care should be quick, easy to use, and fair. In the case of prospectively denied services, patients should be able to obtain a second medical opinion within hours, and in the case of a denial of services that is based on contractual language, they should be able to appeal to an internal neutral decision maker within two days. It also seems reasonable for states to require that all health insurers in their jurisdiction have dispute-resolution procedures that not only meet the requirements outlined in the last answer but go even further.

All patients (not just Medicare patients in HMOs) should have legally established grievance and appeals rights. Some variation is reasonable, but the basic provisions should be uniform, including those governing notification, the right to see and talk to the person who made the decision, and a review of it by a neutral decision maker, along with representation by a qualified advocate, a timely response, and a written explanation of the reasons for the decision. In addition, the state should provide patients who have been turned down by the health plan and their physicians with a neutral and fair appeals process (separate from the judicial system), such as independent arbitration by a knowledgeable panel, which can quickly review and reverse or uphold an adverse decision. The hearing officers for these appeals could come from the state health department, the state attorney general's office, or the insurance commissioner.

Decisions by independent arbitration panels or hearing officers should be binding on the health insurer, but because of the imbalance of power, patients should be able to appeal decisions. In cases requiring treatment within days or weeks, the internal appeals process should take less than forty-eight hours, and the external appeals process no more than another forty-eight hours. Both should be face-to-face; and the burden of proof should always be on the health plan to demonstrate that the wanted treatment is unnecessary or not covered by the contract. In the case of an HMO's decision to discontinue ongoing treatment, whether inpatient or outpatient, treatment should be continued during the expedited appeals process.

Records of all internal and external appeals should be publicly available (although the names and identifying characteristics of patients should be withheld to protect their privacy) for the purpose of comparison and improvement in the quality of care. All costs of nonjudicial appeals should be borne by the health plan. Patients should always have the option to challenge decisions in court, but once a dispute is taken to court, both parties have already lost in terms of time, money, and efficiency in decision making. *The closer to the bedside the dispute can be resolved, in terms of both time and distance, the better.* No health plan that is delivering high quality medical care has anything to fear from a speedy dispute resolution process that treats patients fairly.

The primary problems with existing grievance mechanisms are that they are slow and one-sided. A survey of 196 Kaiser Permanente arbitrations in northern California, for example, found that the final resolution of disputes took an average of more than twenty-eight months.[25] And in the summer of 1997, the California Supreme Court found major problems in the way Kaiser handled arbitration with its dissatisfied members.[26] If physicians cannot or will not act as patient advocates when benefits are denied, some other person will have to assume this role for patients who wish to challenge denials of benefits quickly and effectively. It seems unlikely that a patient would be satisfied with an advocate hired by their health plan, and in any event, it is unlikely that such a person could act independently on the patient's behalf. For any system to succeed in resolving disputes quickly, patients must believe it is fair. I think fairness requires that benefits advocates be provided by an independent organization, such as the state consumer protection agency or the state attorney general's office. Of course, independent consumer groups could also make advocates available for patients. To be feasible, an advocacy program requires predictable funding. An increase in licensing fees paid by all entities doing business as health insurance or claims-management companies seems a reasonable source of funding. Such funding should avoid the preemption under the Employee Retirement Income Security Act (ERISA), because it does not tax group health insurance benefits or premiums.[27]

Relying solely on the ability of patients to exit one health plan and join another is not sufficient to ensure either the rights of patients in managed care plans or improvement in the plans' quality of care. Improving opportunities for enrollees to voice their objections can both enhance patient rights and highlight areas of concern with respect to quality. Most of the managed care backlash has been played out in Congress and the state legislatures. Courts are slower to react but will intervene, especially in cases involving services to Medicare recipients and alleged violations of due process. Prevention is almost always preferable to cure, and the states and the federal government should act to ensure that all patients have access to dispute-resolution mechanisms that are quick, easy to use, and fair, as well as to advocates who can help them use these mechanisms. Supplementing exit with voice can foster choice and enhance patient rights.

May physicians or hospitals discriminate against patients with disabilities?

No. The Americans with Disabilities Act (ADA) prohibits discrimination against all disabled people. A 1998 U.S. Supreme Court decision, *Bragdon v. Abbott*, determined that this prohibition also applies to persons infected with HIV.[28]

Sidney Abbott had been HIV-positive since 1986 but did not yet have AIDS. In 1994, she went to the office of Dr. Randon Bragdon, a dentist in Bangor, Maine, for an appointment. In a pre-examination questionnaire, Abbott noted she was HIV-positive. After examining Abbott's teeth,

Bragdon determined that she had a cavity that needed filling. He informed Abbott that he had a policy against filling cavities of HIV-infected patients in his office but that he would fill the cavity in the hospital if Abbott agreed to pay the additional cost of using the hospital. Abbott declined the offer and brought a lawsuit against the dentist under the ADA, alleging discrimination on the basis of her disability.

The ADA states, "No individual shall be discriminated against on the basis of disability in the full and equal enjoyment of the goods, services, facilities, privileges, advantages, or accommodations of any place of public accommodation by any person who . . . operates a place of public accommodation." The term *public accommodation* is defined as including "the professional office of a health care provider." The prohibition against discrimination contains a qualification that permits discrimination when the person seeking services "poses a direct threat to the health or safety of others."[29]

The Supreme Court certified only two questions for its review: Is asymptomatic HIV infection a disability under the ADA, and should the courts defer to the professional judgment of an individual health care provider who believes a patient's HIV infection poses a direct threat? Justice Anthony Kennedy wrote the Court's opinion, in which four other justices concurred. The opinion begins with the ADA's definition of disability, which is "(A) physical or mental impairment [in a person] that substantially limits one or more of the major life activities of such individual; (B) a record of such impairment; or (C) being regarded as having such an impairment." The Court first considered whether HIV infection itself is a physical impairment. The Court had little problem finding that it is. The Court concluded, "In light of the immediacy with which the virus begins to damage the infected person's white blood cells and the severity of the disease, we hold it as an impairment from the moment of infection [and must be regarded] . . . as a physiological disorder with a constant and detrimental effect on the infected person's hemic and lymphatic systems from the moment of infection."

To qualify as a disability according to the ADA's definition, the impairment must not only be physical or mental but must also limit a major life activity. Abbott argued that since HIV infection could reasonably cause a person to decide not to have a child, it affected reproduction, which she argued is a major life activity. The Court agreed and noted specifically, "Reproduction and sexual dynamics surrounding it are central to the life process itself."

The only question remaining was whether the dentist could use his "professional judgment" of his personal risk of contracting HIV from his patient to refuse to provide treatment in his office. The Court decided that a personal judgment, even one made in good faith, was insufficient under the ADA. In the Court's words, "As a health care professional, petitioner had the duty to assess the risk of infection based on objective, scientific information available to him and others in his profession." Using the standard of objective scientific evidence, the Supreme Court concluded that the Court of Appeals had properly refused to give any weight to the dentist's offer to treat the patient in a hospital, because the dentist had provided no "objective, medical evidence showing that treating [the patient] in a hospital would be safer."[30]

The ADA is a historic civil rights law that properly protects all disabled Americans from many forms of discrimination that result from fear and prejudice. As President George H. W. Bush put it when he signed the act, referring to the estimated forty-three million disabled Americans, "Every man, woman, and child with a disability can now pass through a once-closed door to a bright new era of equality, independence, and freedom." Antidiscrimination laws are not, of course, a guarantee of payment and are no substitute for meaningful health care reform in America.

Health plans, even user-friendly ones, pay physicians and hospitals; they don't deliver care. The next chapter deals with the most important institutions that deliver medical care: hospitals.

NOTES

1. Drew Altman & Larry Levitt, *The Sad History of Health Care Cost Containment Told in One Chart*, Health Affairs, January 2003, W83; Robin Toner & Sheryl Gay Stolberg, *Decade after Health Care Crisis, Soaring Costs Brings New Strains*, New York Times, August 11, 2002, A1.

2. Some of the material on metaphors in this chapter is adapted from George J. Annas, *Reforming the Debate on Health Care Reform by Replacing our Metaphors*, 332 New Eng. J. Med. 744 (1995).

3. Julian Barnes, The History of the World in 10 Chapters, New York: Vintage,

1990, 137. *And see* David Blumenthal, *Health Care Reform at the Close of the 20th Century,* 340 New Eng. J. Med. 1916 (1999) ("Given the persistence and magnitude of [the problems in health care] the current debate over health care policy seems strangely circumscribed and muted.").

4. Physicians' Working Group, *Proposal of the Physicians' Working Group for Single-Payer National Health Insurance,* 290 JAMA 798 (2003).

5. *E.g.,* Ethan Halm et al., *Frequency and Impact of Active Clinical Issues and New Impairments on Hospital Discharge in Patients with Hip Fracture,* 163 Archives of Intern Med. 107 (2003).

6. *As Good as It Gets* is a 1996 film, and when the next major HMO-bashing movie, *John Q,* came out in 2002, the American Association of Health Plans hired a public relations firm to counter it. Barbara Martinez, *Tired of Being Cast as the Villain, HMOs Hire Talent Agency,* Wall Street Journal, July 9, 2002, B1. They had good reason to be concerned. In an opinion poll published earlier in 2002, 53 percent of the respondents said that if they were on a jury in a case against an HMO, they would likely decide for the plaintiff, without being told anything about the case. Only 8 percent said they would favor the HMO. Bob Van Voris, *Pollsters Find No Love for HMOs,* National Law J., February 11, 2002, A1.

7. Richard Knox, *HMO's Creator Urges Reform in Quality of Care,* Boston Globe, May 2, 1999, 1. *See also* Sara Singer, *What's Not to Like about HMOs,* 19 Health Affairs 206 (2000).

8. Laura Landro, *Health Care Reformers Regroup in Jackson Hole,* Wall Street Journal, October 2, 2002, D3; *Pioneer of Managed Care Proposes New Generation of Health Care Delivery,* BNA Health Care Policy Report, February 3, 2003, 167 (quoting Paul Ellwood as saying, "Under managed care we were going to let the market decide—the best method would emerge from that. I no longer believe that. . . . Money doesn't talk at the time you're actually receiving service."). Ellwood's group is not alone. When physician–health system expert Donald Berwick's wife, Ann Berwick, was hospitalized in a major teaching hospital, Boston's Brigham and Women's, he found her care fragmented, disorganized, and plagued by poor communication, and says, "[N]othing I could do made any difference. . . . Now, I have been radicalized." Bernard Wysocki, *Doctor Prescribes Quality Control for Medicine's Ills,* Wall Street Journal, May 30, 2002, A1. These experiences are not unique. Amazingly, only about half of all patients in the U.S. get quality care when measured by standard quality indicators. Elizabeth McGlynn et al., *The Quality of Health Care Delivered to Adults in the United States,* 348 New Eng. J. Med. 2635 (2003).

9. James Childress, Who Should Decide? Paternalism in Health Care, New York: Oxford U. Press, 1982, 7; Susan Sontag, Illness as Metaphor and AIDS and Its Metaphors, New York: Doubleday, 1990. *See also* George Lakoff & Mark Johnson, Metaphors We Live By, Chicago: U. Chicago Press, 1980.

10. W. A. Horwitz, *Characteristics of Environmental Ethics: Environmental Activists' Accounts,* 4 Ethics Behav. 345 (1994). *See also* George Sessions, ed., Deep Ecology for the Twenty-First Century, Boston: Shambhala, 1995, and Edward Wilson, The Future of Life, New York: Alfred A. Knopf, 2002.

11. Willard Gaylin, *Faulty Diagnosis: Why Clinton's Health Care Plan Won't Cure What*

Ails Us, Harper's, October 1993, 57–62. *See also* Daniel Callahan, False Hopes, New York: Simon & Schuster, 1998.

12. Editorial, *Population Health Looking Upstream,* 343 Lancet 429 (1994). *See also* John B. McKinlay, *A Case of Refocusing Upstream: The Political Economy of Illness,* Proceedings of American Heart Association Conferences on Applying Behavioral Sciences to Cardiovascular Risk, Seattle: American Health Association, 1974.

13. There are other candidate metaphors, such as the sports metaphor and the religion metaphor, but none offers the constructive possibilities of the ecology metaphor. Of course, other fields, including the military and religion, themselves make use of the medical metaphor. *See* David Harley, *Medical Metaphors in English Moral Theology, 1560–1660,* 48 J. History of Med. & Allied Sci. 396 (1993); *and* George J. Annas, *The Phoenix Heart: What We Have to Lose,* 15 Hastings Cent. Rep. 15 (June 1985).

14. Vaclav Havel, *The New Measure of Man,* New York Times, July 8, 1994, A27. Havel himself wondered whether emphasis on the environment might itself be a product of "anthropocentrism": "It implies that whatever is not human is just something that envelops man—surroundings that are inferior to him and that he should tend and develop in his own image." Vaclav Havel, *Rio and the New Millennium,* New York Times, June 3, 1992, A1.

15. Albert O. Hirschman, Exit, Voice, and Loyalty: Responses to Decline in Firms, Organizations, and States, Cambridge: Harvard U. Press, 1970.

16. Mark A. Rodwin, *Consumer Protection and Managed Care: Issues, Reform Proposals, and Trade-offs,* 32 Houston Law Rev. 1321 (1996). Patients, of course, retain all of their rights in nursing homes, but enforcing rights in this residential setting has been even more difficult than enforcing them in hospitals. Even federal fines have not had a measurable effect on the quality of health care received by the nation's 1.6 million patients in seventeen thousand nursing homes. *See, e.g.,* Robert Pear, *U.S. Toughens Enforcement of Nursing Home Standards,* New York Times, December 4, 2000, A21.

17. Thomas Bodenheimer, *The HMO Backlash—Righteous or Reactionary?* 335 New Eng. J. Med. 1601 (1996); *see also* David Mechanic, *Managed Care as a Target of Distrust,* 277 JAMA 1810 (1997), and David Mechanic, *Physician Discontent: Challenges and Opportunities,* 290 JAMA 941 (2003).

18. Barbara Martinez, *HMOs' Grip Is Easing, Doctors Say,* Wall Street Jounal, January 16, 2003, D4; Rhonda Rundle, *HMO Denial of Crucial Care Is Rare,* Wall Street Journal, February 19, 2003, D3.

19. Michael Weinstein, *Will Patients' Rights Fix the Wrongs?* New York Times, June 24, 2001, WK1.

20. Medicare recipients need much more accurate information about managed care itself. *See, e.g.,* Susan Edgman-Levitan & Paul Cleary, *What Information Do Consumers Want and Need?* 15(4) Health Affairs 42 (1996).

21. *Grijalva v. Shalala,* 946 F.Supp 747 (D.C. Arizona 1996). This case has been up to the Appeals Court and back and remains unresolved. Nonetheless, it illustrates the major issues involved in patient appeals. *See* Wendy Mariner, *Independent External Review of Health Maintenance Organizations' Medical Necessity Decisions,* 347 New Eng. J. Med. 2178 (2002).

22. *AAHP Urges Respect for Appeals Rights, Additional Safeguards in Medicare HMOs,* BNA's Health Law Reporter, November 7, 1996, 1631. Some HMOs are also giving more authority back to physicians. *See, e.g.,* Milt Freudenhein, *Big HMO to Give Decisions on Care Back to Doctors,* New York Times, November 9, 1999, A1. The U.S. Department of Labor issued new benefit-claims procedures that apply to all self-funded employer health plans (so-called ERISA, or Employee Retirement Income Security Act of 1974 health plans) that state law cannot affect. Pension and Welfare Administration, U.S. Dept. of Labor, Employee Retirement Income Security Act of 1974; Rules and Regulations for Administration and Enforcement; Claims Procedure, 65 FR 70246 (November 21, 2000). *And see* Robert Pear, *Clinton Plans to Issue Rules Expanding Patients' Rights,* New York Times, October 9, 2000, A12.

23. Marilyn Chase, *Knowing When You Need the Expertise of a Specialist,* Wall Street Journal, April 14, 1997, B1. Almost one in three physicians, however, at least sometimes does not even offer useful treatments to his or her patients if the treatments are not covered by the patient's health plan. The most common excuse given is to avoid patient pressure on the physician to "game the system" to get the treatment covered. Matthew Wynia et al., *Do Physicians Not Offer Useful Services Because of Coverage Restrictions?* 22(4) Health Affairs 190 (2003).

24. Eleanor D. Kinney, *Procedural Protections for Patients in Capitated Health Plans,* 22 Am. J. Law & Med. 301 (1996). *See also* Kenneth J. Pippin, *Increasing Consumer Power in the Grievance and Appeal Process for Medicare HMO Enrollees,* 33 U. Mich. J. Law Reform 133 (2000).

25. M. A. Hiltzik & D. R. Olmos, *Kaiser-Justice System's Fairness Questioned,* Los Angeles Times, August 30, 1995, A1.

26. *Engalla v. Permanente Medical Group,* 15 Cal. 4th 951, 938 P.2d. 903 (1997).

27. Wendy K. Mariner, *State Regulation of Managed Care and the Employee Retirement Income Security Act,* 335 New Eng. J. Med 1986 (1996).

28. *Bragdon v. Abbott,* 524 U.S. 624 (1998).

29. Americans with Disabilities Act of 1990, 104 Stat. 327, 42 U.S.C. sec. 12101 et seq.

30. *See* George J. Annas, *Protecting Patients from Discrimination: The Americans with Disabilities Act and HIV Infection,* 339 New Eng. J. Med. 1225 (1998).

IV

Hospitals

The medical care environment of the United States continues to change rapidly, and the role of hospitals as the primary location for medical care continues to diminish. Nonetheless, the most complex and risky procedures are still performed in hospitals, the sickest people will probably always be treated in hospitals, and hospitals will always be the site of most emergency medical care. The country's more than five thousand acute-care hospitals also account for a larger share of total health expenditures than any other segment of the industry (about 35 percent), and about 40 million people are admitted to U.S. hospitals annually, one-third through the emergency department. There are about 500 million additional visits to hospitals by people treated as ambulatory patients.[1] Many hospitals have also become vertically integrated with other health care institutions, such as rehabilitation, long-term care facilities, and home care. Large, for-profit hospital chains also developed in the mid-1990s, although they still control fewer than 20 percent of all hospital beds.

Hospitals are unique, bureaucratic institutions that can be alien and alienating to patients. They can also be dangerous, with risks of death, illness, and serious infection. Experts are correct to caution that you should only go to the hospital if it is absolutely necessary. A major study of adverse events in hospitals, for example, found that 18 percent of all hospital patients experienced a serious, preventable adverse event that led to a longer stay, and the risk of experiencing such an event increased 6 percent for each day in the hospital.[2] David Letterman once provided his listeners with his top ten signs that you're in a bad hospital. I found three particularly humorous, probably because they contain some truth: "Instead of a sponge bath, they send a St. Bernard to lick you. Every couple

63

of minutes, you hear a bugle playing Taps. And, instead of 'patient,' they use the term 'plaintiff.'"

Hospitals are also infamous in U.S. popular culture for their many arbitrary rules, backed up by thinly veiled threats. Perhaps the silliest such rule is that all discharged patients must leave the hospital in a wheelchair. An early 2000 episode of HBO's most successful production, *The Sopranos,* illustrates a particularly unnecessary and annoying application of this rule. Corrado Soprano ("Uncle Junior"), a former Mafia chieftain, has just met with his successor, Tony, in the hospital. He is not sick. Nonetheless, the nurse insists that he leave the hospital in a wheelchair. "Hospital rules," she says. Corrado responds, "So, call a cop." A few minutes later, a very large orderly appears and gestures for Corrado to sit in the wheelchair, saying, "Sir, the chair." Corrado complies. We are left with the impression that the hospital operates very much like the Mafia, on implicit threats of violence for not following their "rules." We are also left wondering, what would happen if Corrado didn't sit in the wheelchair? Would the orderly actually resort to violence and injure him? Or would he simply be asked to leave the hospital, which he was doing in any event? Hospitals are intimidating places, and without knowledge of our rights we are likely to be bullied by threats and to simply comply with unreasonable demands, as even Mafia chieftains do.

Hospitals, nonetheless, are not isolated islands, and physicians are not foreign diplomats with legal immunity. Nor do patients check their legal rights at the hospital door. Medicine must be practiced within the framework of the law of the United States and the state in which the hospital is located. All health care facilities are bound by state and federal regulations, by the standards of the Joint Commission on Accreditation of Healthcare Organizations (JCAHO) if they are so accredited, and by their own bylaws and policies. Public facilities, in addition, must assure that those human rights guaranteed by the U.S. Constitution are afforded to all patients. Perhaps the most important thing for patients or their advocates to realize is that few doctors and nurses understand what the law is on patient rights. Nonetheless, you will encounter people in the hospital who think they know the law, who act like bullies, and who will assure you that you must or can't do something because "it's the law." They are almost always wrong. If someone says they are relying on the law, ask them specifically which law, and ask for a copy of it. This will almost always end the person's reliance on this excuse not to do what you ask. If you read and understand the material in this book, you will know more about the law of patient rights than almost anyone you are likely to encounter in a hospital, health care facility, managed care organization, or doctor's office.

Hospitals seem to be getting better. Nonetheless, because you will be sick as a hospital patient, you will need a knowledgeable advocate to accompany you when you become a hospital patient. It is best if this person (or persons) can be with you twenty-four hours a day during your hospital stay. If you are staying for more than a day, you will need at least two advocates, and probably more, to take shifts staying with you. This may be against hospital "visitor policy," but hospitals are not prisons and cannot require you to be kept in "solitary confinement." Moreover, your advocate is your protector, not a "visitor." This chapter introduces both you and your advocate to the hospital.

How are the hospital's goals determined?

Hospitals are corporations. Economists have traditionally assumed that major corporations were primarily guided by profits, and this assumption is reflected in hospitals in the early twenty-first century. John Kenneth Galbraith, however, has noted that once enough profits have been generated to assure survival, large firms have other goals, usually to maximize growth "consistent with the provision of revenues for the requisite investment." Moreover, as an industry grows more complex, defining the nature of these goals and how they will be implemented is no longer primarily in management's hands. Rather, control is in the hands of production and design experts, whom Galbraith terms the "technostructure."[3]

Corporations are also usefully viewed as living organisms, whose primary goal is to survive and thrive. As Arie de Geus has put it: "The living company does not exist solely to provide consumers with goods, or to return investments to shareholders . . . from the point of view of the organization itself all of these purposes are secondary. Like an organism, the living company exists primarily for its own survival and improvement: to fulfill its potential and to become as great as it can be."[4]

The technostructure composed of middle managers and physicians continues to run most large hospitals, both for-profit and nonprofit, and survival remains a key goal. Once hospitals reach the point at which they can deliver a wide range of competent health care services and have been accepted by the community as quality hospitals, their goals tend to shift and multiply. One common goal is the development of expertise in specialized areas, often backed by increasingly sophisticated and expensive medical equipment. Even in the era of managed care, the senior physicians at major medical centers are often able to dictate to hospital management the types of equipment and staffing necessary to develop specialized capabilities, such as heart and liver transplantation and specialized diagnostic imaging. Up-to-date technology adds to the prestige of both the institution and its medical staff and increases the hospital's marketing advantage.

This institutional quest for glory, with its demands for specialization and subspecialization, makes sense on a regional or multistate level. When every hospital in a community, however, acquires the same array of expensive and redundant equipment, immense waste of medical resources is inevitable. Teaching hospitals add education and research to their goals, as have community hospitals recently. As will become apparent in later chapters, education and research are not always completely compatible with patient care, and care may be compromised by those who rank prestige, education, or research ahead of the care and treatment of individual patients. Nonetheless, as the director of the Massachusetts General Hospital correctly emphasized a quarter century ago: "The first function of any hospital worthy of the name is to serve the sick and the injured."[5]

What kinds of hospitals are there?

The more than five thousand acute-care hospitals in the United States can be classified either by type of ownership or service. Some are owned by the local, state, and federal government. Some, such as HCA and Tenet, are for-profit, private hospitals, also termed proprietary hospitals, and have shareholders. Many of these are a part of a "chain" of hospitals with one corporate owner. The majority of hospitals are private, nonprofit institutions, also called charitable or voluntary hospitals. Hospitals may specialize in particular services, such as pediatrics or orthopedics, or in diseases, such as cancer, but the trend is for hospitals to be "general," capable of handling most medical problems.

What is a teaching hospital?

Teaching hospitals (also called academic medical centers) are affiliated with medical schools and provide a training site for their students and recent graduates of their school and other medical schools. As the fictional Dr. Ben Gideon of the television series *Gideon's Crossing* put it to his residents: "This is a teaching hospital. You're here to learn. We could call it a learning hospital, but that would scare the patients." Recent medical school graduates are supposed to be supervised by a private or senior attending physician and consult with in-house specialists in areas such as infectious diseases, cardiology, pulmonology, endocrinology, and radiology. House staff in their first postgraduate year (PGY) of training may be called PGY-1s, interns, first-year residents, or simply residents. Supervision is provided by residents who are usually at least in their second postgraduate year (PGY-2) of training; by residents in their third, fourth, or fifth year; and by fellows (who are doing specialty training after completing their residency); and ultimately by the attending physician.

Twenty-four-hour-a-day in house physician coverage may not be found in other types of hospitals and is an obvious benefit in teaching hospitals, even though the physicians are often interns and residents. In addition, new physicians and medical students are steeped in the current literature and most recent advances in medical science. Students may have more time to listen to patient concerns and to assess and respond to needs. The time and concern they devote to patients can provide greater insight, and it is not unusual for students to uncover problems that are overlooked by others. On the other hand, teaching hospitals can be tiresome and intrusive, since patients are frequently subject to repetitive examinations, interruptions, and interviews. If your health plan permits it, it is important to choose a hospital based on what care the hospital can provide you. An unusual or complex problem generally warrants a teaching setting, with access to multiple medical opinions, and where the latest technology and the most up-to-date specialists are available. Most routine medical and surgical problems can be adequately managed in a community hospital.

There is a lot of lore about teaching hospitals and the demands put on new physicians (interns, or PGY-1s). By far the most well-known, some say infamous, is a book written in the late 1970s by psychiatrist Stephen Bergman, under the pen name Samuel Shem, *The House of God.* This book has been called an "underground classic" for interns, who continue to read it regularly.[6] In a 1995 introduction, John Updike writes that the book did for "medical training what *Catch-22* did for the military life—displayed it as farce, a melee of blunders laboring to murky purpose under corrupt and platitudinous superiors."[7] Updike noted that although the "freewheeling" novel could not be published today because of its simple stereotypes of race, gender, and age, "the book's concerns are more timely than ever, as the American health care system approaches crisis condition—ever more overused, overworked, expensive, and beset by bad publicity, as grotesqueries of mismanagement and fatal mistreatment outdo fiction in the daily newspapers."[8] The *House of God* is dark humor to be sure, but it is useful and entertaining reading for patient advocates (but not necessarily for patients themselves, who will see little humor in it) who are helping patients in teaching hospitals, and I highly recommend it. After only a few hours in a teaching hospital, for example, readers will understand the fourth law of *The House of God*: "The patient is the one with the disease."

Must a patient in a teaching hospital agree to be examined by medical and nursing students?

No. A patient may refuse to interact with medical and nursing students altogether or refuse to have a specific procedure performed by a student. There has not been much research done on how patients actually feel about being examined by medical students, but a study published in 2000 provides useful insight. One hundred outpatients were interviewed and asked to fill out a questionnaire after the differences among medical students, residents, and fully trained physicians were explained. The patients were also told, correctly, "You should understand that you are never obligated to let a medical student talk to you or examine you."

The results revealed that only 2 percent would refuse to allow a medical student to take their blood pressure, and only 7 percent would refuse to give a medical history to one. However, 36 percent of men would probably or definitely refuse to have a rectal exam performed by a medical student, and 39 percent of women would refuse a pelvic exam. Fully 78 percent would definitely or probably refuse to allow a medical student to perform a spinal tap. The results related to surgical procedures were similar: only 2 percent would refuse to let a medical student watch the surgery; but between 47 and 59 percent of respondents would definitely or probably refuse to allow medical students to make the first incision, to perform a rectal or pelvic examination during surgery, or to intubate them.

The authors, Drs. Peter Ubel and Ari Silver-Isenstadt, conclude that many patients, if properly informed, would agree to participate in medical education in a variety of ways, mostly dependent on the particular participation requested. They conclude, "Just as significantly, enough patients say they would refuse interaction with medical students that we need to heed their request for informed consent. After all, an ethical medical education should teach the precedence of patients' rights."[9] I couldn't agree more.

Who are the house staff in a teaching hospital?

There is a militarylike "pecking order" among hospital physicians that reflects education, experience, and job responsibilities. All physicians are not the same and do not possess equal experience and ability.

Day-to-day care in a teaching hospital is managed by the interns and residents, collectively referred to as the house staff. The *attending physician*, called the *physician of record*, oversees your care. If you are in a managed care plan, the plan itself may have a physician called a hospitalist who will be primarily responsible for you.[10] A hospital is a teaching facility by virtue of the presence of house staff who literally provide physician coverage to the hospital or *house* (a term that originated when doctors actually lived at the hospital). At the same time the house staff are providing physician coverage, they are also developing essential clinical skills in the diagnosis and management of patient problems. They, and the medical school faculty, also supervise and teach *medical students,* who are on the lowest rung and are frequently called on to perform the routine work that the residents prefer not to do.

PGY-1s will spend more time with the patient than any other physician. They spend many long and grueling hours at the bedside, and because of their burdensome schedules there have been proposals over the years to limit the number of hours all house staff are on duty. New work rules took effect in 2003 to limit the total number of hours residents could work to eighty hours a week and twenty-four hours on call at a time (in most circumstances).[11] If properly implemented, these rules should improve patient safety and decrease "fatigue-related depression and anger" that can result in "detachment and a lack of compassion for patients."[12] New graduates usually begin work on July 1, so patients are likely to be seen by a relatively inexperienced PGY-1 if admitted to a teaching hospital during the middle of summer. July through September is a tough time for everyone, although everyone also moves up in July so that experienced personnel are available.

Next in line are PGY-2s, or second-year *residents*. Residents provide a system of checks and balances to ensure safe patient care. They supervise and provide teaching to the PGY-1s in their specialty, such as internal medicine, pediatrics, and surgery. If a patient is uncomfortable with any aspect of care, the PGY-2 should be easily accessible to answer questions.

The patient will see the PGY-1 or PGY-2 at least each morning and evening during rounds, usually conducted between 5:00 A.M. and 10:00 A.M. or between 4:00 P.M. and 7:00 P.M. At that time, a team, usually composed of the PGY-2, several PGY-1s, medical students, and nurses, will go around to visit each patient. The patient may or may not be examined but, at a minimum, should expect to have some communication with the team. A senior member of the medical staff will usually participate in rounds. Because there are many patients to see, this is not a good time to ask questions or request information. Instead, it is best to ask your physician to come back after rounds at a specific time to discuss specific matters with you. This provides you both more time and more privacy. You should not, however, hesitate to speak up. You should not allow discussion to occur over or around you: you have a right to participate in, and to ultimately determine, your own care. You also have a right not to have your private medical information discussed in the hospital corridors or in other public places in the hospital. And when the physician does come to speak with you, the physician should say something like, "I'm here to talk about private medical things—do you want anyone here to stay or leave? It's your call." The physician should sit down for this discussion.

A final system of oversight is provided by the *chief resident* and the staff physician responsible for resident training. Patients will often meet these people on rounds and should request to speak with them at any time they need to. The chief resident is selected based on experience and demonstrated ability, and he or she provides supervision, direction, and education to house staff, as well as manages the residents' schedule. The director of resident training is responsible for all residents and reports to either the chief or assistant chief of the respective department. They in turn report to the medical chief of staff or medical director.

All physicians must wear name tags. Designations such as 3d-year medical student and PGY-1 should appear on the name tag but usually do not. Ask who a person is if it is not clear. If you need to contact any of these people, you can ask either house staff, nurses, or the telephone operator for assistance. Some hospitals have a patient representative who can also provide useful information and help resolve problems. Remember that if you are dissatisfied as a patient or patient advocate, there is always someone else in the physician or hospital management hierarchy that you can talk with. Usually the person to contact is the "administrator on call."

Who are the other doctors in the hospital?

While in the hospital, the patient may be seen by consultants, who are generally subspecialists and should be board certified. This designation is regulated by the medical profession through American specialty boards. There are twenty-four such boards, each of which requires an applicant to complete an internship and three to seven years of approved training and practice before issuing a certificate labeling the doctor a "board-certified specialist." No law requires specialists to be certified, and licensed physicians can call themselves anything. Nonetheless, those who have certification are generally the best, since they have specialized training and have agreed to devote the majority of their practice time to their specialty. It is the patient's right to know whether the consultant is board certified and exactly why the consultant has been called, and you should ask.

Interns, residents, and consultants are medical doctors (MDs). Medical students are just that, students studying to become doctors. Medical students will likely see a patient in a teaching hospital, particularly a university hospital. They are usually in their third or fourth year of school but may have just started. They may be wrongly introduced as "young doctor" or "student doctor." Unless "MD" follows their name on their name tag, they are not physicians. Patients have the right to refuse to be examined or treated by a medical student or any other health provider. Nonetheless, it is important to recognize that bedside training is a critical part of physician preparation. Patients who can accommodate a request to be examined by a student may be making an important contribution to the student's education.

Patients and their advocates should also be aware of the historical "see one, do one, teach one" method of educating medical students, nursing students, and house officers, of course, under supervision. Patients should not hesitate to ask anyone if they have done a particular proposed procedure (such as placement of an I.V. line or a spinal tap) before, and if so, how many times. Patients who do not want to be used for "practice," which can entail both increased pain and risk of injury, have the absolute right to refuse and to have a qualified, experienced person do the procedure instead. You or your advocate should not hesitate to ask about the qualifications and experience of all those proposing to treat you *before* a procedure is performed, and you should expect truthful and nondefensive answers.

Biographical information on most physicians licensed to practice medicine can be obtained by consulting the AMA's *American Medical Directory.* Information can also be obtained from the state or local medical society. For board-certified physicians, *The Directory of Medical Specialists* gives more comprehensive biographies, lists all members of the American Specialty Boards, and gives the requirements for board certification in each specialty.[13]

What is the role of the hospital's nursing staff?

Patients are seen by many people, particularly in teaching hospitals. The amount of time physicians spend at the bedside increases or decreases depending on the seriousness or acuity of the patient's problem. Generally, only the nursing staff is present around the clock. The department of nursing employs the largest number of staff, and departmental salaries constitute a large portion of the hospital's overall wage and salary program, the main reason why there have been so many cutbacks on the number of nurses in hospitals lately.

Registered nurses (RNs) are licensed professionals, whose primary responsibility is to coordinate the patient's care and to take responsibility for its continuity. They are the only professionals always in the hospital twenty-four hours a day in nonteaching hospitals (although all hospitals with an emergency department should have twenty-four-a-day physician coverage as well) and the only ones likely to know about everything that will happen to a particular patient in the hospital.

Generally, RNs assess a patient's needs and plan care to meet these needs. They document both components of this process and evaluate their interventions. Nursing care may include physical care, teaching, resource referral, and emotional support. Nursing presence at the bedside is vital to close patient observation, monitoring, and continuous care. Many hospitals now provide nursing care using a *primary nursing* model. The primary-care nurse is a registered nurse who assumes primary responsibility for patient from the time of admission through discharge. When the primary nurse is not at work, an associate nurse will carry out the plan of care and communicate all pertinent information about the patient to the primary nurse. This system enhances the overall coordination and continuity of care. Most important, a specific nurse is responsible for the patient's care. If primary nursing is practiced on the patient's floor, the patient should expect to be informed of the identity of the primary nurse and to develop a working relationship with the nurse. *The primary nurse can be the patient's most important advocate.*

Many institutions have adopted a decentralized approach to nursing administration. This means that authority and accountability for decision making are delegated to the nurse manager level. In this setting, nurse managers interview, hire, counsel, discipline, and even fire employees. Patients who have concerns and are unable to obtain a satisfactory response from the staff nurse should seek out the nurse manager or the unit manager.

Nurses are often overworked and underpaid, and many hospitals have replaced them with nursing assistants who have much less training.[14] This shortage is related to low pay, low prestige, lack of autonomy, rotating and weekend shifts, and mandatory overtime. The nursing shortage will not change until there is a change in how nurses perceive themselves and in how they are perceived by others, that is, until their critical work is viewed as central by patients and physicians. As nursing specialist Suzanne Gordon tells nurses, they must shed the perception that they are "kind but dumb" and that their work is trivial. "Let's face it," she says to nurses, "the angel image just doesn't work."[15] If this has happened in your hospital, your care and comfort will be compromised, and there is not much you or your advocate can do about it, other than being especially vigilant. Low staffing levels of RNs are associated with increases in patient complications, including pneumonia, upper gastrointestinal bleeding, shock, heart attack, and death.[16]

An investigative report by Michael J. Berens of the *Chicago Tribune,* published in late 2000, revealed that "[o]verwhelmed and inadequately trained nurses kill and injure thousands of patients every year as hospitals sacrifice safety for an improved bottom line." Although few states have mandatory reporting laws, the report found that "at least 1,720 hospital patients have been accidentally killed and 9,584 others injured from the actions or inactions of registered nurses across the country, who have seen their daily routine radically altered by cuts in staff and other belt-tightening . . . that creates a harried work environment that often compromises patient welfare."[17] Most cases involve drug overdoses and monitoring failures. For example, two-year-old Miguel Fernandez received a fatal overdose from a newly graduated nurse who was left alone to perform a complicated medical procedure without proper training. Mary Heidenreich, aged seventy-eight, was killed by an overdose given by a nurse who was overwhelmed with the care of fifteen patients. And thirty-eight-year-old Deedra Tolson bled to death following a hysterectomy, unnoticed by a nurse who had twenty critically ill patients under her care.

As the number of RNs is reduced and less well-trained nurse's aides added to save money, hospitals are becoming more and more dangerous for patients. Nursing leaders recognize the problem but have been powerless to adequately address it. Janice Bussert, the president of the Washington State Nurses Association noted, in response to the *Chicago Tribune* story, that the problem is with the entire hospital system, not with individual nurses. In her words, "Adequate registered nurse staffing is the most critical factor in the delivery of quality, safe patient care because it allows time for appropriate nursing assessment of patients and adjustment in the care to meet their constantly changing needs. Without it, errors will occur. . . . [T]here are limits on time off between shifts and a maximum number of hours that truck drivers and airline pilots can work, but no such limits in the health care industry."[18]

Like physicians, nurses have a variety of levels of education, experience, and responsibility. This can present a confusing picture. The basic education preparing nurses to become RNs varies from two to five years. The designation RN simply indicates that the individual has completed an educational program and passed a state licensing exam. The RN may have received an associate degree from a two-year college, a diploma from a hospital-based three-year program, a baccalaureate degree from a four-year college, or a master's degree or doctorate from a graduate school of nursing. There are also nurses with advanced training, called nurse practitioners or clinical nurse specialists. Nursing assistants can have as little as sixty hours of on-the-job training. If they have passed a certification program, they are CNAs, certified nursing assistants. Each nurse should be identified by a name tag that has RN (registered nurse) or licensed practical nurse (LPN) after their name. Nursing assistants may be called (or call themselves) "nurses," but they are not licensed professionals and should *not* be called nurses. Look at the name tag and ask about credentials. It's your right to know.

Hospitals also have other specialized personnel in such fields as respiratory therapy and physical therapy, transportation, and dietetics, who may also see the patient often, depending on the problem. Some hospitals have more than eighty-five separate job descriptions for various medical personnel. Social workers and chaplains are also available for patients who wish to see them. They can be very helpful in resolving specific problems.

If you are a member of a health plan, the health plan may also assign you a *case manager* who is often a nurse, but who works for the health plan (not the hospital). The case manager's job, as described in the Case

Management Society of America's *Standards of Practice,* is to be "an advocate for the patient as well as the payor to facilitate a win-win situation for the patient, the healthcare team and the payor."[19] Of course, there are often irreconcilable differences between the patient's wishes and the cost of the type of care the patient needs. Case managers can be a very useful source of information about care coordination and treatment alternatives, but they work for your health plan and ultimately cannot be your advocate.

What committees in the hospital structure are most likely to directly affect patient care?

Hospitals may have fifty committees or more, each responsible for various aspects of patient care and the management of the hospital. Some of the more important ones are described below. If the patient has a concern directly involving an area over which one of these committees has responsibility, direct communication with the chair or a member of the committee may produce appropriate action on it. A list of chairpersons and individual members can be obtained from the sponsoring department, for example, executive staff from the department of medicine, quality assurance from administration, pharmacy and adverse drug reactions from pharmacy. Some important committees are the following:

Research and Human Research Committee (Institutional Review Board, or IRB). This committee reviews all proposed research involving human subjects in the hospital or related services. The review should occur before the research is instituted to assure that the scientific design is sound, the potential benefits outweigh the risks, equitable selection of subjects occurs, and the properly documented informed consent of each patient involved is obtained.

Utilization Review Committee. This committee is designed to review the appropriateness of hospital services, including the length of hospital stays and diagnostic tests. Its purpose is to improve the use of hospital services, particularly by eliminating hospital stays that are unnecessarily long, although how long is too long is often contested.

Quality Review Committee. This committee is established to evaluate the quality of patient care—to define and respond to problems in the delivery of good care. The committee reports the results of studies and related recommendations and functions largely as an advisory committee. JCAHO, through its sentinel events reporting requirements, has increased the importance of this committee.

Infection Control Committee. This committee studies data related to the incidence of infections among patients. Infection rates for the surgical staff in particular are tracked and investigated. The committee formulates policies and procedures related to infection control, including tuberculosis, HIV, AIDS, and nosocomial (hospital-acquired) infections.

Nursing Policy and Procedures Committee. This committee establishes and reviews nursing department policies and procedures that govern the delivery of nursing care.

Institutional Ethics Committee (IEC). This committee, or something like it, is a product of the 1980s but exists in all hospitals. It usually develops policy for particular areas (such as DNAR [do not attempt resuscitation] orders and terminating treatment on incompetent patients). The committee may also be available for consultation, but because it usually meets very infrequently, it is unlikely to be of much help in resolving an actual conflict. Contact the chair of the committee to find out.

Where do patients fit into the hospital hierarchy?

The dehumanizing aspects of institutional medical care have been well documented. Autobiographical accounts written by physicians and nurses of their experiences, for example, emphasize that hospitals "show little receptivity to concerns about the patients' experience of life in the hospital."[20] An increased awareness by patients of the pressure to act in a certain way and an increased awareness of patient rights may help patients withstand such pressures and manage to maintain more dignity and autonomy.

In teaching hospitals, it has been noted that "the stress of clinical training alienates the doctor from the patient [and] in a real sense the patient becomes the enemy. *(Goddamnit, did she blow her I.V. again? Jesus Christ, did he spike a temp?)*" The writer who referred to patients as "the enemy," Melvin Konner, was a young anthropologist who had just completed his medical school training. At first, he thought this attitude merely an "inadvertent and unfortunate concomitant of medical training," but he later came to see it as "intrinsic."

Not only stress and sleeplessness but the sense of the patient as the cause of one's distress contributes to the doctor's detachment. This detachment is not just objective but downright negative. To cut and puncture a person, to take his or her life in your hands, to pound the chest until ribs break, to decide on drastic action without being able to ask permission, to render a judgment about whether care should continue or stop—these and a thousand other things may require something stronger than objectivity. They may actually require a measure of dislike.[21]

The notion that "dislike" of, or detachment from, the patient is required to be an effective healer will strike most patients as bizarre and frightening. But even if this is the way things are, this does not mean that this is the way they should be.

Patients may be treated as enemies, as machines whose bodily plumbing becomes coextensive with medical machinery, or as "pathologies" (the stomach ulcer or the gallbladder in room 201, for example). Hospitals tend to reinforce dehumanization by bureaucratization (formal rules, routinized jobs, and excessive paperwork) and heavy reliance on technology. But consumer pressure, the move for a national health plan, and other changes are working against dehumanization. As Yale surgeon-writer Sherwin Nuland has perceptively put it: "Every person who comes to the hospital is sick in his own way and requires a level of personal attention, even devotion, that will ever frustrate the purveyors of total efficiency."[22] Vigorous enforcement of patient rights, along with constant pressure to treat patients as individuals and changes in medical education, can help make this model a reality.

The view the hospital staff will take of the patient varies from hospital to hospital. U.S. hospitals in the nineteenth century were heavily class structured. Only the poor went to hospitals, and "every aspect of the patient's life was subject to the institution's paternal oversight."[23] Patients were expected to work in the wards to the extent that their health permitted, no reading was allowed without permission, and use of profane language could result in discharge. Visitors were controlled by a "rigid system of passes." Patients were, in short, treated like children.

By the 1930s and 1940s, many hospitals adopted the posture that hospital patients should be treated like guests, and the hospital should act as if it were a hotel that rents space to patients and their physicians. This view continued into the 1950s and 1960s, but because it shut the hospital administration out of the medical care arena, it ultimately became untenable. Since then, as laws have made the hospital's duties to patients more explicit, the hotel model has withered. In the 1990s, as health care began to be seen by many as a commercial product, some hospitals came to view patients as consumers. With the advent of informed consent and the view that it is good for both patients and providers for patients to be active participants in their care, a new partnership model is developing in which patients are seen as partners in care.

The partnership model is supported by patient rights, with the recognition that each patient is an individual with unique values who has the right to make his or her own decisions. The partnership model also requires the hospital staff and physicians to engage the patient as a unique individual. Although this may seem more difficult, the partnership model is likely to produce added professional satisfaction for physicians and nurses as well. Patients should insist on being treated at least as partners, lest their caregivers mistakenly conclude that patients want to be treated like children, guests, or passive consumers.

Might a patient be seen as a troublemaker for asserting his or her rights?

Of course. Asserting rights, sometimes even asking questions, runs a risk. Judith Lorber's study of "good" and "problem" patients makes this point.[24] Her work bears out other studies indicating that hospital rules are for the benefit of staff, not patients, and that doctors and nurses act in ways that reduce patient autonomy and encourage compliance. The chief method of minimizing troublemaking by patients is to withhold information of things patients might complain about.

Lorber says that most patients resent submission but feel that submissiveness is the proper posture, lest their care suffer. Her study was done in a general hospital in the 1970s, using elective surgery patients. Although younger and better-educated patients tended to resist conforming attitudes and behavior more, most of the patients tended to comply with orders unquestioningly (only 24 percent of patients disagreed with their doctors at least once). Patients who were cooperative, stoic, and uncomplaining were labeled "good patients" by staff, while those demanding time and attention thought to be disproportionate to their medical condition were the "problem patients." The staff did expect patients to make them aware of their needs. Nonetheless, those labeled "problem patients" were more likely to be tranquilized or discharged early.[25]

Even today, patients are sometimes labeled as troublemakers for exercising their right to decide their own fates. Yet autonomy requires accepting responsibility for one's action, even if adverse consequences result. Without increased pressure on hospitals to recognize patient rights, those who do exercise their rights will continue to risk being seen as troublemakers, and the hospital environment will not change.

What is the Joint Commission on Accreditation of Health Care Organizations?

The Joint Commission or JCAHO is the only private hospital-accrediting agency of national significance. It was founded as the Joint Commission on Accreditation of Hospitals (JCAH) in 1952 by the American Medical Association, the American Hospital Association, the American College of Physicians, the American College of Surgeons, and the Canadian Medical Association (which has since formed its own group in Canada). Representatives of the American Association of Homes for the Aging and the American Nursing Home Association were added later, and the name was changed to its current name in 1988. The organization inspects facilities on a voluntary basis and designates them "accredited" if they measure up to a set of published capability criteria. Although submission to such an examination is optional, since 1965, a JCAH-accredited facility has been automatically eligible to be certified as a reimbursable provider under Medicare, provided it also complies with federal utilization requirements. Until 1970, JCAH standards mainly dealt with the medical staff organization, record keeping, and the hospital's physical plant. New standards have since been added in areas such as patient rights, sentinel events reporting, pain management, the emergency department, anesthesia, nursing, infection control, and ambulatory care.

Unfortunately, the fact that a hospital has been accredited by JCAHO is no assurance that proper care is delivered in the hospital. A two-year study by the U.S. Department of Health and Human Services Office of the Inspector General, published in 1999, for example, concluded that JCAHO relies on survey procedures that are inadequate for detecting substandard levels of care; also, on-site inspectors are poorly prepared and permit hospitals to determine the records that will be reviewed. JCAHO's approach has been collegial rather than regulatory. Among the recommendations were calls for unannounced inspections and making all hospital-performance data available to the public. As deputy inspector George F. Grob put it, "Hospitals are dangerous places to be, and people ought to know what they are getting into."[26] JCAHO has taken some tentative steps to reform itself, but patients and their advocates cannot rely on this "old boy" secret network to protect them.[27]

Since JCAHO is not a patient-protection or regulatory agency, and since its record of protecting patients has been so poor, I continue to believe that JCAHO should be replaced with a public federal regulatory agency that will not only accredit hospitals but will also make its findings available to the public, make patient safety and protection its first priority, and go out of its way to solicit and investigate complaints against hospitals by patients and members of the public. Until such a public agency is created, patients and their advocates should insist that hospitals at least adhere to the JCAHO standards on patient rights.

Which standards of the Joint Commission are most relevant to patient rights?

Patient rights are dealt with in a section of the *2003 Hospital Accreditation Standards* entitled "Patient Rights and Organizational Ethics." It provides in relevant part:

Standard: The hospital addresses ethical issues in providing patient care.

A mere listing of patient rights cannot guarantee that those rights are respected. Rather, a hospital demonstrates its support of patient rights through the processes by which staff members interact with and care for patients. These day-to-day interactions reflect a fundamental concern with and respect for patients' rights. All staff members are aware of the ethical issues surrounding patient care, the hospital's policies governing these issues, and the structures available to support ethical decision making.

The hospital establishes and maintains structures to support patient rights, and does so in a collaborative manner that involve the hospital's leaders and others. The structures are based on policies, procedures, and their philosophical basis, which makes up the framework that addresses both *patient care* and *organizational* ethical issues, including the following:

a. The patient's right to reasonable access to care;

b. The patient's right to care that is considerate and respectful of his or her personal values and beliefs;

c. The patient's right to be informed about and participate in decisions regarding his or her care;

d. The patient's right to participate in ethical questions that arise in the course of his or her care; including issues of conflict resolution, withholding resuscitative services, forgoing or withdrawal of life-sustaining treatment, and participation in investigational studies or clinical trials;

e. The patient's right to security and personal privacy and confidentiality of information;

f. The issue of designating a decision maker in case the patient is incapable of understanding a proposed treatment or procedure or is unable to communicate his or her wishes regarding care;

g. The hospital's method of informing the patient of these issues identified in this intent;

h. The hospital's method of educating staff about patient rights and their role in supporting those rights; and

i. The patient's right to access protective services.

In addition, each patient must receive a written statement of his or her rights. This is because

[a]dmission to the hospital can be a frightening and confusing experience for patients, making if difficult for them to understand and exercise their rights. A written copy of the hospital's statement of patients' rights is given to patients when they are admitted and is available to them throughout their stay. This statement is appropriate to the patient's age, understanding and language.

The hospital may also post a copy of its patients' rights document in public areas accessible to patients and their visitors. When written communication is not effective (for example, the patient cannot read or the patient's language is rare in the patient population served), the patient is informed again of his or her rights after admission, in a manner that he or she can understand.[28]

These standards have eclipsed and effectively replaced the 1973 American Hospital Association's (AHA) *Patient Bill of Rights.*[29] Most of the other provisions address advance directives and organ donation, subjects dealt with in chapters 12 and 14 of this book.

What is the legal significance of the Joint Commission standards, the AHA Bill of Rights, and other similar documents on patient rights?

The thrust of the JCAHO standard is to encourage etiquette and courtesy and to summarize fairly basic concepts relating to firmly established legal rights derived from informed consent. Commenting on the AHA Patient Bill of Rights, Dr. Willard Gaylin termed the title "not only pretentious, but deceptive" and described the entire AHA effort as akin to "the thief lecturing his victim on self-protection."[30] Hospitals have a long way to go to equal strides taken in the areas of employer-employee, landlord-tenant, and debtor-creditor relationships. Nonetheless, the AHA document served important symbolic purposes and helped legitimate the entire patient rights movement.[31]

Some states have adopted a patient bill of rights for hospitals by regulation, resolution, or statute, and almost all states have adopted managed care reform laws, many of which are inaccurately described as patient bills of rights. In states with hospital bills of rights, hospitals are legally required to follow the standards set forth in these acts. These enactments are primarily a restatement and codification in one place of existing statutory and common law rights of patients. Thus, citizens in other states possess most, if not all, of these rights as well. Nonetheless, formal statutory enactment of a patient bill of rights is a powerful educational tool and can promote enforcement of patient rights in the state. In addition, all hospitals that admit patients covered by Medicare must adhere to specific patient rights.[32]

When can patients hold hospitals responsible for the actions that result in harm?

In general, violation of a rule or regulation that is designed primarily for the safety of the hospital is evidence of malpractice if the violation causes an injury to the patient.[33] This rule was applied in one case in which a consultation was not sought when it should have been. The court cited the Joint Commission standards (since the hospital was accredited and had agreed to be bound by these standards) on consultation, which provided in part: "The patient's physician is responsible for requesting consultation when indicated. It is the duty of the hospital staff through its chief of service and executive committee to make certain that members of the staff do not fail in the matter of calling consultants as needed."

Hospitals are responsible for the negligent acts of their employees (the doctrine of *respondeat superior*) and for failure to fulfill the duty the hospital owes to its patients directly (the doctrine of *corporate responsibility*). The following examples illustrate areas in which a hospital may be liable for its action or inaction. The list is not meant to be exhaustive: A hospital may be held liable for failure to take reasonable steps to protect the rights and welfare of patients. Simple examples include failure to count instruments after surgery and failure of a hospital radiology department to obtain and check the medical history of a patient referred for X-ray.

Good practice requires that all equipment be properly maintained. Nurses and technicians are also required to read the patient's "signals of danger" and bring these to the immediate attention of a doctor, and if the doctor persists in a course of action that may be to the detriment of the patient, the nurse has an obligation to report this to a hospital administrator to ensure the patient's safety. A facility may not transfer a patient if it will worsen the patient's condition; must not injure a bedridden patient while turning the patient over; nor permit a patient to be burned by a heating lamp, hot-water bottle, or similar device.

Hospitals that are substandard in infection control can also be successfully sued if this could be shown to be the cause of the patient's infection. The Centers for Disease Control and Prevention have estimated that about 5 percent of all patients admitted to hospitals, or almost two million annually, contract an infection while in the hospital, and twenty thousand die as a result (more than die from AIDS). The problem is getting worse as more and more common bacteria become resistant to antibiotics.

One easy way to help prevent patients from acquiring infections is for physicians and nurses to wash their hands between patients (or to change gloves). As Dr. Robert A. Weinstein, the director of infectious diseases for Chicago has put it, "Hands are the most dangerous things in the hospital."[34] Nonetheless, surveys have shown that fewer than 20 percent of physicians in intensive-care units, for example, properly washed their hands.[35] In 2002, the Centers for Disease Control and Prevention issued detailed recommendations on hand washing in health care settings. These should help, but patients will not be particularly comforted by the first recommendation, which seems so obvious it is somewhat distressing that it had to be written down: "When hands are visibly dirty or contaminated with proteinaceous material or are visibly soiled with blood or other body fluids, wash hands."[36] Patients and their advocates should ask physicians and nurses whether they have washed their hands and insist on it if they have not. This will help everyone to deal with the hospital infection problem and perhaps even save the patient's life from this predictable complication.

TIPS FOR ADVOCATES

- **Stay with your patient as much as possible.** Hospitals are dangerous places and are often understaffed.
- Make sure you **know the identity of the physician who is in charge** of the patient's care and how to contact the physician.
- Get to **know the nurses caring for the patient** and their qualifica-

tions and the nurse manager. Go to the director of nursing or patient care services with problems. If this doesn't work, ask to speak with the administrator on call.

• **Understand the patient's diagnosis, prognosis, and alternative treatment options and their risks and benefits.**

• Get to know the resources to help you in the hospital, including the unit clerk, nurse manager, patient representative, the ethics committee, the quality assessment coordinator, the risk manager, the library, and other resources available.

• The patient has no obligation to agree to be touched or treated by a medical or nursing student (or by anyone else for that matter).

• Make sure you and the patient both **know all the medications the patient should be taking,** what each is for, and the proper doses and times they should be administered. Question everything that you or the patient are unsure is correct.

• Schedule time(s) to discuss the patient's care with the patient's physician of record.

• **Review the patient's medical record on a regular basis** and make sure you and the patient understand it.

• Ask everyone who wants to touch the patient if the person has washed their hands and insist that they either wash their hands or use new gloves. This is not an unreasonable request.

• Keep a notebook to record the above information.

Notes

1. *See generally* Agency for Health Care Research and Quality, Hospitalization in the United States, 1997, Silver Spring, Md.: AHRQ Pubs., 2000

2. Lori Andrews et al., *An Alternative Strategy for Studying Adverse Events in Medical Care,* 349 Lancet 309 (1997).

3. John K. Galbraith, The New Industrial State, Boston: Houghton Mifflin, 1967, 176. As Galbraith notes, the goal of expansion "in the output of many goods is not easily accorded a social purpose. More cigarettes cause more cancer. More alcohol causes more cirrhosis. More automobiles cause more accidents, maiming and death, more preemption of space for highways and parking, [and] more pollution of the air and the countryside" (*Id.,* at 164).

4. Arie de Geus, The Living Company, Boston: Harvard Business School Press, 1997, 11.

5. John Knowles, *The Hospital,* Scientific American, September 1973, 143.

6. W. Marston, *Medicine's Steamy Side, for and about Interns,* New York Times, July 6, 1999, 6.

7. John Updike, introduction, Samuel Shem, The House of God, New York: Dell, 1995, 5.

8. *Id.,* at 8.

9. Peter A. Ubel & Ari Silver-Isenstadt, *Are Patients Willing to Participate in Medical Education?* 11 J. Clinical Ethics 230 (2000).

10. S. Z. Pantilat, A. Alpers & R. M. Wachter, *A New Doctor in the House: Ethical Issues in Hospitalist Systems,* 282 JAMA 171 (1999).

11. Ingrid Philibert et al., *New Requirements for Resident Duty Hours,* 288 JAMA 1112 (2002); Robert Steinbrook, *The Debate over Residents' Work Hours,* 347 New Eng. J. Med. 1296 (2002); Debra Weinstein, *Duty Hours for Resident Physicians: Tough Choices for Teaching Hospitals,* 347 New Eng. J. Med. 1275 (2002).

12. David Gaba & Steven Howard, *Fatigue among Clinicians and the Safety of Patients,* 347 New Eng. J. Med. 1249, 1253 (2002); *but see* Jeffrey Drazen & Arnold Epstein, *Rethinking Medical Training: The Critical Work Ahead,* 347 New Eng. J. Med. 1271, 1272 (2002) ("We risk exchanging our sleep-deprived healers for a a cadre of wide-awake technicians.").

13. For more information on the twenty-four medical specialty boards and to find out if a particular physician is a member of one or more of them, go to their Web site (www.abms.org).

14. Claire Fagin, *Nurses, Patients and Managed Care,* New York Times, March 16, 1999.

15. Sarah Corbett, *The Last Shift,* New York Times Magazine, March 16, 2003, 58, 60.

16. Jack Needleman et al., *Nursing Staffing Levels and the Quality of Care in Hospitals,* 346 New Eng. J. Med. 1715 (2002); *see also* Susan Jacoby, *The Nursing Squeeze: Nationwide Shortage Puts Hospital Patients at Higher Risk of Complications, Death,* AARP Bulletin, May, 2003, 6.

17. Michael J. Berens, *Nursing Mistakes Kill, Injure Thousands,* Chicago Tribune, September 10, 2000, 20.

18. *Nurses Counter Chicago Tribune Series on Medical Errors,* PR Newswire, September 13, 2000 (available at www.prnewswire.com).

19. Case Management Society of America, Standards of Practice for Case Management, Little Rock: CMSA, 1995, 10.

20. R. Zussman, *Life in the Hospital: A Review,* 71 Milbauk Q. 167 (1993).

21. Melvin Konner, Becoming a Doctor, New York: Penguin, 1988, 373. *See also* Perri Klass, A Not Entirely Benign Procedure, New York: Putnam, 1987, 373; *see also* S. Hoffman, Under the Ether Dome, New York: Scribner's, 1987, and Samual Shem, House of God, New York: Dell, 1978.

22. Sherwin Nuland, *The Hazards of Hospitalization,* Wall Street Journal, December 2, 1999, A22.

23. Charles E. Rosenberg, The Care of Strangers, New York: Basic Books, 1987, 117.

24. Judith Lorber, *Good Patients and Problem Patients: Conformity and Deviance in a General Hospital,* 16 J. Health & Social Behavior 213 (1975).

25. *Id., and see* Ruth Macklin, Mortal Choices, Boston: Houghton Mifflin, 1987, 214–16.

26. S. Murray, *Medicare's Oversight Program for U.S. Hospitals Is Criticized,* Wall Street Journal, July 21, 1999, B7.

27. Some courts have reached a similar conclusion about JCAHO. In one case, for example, when JCAHO was called JCAH, five of eight dialysis patients at a JCAH-accredited hospital were negligently dialyzed with water that contained excessive amounts of aluminum. They suffered speech disturbances, seizures, walking disorders, and the potentially fatal disease of dialysis dementia. The patients settled a lawsuit with the state of Louisiana, which then sued the JCAH for negligence in its inspection. A Louisiana court of appeals found in favor of the JCAH, ruling that the JCAH surveys and accreditation are not done for the benefit or protection of hospital patients:

The duty to survey did not include within its scope the protection of hospital patients against injury from inattention and possible malpractice of certain hospital personnel and the malfunctioning of certain equipment. . . . [T]he purpose of the JCAH survey was to foster *self-improvement by the hospital.* Any benefit in favor of the hospital patients which resulted from the contractual agreement was merely incidental. JCAH did not contract to monitor, regulate or supervise the standard of [the hospital's] patient care. In fact, JCAH had no authority to mandate compliance with accepted medical standards or to require remedial action. *State v. Joint Commission on Accreditation of Hospitals,* 470 So. 2d 169, 177–178 (La. 1985) (emphasis in original).

And see Timothy Jost, *The Joint Commission on Accreditation of Hospitals: Private Regulation of Health Care and the Public Interest,* 24 B.C.L. Rev. 835 (1983).

28. Joint Commission on Accreditation of Healthcare Organizations, 2003 Hospital Accreditation Standards, Chicago: Joint Commission, 2003, 83.

29. The text of the AHA Bill of Rights appears at note 20 in chapter 1.

30. Willard Gaylin, *The Patient's Bill of Rights,* Saturday Review of Science, March 1973, 22.

31. *E.g., Fonda v. St. Paul City Ry.,* 71 Minn. 438, 74 N.W. 166 (1988); Agency for Health Care Research and Quality, *supra* note 1; and *Stone v. Proctor,* 259 N.C. 633, 131 S.E. 2d 297 (1963); *Pederson v. Duouchel,* 72 Wash. 2d 73, 431 P.2d 973 (1967); *Magana v. Elie,* 108 Ill. App. 3d 1028, 439 N.E.2d 1319 (1982); *Hahn v. Suburban Hospital Assoc.,* 461 A.2d7 (Md. Ct. App. 1983); *Kapuschinsky v. United States,* 248 F. Supp. 732 (D.S.C. 1966); and *Jackson v. Power,* 743 P.2d 1376 (Alaska 1987). In a survey of nurses, for

example, adoption of a patient bill of rights was listed as the most common way of changing hospital policy regarding patient rights. More importantly, nurses at hospitals where the bill of rights was taken seriously reported greater job satisfaction and pride in the quality of patient care.

If adopted as official hospital policy, a patient bill of rights can also be used in court as evidence of a standard of care to which the hospital and its staff can be held. In some early cases, a few courts concluded that to permit the introduction of self-imposed standards into evidence would only discourage the use of such standards, but the modern trend is to allow them into evidence. The Joint Commission standards and hospital bylaws, for example, have been admitted to serve as "evidence of custom" to aid the jury in determining the standard of care to which the hospital should be held. A court might even allow the admission of a document such as the AHA Bill of Rights, even if the defendant hospital had not officially adopted it, on the grounds that it would give the jury an indication of industry custom as practiced by other hospitals.

32. A hospital that admits Medicare-covered patients must protect and promote each patient's rights.

(a) Standard: Notice of rights.
  (1) A hospital must inform each patient, or when appropriate, the patient's representative (as allowed under State law), of the patient's rights, in advance of furnishing or discontinuing patient care whenever possible.
  (2) The hospital must establish a process for prompt resolution of patient grievances and must inform each patient whom to contact to file a grievance. The hospital's governing body must approve and be responsible for the effective operation of the grievance process and must review and resolve grievances, unless it delegates the responsibility in writing to a grievance committee. The grievance process must include a mechanism for timely referral of patient concerns regarding quality of care or premature discharge to the appropriate Utilization and Quality Control Peer Review Organization. At a minimum:
    (i) The hospital must establish a clearly explained procedure for the submission of a patient's written or verbal grievance to the hospital.
    (ii) The grievance process must specify time frames for review of the grievance and the provision of a response.
    (iii) In its resolution of the grievance, the hospital must provide the patient with written notice of its decision that contains the name of the hospital contact person, the steps taken on behalf of the patient to investigate the grievance, the results of the grievance process, and the date of completion.
(b) Standard: Exercise of rights.
  (1) The patient has the right to participate in the development and implementation of his or her plan of care.
  (2) The patient or his or her representative (as allowed under State law) has the right to make informed decisions regarding his or her care. The patient's rights include being informed of his or her health status, being involved in care planning and treatment, and being able to request or refuse treatment or services deemed medically unnecessary or inappropriate.

(3) The patient has the right to formulate advance directives and to have hospital staff and practitioners who provide care in the hospital comply with these directives, in accordance with § 489.100 of this part (definition), § 489.102 of this part (requirements for providers), and § 489.104 of this part (effective dates).

(4) The patient has the right to have a family member or representative of his or her choice and his or her own physician notified promptly of his or her admission to the hospital. (64 Fed. Reg. 36070, 36088 [July 2, 1999])

33. *Darling v. Charlestown Memorial Hospital,* 33 Ill.2d. 326, 211 N.E.2d. 253 (1965). As a result, a malpractice award was upheld. In reaction, JCAHO revised this standard by lowering it to state only that "the use of consultations, and the qualifications of the consultant, should be reviewed as part of medical care evaluation." JCAHO later dropped it altogether.

34. *Doctors Are Reminded, "Wash Up!"* New York Times, November 9, 1999, D1.

35. *See, e.g.,* K. B. Kirkland & J. M. Weinstein, *Adverse Effect of Contact Isolation,* 354 Lancet 1177 (1999), and D. Pittet, et al., *Compliance with Handwashing in a Teaching Hospital,* 130 Annals Internal Med. 126 (1999).

36. Hand Hygiene Task Force, *Guideline for Hand Hygiene in Health Care Settings,* 51 Morbidity and Mortality Weekly Report 1 (2002); *see also* Didier Pittet & John Boyce, *Hand Hygiene and Patient Care: Pursuing the Semmelweis Legacy,* Lancet, Infectious Disease Rev., April 2001, 9, and John Burke, *Infection Control: A Problem for Patient Safety,* 348 New Eng. J. Med. 651 (2003). Infection-control protocols, featuring hand washing, are also the only programs that have had a proven effect on hospital safety as demonstrated by a controlled clinical trial which showed that implementation decreased hospital-acquired infection rates by 32%. *See* Lucian Leape, *Reporting of Adverse Events,* 347 New Eng. J. Med. 1633, 1634 (2002).

V

Emergency Medicine

Emergency medicine, usually centered in a hospital emergency medicine department, presents both health care professionals and patients with unique problems. In an ideal physician-patient interaction, the patient voluntarily enters the relationship, the physician gets to know the patient and has an opportunity to discuss treatment options in detail, and there is time for reflection. In an emergency department, the patient is often brought in by ambulance, the police, or others; does not choose the physician; and there is rarely opportunity for detailed discussion of treatment options. The pain or fear that drives people to seek medical advice is also often more extreme in the emergency setting.

In some cases, the situation may be even worse: the patient may be under the influence of drugs or alcohol or be suffering a severe psychotic episode and actually be hostile to the nurses and physicians who are trying to help.[1] People who are homeless or live alone may also be brought to the emergency department by police because they are intoxicated and there is no other safe place for them. For this group, which society seems to have abandoned, emergency care offers no long-term solution and frustrates care for others who need it. As one astute physician-administrator has described it, "The emergency ward is what the church had been in the Middle Ages: A sanctuary for those with any form of disease—social, psychic, or somatic."[2] Emergency medicine departments have been usefully described as the country's medical "safety net."[3] Emergency departments have also been lauded as places every uninsured person can go to for care, and they can be used as an excuse not to work to provide universal health care insurance for all.[4]

Emergency medicine is now a recognized and valued specialty, and the people working in emergency departments are usually highly skilled and knowledgeable. In fact, even if you have a personal physician, when you need urgent treatment, your physician will usually advise you to go immediately to the nearest emergency department.

Do hospitals have a duty to treat anyone who arrives at an emergency department who needs emergency medical treatment?

Yes. The rule is that if a person is experiencing a medical emergency, a hospital with emergency facilities is legally required to provide appropriate treatment or to arrange for appropriate treatment elsewhere if the hospital is unable to provide it. No completely satisfactory definition of a medical emergency has ever been formulated. In general, however, a medical emergency is an injury or medical condition likely to cause death, disability, or serious illness if not attended to immediately. To encourage people to come to emergency departments early, state laws generally provide that health plans must pay for emergency department visits if a "prudent layperson" would have believed emergency care was needed. A triage nurse will generally decide if a person must be seen immediately or can wait. A screening exam will be done by a physician, a physician's assistant, or a nurse practitioner.

The legal obligation to treat is the hospital's; nonetheless, the physician's role is central. It is the physician's duty to screen the patient to determine whether or not an emergency situation exists. If an emergency does exist, both law and medical ethics require the physician to treat the patient or to find someone who can. The broadest definition of emergency services is that of the American College of Emergency Physicians, most recently reaffirmed in 2002, which defines *emergency services* as "those health care services provided to evaluate and treat medical conditions of recent onset and severity that would lead a prudent layperson, possessing an average knowledge of medicine and health, to believe that urgent and/or unscheduled medical care is required."[5] This definition is motivated in part to satisfy third-party payers, especially under managed care, but it is also one that most laypeople (and state legislators) find reasonable. Emergency treatment (in an emergency department) is the great exception to the general American rule that physicians and hospitals are free to choose their own patients.

Popular culture reflects the critical importance of emergency care to Americans. The same week that President Clinton withdrew his national health insurance plan from the U.S. Senate, for example, the TV drama

ER made its debut. It soon became the number-one TV show in the United States, temporarily supplanted by *Who Wants to Be a Millionaire?* *ER's* incredible popularity for more than six years was based partially on the love Americans have for TV dramas devoted to sex and violence. But much more important, I believe (since many TV shows feature sex and violence), is that the physicians and nurses portrayed in *ER* always do their best to treat anyone who arrives in their emergency department with skill and respect, regardless of the patient's race, social class, or ability to pay. *ER* is thus more than just another TV show: it is emblematic of the importance Americans place on equal access to emergency care.

What are examples of emergency conditions?

Examples of emergency conditions that require the *immediate* attention of a physician are mostly easily recognized, and include the following:

- Chest pain
- Excessive bleeding (hemorrhage)
- Ingestion or exposure to poison or drug overdose
- Anaphylactic reactions (allergic response)
- Head injury leading to bleeding within the brain
- High fever, especially with children and the elderly
- Breathing problems
- Neck, chest, or abdominal injuries
- Abdominal pain
- Changes in personality or level of consciousness[6]

An emergency condition can also include broken bones and cuts that require stitches. The leading case explicitly dealing with the right to receive emergency treatment, for example, involved a four-month-old baby with diarrhea and fever.[7] The family physician had prescribed medication by phone on the second day of the illness and saw the child during office hours on the third day. The child did not sleep at all the third night, and on the morning of the fourth day, the parents, knowing their doctor was not in his office that day, took their child to a hospital emergency department. The nurse on duty refused to examine the child, telling the parents, among other things, that hospital policy forbade treating anyone already under a doctor's care (and not experiencing a "frank emergency") without first contacting the doctor, which she was unable to do. The

parents took their child home and made an appointment to see their
family doctor that night. The child died of pneumonia later that same
afternoon.

The court ruled that the parents could recover damages from the hospital for refusal to treat an "unmistakable emergency." The court found
that the "frank emergency" exception to treating a patient already under
a doctor's care "implied recognition of this duty." But the court also reasoned that the public should be able to rely on an established custom of
hospitals to render emergency assistance in their emergency departments.
This is because a person who requires emergency assistance but is refused
treatment at a place where there is a reasonable expectation of that treatment, is made worse by having treatment delayed as he or she seeks treatment elsewhere. The court applied the legal principle (the negligent termination of gratuitous services) that if a person voluntarily undertakes to
render services to another, service may not be refused or negligently terminated to the detriment of another person who has *reasonably relied on
the representation that the service would be provided.*[8] An analogy is that a
lifeguard at a beach, even an unpaid volunteer, must come to the assistance of a swimmer in trouble, since the swimmer may have reasonably
relied on the lifeguard's presence and implicit promise of help when deciding to swim at that particular beach. The case was sent back for a trial on
the question of whether a reasonably prudent qualified emergency department nurse would have assessed an "unmistakable emergency."

Physician and author Jerome Groopman tells the story of his own son
to illustrate the difficulties involved in both accurately assessing an emergency and communicating with emergency department residents in a busy
teaching hospital. Groopman and his physician-wife brought their nine-
month-old son Steven to the emergency ward of Boston Children's Hospital in the early evening. The resident made the proper diagnosis of an
intestinal blockage by about midnight. Nonetheless, the resident insisted
that surgical treatment could wait until the following morning and informed Groopman, "In my clinical experience we can safely observe your
son overnight." Groopman's wife, Pam, was not satisfied, believing that
her son needed much more immediate treatment, and that the resident
was not listening to her. Groopman decided to go over the resident's head
and called the chief of medicine at home. An expert was dispatched to the
hospital who concluded that since his son Steven's bowel could burst at

any time, possibly killing him, surgery should be performed immediately. Successful surgery was done, perhaps saving the child's life. Groopman urges all of us to trust our own instincts about our children and to insist that diagnostic tests be done and experts be called for second opinions when no satisfactory reason is given for not calling one.[9]

In 2000, a very similar case occurred again at Boston Children's Hospital when residents told the parents of thirteen-month-old Taylor McCormack that surgery to replace a tube that had been placed to drain fluid from her brain could be safely postponed until the morning. While waiting in a non-intensive-care room where she could not be properly monitored, Taylor stopped breathing, was resuscitated, but died six days later. An examination of the case found that the attending physician had fallen asleep with his pager set on vibrate and had slept through several pages to him made by the residents. Another physician noted, "[T]he residents should not have managed this case alone." For Taylor's father, John McCormack, however, there was only one mistake that mattered, his own decision "not to question the postponement of Taylor's surgery."[10]

The breakdown of communication between resident and attending, and between physicians and families, in emergency situations is not, of course, unique to Boston Children's Hospital. It is systemic. Parents are the natural advocates for their children, and when postponing treatment seems wrong or arbitrary, parents need to speak with the attending physician personally and refuse to take no for an answer. Family members must feel free to question decisions and demand reasonable responses as to why waiting or not calling an attending or supervising physician is appropriate (it often is appropriate to wait). Perhaps the most important lesson is to be clear when you believe you need to talk to the attending physician. Ultimately, the attending physician is in charge of the care and is accountable for it.

A state may also impose a duty on hospitals to administer emergency care by statute or regulation. In emergencies, no distinction is made between the duty of private and public hospitals, and no hospital may refuse treatment on the basis of the prospective patient's race, religion, or national origin.[11] Under the Americans with Disabilities Act, no hospital may refuse to treat a patient who has an emergency condition because the patient is HIV positive or has AIDS or any other specific medical disability.[12]

What is patient "dumping"?

Uninsured patients are at risk of being denied treatment in emergency departments because treatment is expensive. Dumping historically refers to the practice of transferring undesirable patients to another facility. In his irreverent *House of God,* Samuel Shem describes gomers ("get out of my emergency room") as "human beings who have lost what goes into being human beings." Gomers are elderly, demented patients, usually transferred from nursing homes, with multiple illnesses that medicine cannot cure. Law number one in the *House of God* is "Gomers don't die."[13] The problem of medical residents in the 1970s, according to Shem, was to keep such patients out of the emergency department (and therefore out of the hospital) because they would make the hospital staff's lives miserable, and there was nothing they could do for them. In the 1990s, the incentives shifted. The new cry was to keep the uninsured and the poor, especially those with AIDS (the "new gomers"), out of the emergency departments, based on economic law number one of the House of Adam Smith: "Poor People Can't Pay."[14]

It is not only the rise of for-profit medicine that has challenged our traditional social commitment to provide emergency services to rich and poor alike but also the erosion of this social commitment on the part of the government itself. And it is not only public hospitals that are the recipients of economic dumps. As Emily Friedman, an early chronicler of the phenomenon, noted twenty years ago, "Catholic institutions in many cities, and children's hospitals in a few, appear to be receiving significant numbers of economic transfers."[15] It was almost inevitable that the federal government would take action to prevent patient dumping: that action is EMTALA.

What are the EMTALA rules?

In April 1986, Congress adopted the Consolidated Omnibus Budget Reconciliation Act of 1985 (COBRA).[16] An amendment to COBRA, entitled the Emergency Medical Treatment and Active Labor Act, or EMTALA, and known variously as EMTALA, COBRA, and the anti-dumping rules, established criteria for emergency services and care of women in active labor in hospitals that admit Medicare patients (almost all do) and criteria for safe transfer of patients between hospitals. The purpose of EMTALA was to outlaw the practice of hospitals (usually private) "dumping" emergency patients onto other hospitals (usually public) because of inability to pay for services. Under EMTALA:

1. A hospital must provide all patients with a medical screening examination to determine if an emergency medical condition exists;

2. A hospital must provide stabilizing treatment to any individual with an emergency medical condition or woman in active labor prior to transfer;

3. If the hospital cannot stabilize the patient, the patient may be transferred to another hospital:

    a. if the responsible physician certifies in writing that the benefit of the transfer outweighs the risk;

    b. if the receiving hospital has space and personnel to treat the patient and has agreed to accept the patient;

    c. if the transferring hospital sends medical records with the patient; and

    d. if the transfer is made in appropriate transportation equipment with life support if necessary.

4. If a hospital knowingly and willfully, or negligently violates any of these provisions, it can be terminated or suspended from the Medicare program; and

5. If a physician or hospital knowingly violates the law, a civil monetary penalty of up to $50,000 can be imposed on each of them for each violation of the law.

The Centers for Medicare and Medicaid Services (CMS), formerly called Health Care Financing Administration, has the primary responsibility for enforcing the law, and the Office of Inspector General of the U.S. Department of Health and Human Services is responsible for applying most penalties.

How is managed care related to EMTALA?

Managed care did not cause patient dumping, but by focusing on the cost of care, it has put more pressure on emergency department personnel to obtain approval before treating. An illustrative case is that of Dawnelle Barris, who brought her eighteen-month-old daughter Mychelle to the emergency department of Martin Luther King/Drew Medical Center in

Los Angeles County. Mychelle had had episodes of vomiting and diarrhea, was lethargic, had trouble breathing, and had a fever of 106.6 degrees. She was examined in the pediatric emergency department by a physician who, believing the fever might be bacterial, wanted a blood culture to rule out a bacterial infection. He did not order it, however, because he believed that since Mychelle was a member of the Kaiser Foundation Health Plan, he would need special authorization from them for the test. Instead, following Kaiser's Emergency Prospective Review Program's protocol, he called Kaiser to arrange transfer of Mychelle to a Kaiser facility and for permission to do a blood test in the meantime. Permission to do the blood test was denied. Antibiotics were not started. This transfer was done solely for economic reasons.

About an hour later, Mychelle had a seizure. An hour after that, she was transferred by ambulance to Kaiser, where she died shortly thereafter. A blood culture performed at autopsy found streptococcus bacteria, readily treated by antibiotics. The death certificate indicated that the bacteria had been present for ten hours. Mychelle's mother sued. A jury found in her favor, against the County of Los Angeles and the emergency department physician, for failure to stabilize Mychelle before transferring her as required by EMTALA. The jury returned a verdict of $1.35 million.[17]

EMTALA has not put an end to patient dumping. Public Citizen's Health Research Group noted that by 2001, 10 percent of the nation's hospitals had violated the act.[18] With hundreds of complaints a year from patients who had been denied emergency care, the Clinton administration issued new guidelines in 1999, restating EMTALA to improve compliance. The guidelines state, among other things:

Under [EMTALA] a hospital must provide to any person who comes seeking emergency services an appropriate medical screening examination sufficient to determine whether he or she has an emergency medical condition, as defined by statute.

If the person is determined to have an emergency medical condition, the hospital is required to stabilize the medical condition of the individual, within the capabilities of the staff and facilities available at the hospital, prior to discharge or transfer. . . .

If the patient's medical condition cannot be stabilized before a transfer requested by the patient (or responsible medical personnel determine that the medical benefits of such transfer outweigh the risks), the hospital is required to follow very specific statutory requirements designed to facilitate a safe transfer to another facility.

A hospital may not delay the provision of an appropriate medical screening examination or further medical examination and stabilizing medical treatment in order to inquire about the individual's method of payment or insurance status.[19]

The guidelines also make it clear that managed care contracts or agreements do not supersede the hospital's EMTALA obligations. Specifically, the guidelines state:

Notwithstanding the terms of any managed care agreements between plans and hospitals, the anti-dumping statute [EMTALA] continues to govern the obligations of hospitals to screen and provide stabilizing medical treatment to individuals who come to the hospital seeking emergency services regardless of the individual's ability to pay. . . . [N]o contract between a hospital and a managed care plan can excuse the hospital from its anti-dumping statute obligations.

The guidelines permit "qualified medical personnel" to do medical screening but require a physician to make the determination that a patient with an emergency condition should be transferred to another hospital for treatment.

Patients may, as discussed later in this book, refuse any medical treatment and change their minds and leave the emergency department against medical advice. The guidelines reinforce this general rule but also advise the hospital to (1) offer further medical treatment to the patient, (2) inform the patient of the benefits of additional screening and treatment and of the risks of leaving, and (3) "take all reasonable steps to secure the individual's written informed consent to refuse such examination and treatment." Patients, of course, do not have to sign anything prior to leaving the emergency department. Hospitals should document the patient's actions in the medical record.

EMTALA also provides that a private malpractice action under state law can be initiated by any person who suffers harm resulting from the hospital's violation of the law. Because private attorneys seldom accept malpractice cases unless there has been severe injury, however, this has not been very effective. Until effective governmental enforcement is forthcoming, it is critical for those who accompany people in emergencies to emergency departments to *insist* (loudly if necessary) that they be treated (and not transferred except for better care), and that the law be complied with.

This does not solve the problem of a disagreement between the emergency department physician who believes a diagnostic test is needed and the managed care plan that refuses to authorize it. The physician can, of course, perform the test anyway, but the physician and the patient know that the patient will be billed directly for the test, the bill will be high, and the patient will be expected to pay it or fight it out with the managed care plan. In this circumstance, it is best to make an informed decision with the emergency department physician, and if you and the physician think the test is needed, document the reasons for it (and get a copy of your medical record with this in it), have the test done, and insist that your health plan pay for it.

Does EMTALA apply to all patients?

Yes. One extreme example is a court ruling that EMTALA requires hospitals even to stabilize an infant with anencephaly (absence of any upper brain). According to the Fourth Circuit Court of Appeals, Congress, in passing EMTALA, provided no exception for anencephalic infants (or anyone else). In the court's words, "a straightforward application of the statute obligates the hospital to provide respiratory support to Baby K (an anencephalic child) when she arrives at the emergency department of the hospital in respiratory distress and treatment is requested on her behalf."[20] While this is correct, I think the court went too far in applying this rule somewhat woodenly in this case.

The hospital suggested two basic reasons why the EMTALA rule should not apply to Baby K. The first was that Baby K's emergency condition was not respiratory distress but anencephaly. The court disagreed, noting that it was her respiratory distress, not her anencephaly, that brought her to the emergency department. Second, Congress did not "intend to require physicians to provide medical treatment outside the prevailing standard of medical care" in passing EMTALA. The appeals court seemed to agree with the hospital that the "prevailing standard of medical care for infants with anencephaly is to provide only warmth, nutrition, and hydration." Nonetheless, the court held that the language of the law was "unambiguous" and included no such limitation on the hospital's responsibility to stabilize emergency conditions.

The court concluded that EMTALA makes no exception either for anencephalic infants or for "comatose patients, those with lung cancer, or those with muscular dystrophy—all of whom may repeatedly seek emergency stabilizing treatment for respiratory distress and also possess an underlying medical condition that severely affects their quality of life and ultimately may result in their death." The dissenting judge argued that EMTALA was enacted to prevent patients from being dumped for economic reasons and that since economic dumping was not an issue with Baby K, the statute was irrelevant. He also argued, correctly I believe, that it was wrong to consider Baby K's treatment as involving a series of discrete emergency conditions; rather, her care should be "regarded as a continuum," since there is "no medical treatment that can improve her condition [of permanent unconsciousness]."[21]

How long must a patient wait to be seen?

Emergency patients should be seen within a reasonable time,[22] and in case of a real emergency, this means very quickly. In one case, a patient entered the emergency department bleeding from a shotgun wound in his arm. He was observed but not treated for two hours, at which time he was transferred to another hospital. He died shortly after arrival. The court understandably found the hospital responsible for the results of the delay in rendering aid.[23] It is often unrealistic, however, to expect to be seen immediately. A reasonable triage system, which includes an evaluation by a triage nurse or other health care professional, should ensure that those persons requiring *immediate* treatment (for example, chest pain, bleeding, major trauma) to safeguard their life or health will obtain it.

The majority of patients who do not arrive by ambulance do not require immediate treatment. It is not uncommon to have to wait from one to six hours to be treated if you do not require immediate attention. It is important to realize that patients are not seen on a first-come, first-served basis, but that the sickest and most critical patients are seen first. A few sophisticated emergency departments actually post expected waiting times, and this seems like a good idea.

Does a patient have a right to be examined by a physician?

A patient usually does, but not always. There is a legal right to be screened by competent triage personnel, and if the patient is determined to have a medical emergency, the patient has a right to be seen and examined by a physician. Initial screening or triage, however, will usually be done by a nurse or physician's assistant but is occasionally done by a clerk. The triage nurse determines the need for immediate medical intervention and decides how long the patient can reasonably wait to see a physician.

A hospital that operates an emergency department must, to be accredited, have a "licensed independent practitioner with appropriate clinical privileges to determine the scope of assessment and care for patients in need of emergency care."[24] Although this standard does not specify the profession of the "licensed practitioner," the case law that exists indicates that if there is reasonable basis for suspecting an emergency exists, a patient has a right to be examined and treated by a physician. In one case, for example, an automobile accident victim was brought in with back pain. A nurse examined him and found no injury. She refused to call a doctor or admit the patient. The following day, in another hospital, he was found to have a broken back. The first hospital was held responsible for not having had a physician examine the patient.[25]

Similarly, in another case, the patient was taken to an emergency ward with chest pain and shortness of breath. He told the nurse on duty he thought he was having a heart attack. Because he did not have the proper type of health insurance, however, she refused to admit him or call his physician to the hospital. The patient returned home and died, and the court decided that the hospital could be found liable for the death.[26]

When has a hospital met its duty to provide emergency treatment?

A hospital must continue to provide emergency treatment until a patient can be transferred or discharged without harm. In one case, a woman with a stab wound was examined and had her wound cleansed and dressed by an intern. She was then transferred to another hospital where she died a short while later during exploratory surgery. The court found that the hospital had not supplied adequate emergency treatment prior to ordering a transfer, and that this contributed to the patient's death.[27] Another case involved a victim of an auto accident. After pulse and blood pressure checks and a brief abdominal exam, the intern in charge left the person unattended. After about forty-five minutes, the patient was transferred to another hospital, where he died thirty minutes later from internal injuries. The court found that the hospital had failed to provide adequate emergency treatment.[28]

A particularly infamous transfer case involved Michael Thompson, a thirteen-year-old boy who was pinned against a wall by an automobile that had fallen off a jack and was rushed by ambulance from the scene directly to the Boswell Memorial Hospital in Sun City, Arizona.[29] He arrived at 8:33 P.M. and was examined and treated by the emergency room physician who found that Michael's left thigh was severely lacerated; there was no pulse in the leg; the left foot and toes were dusky, cool, and clammy; and the bone was visible at the lower end of the laceration near the knee. The physician administered fluids, ordered blood, and called in an orthopedic surgeon.

The surgeon examined Michael, consulted by phone with a vascular surgeon, and determined that Michael's condition was "stabilized" and that he was "medically transferable." At 10:13 P.M., he was placed in an ambulance and transferred to the county hospital where his condition worsened. His condition later stabilized, and surgery was performed at about 1:00 A.M. Michael survived but had serious residual impairment of the left leg, caused by the delay in restoring blood flow, which stopped when the femoral artery was cut.

The hospital stipulated that the surgery could have been performed at Boswell, and that the transfer was "for financial reasons." A Boswell administrator testified that emergency "charity" patients are transferred from Boswell to County whenever a physician, in his or her professional judgment, determines that "a transfer could occur." The emergency room physician did so determine, and a witness for the plaintiff testified that the physician had told Michael's mother, "I have the shitty detail of telling you that Mike will be transferred to County." His mother "begged" the doctor not to send her son there. The primary question before the court was whether the hospital violated the law in transferring this child solely because he lacked the proper insurance. The court reaffirmed Arizona law that "as a matter of public policy, licensed hospitals in this state are required to accept and render care to all patients who present themselves in need of [emergency] care. The patient may not be transferred until all medically indicated emergency care has been completed . . . without consideration of economic circumstance." The court concluded that the child had an emergency condition, that emergency surgery was the indicated treatment, and accordingly, that the hospital had a legal duty to provide that emergency surgery.

What is the physician's role in transfer?

The physician's role is pivotal, since no patient will be transferred unless a physician certifies that the patient is stable and can be safely transferred. If immediate treatment is necessary, it must be provided. If the physician certifies that the patient can be safely transferred without foreseeable risk to his or her health or any decrease in the chance for recovery, the patient can legally be transferred. But what if the county hospital (or tertiary care center) refuses to take the patient? It could do so, for example, if it is itself overwhelmed with emergency patients and is therefore "on divert." The physician can either arrange for the patient to stay at the original hospital or discharge the patient. In this regard, an Arizona court held that "since cessation of hospital care may not be medically indicated despite the cessation of the emergent condition . . . the private hospital may not simply release a seriously ill, indigent patient to perish on the streets."[30] The hospital's obligation to provide care *after* the emergency condition is stabilized *continues* until the patient is properly transferred or is medically fit for discharge from the hospital, and the physician should ensure that the hospital meets this care obligation.

There may be some cases, especially in smaller, community hospitals, in which the hospital does not have the properly trained staff, either on site or on call, to stabilize the patient prior to transfer to a facility that does have physicians (for example, thoracic surgeons) who can treat the patient properly. In this case, a decision to transfer must be made based on the physician's medical judgment that it is in the patient's best interests to be transferred to receive acceptable care. Of course, this decision is very difficult because the patients who most need to be transferred for specialized care will be the sickest and thus those who are in the most danger of death or further injury if transported by ambulance.

May an emergency department lawfully require prepayment or demonstration of an ability to pay as a condition of rendering treatment?

No. Both EMTALA and case law require emergency treatment to be rendered regardless of ability to pay. In one case, for example, an eleven-year-old boy was taken to a hospital for an emergency appendectomy.[31] Two hours later, after having been placed in bed and given medication, he was discharged by the hospital because his mother could not immediately pay $200. Although the court properly treated the case as an issue of negligent discharge rather than as one of refusal to administer emergency aid, the case is an example of a court finding that essential hospital treatment must be administered without regard to cost or ability to pay.

May emergency patients be restrained against their will?

They may be restrained only as a last resort, for example, if patients are homicidal, suicidal, physically threatening others, or in real danger of hurting themselves (e.g., consistently trying to climb over guard rails because drunk). Restraint is an enormous affront to dignity and autonomy. Federal regulations, promulgated in July 1999, apply to all patients in hospitals that participate in Medicare and Medicaid programs and include the following standard for the use of "restraint for acute medical and surgical care":

(1) The patient has the right to be free from restraints of any form that are not medically necessary or are used as a means of coercion, discipline, convenience, or retaliation by staff. . . . (2) A restraint can only be used if needed to improve the patient's well-being and less restrictive interventions have been determined to be ineffective. . . . (3) The use of restraint must be . . . in accordance with the order of a physician or other licensed independent practitioner . . . never written as a standing [or as needed] order. . . . (4) The condition of the restrained patient must be continually assessed monitored, and reevaluated.[32]

This rule, while reasonable, does not make it clear enough that *competent patients, even in an emergency department, have a right to refuse any medical treatment and that the use of restraints can never be justified as a means of forcing treatment on a competent patient just because the doctor disagrees with the patient's decision to refuse treatment.* A case decided in spring 1999 by the Massachusetts Supreme Judicial Court, which did not involve the new regulations, illustrates this and related issues.[33]

Catherine Shine, who was twenty-nine years old at the time, suffered a severe asthma attack on a Sunday morning in March 1990 while at her sister Anna's apartment. Anna suggested that they go to Massachusetts General Hospital. Catherine agreed reluctantly. They went to the emergency department at 7 A.M., where Catherine was given oxygen and medication through an oxygen mask. Catherine soon removed the mask, reporting that the medication gave her a headache, and said she wanted to leave the hospital. This behavior alarmed her treating nurse. Blood gas results, obtained at about 7:30 A.M., showed that she was "very sick." Dr. José Vega, the only attending physician on duty in the emergency department that morning, examined Catherine and concluded that intubation was necessary. Catherine refused, and Vega agreed to continue treatment with the oxygen mask. Anna, meanwhile, telephoned her father, a physician, who agreed with Catherine.

When Anna returned to Catherine's room, Catherine told Anna to "run," and they ran down the corridor to an exit door, where they were forcibly apprehended by a physician and a security guard. Catherine was returned to her room, and Vega immediately ordered her placed in four-point restraints. Anna was removed from the room and not allowed to speak with her sister or observe her treatment. At approximately 8:25 A.M., forcible intubation commenced. Catherine had been in four-point restraints for about forty-five minutes. No one ever questioned Catherine's competence to consent to treatment, nor was there any basis to question her competence. Of course, after forty-five minutes in four-point restraints her breathing may have become severely compromised, and she herself even more frightened and confused. The act of restraining Catherine itself seems to have transformed a potentially serious situation into a frank emergency: the treating physician thus creating the very problem he should have been trying to avoid. Catherine never consented to intubation, and Vega testified that he never discussed the risks and benefits of intubation with Catherine, Anna, or their father. Catherine's condition subsequently improved, and she was released from the hospital the following day.

Evidence was presented at trial that Catherine had been severely traumatized by her mistreatment at the hospital. She had nightmares, cried constantly, was unable to return to work for several months, became obsessed about her medication, and swore repeatedly that she would never go to a hospital again. Approximately two years later, in July 1992, Catherine had a severe asthma attack while at home with her fiance and her brother. She refused to be taken to the hospital. Her brother, nonetheless, called an ambulance, which transported her to a nearby hospital after she became unconscious. After unsuccessful medical treatment, she died. The Massachusetts Supreme Judicial Court reversed a jury verdict for the hospital because the jury was not properly instructed on the law, which states:

If the patient is competent, an emergency physician must obtain her consent before providing treatment, even if the physician is persuaded that, without the treatment, the patient's life is threatened. If the patient's consent cannot be obtained because the patient is unconscious or otherwise incapable of consenting,

the emergency physician should seek the consent of a family member if time and circumstances permit.

The only justification for the use of restraints in an emergency is to prevent patients from physically harming themselves or others, and even then, they should be used only for the shortest time possible. Catherine Shine, as a competent adult patient, also had a legal right to leave the hospital at any time she decided to leave.[34]

Do emergency department patients have a right to have a friend or relative with them during treatment?

Yes, but there may be times when this right can be reasonably restricted. As the case of Catherine Shine illustrates, it can be essential to have your advocate with you at all times during emergency department treatment to avoid mistreatment. Obviously, when you have a serious emergency condition, you will be in no shape to be your own advocate. Emergency department physicians sometimes argue that they have no time for crowd control—but one person is not a crowd. The only persuasive reasons hospitals may have to exclude your advocate are that there is a frank and immediate emergency, and standard treatment of the emergency will require a major invasive procedure (in which case, the treatment room becomes substantially similar to an intensive care unit, and your advocate's presence would compromise the safety or medical care of another patient or patients in the room. There may also be some exceptionally rare cases in which the behavior of your advocate is so disruptive or threatening that emergency department staffs reasonably fear for their own safety, and then your advocate will be asked to leave or be escorted out.

The issue of family members in the emergency department during treatment has become a major one over the past five years. There seems to be general agreement that parents should always be able to stay with their child if that is their wish.[35] The role of other family members and of patient advocates is less certain. The Emergency Nurses Association has strongly advocated the routine presence of families with their loved ones during procedures, including attempted resuscitation, on the basis that it meets the psychological and emotional needs of both the patient and family members. Since most emergency resuscitations are unsuccessful,

the family presence will also aid in the grieving process. Many physicians and hospitals support this policy, although at least some trauma surgeons object strenuously to it, mostly on the basis that families will not understand serious, invasive procedures; might attack or threaten the surgeon; and could distract the surgeon from doing his or her job as skillfully as possible and thus endanger the patient's well-being.[36]

The trend is toward making both hospitals and emergency departments more open and making them more welcoming of family members. Nonetheless, there is resistance from physicians ranging all the way from physicians in training (interns and residents) to senior trauma surgeons, who are used to having their way. If you are a competent, conscious emergency patient, you have the right to have a person of your choice with you at all times if you believe that the person's presence and advice is necessary for you to provide informed consent to treatment and if your advocate does not in any way endanger the health or safety of other emergency patients. Of course, if you are unconscious, someone else must make decisions for you, and if you have previously designated a friend or member of your family to take this responsibility, then that person also has a legal right to stay with you. On the other hand, once it has been determined (however quickly) that a serious invasive procedure will be done, then there is no real role for an advocate to play to protect you, and it may be reasonable for the physicians performing the procedure to insist that the advocate leave them to do their job. Reasonableness and common sense should help you determine how to respond to a request to leave if you are an advocate, or whether to let your advocate leave if you are the patient. To help support their children, and to be available to answer questions and give or withdraw consent, parents should stay with their children during almost all procedures.

What can be done to help guarantee that people experiencing a medical emergency will be treated promptly in a hospital emergency department?

Four actions seem reasonable:

> • Professional associations should reaffirm the ethical requirement of their members to assist all those needing emergency medical care and should permit transfer only for better care.
> • States, through statutes and regulations, should define *emergency*

broadly (rather than narrowly), such as by adopting the "reasonably prudent person" standard, and they should add criminal penalties for hospitals, physicians, and nurses in emergency departments that refuse such services.

• Uninsured individuals should be encouraged to carry cards that set forth the federal law and their state's law regarding emergency treatment; these cards should contain a form for the emergency room physician to sign certifying that no emergency condition exists if he or she refuses to treat them for what they consider an emergency situation, and that transfer can be accomplished without risk and will provide superior services should transfer be ordered.

• EMTALA should be amended to provide that hospitals be required to provide written notification to all patients of their rights under EMTALA; that tertiary hospitals be required to accept patients from small, underequipped hospitals when tertiary care is needed by the patient (to prevent "reverse dumping"); and that periodic, random reviews of hospital transfers be conducted by CMS to ensure that the law is being followed.

Other approaches should also be explored. One is to develop emergency transfer protocols and a mechanism to enforce them. State departments of public health could usefully adopt such protocols as regulations, with input from the hospitals in the state, and enforce them by retrospective review of individual emergency transfers. Noncomplying hospitals could be eliminated from emergency systems, such as the 911 network; fined; or their emergency department's license or permit revoked. Noncompliant physicians and nurses could also be disciplined through the offices of state physician and nurse licensing agencies. Some health plans, such as health maintenance organizations (HMOs), also have overly restrictive policies regarding the use of hospital emergency rooms by their subscribers. If you are a member of a health plan, you should know what its policy is regarding emergency treatment, and if it is too restrictive, you should make your concerns known to the plan and other subscribers and try to get the policy changed. It is far better to try to improve emergency department and health plan policies while you are healthy than to try to fight for your right to emergency care when you need it.

The only right to medical care that free-living U.S. citizens have is the right to be treated in an emergency for an emergency condition. During the 1970s, it seemed that this right was secure and could be the basis for expanding "the rights to medical care" in the country. At the beginning of the new century, even this limited right remains in danger of shrinking significantly because of closing and shrinking emergency departments. Everyone interested in fairness, equity, and a medical care system that at least responds to emergencies without first inquiring into the patient's finances must condemn this trend. Of course, hospitals should be paid for emergency services, and we need to work out a payment mechanism that is universally acceptable. The emergency department rule must remain: treat first and ask about ability to pay later.

Does a government-declared state of emergency affect a person's right to emergency care and to refuse treatment?

A person experiencing a medical emergency has a legal right to be treated in a hospital's emergency department, but local hospitals with emergency departments are likely to be quickly overwhelmed if a state of emergency is declared because large numbers of people have been or may have been exposed to a toxic chemical or biological substance. Americans will, as they did in the anthrax letter attacks in 2001, likely line up at emergency departments to be screened and treated. This is appropriate, and it is well recognized that the first sign of any biological attack is likely to be recognized in a patient seeking care in an emergency department, and that thereafter emergency departments will be quickly overwhelmed and care will have to be provided at other sites.

A state of emergency can be variously defined by both the state and federal governments, but in the wake of September 11, there has been increasing attention paid to the idea of a state of emergency. Many state legislatures, for example, have enacted new laws to strengthen the authority of their public health departments to respond to emergencies in a quasi–martial law manner. There have even been proposals to give public health officials emergency powers to force physicians to screen, vaccinate, and quarantine people without their consent.[37] Such laws, I believe, are not only unconstitutional because they conflict with the patient's constitutional right to refuse any medical treatment but are also dangerous because they are likely to engender fear and mistrust in the public (that otherwise would actively seek out care), leading potentially infected people to flee from medical help.[38] Historically, Americans have tried to be helpful to each other in emergency situations, including September 11 itself. Cooperation with physicians, public health officials, and the public based on trust should be presumed, and disaster planning should encourage cooperation and not be based on fear and force. Americans are not the enemy and should not be treated as the enemy in a bioterrorist-induced emergency.

TIPS FOR ADVOCATES

• If you (as a "reasonably prudent person") think the patient has an emergency condition, **you should insist that the patient be seen by a physician as soon as possible.** (The emergency patient with an emergency condition has a legal right to be seen and evaluated by a physician, or qualified triage nurse or physician's assistant, to determine whether or not the condition is an emergency.)

• **The hospital's emergency department cannot insist that the patient pay or provide proof of insurance before screening and evaluating the patient.**

• **Keep asking questions until you are satisfied that your patient's problems have been properly diagnosed and are being reasonably treated.**

• **The emergency patient may not be transferred to another hospital while an emergency condition exists and the transfer cannot safely be made.** It is your job to let the emergency department staff know that you know the law, and you should insist this doesn't happen.

• **You should stay with the patient at all times.** You have a legal right to stay with the patient if the patient wants you to as the patient's advocate, not as a visitor. (The emergency department staff could reasonably request or require you to leave if your presence threatens the health or safety of other patients in the emergency department or you are so disruptive that the nursing and medical staff cannot perform their jobs, or if major invasive procedures are being performed.)

• **Bring a copy of any health care proxy document with you to the emergency department.**

NOTES

1. Arthur Sanders, *Unique Aspects of Ethics in Emergency Medicine* (in) K. V. Iverson et al., eds., Ethics in Emergency Medicine, 2d ed., Tucson, Ariz.: Galen Press, 1995, 7–10; *and see* Web site of American College of Emergency Physicians (www.acep.org).

2. John Knowles, *The Hospital,* Scientific American, September 1973, 136; *and see* Robert Brook & R. Stevenson, *Effectiveness of Patient Care in an Emergency Room,* 283 New Eng. J. Med. 904 (1970); Randy Kennedy, *Desperately Ill Foreigners at U.S. Emergency Rooms,* New York Times, July 1, 1999, 1.

3. *See* American College of Emergency Physicians, Defending America's Safety Net, Dallas: ACEP, 1999 (available at www.acep.org/practice). *See also* Jennifer Steinhauer, *Emergency Room to Many, Remains the Doctor's Office,* New York Times, October 25, 2000, A1 ("[V]isits to emergency rooms grew 3% a year from 1997 to 1999, and have risen 6 to 8% in the last year.").

4. Health policy expert Emily Friedman has personally noted that this political argument is logistically, practically, medically, and socially wrong. It is logistically wrong, she noted, because many hospitals are just hanging on financially and cannot shoulder the burden of the uninsured alone. It is practically wrong because charitable care is "notoriously unreliable and no substitute for the security insurance provides." It is medically wrong because last-minute care is neither preventive nor comprehensive. And it is socially wrong because having people "beg" for care and wait for hours in an emergency department, only later to be terrorized by bill collectors, "does not protect human dignity." Emily Friedman, Concluding remarks to the National Summit on the Uninsured Conference, Albuquerque, New Mexico, September 8, 2000. Emergency departments on both coasts are also becoming more crowded. *See, e.g.,* Kelly St. John, *Critical Condition: Emergency Wards in Bay Area Are Overwhelmed,* San Francisco Chronicle, November 20, 2000, 1, and Larry Tye, *Hospital Deaths Spur ER Debate,* Boston Globe, November 27, 2000, B1.

5. American College of Emergency Physicians' Web site (www.acep.org) contains this and other ACEP policies.

6. Some leading textbooks on emergency medicine are Peter Rosen et al., Emergency Medicine: Concepts and Clinical Practice, 4th ed., 3 vols., St. Louis: Mosby, 1998; James Roberts & Jarris Hedges, eds., Clinical Procedures in Emergency Medicine, 3d ed., Philadelphia: W. B. Saunders, 1997; Gary Fleisher & Stephen Ludwig, eds., Textbook of Pediatric Emergency Medicine, 4th ed., Baltimore: Williams & Wilkins, 1999; and Lester Haddad et al., eds., Clinical Management of Poisoning and Drug Overdose, 3d ed., Philadelphia: W. B. Saunders, 1998.

7. *Wilmington General Hospital v. Manlove,* 54 Del. 15, 174 A.2d 135 (1961).

8. Other courts have arrived at the same conclusion. *See, e.g., Stanturf v. Sipes,* 447 S.W.2d 558 (Mo. 1969), *Williams v. Hospital Authority of Hall County,* 119 Ga. App. 626, 168 S.E.2d 336 (1969).

9. Jerome Groopman, Second Opinion, New York: Viking, 2000. Groopman also notes that some physicians may be too quick to operate in the same circumstances and tells the story of Ellen O'Connor whose six-month-old daughter Sandra was also diagnosed with an intestinal blockage. The physician recommended exploratory surgery, but O'Connor felt

her child was not in serious trouble and asked if any other test was available. She was told ultrasound could confirm it, but that it was expensive and required a specialist to come in. She insisted, and ultimately an ultrasound was performed that proved there was no blockage. O'Connor said her decision was hard, but that she had to stand up for her child. In her words, "[W]e needed to be sure they were right. It was my baby." (at 37). *See also* J. Hector Pope et al., *Missed Diagnoses of Acute Cardiac Ischemia in the Emergency Department*, 342 New Eng. J. Med. 1163 (2000).

10. Anne Barnard, *A Death at Children's Reverberates*, Boston Globe, August 7, 2001, 1; Anne Barnard, *Teaching Hospital's Dilemma: Instruction vs. Care*, Boston Globe, August 10, 2001, B1, and Anne Barnard, *Grieving father targets medical malpractice*, Boston Globe, July 14, 2003, A1 (John McCormick lobbies against malpractice award caps).

11. *Williams v. Hospital Authority, supra* note 8; *see also Jackson v. Power*, 743 P.2d 1376 (Alaska, 1987), and *Cypress v. Newport News Gen. & Nonsectarian Hospital Ass'n.*, 375 F.2d 648 (4th Cir. 1967).

12. *See, e.g.*, George J. Annas, *Protecting Patients from Discrimination: The Americans with Disabilities Act and HIV Infection*, 339 New Eng. J. Med. 1255 (1998), and *Bragdon v. Abbott*, 524 U.S. 624 (1998), discussed in this book at the end of chapter 3.

13. Samuel Shem, The House of God, New York: Dell, 1995, 43.

14. *See* Arnold Relman, *Economic Consideration in Emergency Care: What Are Hospitals For?* 312 New Eng. J. Med 372 (1985), *and* David Himmelstein et al., *Patient Transfers: Medical Practice as Social Triage*, 74 Am. J. Public Health 494 (1984).

15. Emily Friedman, *The Dumping Dilemma: The Poor Are Always with Some of Us*, Hospitals, September 1, 1982, 53. *See also* Ken Wing, *Medicare and President Reagan's Second Term*, 75 Am. J. Public Health 782 (1985).

16. P.L. 99-272, codified, 42 USC sec. 1395(dd). *See generally* Lawrence Singer, *Look What They've Done to My Law, Ma: COBRA's Implosion*, 33 Houston L. Rev. 113 (1996).

17. *Barris v. County of Los Angeles*, 20 Cal. 4th 101, 972 P.2d 966 (1999). The amount was later reduced to $250,000, the limit on noneconomic damages in a malpractice suit in California.

18. *See, e.g.*, Public Citizen Health Research Group, *Hospitals in Nearly Every State Violate Federal Dumping Laws*, July 12, 2001 (available at www.citizen.org). On the difficulty of applying the law against physicians, *see Cherukuri v. Shalala*, 175 F.3d. 446 (6 Cir. 1999).

19. Dept. of Health and Human Services, Office of Inspector General, *OIG/HCFA Special Advisory Bulletin on the Patient Anti-Dumping Statute*, 64 Fed. Reg. 61353 (1999). The Bush administration's changes in the EMTALA regulations applied to "Medicare-participating hospitals" did not alter these obligations. 68 Fed. Reg. 53222 (September 9, 2003).

20. *In the Matter of Baby K*, 16 F.3d 590 (4th Cir. 1994).

21. After the Baby K case, a survey of forty-three children's hospitals was done with responses obtained from all neonatal intensive-care unit directors, all ethics committee chairpersons, and twenty-two emergency department directors. None of these respondents could recall that their hospital ever ventilated an anencephalic infant upon parental demand. Nonetheless, the surveyors concluded from their phone interviews that because of the possibility of "unwanted litigation and adverse publicity," these hospitals would have

done the same thing Fairfax Hospital did in the face of a mother who insisted on treatment. The surveyors thus concluded that the status quo is to provide futile treatment on demand, and that this "does nothing more than confirm that physicians will do whatever patients and families want, regardless of the treatments' benefits." Lawrence Schneiderman & S. Manning, *The Baby K Case: A Search for the Elusive Standard of Medical Care,* 6 Cambridge Q. Healthcare Ethics 9 (1997).

22. Joint Commission on Accreditation of Healthcare Organizations, 2003 Accreditation Manual for Hospitals (2003).

23. *New Biloxi v. Frazier,* 245 Miss. 185, 146 So. 2d 882 (1962).

24. Joint Commission, *supra* note 22, at 102.

25. *Citizen's Hospital Assoc. v. Schoulin,* 48 Ala. App 101, 262 So.2d 303 (1972).

26. *O'Neill v. Montefiore Hospital,* 11 A.D.2d 132, 202 N.Y.S.2d 436 (1960).

27. *Jones v. City of New York,* 134 N.Y.S.2d 779 (Sup. Ct. 1954), *modified,* 286 A.D.2d 825, 143 N.Y.S.2d 628 (1955).

28. *Methodist Hospital v. Ball,* 50 Tenn. App. 460, 362 S.W.2d 475 (1961). *See also Mulligan v. Wetchler,* 39 A.D.2d 102, 332 N.Y.S.2d 68 (1972).

29. *Thompson v. Sun City Community Hospital,* 141 Ariz. 597, 688 P.2d 605 (1984).

30. *St. Joseph's Hospital v. Maricopa Co.,* 142 Ariz. 94, 98, 699 P.2d 986, 990 (1984).

31. *LeJeune Road Hospital v. Watson,* 171 So. 2d 202 (Fla. Dist. Ct. App. 1965); *Tabor v. Doctors Memorial Hospital,* 501 So. 2d 243 (La. Ct. App. 1987).

32. Health Care Financing Administration, Department of Health and Human Services, *Medicare and Medicaid Programs: Hospital Conditions of Participation, Patients' Rights,* 64 Fed. Reg. 36070 (1998).

33. *Shine v. Vega,* 429 Mass. 456, 709 N.E.2d 58 (1999).

34. *See generally* George J. Annas, *The Last Resort: The Use of Restraints in Medical Emergencies,* 341 New Eng. J. Med. 1408 (1999).

35. *See, e.g.,* Alfred Sacchetti et al., *Acceptance of Family Member Presence During Pediatric Resuscitations in the Emergency Department: Effects of Personal Experience,* 16 Pediatric Emergency Care 85 (2000) (survey concluding that opinions on family presence are strongly influenced by personal experience); Alfred Sacchetti et al., *Family Member Presence During Pediatric Emergency Department Procedures,* 12 Pediatric Emergency Care 268 (1996) (family presence is favored by family members); and Ellen Tsai, *Should Family Members Be Present During Cardiopulmonary Resuscitation?* 346 New Eng. J. Med. 1021 (2002) (argues that family members should be given the opportunity to be present).

36. Stephen Helmer et al., *Family Presence During Trauma Resuscitation: A Survey of AAST and ENA Members,* 48 J. Trauma: Injury, Infection and Critical Care 1015 (2000); *see also* Steve Findlay, *Some Hospitals Now Let Family Members in ER's,* USA Today, February 26, 1998, 1, and Robert Davis, *Bedside in the ER,* USA Today, March 7, 2000, 1.

37. James Hodge & Larry Gostin, *Protecting the Public's Health in an Era of Bioterrorism: The Model State Emergency Health Powers Act* (in) Jonathan Moreno, ed., In the Wake of Terror: Medicine and Morality in a Time of Crisis, Cambridge: MIT Press, 2003, 17–32.

38. George J. Annas, *Terrorism and Human Rights* (in) Jonathan Moreno, *supra* note 37, at 33–50; George J. Annas, *Bioterrorism, Public Health and Civil Liberties,* 346 New Eng. J. Med. 1337 (2002).

VI

Informed Choice

I nformed consent, more accurately termed *informed choice*, is the most important legal doctrine in the doctor-patient relationship and in health care facilities. Information is power, and because information sharing inevitably results in decision sharing, the doctrine of informed consent has helped transform the doctor-patient relationship. It is not only important because of its implications for power and accountability but also because many other patient rights are either derived from or enhanced by the doctrine of informed consent. The basic concept is simple: a doctor may not treat a patient until the doctor has given the patient some basic information about what the doctor proposes and the alternatives, and the patient has chosen which course of treatment, if any, to take. The overwhelming majority of Americans agree with this proposition and the foundation on which it stands: people have a right to decide whether or not to have their bodies invaded because of their overwhelming interest in bodily integrity and self-determination. Put more simply, it's the patient's body. The patient is the one who must experience the medical invasion and live with its consequences. There is no obligation to accept any medical treatment, and it is remarkable that anyone ever considered it acceptable practice to treat an adult without informed consent.

Physicians have no roving mandate to treat whoever they believe is in need of their services. The notion that the doctor "knows best" and should therefore make decisions for the patient is known as medical paternalism; the physician-father makes decisions for the patient-child. Paternalism is an old-fashioned idea that has been totally discredited, although some dinosaurs still roam hospital corridors. As one court summarized the law at the dawn of the twentieth century: "Under a free government at least, the free citizen's first and greatest right which underlies all others—the right to the inviolability of his person, in other words, his right to himself, is the subject of universal acquiescence, and this right necessarily forbids a physician . . . to violate without permission the bodily integrity of his patient by a major or capital operation."[1]

In the most important study of informed consent to date, the President's Commission for the Study of Ethical Problems in Medicine concluded that informed consent has its foundations in law and is an ethical imperative as well. It also concluded that "ethically valid consent is a process of shared decision making based upon mutual respect and participation, not a ritual to be equated with reciting the contents of a form that details the risks of particular treatments." Its foundation is the fundamental recognition "that adults are entitled to accept or reject health care interventions on the basis of their own personal values and in furtherance of their own personal goals."[2]

In *Love, Medicine, and Miracles,* surgeon Bernie Siegel underlined the importance of informed consent and shared decision making to enhancing the doctor-patient relationship and avoiding malpractice lawsuits: "Shared responsibility increases cooperation and reduces the resentments that often lead to malpractice suits. Second-guessing and recrimination are unlikely when decisions are based on a mutual assessment of what is right for the patient now, not on predictions about the unknowable future. . . . The physician must remember that it's the patient who must make the choice and then *live with it.*"[3]

This chapter explores the doctrine of informed consent, including where it comes from, what it means in practice, how patients can be sure they have been properly informed, and the right to refuse or place conditions on consent. Unique problems involving dying patients are dealt with in chapters 12 and 13, and issues involving surgery, as well as consent and refusal of treatment for children, are discussed in the following chapter. Many states have specific statutes on informed consent.[4] Nonetheless, the doctrine of informed consent is substantially similar across the country. Where it differs is usually based on the trend toward requiring more, rather than less, disclosure and toward measuring the doctor's obligation by reference to what patients need to know to make their own decisions (often termed material information) rather than by what doctors typically tell their patients. The goal of the doctrine of informed consent is to enhance and encourage a responsible patient-physician partnership designed to share information and to provide the patient with the right to make the final decision about treatment.

What is the difference between consent and informed consent (informed choice)?

Historically, the unauthorized performance of a medical or surgical procedure was dealt with by the law of battery, a legal term for any intentional, unauthorized, offensive touching. Examples of battery include a punch in the face, an unwanted kiss in the dark, or a push down the stairs. Some courts use the terms *assault, battery,* and *assault and battery* interchangeably. In one famous opinion, Judge Benjamin Cardozo wrote: "Every human being of adult years and sound mind has a right to determine what shall be done with his own body; and a surgeon who performs an operation without his patient's consent commits an assault for which he is liable in damages."[5]

Since battery connotes an unauthorized touching, it is most applicable either when the physician treats a patient without obtaining any consent or when the doctor properly obtains consent for one type of an operation but does another (for example, when a doctor operates on the wrong ear). The modern trend is to discard the battery model for all but these glaring types of misconduct (because in most cases treatment is in fact authorized) and to examine the physician's lack of disclosure of material information to the patient as negligence.

Under the negligence theory, the doctor has an affirmative duty to the patient, based on the fiduciary (trust) nature of the doctor-patient relationship, to disclose relevant, material facts about a proposed treatment. If material risks are not disclosed, and if the patient suffers an undisclosed material risk, the patient may sue the doctor for negligence. The distinction between suing in battery or negligence may seem only semantic. But in many states, a patient is still required to present expert evidence by a physician to prove how much the "average doctor of good standing" discloses (since in these states customary medical practice defines how much the doctor must tell the patient). In a battery lawsuit, expert opinion becomes irrelevant because the doctor's privilege to touch the patient ends when the doctor exceeds the scope of the patient's consent.[6] The choice between battery or negligence may also determine the period of time during which the lawsuit can be brought (statute of limitations), the nature and extent of the damages that can be recovered, and the test used to prove that the patient's injury was caused by the physician.

What is the doctrine of informed consent?

The doctrine of informed consent, simply stated, is that *before* a patient is asked to choose to undergo any treatment or procedure that has risks, the patient must be provided with information. This information includes at least the following, which must, of course, be presented in *language the patient can understand:*

- A description of the recommended treatment or procedure
- A description of the risks and benefits of the recommended procedure, with special emphasis on risks of death or serious bodily disability
- A description of the alternatives, including other treatments or procedures, along with the risks and benefits of these alternatives
- The likely results of no treatment
- The probability of success and what the physician means by success
- The major problems anticipated in recuperation and the amount of time during which the patient will not be able to resume his or her normal activities
- Any other information generally provided to patients in this situation by other qualified physicians[7]

As can readily be seen from this list, there is nothing profound or mysterious about informed consent: it is based on common sense and includes what almost anyone would need to know to make a decision about whether or not to accept a treatment recommendation by a physician. Some physicians have argued that the doctrine puts physicians at a disadvantage, because it is difficult to determine what risks should be disclosed. The courts have generally answered as follows: the risks that must be disclosed are *material* risks, that is, those risks that might cause a reasonable patient to decide not to undergo the recommended treatment (and choose either an alternative treatment or no treatment at all). Another way to think about the materiality or importance of a risk is by multiplying the probability that a risk will occur by the magnitude of that risk.[8] For example, even a one in ten thousand risk of death must always be disclosed, but not a one in ten thousand risk of a two-hour headache.

All information must, of course, be presented in language the patient can understand, and treatment should not proceed until the health care provider is satisfied that the patient actually does understand the information presented and decides to proceed.

How good are doctors and patients at communicating probabilities?

Most Americans have a difficult time with probabilities, and this is illustrated by the tremendous growth and profitability of the gambling industry in the United States. Probabilities become even harder to communicate and understand when questions of personal survival, success rates, and quality of life outcomes are under discussion.

Physicians use a wide variety of expressions to describe likely outcomes, for example, the likelihood of a particular side effect of a drug actually occurring. The terminology chosen is often based on severity of the possible side effect. In one study, for example, in which physicians were asked to choose the word *rare* (defined as less than one per thousand) to describe a side effect of a drug, physicians were much more likely to minimize the probability of a side effect if the drug was a beta-blocker (prescribed to prevent heart attacks) than an antihistamine (for nasal congestion). The physicians used *rare* 60 percent of the time for a beta-blocker side effect and only 20 percent of the time for an antihistamine side effect, whereas the actual probability of experiencing a side effect from the two drugs was the same. The point is that context matters, and that the meaning of an expression may be very different depending on the specific condition involved.[9]

Another study explored the meaning of a set of common expressions, including, in the order from most certain to be successful to most certain not to be successful, *certain, almost certain, very likely, probable, likely, frequently, not unreasonable, possible, unlikely, improbable, almost never,* and *never.* Studies of how physicians use these expressions have revealed a wide range in their meanings. Basically, this study showed very little variation in the meaning of probabilities at the extremes (certain means always, and never means never). In the middle range of expressions, however, there can be a wide variation in meaning, with words like *probably, likely,* and *frequently* having large potential variations, so that one physician may mean 70 or 80 percent of the time when using a word such as *probable,* whereas another physician using the same word may mean only 40 to 50 percent of the time.[10]

In a study of patients, one-third wanted only numerical probability information, one-third wanted only verbal expressions of probability, and the rest either didn't care or wanted both numbers and words. The study had results similar to the physician study in the middle range of verbal expressions of probability. It also showed that patients make no distinction between the following pairs of words: *likely* and *frequently, possible* and *not unreasonable, improbable* and *unlikely.* The study recommended that physicians drop one term from each of these pairs to improve communication.[11]

The lesson from all of these studies is that you should ask for both the numerical value your physician puts on the likelihood of success (or side effects), as well as the verbal description of that probability. Of these two, the most meaningful is the actual number, although precision is often illusory. For example, whether that number is itself meaningful depends on the data in the medical literature about side effects, and success may also depend on the actual experience of the physician. Trying to be as accurate and realistic as possible about risks is reasonable. On the other hand, both physicians and patients must accept the fact that uncertainty is inherent in medicine.[12] Even with the best data and outcome studies, there can be no guarantees regarding risks and outcome in individual cases.[13]

Do physicians and patients value treatment outcomes the same?

No. If the value physicians placed on particular outcomes and risks were the same as their patients, informed consent would be much less important to patients. But doctors and patients really do have different values. One study, for example, compared alternative treatments for cancer of the larynx. The first alternative, surgical removal of the larynx, would result in a three-year survival rate of 60 percent, but with loss of normal speech. Radiation therapy, on the other hand, had a 30 to 40 percent three-year survival rate, but it preserved normal speech. Physicians tended to think that surgery was best because it had the best survival rate. A survey of healthy volunteers, using utility theory, disclosed that 20 percent of them would choose radiation instead of surgery to preserve their quality of remaining life, and another 24 percent would try the radiation first and only agree to surgery later if needed.[14]

The point, of course, is that there is no right or wrong answer about trading off quality of life for a statistical increase in quantity of life. The only person who can make this trade-off is the patient. It is the primary role of the informed consent doctrine to make sure the physician provides the patient with enough accurate information so the patient can make an informed choice about what course is right for him or her.

Do patients have a right to know their prognosis?

Yes, but the patient may have to ask. I think prognosis information is always material, but courts have only required it to be disclosed without a specific request after a factual determination that it was material in a particular case. Therefore, it is best for the patient to ask the physician about prognosis (likely outcome with and without treatment). This question was put before the California Supreme Court, the court with the most experience in deciding informed consent cases, in 1993.

The leading case that outlined the basic requirements for informed consent was decided by the California Supreme Court in 1972, *Cobbs v. Grant.*[15] Ralph Cobbs had an ulcer and his surgeon, Dr. Dudley Grant, recommended an operation on his small intestine. Grant did not tell his patient that this operation carried two further, small risks: losing his spleen and developing a stomach ulcer. Both of these risks materialized after the surgery, and Cobbs sued, arguing that he never would have consented to the surgery had he been properly informed of the risks.

The California Supreme Court concluded that physicians have a duty to provide certain information because sick people necessarily are dependent on their physician. Physicians are licensed by the state to "practice medicine," and medical practice is not just routine business in which commercial deals are made on an arms-length basis. Instead, the doctor-patient relationship is intensely personal and unbalanced. The patient must trust the physician. This trust carries obligations to disclose; and trust will be misplaced if at least basic, material information is not shared by the physician with the patient.

A later California case, *Truman v. Thomas,*[16] involved the refusal by a young mother to have a Pap smear. The court concluded that material information had to be disclosed even if the patient refused a test or treatment (and thus would not be touched or treated by the physician). Otherwise, the court said, patients would not have a real choice because they would not be able to "meaningfully exercise their right to make decisions about their own bodies." And in another California case, *Moore v. Regents of University of California*,[17] about creating an immortal cell line from a diseased spleen that a surgeon had removed from John Moore, the court held that the physician must disclose "personal interests unrelated to the patient's health, whether research or economic, that may affect the physician's personal judgment." This disclosure was required so patients could learn if a physician had an ulterior motive (such as a personal research or commercial interest) in making a particular treatment recommendation.

Nonetheless, when the California Supreme Court was confronted with the question of whether physicians must disclose a patient's life expectancy as predicted by mortality statistics, it said no, because the court found it would not have added substantially to what the plaintiff already knew. The court thought, for example, that "statistical morbidity values derived from the experience of population groups are inherently unreliable and offer little assurance regarding the fate of the individual patient." The patient in the case *Arato v. Avedon*,[18] forty-two-year-old electrical contractor Miklos Arato, had pancreatic cancer, which was 95 percent fatal within one year. Nonetheless, his physician recommended interventions without disclosing their very small chance of success. The California Supreme Court concluded:

Rather than mandate the disclosure of specific information as a matter of law, the better rule is to instruct the jury that a physician is under a legal duty to disclose to the patient all material information—that is, information which would be regarded as significant by a reasonable person in the patient's position when deciding to accept or reject a recommended medical procedure—needed to make an informed decision regarding a proposed treatment.

I think the court's opinion was too narrow because prognosis is *always* material, since it indicates whether the patient is likely to survive, and the probable quality of life with and without the proposed treatment. In other words, the issue of informed consent in this instance centers on the disclosure of the *success rate* of the proposed treatment in terms of the prospects for long-term survival and the patient's quality of life. This is what patients need to know, and prognosis information is the type of material information patients have a right to—not only because it is the patient's body but, more importantly, because it is the patient's life.[19]

Does a patient have a right to know his or her physician's experience with a patient's disease or condition?

Yes. Although if experience information is not provided by the physician, the patient may have to ask for this information. In a 1996 case, for example, a patient, Donna Johnson, was diagnosed as having an enlarging brain aneurysm, and surgery was recommended by her neurosurgeon.[20] Following surgery, Johnson, who had no physical impairments prior to the surgery, was unable to walk or control her bowel and bladder, and her vision, speech and upper body coordination were impaired. She sued her surgeon for failure to disclose not only his lack of experience, but also the availability of more qualified surgeons in the area. Johnson specifically argued that the surgeon understated the risks and should have told her that he had only done nine aneurysms, and none like the one the plaintiff had, and that there were many more qualified neurosurgeons close by. Relying both on basic informed consent doctrine and a specific Wisconsin statute on informed consent, the Wisconsin Supreme Court concluded that this information should have been disclosed because it was "material." In the court's words, "[H]ad a reasonable person in the plaintiff's position been aware of the defendant's relative lack of experience in performing basilar bifurcation aneurysm surgery, that person would not have undergone surgery with him."

The lesson from this case is obvious: informed consent requires some basic knowledge about risks and benefits. The physician's personal experience and the availability of more experience physicians is material to the patient's decision and therefore should be disclosed to the patient. If the physician does not disclose his or her experience, especially with complex problems that can have serious side effects, you (and your advocate) should be sure to ask. It is, after all, you, not the physician, who will be undergoing the treatment, and you who will have to live with its consequences.

Why did the courts adopt the doctrine of informed consent?

The doctrine of informed consent was articulated by the courts for two basic reasons: to promote patient self-determination and to promote rational decision making.[21] The reason that it is seen as reasonable to require physicians to provide information is that patients are generally ignorant of medical sciences and so are "abjectly dependent" on their physicians for information needed to make a personal decision about treatment.[22]

Another way to think of it is that caveat emptor (let the buyer beware) is not an appropriate or useful model for the doctor-patient relationship. The patient *should* be able to trust that the doctor will share such critical information.

It has, however, been persuasively suggested by Jay Katz that as courts view it, informed consent is too arbitrary a conceptionalization of the doctor-patient relationship, and that the reality is one of psychoanalytical richness, ambiguity, and uncertainty in which the patient often plays the part of the child and the doctor that of the parent.[23] This is certainly true: the doctor-patient relationship is much more complex than simple information exchange. Katz is also correct when he underscores that sharing uncertainty (rather than "guesstimated" numbers) can be as important as sharing other information, and that theory of informed consent is seldom reflected in real encounters between physicians and patients. Nevertheless, to encourage dialogue the law properly defines the disclosure rules so that doctors know what is expected of them and patients can obtain the basic information they need to decide about treatment. Information disclosure will not necessarily result in an ideal doctor-patient relationship, but it should help enhance patient autonomy and participation in decision making, and no ethical doctor-patient relationship can exist without it.

Has informed choice and patient autonomy gone too far?

My own view is that courts have not gone far enough in promoting honest and full disclosure of relevant information to patients, and that is why patients and their advocates may have to insist that specific information, such as the physician's experience, be discussed. There are, however, some commentators who think patient choice has been put on too high a pedestal, and that what sick people really want is kindness and caring rather that simply more information. This view has been articulated from two perspectives. The most intriguing one is from a law professor, Carl Schneider, who thinks that medical ethicists and lawyers are taking autonomy too seriously, when, in fact, sick people themselves are often in no position to act as autonomous individuals. This is certainly true when patients are heavily medicated and may appear to be lucid to people who don't know them. As Schneider accurately observes, patients often choose interventions immediately after they are presented with them, based on things such as "intuition, instinct, and impulse" rather than through some rational weighing of risks and benefits. He also thinks that, at least in the case of major medical illnesses, physicians are likely to make better medical decisions than patients because "emotions distort decisions."

For all his caveats, however, Schneider ultimately does not conclude that we should do away with informed consent but rather that we should focus more on what he thinks patients really want: a competent physician who cares about them. He sets forth ten rules that physicians should follow: (1) do not keep people waiting, (2) respect privacy, (3) introduce yourself to strangers, (4) grant other adults the same courtesy in titles you accord yourself, (5) take the time you need to talk to the patient, (6) listen, and seem to listen, (7) say please and thank you, (8) express sympathy when you deliver bad news, (9) return your phone calls, and (10) think about the effect on your patients of what you do and say.[24]

These are all matters of common courtesy and ones we can probably all agree with. The problem, of course, is that this series of Miss Manners—type rules of etiquette deals only with surfaces, not substance. Yes, autonomy, especially in the face of severe illness and possible death, is difficult, even terrifying. When you become very sick you may prefer not to participate in a dialogue about your prognosis and medical options. I think you should, nonetheless. It's your body and your life. I also think that you should pick an advocate who will help you to make the decision that you think is best for you.

Schneider is not, however, alone in advising physicians to act as if they care about patients, even if they don't. Physician commentators viewing the doctor-patient relationship from another perspective have gone so far as to suggest that physicians learn how to pretend they care. In their view, since empathy with all patients is impossible, but all patients want to believe that their physicians care about them, physicians should at least act as if they care and take acting lessons to become "better actors than they are now." The physicians suggested, in an article in the British medical journal, the *Lancet,* that Lawrence Olivier and Marlon Brando could be their role models to help them either to simulate or stimulate "the appropriate emotional response."[25] It is probably true that most of us want a physician who cares about us; but this is almost always too much to expect from physicians who, unlike TV's Marcus Welby, must deal with more than one patient a week. We do want a doctor who cares. But we don't expect acting.[26] What we can realistically expect, however, is honesty and competence. These qualities can best be displayed in the context of a full discussion of the patient's condition and the reasonable medical alternatives to deal with it. What we can also realistically expect is that the ultimate decision about treatment will be ours. The authenticity of the final treatment decision is what the doctrine of informed consent seeks to protect.

Of course, because you may be very sick, you will likely need an advocate to help you understand your options and help you choose among them. Your advocate may even make some decisions for you: that is also your choice, a choice that is fully supported by the doctrine of informed consent as well.

Is informed consent important in an outpatient clinic and in a doctor's office?

Yes. As important as informed consent is to crisis-oriented medical treatment, it is even more critical to elective procedures, especially when there is a possibility that the patient's condition might worsen as a result of the treatment. This point was illustrated in a case of Chung Hunter, a pregnant woman who had skin blotches on her face. She was treated by Dr. Walter Brown, who used a procedure called dermabrasion in which he, in effect, sanded a layer of skin off her face. Instead of removing the blotches, the procedure actually made them more noticeable. There was evidence that Brown did not mention the possibility of failure, and that he knew the probability of a good result was only about 50 percent. The court noted that this was "an elective thing," because "there was no emergency" and the "patient's health was not at stake." Brown therefore was obligated "to disclose to his patient all material facts which reasonably should be known if his patient is to make an informed and intelligent decision. . . . Arguably, one of the facts needed . . . was the percentage probability that the contemplated surgery would improve her appearance." The case was sent back for a jury determination of the sufficiency of the doctor's disclosures.[27]

Other examples of procedures that may produce distressing failures are plastic surgery and vasectomy.[28] In all of these instances, patient knowledge of the *probability of success* is critical to providing informed consent to the treatment.

What does it mean to say that consent must be competent and voluntary?

In general, the patient's consent must be *competent, voluntary, informed, and understanding*. Information and understanding have been discussed.

Voluntary is relatively simple. The patient must not be medicated, intoxicated, under extreme distress, or be threatened by the physician when giving consent. In one case, for example, a patient who had been given a sleeping pill (Nembutal) was awakened in the middle of the night and asked to sign a consent form for a hernia operation and repair of a hydrocele. The patient testified that he could not remember the event, and the court found that consent obtained under such circumstances was not valid because it was unlikely he was able to understand what was happening.[29] The paradigm case for involuntary consent is when someone holds a gun to another's head and says, "Sign this."

Competence (sometimes referred to as capacity to understand) is somewhat more difficult to understand. The most important thing to know is that *the law presumes every adult is competent.* The burden of proof is on the person who would try to take an individual's right to make decisions away on the basis of "incompetence." The second most important thing to know is that a person is not incompetent simply because the person refuses treatment or disagrees with the physician. If this were so, the entire doctrine of informed consent would collapse into a right to agree with your doctor. Nonetheless, almost the only time competence is likely to be challenged in the hospital is when a patient disagrees with a doctor's recommended treatment or refuses to be treated altogether.

The most useful way to think about competence in the health care setting is that an individual is competent to consent or refuse treatment so long as the individual is able to understand the information needed to give informed consent for the proposed treatment. In this sense, the requirement of *understanding* is somewhat redundant, since competence itself requires understanding. Relatives, friends, or even the physician can thus determine competence, because it is primarily a question of fact (although only a judge can actually adjudicate an individual incompetent and appoint a guardian with legal authority to make decisions for the individual). Although there is no magic formula, one way to test competence is to determine if the patient can answer the following questions:

1. What is your present condition?
2. What is the treatment that is being recommended for you?
3. What do you and your doctor think might happen to you if you decide to accept the treatment? [This could be modified in appropriate circumstance to ask specifically about risks involved in the treatment, including those of most concern to the patient.]

4. What do you and your doctor think might happen to you if you decide not to accept the recommended treatment?

5. What are the alternative treatments available (including no treatment) and what are the probable consequences of accepting each?[30]

Since competence ultimately rests on an ability or capacity to understand and appreciate the nature and consequences of one's decision, it is appropriate to test this ability in the medical care setting by using a basic informed consent interview. In this interview, the nature of the proposed treatment, its likely risks and benefits, the alternatives, their risks and benefits, and the likely consequences of no treatment would be carefully explained. Thereafter (ideally before the patient is asked to consent), a determination would be made as to whether or not the patient actually understands this basic information. By making a capacity determination *before* asking for consent, the "outcome approach" pitfall of labeling a patient incompetent solely on the basis of the patient's refusal is avoided.[31] The consent of the family, or anyone else, is, of course, neither necessary nor appropriate if the patient is competent.

May a family member or the next of kin consent for a patient if the patient is incapable and the patient's choice is not known?

As a general rule, a family member or next of kin may. There is a longstanding medical custom of deferring to the next of kin when treatment decisions concerning incompetent patients must be made. In cases in which there are no real treatment options and treatment is in the best interest of the patient, this presents no major legal or ethical problems. Technically, however, only a guardian can make a legally binding treatment decision for an incompetent person. And a guardian may only be appointed by a judge, and only after the judge has determined that the individual is in fact incompetent.[32] Since guardians are required to make decisions consistent with their ward's "best interests," however, and since courts are likely to defer to the family's judgment of best interests in any event, there is often little to be gained by having a legal guardian appointed.[33] It is primarily when treatment that seems to be in the patient's best interests is being refused by the family or next of kin, or when there is an unresolvable disagreement among family members, that it is appropriate to have a court-appointed guardian make the decision.

One reason family members are often asked to consent on behalf of an incompetent person is simply that it is time-consuming, expensive, and burdensome to have a guardian appointed by a court. Moreover, by consenting to the treatment, the relatives effectively waive their own right to sue the physician for any action based on failure to obtain consent. Their consent also demonstrates that the physician consulted someone likely to know the patient and be concerned about the patient's well-being, and this will likely be sufficient to persuade the patient not to sue for failure to obtain consent should the patient recover.

When is a physician justified in not giving a patient full information about a proposed treatment or procedure?
There are four major justifications:

- If it is an emergency situation, in which immediate treatment is needed to preserve the patient's life or health and the patient is unconscious or incompetent and there is no time to locate a family member or other decision maker.
- If the risks are minor and well known to the average person (such as the risks involved in drawing blood).
- If the patient does not want to know the specific risks and, understanding that there are risks of death and of unspecified serious bodily disabilities, asks not to be informed of them in detail (in this case the patient may be asked to sign a "waiver of informed consent" form, and this is perfectly appropriate).
- The fourth is more theoretical than real: the "therapeutic privilege" under which the physician need not inform the patient of the risks involved if the physician has *objective* evidence that this information would so upset the patient that the patient would be unable to make a rational decision. Under these circumstances, the physician must, however, give the information to another person designated by the patient. This privilege only applies in the rarest of situations, and the burden of proving its application rests on the physician.

The California Supreme Court has put this fourth exception in the following terms: "A disclosure need not be made beyond that required within the medical community when a doctor can prove by a preponderance of the evidence that he relied on facts that would demonstrate to a reasonable [person] the disclosure would have so seriously upset the patient that the patient would *not have been able to dispassionately weigh the risks* of refusing to undergo the recommended treatment."[34] I know of no case in which this doctrine has actually been used as a successful defense to nondisclosure.

A better legal and ethical rule is that physicians must always inform competent patients of all material information, but the manner in which the information is conveyed (including the time, place, and language used) can vary depending on the patient's circumstances. Some doctors have complained that they might be held liable for telling patients too much, but no court has ever held a doctor liable for giving a patient too much accurate information. On the other hand, if a patient makes an informed waiver of the basic informed consent information, the physician is required to honor it and may not inflict unwanted information on the patient. This should rarely happen, since patients should take their role in shared decision making seriously, and their advocates should strongly encourage patients to make important treatment decisions themselves. Under the extreme time pressures imposed by managed care, extended conversation with the patient is discouraged, and requests not to know may be accommodated without adequate discussion.

Treatment may also be rendered without going through the formalities of consent if the life or health of the patient is in immediate danger and obtaining consent is impossible. For example, if the victim of an automobile accident is brought in bleeding and unconscious, and no relative can be reached, treatment to save his life may be commenced immediately. Although this has sometimes been justified as implied consent, the more accurate view is that society gives doctors a privilege to treat patients under such extreme conditions without obtaining their consent. No one consents to anything simply by being in an accident or having a heart attack.

What is the purpose of the consent form?

Informed consent is not a form.[35] Nonetheless, the consent of the patient is put in writing for the same reason that most contracts are in writing: to document the exact terms of the consent in case of future disagreement. For example, if a patient later sues a doctor or a hospital and alleges lack of informed consent, the doctor will be able to present the written consent form in court as *evidence that consent was in fact obtained.* If the form is specific in its terms, and if it was voluntarily signed by a competent patient who understood the information set forth in the form, the patient has very little chance of winning such a lawsuit.[36] There are, nonetheless, very few situations other than medical research (discussed in chapter 9) in which a written consent form is legally required. The form is *not* consent but only some evidence that the consent process occurred.

What is the legal effect of signing a blanket consent form?

A blanket consent form is one that covers (like a blanket) almost everything a doctor or a hospital might do to a patient, without mentioning anything specifically. Many hospitals continue to require patients to sign such forms on admission. A typical form reads: "I, the undersigned, hereby grant permission for the administration of any anesthetic to, and for the performance of any operation upon myself as may be deemed advisable by the surgeons in attendance at No Mercy Hospital." The general rule is that a blanket consent form is legally inadequate for any procedure that has risks or alternatives. Usually, the more vague and indefinite the terms in the consent form, the more the contents of the form will be construed *against* the doctor or the hospital by a court.[37]

In one case, for example, a woman had consented only to a simple appendectomy, but the surgeon decided to also perform a total hysterectomy. She had signed the following consent form:

Authority to Operate

I hereby authorize the physician or physicians in charge to administer such treatment and the surgeon to have administered such anesthetics as found necessary to perform this operation which is advisable in the treatment of this patient.

The court had little difficulty deciding that this "so-called authorization is so ambiguous as to be almost completely worthless." The court determined to give it "no possible weight under the factual circumstances" of the case.[38] Blanket forms can, however, be properly used on admission to the hospital as proof of consent to noninvasive "routine hospital procedures" (such as taking blood pressure), as long as specific informed consent is obtained whenever any invasive procedure is contemplated. Even in states with statutes that say the patient's signature on the consent form is conclusive evidence that informed consent was obtained, the signed form is only evidence that the informed consent process took place, and the patient may still present evidence that it did not.[39]

What should an "informed" consent form contain?

No form is necessary at all for consent. But if there is a form, the form should contain all of the information needed to comply with the elements of informed consent, that is, a description of the proposed procedure, its risks and benefits, the alternatives and their benefits and risks, the risks of nontreatment, the success rates, problems of recuperation, and other necessary information. In general, the consent form will also contain the name of the physician involved. It may also include specific clauses dealing with photographs and disposition and use of removed tissues, organs, and body parts. Patients have the right to cross out any clauses they do not agree with or consent to. If there is something in the form you do not understand or agree to, however, this should be discussed with your physician to see if you can reach an agreement about it.

It should be emphasized that although the patient may put some limits on a surgeon's authority in the written consent form, a surgeon who believes that the limitations are so strict the surgeon cannot proceed with the operation consistent with good medical practice might be justified in declining to perform it. And the surgeon has the right to have all patient-imposed conditions noted in the record, together with the fact that the risks of such conditions have been fully explained and agreed to by the patient.

What do most patients think of consent forms?

In one study,[40] the first question was, "What are consent forms for?" Approximately 80 percent of patients responded, "To protect the physician's rights." The authors were upset at this response, but the patients, of course, were correct. That *is* the primary function of *forms.* If forms are also to protect the patient, three simple steps are necessary: (1) the forms must be complete; (2) they must be in lay language; and (3) patients must be given a copy and time to think over the information contained therein before being asked to sign them. The reason none of this is usually done is that informed consent is not usually taken seriously in the hospital setting. It is seen as a luxury that is secondary to caring for the medical "needs" of the patient, and besides (it is often argued), it really does not matter anyway because patients cannot remember what they have been told.

A survey done for the President's Commission for the Study of Ethical Problems in Medicine confirms the conclusion that the public strongly supports the doctrine of informed consent. Eighty-eight percent of the public believes a patient's right to information about treatment risks and alternatives should be protected by law, and only about one in five thinks that the time doctors spend discussing diagnosis, prognosis, and treatment could be better spent taking care of patients. A majority of the public (52 percent, as compared with 32 percent of physicians) believes that the requirements for informed consent are "clear and explicit"; and although 73 percent of physicians think the doctrine places too much emphasis on the disclosure of remote risks, less than half (44 percent) of the public feels that way. More than 40 percent of both patients and physicians believe that the amount of information disclosed should be based on what the particular patient needs to know rather than on what "a reasonable patient" needs to know, or based on a disclosure standard set by physicians themselves.[41] There is no reason to believe that the results of any of these studies would be different if they were repeated today.

Are clauses in consent forms in which a patient agrees not to sue a care facility or physician enforceable?

No. Patients cannot effectively waive their right to sue a health care facility or physician in the event of malpractice (unless state law provides for binding arbitration upon mutual agreement). The leading case involved a patient in a nonprofit hospital. He signed a consent form that included the following clause:

RELEASE: The hospital is a non-profit, charitable institution. In consideration of the hospital and allied services to be rendered and the rates charged therefore, the patient or his legal representative *agrees to and hereby releases* the Regents of the University of California [the hospital was maintained by the University], and *the hospital from any and all liability for the negligent or wrongful acts or omissions of its employees,* if the hospital has used due care in selecting its employees.[42]

The main issue in the case was the validity of this clause. The California Supreme Court found that the patient was at a great disadvantage in bargaining, as compared with the hospital, and thus was almost forced to sign any agreement the hospital presented to him. The court found further that this agreement affected the public interest (since the hospital held itself out as one that would perform services for any person who qualified by their medical condition for service), and that requiring such a waiver as a condition of treatment was illegal and void as against public policy. The same reasoning would likely be applied to void such a clause in almost any consent form. A clause requiring that all disputes be settled by binding arbitration is, however, enforceable if the state has an arbitration statute that so provides.

May consent be given without signing a consent form?

Yes. As noted previously, the primary reason for writing is to maintain a permanent record of what was agreed to. No writing is required to make most contracts, and *no written form is required to make consent to treatment valid.* Consent may also be implied by actions, such as the voluntary submission to treatment.

One of the first consent cases to reach the courts in the United States, for example, involved a woman who was given a smallpox vaccination. There was no explicit verbal or written consent. The court concluded that she consented to it by standing in the vaccination line, observing what was happening, and holding up her arm for the doctor.[43] The basis for allowing voluntary submission to imply consent is that the patient understood what was going on and should have been aware that her actions would be interpreted by a doctor as consenting to the procedure. For a more complex procedure, such as electroconvulsive therapy, consent by action or inaction alone is never sufficient.[44]

May a patient withdraw consent after signing a consent form?

Yes! *Consent* must be freely given, and so given, it *can be freely withdrawn at any time.* This is the rule, but there are practical limitations. For example, once a patient is under general anesthesia, it is obviously too late for the patient to change his or her mind.

A written consent form does not affect your ability to change your mind and withdraw consent. After orally indicating your change of mind, it may be a good idea either to obtain and destroy the original consent form or to execute another form—this time a "nonconsent form," noting on it the date and time of day your consent was withdrawn.

May a patient refuse treatment?

Yes. *A competent patient may refuse any treatment.* There are some very difficult issues involving children, which are discussed in the following chapter. There are also some unique issues dealing with potentially lifesaving or life-prolonging treatment discussed in chapter 12. The only other major difficult categories of patients are mentally ill patients and those with communicable diseases. In general, even mentally ill patients are competent to refuse treatment—although if they are dangerous, they may be confined to an institution for the mentally ill against their will.[45] Likewise, competent individuals with contagious diseases may refuse treatment, but public health authorities may be able to quarantine or involuntarily hospitalize and isolate them if they are a danger to others.[46]

The reason for refusal may be as rational as the slim chances for success or as "irrational" as a fear of hypodermic needles. No matter what the reason, the refusal is just as legally binding on the doctor and the hospital. As a leading legal textbook explains:

The very foundation of the doctrine of informed consent is every man's right to forgo treatment or even cure if it entails what for him are intolerable consequences or risks, however warped or perverted his sense of values may be in the eyes of the medical profession, or even of the community, so long as any distortion falls short of what the law regards as incompetency. *Individual freedom here is guaranteed only if people are given the right to make choices which would generally be regarded as foolish.*[47]

What is a hospital's duty to a patient who refuses a specific treatment?

It is the obligation of the hospital, in the face of a patient's refusal, to make sure that no member of the hospital staff performs the refused procedure. If the hospital does not successfully prevent unauthorized procedures, it may be legally liable to the patient to the same extent as the doctor or other staff person who performs the procedure.

The hospital is also legally obligated to continue to render the best medical care possible within the limitations imposed by the patient's refusal. Only if you consistently refuse to participate in *any* treatment would the hospital, after making diligent attempts to verbally persuade you to change your mind, be justified in asking you to leave. Under these circumstances the hospital will probably ask you to sign a release form that explains the proposed treatment to you, sets forth your refusal to consent to it, and releases the hospital from liability for the consequences of the refusal.[48] This release is binding on you. You cannot refuse treatment and then hold the hospital liable for respecting your wishes.

How does a patient (or advocate) know if he or she has been properly informed?

The following checklist will help a patient determine the quality of informed consent. This list should be reviewed *before* you sign the consent form.

- I know the name and nature of my injury, illness, or disability, and I know what the dangers or disadvantages of not treating it are.
- I know the nature of the procedure that is recommended for the specific purpose of dealing with my problem.
- I know whether or not there are other ways of treating my problem, and if there are, I have been told of the risks and benefits of these other procedures. *I believe that the procedure proposed is the best one for me.* I know what the advantages and benefits of this procedure are. (List the alternatives.)
- I know what the risks, disadvantages, and side effects of this procedure are. (List these if you can.)
- I know the experience my physician has in treating my condition. (What is it?)
- I know what the probability of success is, and what my physician means by "success." (What is it?)
- I know what my prognosis is and what is likely to happen if I am not treated. (What is it?)
- I understand all that I have been told, and I can explain the procedure in my own words. (Try to explain it to your closest friend or relative.)
- My doctor has answered all of my questions openly and has offered to discuss any additional concerns with me. *(Make sure all your questions are answered before you sign the consent form.)*
- I understand the meaning of all the words in the consent form. (If not, have them explained to you.)
- I agree to everything in the form I signed and have crossed out

things I did not agree with (or added in some new requirements), and my doctor is aware of these changes. *(If you do not agree to everything in the form, do not sign it.)*

  • I have a clear head and alert mind, and I am not so anxious or so harassed that I feel my decision is not my own free choice.

  • I think that the benefits I might get from this procedure are sufficiently important to me to outweigh the risks I am taking. (Or you should reconsider your decision.)

  • I know I do not have to consent to this procedure if I do not want to.

When doctors and patients take informed consent seriously, the doctor-patient relationship can become a partnership, with shared authority, shared decision making, and shared responsibility for outcomes. This is a constructive and humane goal for both patients and physicians.

The law has championed this movement toward shared decision making through shared information but may not have gone far enough to help ensure that patients in fact get the information they need. As is explained in detail in chapter 15, a patient cannot win a lawsuit against a physician for failure to disclose the information needed for an informed consent unless a physical injury is suffered (either a nondisclosed risk is actually suffered by the patient or an undisclosed alternative treatment would have been selected and been less harmful to the patient).

It has therefore been suggested that patients should be able to sue physicians who fail to disclose risks and alternatives, because this is an affront to the patient's dignity as a person and denies the patient the right to rational participation in his or her own health care.[49] This dignity tort is similar to suing in cases of battery (although the injury inflicted is neither intentional nor physical), and the amount of money awarded to the patient would depend on the jury's assessment of the actual affront to the patient's dignity inflicted by denying the patient the right to participate in the treatment decision. If information sharing does not soon become the norm, the courts will likely recognize this type of lawsuit in the future. A major lawsuit alleging just this type of a dignitary harm in the context of a research trial in which informed consent was not obtained from poor, Hispanic pregnant patients was settled in 2000, and this case may help set the standard for dignitary harm lawsuits.[50]

TIPS FOR ADVOCATES

• **No one should be asked to agree to treatment until there is a diagnosis, a prognosis, and all reasonable medical alternatives have been explained.** Use the checklist in this chapter to make sure the patient has all information needed to make his or her own decision.

• **Ask questions if more information is needed and seek a second opinion from another physician expert in the area of the patient's disease if you think it would be helpful.**

• Signing a consent form is not necessary for informed consent but is meant to document it. **If the patient is asked to sign a consent form: (1) make sure it contains the same information that has been explained orally; (2) cross out any statements the patient does not agree with; and (3) keep a copy of it for future reference.**

• **Informed consent is a legal doctrine that protects the right of patients to make their own choices regarding medical treatment.** Sometimes you must remind physicians (and even nurses) that it is the patient's body and the patient who must live with the consequences of the treatment.

• **Don't let the patient sign any form if the patient is medicated (or premedicated for surgery) or the patient is not satisfied that he or she understands the information in the form.**

• **The patient's competence to consent to or refuse treatment can be determined by asking the patient questions about the elements of informed consent. If the patient understands what the physician wants to do and what is likely to happen if the physician does (or doesn't) do it and what the alternatives are, the patient is likely competent.**

• **Adults are presumed competent by law, and the burden of proving they are not is on the person who wants to "declare" the patient incompetent.**

- **If a patient is incompetent, the personal advocate, nearest relative, or health care agent can usually make medical decisions for the patient—the physician cannot.**

- **Patients can withdraw their consent at any time.** It is useful to put the refusal in writing and get it into the patient's chart.

- **Patients have the right to refuse any medical treatment and to leave the hospital against medical advice.**

- **No one may discriminate against or retaliate against a patient just because the patient refuses treatment.**

NOTES

1. *Pratt v. Davis,* 118 Ill. App. 161, 166 (1905), *aff'd,* 244 Ill. 30, 79 N.E. 562 (1906).

2. President's Commission for the Study of Ethical Problems in Medicine and Biomedical and Behavioral Research, Making Health Care Decisions, Washington, D.C.: Government Printing Office, 1982, 2–3. *See generally Empirical Research on Informed Consent: An Annotated Bibliography,* Hastings Center Report, Supp., January 1999, S1–S42.

3. Bernie Siegel, Love, Medicine, and Miracles, New York: Harperennial & Row, 1990, 52 (emphasis in original). Physicians may, however, seriously underestimate risks. *See* S. F. Kronlund & W. R. Phillips, *Physician Knowledge of Risks of Surgical and Invasive Diagnostic Procedures,* 142 West. J. Med. 565 (1985).

4. *See, e.g.,* Lori Andrews, *Informed Consent Statutes and the Decisionmaking Process,* 5 J. Legal Med. 163 (1984), and Lori Andrews, Future Perfect, New York: Columbia U. Press, 2001.

5. *Schloendorff v. New York Hospital,* 211 N.Y. 127, 129, 105 N.E. 92, 93 (1914).

6. *E.g., Perry v. Shaw,* 88 Cal. App 4th 658, 106 Cal Rptr.2d 70 (2001); *and see Scott v. Wilson,* 396 S.W.2d 532 (Tex. Civ. App. 1965), and *Montgomery v. Bazez-Sehgal,* 568 Pa. 574, 798 A.2d 742 (2002).

7. *See, e.g.,* Jon Waltz & Fred Inbau, *Medical Jurisprudence* (in) Liability for Failure to Obtain "Informed Consent" to Customary Therapy, New York: MacMillin, 1971, 152–68; Marcus Plante, *An Analysis of "Informed Consent,"* 36 Fordham L. Rev. 639 (1968); Marjorie Shultz, *From Informed Consent to Patient Choice: A New Protected Interest,* 95 Yale L.J. 219 (1985); Laurel Hanson, *Informed Consent and the Scope of a Physician's Duty to Disclose,* 77 N.D.L. Rev. 71 (2001); *Natanson v. Kline,* 186 Kan. 393, 350 P.2d 1093 (1960); *Cobbs v. Grant,* 8 Cal. 3d 229, 502 P.2d 1 (1972); *Canterbury v. Spence,* 464 F.2d 772 (D.C. Cir. 1972), *cert. denied,* 409 U.S. 1064 (1972); *Brown v. Dahl,* 705 P.2d 781

(Wash. App. 1985); and *Hook v. Rothstein,* 316 S.E.2d 690 (S.C. Ct. App. 1984). The statutes remain divided about evenly between those using the patient-centered standard and those using the professional standard for disclosures. *See* Barry Furrow et al., eds., Health Law, St. Paul: West Pub., 2001, 355.

8. E. Coruch & R. Wilson, Risk/Benefit Analysis, Cambridge: Ballinger, 1982.

9. R. E. A. Mapes, *Verbal and Numerical Estimates of Probability in Therapeutic Contexts,* 13 Soc. Sci. Med 277 (1979).

10. Augustine Kong et al., *How Medical Professionals Evaluate Expressions of Probability,* 315 New Eng. J. Med. 740 (1986); *and see* Frederick Mosteller & Cleo Youtz, *Quantifying Probabilistic Expressions,* 5 Statistical Sci. 2 (1990).

11. Dennis Mazur & David Hickam, *Patients' Interpretations of Probability Terms,* 6 J. Gen. Int. Med. 237 (1991).

12. Sam Gorovitz & A. MacIntyre, *Toward a Theory of Medical Fallibility,* 1 J. Med. Philosophy 51 (1976).

13. Sandra Tanenbaum, *What Physicians Know,* 329 New Eng. J. Med. 1268 (1993). *See also* Thomas Gutheil et al., *Malpractice Prevention Through the Sharing of Uncertainty: Informed Consent and the Therapeutic Alliance,* 311 New Eng. J. Med. 49 (1984).

14. Barbara McNeil et al., *Speech and Survival: Tradeoffs between Quality and Quantity of Life in Laryngeal Cancer,* 305 New Eng. J. Med. 982 (1981). *And see* Barbara McNeil et al., *Fallacy of the Five-Year Survival in Lung Cancer,* 299 New Eng. J. Med. 1397 (1978), and Sharon Imbus & Bruce Zawacki, *Autonomy for Burned Patients When Survival Is Unprecedented,* 297 New Eng. J. Med. 308 (1977).

15. *Cobbs v. Grant,* 8 Cal.3d 229, 104 Cal.Rptr. 505, 502 P.2d 1 (1972). The *Cobbs* court described the patient as being "abjectly dependent" on the physician for information. This is no longer true in the Internet age; nonetheless, many patients know almost nothing about health care. *See, e.g.,* Julie Gazmararian et al., *Health Literacy among Medicare Enrollees in a Managed Care Organization,* 281 JAMA 545 (1999).

16. *Truman v. Thomas,* 27 Cal.3d 285, 165 Cal.Rptr. 308, 611 P.2d 902 (1980).

17. *Moore v. Regents of University of California,* 51 Cal.3d 120, 217 Cal.Rptr. 146, 793 P.2d 479 (1990).

18. *Arato v. Avedon,* 5 Cal. 4th 1172, 23 Cal.Rptr.2d 131, 858 P.2d 598 (1993).

19. Alex Capron, *Duty, Truth, and Whole Human Beings,* 23(4) Hastings Center Report 13 (July 1993).

20. *Johnson v. Kokemoor,* 199 Wis.2d 615, 545 N.W.2d 495 (1996).

21. George J. Annas, Leonard H. Glantz & Barbara F. Katz, Informed Consent to Human Experimentation, Cambridge: Ballinger, 1977, 33–38.

22. *Cobbs v. Grant,* 8 Cal. 3d. 229, 502 P.2d 1 (1972). Patient dependency and physician control is also reinforced by the setting of doctor-patient interactions in which the doctor may stand, fully clothed, while the patient is lying down, often clothed only in a johnny, in a hospital bed. *See* John Stoeckle, ed., Encounters Between Patients and Doctors, Cambridge: MIT Press, 1987.

23. Jay Katz, The Silent World of Doctor and Patient, New Haven: Yale U. Press, 1984.

24. Carl E. Schneider, The Practice of Autonomy: Patients, Doctors, and Medical Decisions, New York: Oxford U. Press, 1998, 221–27.

25. Hillel Finestone & David Conter, *Acting in Medical Practice*, 344 Lancet 801 (1994); and Chris McManus, *Department of Theatrical Medicine?* 344 Lancet 767 (1994).

26. J. Urschel, *Doctors Won't Win Any Awards by Acting*, USA Today, September 21, 1994, 11A; *and see* C. Charles, A. Gafni & T. Whelan, *How to Improve Communication Between Doctors and Patients*, 320 Brit. Med. J. 1220 (2000).

27. *Hunter v. Brown*, 4 Wash. App. 899, 484 P.2d. 1162 (1971), *aff'd*, 81 Wash. 2d. 465, 502 P.2d. 1194 (1972).

28. In *Sullivan v. O'Connor*, 363 Mass. 579, 296 N.E.2d 183 (1973). The patient, a female entertainer, sued her physician, who she alleged had guaranteed her that her nose would be gracefully shaped following surgery. In fact, it became more grossly disfigured. She was awarded damages on the theory that the doctor had entered into a contract with her to alter her nose for the better and had guaranteed the results. In *Hackworth v. Hart*, 474 S.W.2d 377 (Ky. 1971), the doctor had told a man that a vasectomy was "a foolproof thing, 100 percent," and the court held that this stated a cause of action against the doctor when the man's wife became pregnant. Here, disclosure of the *probability of success* would seem critical, since the *only* purpose for having the procedure performed was complete sterilization.

29. *Demers v. Gerety*, 85 N.M. 641, 515 P.2d 645 (1973).

30. George J. Annas & Joan Densberger, *Competence to Refuse Medical Treatment: Autonomy v. Paternalism*, 15 Toledo L. Rev. 561 (1984).

31. *Id.*, at 578. *And see* Lawrence Markson et al., *Physician Assessment of Patient Competence*, 42 J. Am. Geriatics Suc. 1074 (1994).

32. Annas & Densberger, *supra* note 30, at 561–78. *And see* Applebaum & Grisso, *Assessing Patients' Capacity to Consent to Treatment*, 319 New Eng. J. Med. 1635 (1988).

33. *See Petition of Nemser*, 51 Misc. 2d 616, 273 N.Y.S.2d 624 (Sup. Ct. 1966).

34. *Cobbs v. Grant*, 502 P.2d 1, 12 (1972) (emphasis added).

35. National Bioethics Advisory Commission, Ethical Policy Issues in Research Involving Human Participants, Bethesda, Md.: National Bioethics Advisory Commission, August 2001.

36. *E.g., Karp v. Cooley*, 349 F. Supp. 827 (S.D. Texas 1972), *aff'd*, 493 F.2d 408 (5th Cir. 1974), *cert. denied*, 419 U.S. 845 (1974) (involving the consent form for the first human artificial heart implant).

37. *E.g., Valdez v. Percy*, 35 Cal. App. 2d 485, 96 P.2d 142 (1939); *Moore v. Webb*, 345 S.W.2d 239 (Mo. 1961).

38. *Rogers v. Lumbermens Mutual Casualty Co.*, 119 So. 2d 649, 652 (La. 1960).

39. *Parikh v. Cunningham*, 493 So. 2d 999 (Fla. 1986).

40. Another significant finding of this survey was the way patients view the consent process: 80 percent thought the forms were necessary; 76 percent thought they contained just the right amount of information; 75 percent thought the explanation given was important; 84 percent understood all or most of the information; and 90 percent said they would try to remember the information contained on the forms. This suggests that patients understand the informed consent process very well and that for almost all patients informed consent is very important. Barrie Cassileth et al., *Informed Consent: Why Are Its Goals Imperfectly Realized?* 302 New Eng. J. Med. 896 (1980).

41. President's Commission, *supra* note 2, at 105. Forms alone, of course, guarantee

neither that useful information is conveyed nor that it is understood. *See* S. Jaffee et al., *Quality of Informed Consent: A New Measure of Understanding among Research Subjects,* 93 J. Nat'l Cancer Inst. 139 (2001); A. Luck, S. Pearson, G. Maddern & P. Hewett, *Effects of Video Information on Pre-colonoscopy Anxiety and Knowledge: A Randomized Trial,* 354 Lancet 2032 (1999); and Rebecca Jean Gordon-Lubitz, *Risk Communication: Problems of Presentation and Understanding,* 289 JAMA 95 (2003).

42. *Tunkl v. Regents of University of California,* 60 Cal. 2d 92, 94, 32 Cal. Rptr. 33, 34, 383 P.2d 441, 442 (1963) (emphasis added).

43. *O'Brien v. Cunard S.S. Co.,* 154 Mass. 272, 28, N.E. 266 (1891).

44. *E.g., Woods v. Brumlop,* 71 N.M. 221, 377 P.2d 520 (1962).

45. George J. Annas, *Control of Tuberculosis—The Law and Public Health,* 318 New Eng. J. Med. 585 (1993).

46. This is based on the broad "police powers" that states have (and can exercise through their departments of public health) to protect the health and safety of the public.

47. Fowler Harper & Fleming James, *The Law of Torts* (1968 Supp.) sec. 17.1, 61. This remains the current rule. *See* President's Commission, *supra* note 2.

48. A typical release form is the following:

I, [name], refuse to allow anyone to [treatment]. The risks attendant to my refusal have been fully explained to me, and I fully understand that I will in all probability need [treatment], and that if the same is not done, my chances for regaining normal health are seriously reduced, and that in all probability, my refusal for such treatment or procedure will seriously imperil my life. I hereby release the Hospital, its nurses and employees, together with all physicians in any way connected with me as a patient, from liability for respecting and following my express wishes and direction.

The form will also contain a clause setting forth religious objections if that is the basis for the patient's refusal. Some states also require hospitals to make sure proper consent is obtained. *Rogers v. T. J. Samson Comm. Hospital,* 276 F.3d 228 (6 Cir. 2002).

49. *See* Wendy Mariner, *Informed Consent in the Post-Modern Era,* 13 Law & Social Inquiry, 385 (1988), and Alan Meisel, *A "Dignitary Tort" as a Bridge Between the Idea of Informed Consent and the Law of Informed Consent,* 16 Law, Medicine & Health Care 210 (1988). Physicians recognize that informed consent can be used educationally and can positively and powerfully affect a doctor-patient alliance or partnership to their mutual benefit. As Dr. Drummond Rennie has advised his physician colleagues: Physicians must do more than just "improve consent forms" but must see "education . . . as a worthwhile therapeutic goal . . . to give patients equality in the covenant by educating them [as a counselor and advocate] to make informed decisions" (*Informed Consent by "Well-Nigh Abject" Adults,* 23 New Eng. J. Med. 917, 918 [1980]).

50. *See* Peter Aronson, *A Medical Indignity,* National L.J., March 27, 2000, 1.

VII

Choices about Surgery and Children's Care

This chapter continues the discussion of informed choice by applying the doctrine of informed consent to surgery and to decisions for children. Although all of the principles addressed in the informed choice chapter apply to surgery, surgery deserves its own chapter because of the large number of surgical procedures performed and because surgery has such a dramatic impact on the patient, for better or worse. Likewise, children need others to make decisions for them, and this can make decision making difficult. There are approximately seventy million surgical procedures done annually in the United States, about one surgical procedure for every four people. The likelihood of any particular person undergoing a surgical procedure in any year, however, is less than this because some people have multiple operations.

About thirty million surgical procedures are now done on an outpatient or day-surgery basis. Nonetheless, surgery still accounts for most hospital admissions, more than half of all health care expenditures, and more than half of all malpractice allegations and lawsuits. Because the indications for surgery are often controversial and often involve questions of preferred lifestyle, this is an area in which you are your own most important advocate. As one surgeon has warned, "Remember this about surgery: There are risks. There are benefits. There are choices. There are alternatives. It is your body. It is your life. The final decision is yours."[1]

Should patients routinely seek a consultation or a second opinion before entering the hospital or agreeing to elective surgery?

Yes. Patients should almost always get a second opinion before undergoing surgery.[2] Hospitals can be dangerous places, and people should only go there when it is medically necessary. For example, patients may be injured by physicians (iatrogenic injury), may become infected in the hospital (nosocomial infections), and may be given the wrong drugs. In one study of eight hundred consecutive admissions to a major hospital, for example, more than one-third developed a major or minor iatrogenic injury, which in fifteen of these patients directly contributed to the patient's death.[3] An average-sized, three-hundred-bed hospital will conservatively experience eleven thousand medication errors annually, or more than thirty medication errors daily.[4] Errors are also commonplace in surgery.[5] Because surgery has been overutilized in the United States, and because it is dangerous, some insurance companies and health plans *require* their subscribers to get a second opinion before elective surgery is approved for payment. This is good advice.

The treatment preference of your surgeon is the most important thing that influences the type of surgery you are likely to get. For example, in one study of women undergoing surgical treatment for breast cancer, the choice was between removal of the breast (mastectomy) and removal of the tumor only (lumpectomy), both of which have substantially equal long-term survival rates. The patients' choice of lumpectomy varied drastically among surgeons, from 9 to 81 percent. The researchers concluded that the preference of the surgeon (including unconscious bias) accounted for this difference, not the preferences of the patients. The researchers also concluded that surgeons should share more information with patients, but that ultimately the patient herself must ask the right questions to understand her options.[6]

If surgeons cannot agree on what the best treatment is, how can a patient decide which advice to accept?

The answer to this question depends upon knowing *who* is going to be operated on and who must live with the consequences of the operation. As surgeon George Crile has put it: "There is no answer to this question, because there is no 'best' treatment. For example, are we speaking of best in terms of eradicating the disease, or best in terms of the safety of the patient, or best in terms of the comfort of the patient—malpractice suits, the size of fee, or the time and trouble required to perform the operation?"[7] As he and others have noted, there may be very important differences among alternative treatment options in terms of lifestyle and quality of life, as well as in terms of survival. These outcomes will be valued or discounted by you on the basis of your own lifestyle and values. Making a choice among treatment alternatives, in other words, is not a medical decision but a personal value-laden one: only you can decide what is right for you.

The new emphasis on evidence-based medicine in the United States should result in both better-informed patients and savings in medical expenditures. These studies will identify treatments and procedures falling into a variety of efficacy categories.[8]

Dr. Jack Wennberg has suggested, correctly I believe, that patients should make final treatment choices based in large measure on their own evaluation of outcomes data, as applied to their own lives. An early Wennberg study, for example, demonstrated that prostate cancer surgery was performed primarily to relieve symptoms. When the patients themselves were queried, however, their attitudes toward their symptoms varied; some were not bothered much at all by them. Patients also differed from doctors in their views of treatment risks, "particularly surgery-induced impotence and operative mortality." The key to "reducing variations between physician and patient goals," in Wennberg's words, thus depends not on learning more from laboratory findings or clinical exams but "on learning what patients want, and this can only be ascertained by asking patients . . . [who should be informed] that they indeed have a choice and that their choice should depend on their own preferences."[9] When fully informed of the risks and benefits, only one of five severely symptomatic men in this study actually chose prostate surgery.

Does a patient have a right to know the experience of his or her surgeon with a particular operation?

Yes. Knowing the experience of the surgeon (and anesthesiologist) is a vital piece of information you need to make an informed choice. If the surgeon or anesthesiologist refuses to tell you what his or her experience is with the recommended procedure, you should get another surgeon. Surgeons who perform operations frequently have better outcomes than those who perform the same procedure less frequently. In addition, some hospitals have much poorer outcomes for specific types of surgery than others.[10]

As important as the experience and outcome history of the surgeon and hospital are, the experience and competence of the anesthesiologist can be equally important. Some of the gravest risks of surgery are from anesthesiology. You should feel comfortable with the anesthesiologist (who may first show up to talk with you just before surgery) and the type of anesthesia that will be used. No question is too trivial, and you should not consent to anesthesia until you are satisfied that the person in charge of anesthesia during the operation is competent and knows your medical history, including prior drug reactions and allergies, completely.

Are all surgeons equally competent?

Of course they are not. Surgeon-writer Atul Gawande also reminds us that physicians, like everyone else, have good and bad days and can suffer from depression and other mental illnesses, have drug and alcohol addiction, and experience burnout. In his words, "Good doctors can go bad, and when they do the medical profession is almost entirely unequipped to do anything about it."[11] He recounts the case of one surgeon, Hank Goodman, who suffered burnout and continued to practice medicine, much to the detriment of his patients. In one case, for example, he had operated on a woman's knee to relieve persistent swelling. A week later, the patient returned with fever and intense pain. Although Goodman removed foul-smelling pus from the knee, he refused to reoperate to drain it, telling his assistant, "Ah, she's just a whiner." When the patient again returned, a week later, he did finally drain the wound, but it was too late. The infection had eaten away the cartilage and "her entire joint was destroyed and she was never able to run or even bend over to pick up her child again." It is often a matter of months, even years, before other physicians take any action to restrain the destructive conduct of their colleagues because, Gawande argues, physicians just don't have "the heart" for it. Moreover, he notes, the people in the best position to see how dangerous a surgeon has become, are often "in the worst position to do anything about it: junior physicians, nurses, ancillary staff." This means that just as you should drive defensively, you (and your advocate) will have to take steps to protect yourself.

Does a patient have the right to know a surgeon's HIV status?

The purpose of the doctrine of informed consent is to provide patients with enough information so that the patient can decide which, if any, surgery is right for the patient. The HIV status of the surgeon is not information, such as treatment alternatives, that is generally known to the medical profession but not to lay patients. Rather, it is private, personal medical information that is not generally known to anyone else. In this situation, the surgeon is also a patient with privacy rights.

Although you have a right to ask for any information you think is relevant from your surgeons, I believe you should not ask this question, and surgeons should not respond to this question. This is because there is no objective medical evidence that a surgeon with HIV infection places you as a surgical patient at any measurable added risk, and disclosure of such information could seriously harm the surgeon because of the continuing irrational fear and prejudice that still often surrounds HIV. The fact that you or other patients may want to know personal information about surgeons (including religion or sexual preference, for example) does not translate into an obligation on the part of surgeons to disclose it.

If a surgeon really is a danger to his or her patients, the surgeon should be disqualified from performing surgery. Consent to being operated on by a surgeon who is under the influence of drugs or alcohol, for example, does not excuse the surgeon from harming the patient if he or she operates while under the influence. Surgeons who are under the influence of drugs or alcohol should simply not be permitted to perform surgery. Ultimately, the question of HIV status is a private, personal one, at least until it is scientifically shown that HIV infection places the patient at increased risk. As long as that case cannot be made, you should not be concerned about the HIV status of your surgeon.[12]

Does information about alternative treatments actually affect decisions patients make regarding surgery?

Yes. In the case of breast cancer, for example, in which some controversy still exists over which treatment is most effective, more than a dozen states have passed laws specifically requiring that surgeons disclose alternative treatments to their patients. A survey of breast cancer treatment by the American College of Surgeons indicates that these laws have directly affected the treatment decisions women make.[13]

It is not logical to enact statutes on informed consent that apply only to specific diseases, since this implies that each disease or body part should have its own statutory disclosure requirements; instead, a general rule requiring informed consent should simply be applied to *all* treatments. Nonetheless, it is easily understandable why breast cancer treatment was singled out for special legislative action.

Psychiatrist and the world's leading expert on informed consent, Yale professor Jay Katz, has outlined the history of breast cancer treatment and consent. He notes, for example, that radical mastectomy was first proposed as a breast cancer treatment by William Halsted in 1894. Halsted's proposal was based on a claim of fifty cures that has never been duplicated. His method was unchallenged in medicine until the 1950s, and it was not until the 1970s that alternatives were seriously and widely considered and studied. We have learned much more about breast cancer and have learned that "surgery, from its most limited to its most extensive varieties, as well as radiation therapy, chemotherapy, hormone therapy and immunotherapy in various combination and permutations of their own and with surgery have therapeutic impact. . . . [W]e seem to know that some treatment is better than none." But which treatment? In Katz's view, this uncertainty provides the physician with an opportunity and obligation to share uncertainty in treatment with the patient:

What we do not know . . . is which treatment is best. Most likely any or all of the theories of cure will be modified or discarded over time. They attest to our vast ignorance about the big picture. . . . Of importance to decision making between physician and patient is the fact that, if they are so inclined, physicians can now make clearer distinctions between what they know and do not know. Thus, they can offer patients a variety of treatment options based on pieces of evidence from available data. *There is no certainty about the available knowledge, but its uncertainty can be specified.* This crucial point holds true for the treatment not only of breast cancer but for many other diseases as well.[14]

Marcia Lynch, in her poem *Peau d'Orange,* has described how difficult it is for patients confronted with a diagnosis of breast cancer not to resort to magical thinking instead of trying to weigh treatment options rationally. To her doctor she says:

I prayed you to pull magic
out of your black leather bag

And later promises her doctor the impossible:

If you lift the chill
that unravels my spine,
I will send you stars from the
Milky Way.

send them spinning down,
dancing a thousand-fold. Please
let me grow old.[15]

The medical literature also confirms that physicians have great difficulty discussing mortality and complication rates of surgery, especially cancer surgery, with patients.[16] Surgeons are usually also much more willing to discuss treatment options with you than to discuss your prognosis.[17]

How can a patient be sure that the surgeon selected to perform the surgery actually does the surgery?

The best you can do is to tell your surgeon that it is very important to you that the surgeon himself or herself perform the surgery, and obtain the surgeon's agreement (which need not be in writing). Then write on the operative consent form words to the effect "all surgery to be performed personally by Dr. [name of surgeon]." This agreement is a contract between you and the surgeon. In one case, a patient consented to having one surgeon perform the surgery, but another member of his group actually performed it without the patient's consent. The court ruled that a patient "has the right to choose the surgeon who will operate and to refuse to accept a substitute. . . . [C]orrelative to that right is the duty of the doctor to provide his or her personal services in accordance with the agreement with the patient."[18] Put another way, by another court, "the basic tenet [of the contract between doctor and patient] is that the physician with whom the patient has contracted is obligated to perform the services."[19]

Another court, summarizing the law as it applies to doctor-patient agreements, has noted that doctors and patients can define the specific role of the surgeon in any reasonable way they agree to. The court notes that failure of the surgeon to live up to the agreement could be a violation of a number of legal duties, including "lack of informed consent, negligent delegation, and a breach of contract, not to mention the risk of a claim of misrepresentation or fraud." The court concludes that while not legally necessary, "it would be prudent for the written form presented to the patient either to set forth any special understanding in this regard or note affirmatively that there is no such understanding."[20]

This means that if there is a surgeon in training involved in your surgery, you should be informed of this and told exactly what the resident will be doing (e.g., opening, closing the wound). You, of course, have a right to refuse any such participation by a surgical resident. The argument that surgeons have to learn somehow does not mean that they have to learn on you—since you (not the surgeon in training) are the one who must live with the consequences of their learning experiences. Like other physicians, surgeons have become especially adept at rationalizing either not informing patients about the role of residents or deceiving patients with ambiguous or meaningless phrases. Atul Gawande, among the most thoughtful of all young surgeons, candidly acknowledges, "Given the stakes, who in his right mind would agree to be practiced upon?" Gawande thinks that "the future of medicine" is dependent upon such learning and wonders, "If everyone cannot have a choice, maybe it is better if no one can."[21] But this is self-serving nonsense. If it is true that every patient would refuse the request of the surgical residents, the answer is not to lie to patients but to understand why patients see the requests as unreasonable and to work to make surgical training both more reasonable and more honest. Of course, if you have other conditions that are unreasonable, the surgery may simply not be done at all. Requiring that surgery be performed without blood transfusions, for example, may or may not be reasonable depending on the type of surgery involved.[22]

May medical students perform examinations on surgical patients while they are under anesthesia?

Medical students, like anyone else, may only touch or examine patients during surgery with the prior informed consent of the patient. This does not have to be in writing, but there are reports of some hospitals simply adding a line to their standard surgical consent form that reads something like "medical students may be involved in my care" and considering this adequate consent for medical students to do invasive examinations, such as pelvic exams, while the patient is under anesthesia.[23] This is, of course, NOT informed consent to anything, since it does not tell the surgical patient what will be done and why, that it is not necessary, and that you can refuse without any effect on your care. If any language like this appears on your consent form, simply cross it out and tell the surgeon you do not consent to any medical students touching you during surgery (an unconsented-to touching during surgery is a battery and could be considered a form of sexual molestation). Surveys of medical students in 2003 in both England and the United States shockingly indicated that it is still not uncommon, especially in obstetrical clerkships, for medical students to perform pelvic examinations during surgery without patient consent.[24] This is intolerable and teaches students that consent is not important if obtaining it makes the student (or the surgeon) uncomfortable. Some surgeons justify the practice by saying that examination under anesthesia is less painful for the woman, that it allows students a better opportunity to palpate internal organs, and that (they believe) obtaining consent is an unnecessary stressor for an already anxious patient. As the author of one of the studies, Dr. Peter Ubel, responded: "This concern for patient well-being is genuine, but the implicit, perhaps even intended message that is delivered to the medical students is that to do no harm, they should not ask and they should not tell."[25]

If a surgeon discovers an unforeseen condition during an operation may the surgeon treat that condition if the patient has not consented to it?

When a surgeon discovers a condition that requires immediate attention, an additional procedure may be performed on the patient without consent if the newly discovered condition constitutes an emergency. For example, in one case a surgeon operated on a woman he thought had a tubal pregnancy but discovered that she had acute appendicitis. A court concluded that the removal of the appendix was permissible.[26]

Even when no emergency exists, a procedure may be extended when the extension is minor and reasonably within the scope of the consented-to procedure. In one case, a physician performing an appendectomy discovered enlarged cysts on the patient's ovaries and punctured them. The court, holding this extension proper, stated: "[T]he surgeon may extend the operation to remedy any abnormal condition in the area of the original incision whenever he, in the exercise of his sound judgment, determines that correct surgical procedure dictates and requires such an extension of the operation originally contemplated."[27]

On the other hand, no nonemergency extension is permissible that would result in the loss of an organ or a normal body function. For example, a surgeon who removed a patient's ovaries during an appendectomy, when he discovered they were diseased, was found liable for this extension of the operation.[28] The scope of the operation should also not be extended beyond the operative field originally consented to. In one case, for example, a patient consented to an operation on her right ear, and the surgeon decided that the left ear also needed surgery and also operated on that ear while she was still under anesthesia. The court concluded that the operation on the left ear constituted a battery.[29]

The general theory behind the cases permitting extension of the operations is that a patient consents both to having a specific condition treated and to assuming certain risks. As long as the procedure is extended only to treat the general problem the patient sought to have treated, and the procedure does not increase the risk or cause disabilities the patient did not contemplate, the extension will likely be deemed proper. Of course, if you expressly forbid any extension of the operation, it should not be undertaken.

If it is possible to foresee that an extension of a surgical procedure may be necessary before the procedure is performed, your explicit consent to such an extension should be sought. You should make your own feelings on extensions of surgery known to your surgeon. Likely areas where extensions might occur should be specifically discussed, and you should make a decision about each before surgery. For example, your exact condition may be uncertain until the surgeon actually operates, but you can discuss the likely options before the surgery.

May a physician treat an emancipated minor without parental consent?

Yes. An emancipated minor is one who is no longer under the care, custody, and control of his or her parents. A married minor or a minor who is in the armed forces is always considered emancipated. Generally, minors who are living apart from their parents and are self-supporting are emancipated for the purpose of consenting to medical care. Some states have codified the emancipated minor rule. In Massachusetts, for example, a minor who is living apart from the minor's parents or guardian and is managing his or her own financial affairs may consent to medical treatment by statute, with certain exceptions.[30]

May mature minors consent to medical or surgical care?

Yes. No court in recent history has found any health care provider liable for treating a minor older than the age of fifteen without parental consent, when the minor consented to the care. Courts have found that a nineteen-year-old (when the age of majority was twenty-one) could consent to the use of a local anesthetic even though his mother had specifically stated she wanted a general anesthetic administered,[31] that a seventeen-year-old could consent to a vaccination required by his employer,[32] and that a seventeen-year-old could consent to the minor surgical care necessary to treat an injury incurred when her finger was caught in a door.[33] In essence, the mature minor rule means that when the minor is capable of understanding the nature and consequences of the medical treatment (the information needed to give an informed consent), the minor is able to consent to his or her own medical care.

Cases using the mature minor rule involve older minors; treatments that are rendered for the benefit of the minor (not using the minor as an organ transplant donor or blood donor); and treatments that are necessary, and some reason exists for not seeking permission of a parent, including the refusal of the minor to do so. Additionally, the treatment usually involves standard and relatively low-risk procedures.

Are there other situations in which a minor may consent to his or her own medical or surgical treatment?

Yes. More than half the states have laws permitting minors to be treated for several diseases or conditions without parental consent. A significant number of states permit children to consent to treatment of alcohol and drug dependency. A large number of states also permit pregnant minors to consent to medical care associated with the pregnancy and pregnancy prevention, including contraception and venereal disease treatment (although many states exclude consent to abortion from these statutes). Other states include mental health care and treatment after sexual assault.

As a practical matter, there is no case in which a physician who has treated a minor for pregnancy or drug or alcohol dependence has been successfully sued by parents for rendering such care, even when no statute exists permitting such treatment without parental consent. It is extremely unlikely that in situations in which minors refuse to consult their parents, care providers who render standard medical treatment to minors for pregnancy, drug or alcohol disease, sexually transmitted diseases, or any other communicable disease would be held liable merely for rendering such care. Minors with good reasons for not wanting their parents to know about these conditions should expect physicians to treat them without parental consent.

If a parent refuses to consent to the treatment of his or her child, may the hospital treat the child?

There are certain instances when a hospital may treat a child even if the parent refuses to consent. When a child's life is in danger, and the parents will not permit treatment, a hospital can seek a court order, and courts will authorize treatment if a physician believes it is necessary to save the child's life. The hospital must, however, go to court and have someone (usually a member of its staff) appointed the guardian of the child for the purpose of consenting to the treatment. In an emergency, this can be done over the phone. If there is not even time for a phone call, emergency treatment can be rendered without any consent if immediate treatment is needed to save the child's life or preserve the child's health.

Conflict can arise when parents refuse to consent to treatment on the basis of their religious convictions. In a typical case, parents, who were Jehovah's Witnesses, refused to grant permission for the necessary blood transfusions in the treatment of their infant son's heart abnormality. The hospital went to court and had the superintendent of the hospital appointed guardian of the child for the purpose of consenting to the surgery. The superintendent then consented to the blood transfusion.[34]

In an unusual case, a court ordered an operation to correct a condition that did not endanger the life of the minor. A fifteen-year-old boy was suffering from Von Recklinghausen's disease, which caused a severe facial deformity. The mother, a Jehovah's Witness, would not consent to the blood transfusion necessary to the operation. The court permitted the operation to proceed without the mother's consent.[35] More commonly, courts will not interfere in a non-life-threatening parental decision. For example, the court would not override a father's refusal to consent to a surgical procedure necessary to repair his son's harelip and cleft palate.[36] The most extreme and unusual cases involve the separation of conjoined infant twins in which one will necessarily be killed in an attempt to "save" the other. In the United States, the decision to operate has been left to the parents. In the United Kingdom, however, a court ordered such a separation over the objections of the parents in late 2000. British law required that the judge make an independent assessment of the best interests of the children rather than simply review the reasonableness of the parental refusal.[37]

Who is responsible for the payment of a minor's medical bills?

One of the advantages of minority is the right to disaffirm or refuse to fulfill a contract. This means that a minor may be able to avoid the obligation to pay for services rendered by a physician or in a hospital. One exception to this rule is that minors are "liable for the reasonable value of necessaries furnished" to them.[38] Necessaries include what is reasonably needed for the minor's subsistence, including food, lodging, and education. Legally, doctor and dentist fees and bills for medicines are considered necessaries, so a minor is obligated to pay for them.

The minor's parents might also be responsible for the cost of necessaries supplied to an unemancipated minor. But parents are not responsible for the necessaries of an emancipated minor. And for a parent to be responsible for the medical bills of an unemancipated minor, it must be shown that the parent negligently failed to provide such services, even though the parent knew they were necessary for the well-being of the child.

If a parent does consent to treatment, may a child nonetheless refuse to undergo the treatment?

There is very little law on this question. In general, however, it seems correct to conclude that a minor who is competent to consent to treatment has the right to refuse the treatment as well, at least as long as neither death or serious permanent disability is involved. In one case, a mother wanted to force her sixteen-year-old, unmarried, pregnant daughter to have an abortion over the minor's objections. A state statute gave a minor the same capacity to consent to medical treatment as an adult when the minor sought treatment concerning pregnancy. The court found that medical treatment concerning pregnancy included abortion, stating: "The minor, having the same capacity to consent as an adult, is emancipated from control of the parents with respect to medical treatment within the contemplation of the statute. We think it follows that if a minor may consent to medical treatment as an adult upon seeking treatment or advice concerning pregnancy . . . [she] has the right to forbid."[39]

May a doctor or hospital tell a child's parents about the child's condition or treatment over the child's objection?

As discussed more fully in chapter 11, the doctor has a legal duty not to disclose information received from the patient or the treatment provided to the patient. Is there anything in the parent-child relationship that should deprive the child of confidential dealings with a doctor?

The parent is generally the consenting party, and to provide informed consent, the parent needs complete information from the doctor. On the other hand, if the child has the capacity to consent to care, the child should have a right to a confidential relationship with a doctor. The confidentiality rules the physician will follow should be discussed with and understood by both parent and adolescent before treatment begins.

May a hospital prevent or restrict visits to children by parents?

In general, if the law or the hospital requires the parent's consent for treatment of the child, the hospital cannot prevent or restrict parents from being with their children while in the hospital for treatment. Restrictive visiting hours for parents, where they still exist, have their roots firmly planted in a past that no longer has any relevance. When Children's Hospital of Boston was founded in 1869, for example, its purpose included bringing children "under the influence of order, purity and kindness." To isolate children from their less-than-desirable working-class home environments, visiting hours were restricted to one relative at a time, from eleven A.M. to noon on weekdays only. The intent and effect was to bar working parents from frequent contact with their children.[40] Modern hospitals have attempted to come up with other reasons to restrict visits by parents (for example, it makes children without parents who can stay with them uncomfortable); however, none have any more validity that the 1869 visiting restrictions.

Nevertheless, it was not until the 1950s that some in the medical profession began to view as paradoxical the fact that "when a young child needs his mother most, when the child is ill and perhaps in pain, she is generally not allowed to be with the child for more than brief visits."[41] Since then, trends have continued toward liberalizing visiting hours in pediatric wards and hospitals, and parents who insist can stay with their child in almost every modern hospital.

In Boston, a consumer group called Children in Hospitals was organized in the early 1970s to support parents who want to stay with their children in the hospital and to encourage hospitals to broaden their visiting policies.[42] It was founded by a mother who demanded and was granted the right to stay with her ten-month-old daughter during a hospitalization. At one point, a nurse put some drops in the child's eye and left. The baby started screaming and would not open her eyes. Twice the mother carried the child out to the nursing station and was given no satisfaction. After a third try, she persuaded the nurse to check to be sure the right drops had been administered. The nurse discovered that the drops were iodine for the baby to drink prior to a brain-wave test. Her eyes were immediately flushed out, and luckily no permanent damage was done.

The legal right to be with one's children derives from the doctrine of informed consent. Parents may not be able to give informed consent for their children if they are not able to be with them constantly to monitor their reactions (which they can interpret better than anyone else because of their experience with their children). Also, parents have the right to withdraw their consent to treatment at any time, and this right can only be meaningfully exercised if the parent is continuously present with the child to determine that circumstances have changed to such an extent that consent should be withdrawn. Parents whose request to stay with their child is refused can limit any consent they are asked to give or form they are asked to sign with the condition that they be permitted to stay with their child. If they are thereafter denied the right to stay with their child, they can terminate their consent, and the hospital may no longer legally treat their child.

The only reasonable limits a hospital probably is allowed to place on parental presence involve actual interference with the hospital's ability to care for other patients (not the parent's own child, since the parents and not the doctor or hospital have the ultimate treatment obligation and authority). This means that parents, if they so desire, have the legal right to stay with their children during all tests and procedures, the induction of anesthesia, and to be present in the recovery room when the child regains consciousness.

What can parents do to make hospitals more responsive to their needs?

Parents can take the following actions to improve hospital care of their children:

- Question hospital policy *before* your child is admitted.
- Select the doctor and hospital best able to make the arrangements you want.
- Negotiate directly with the chief of pediatrics or the chief of anesthesia, never with the admissions office or floor nurses.
- Publicize your experiences, both favorable and unfavorable.
- Form parent groups to work for the changes in hospital policy you want.

Can assertiveness and attempts to be independent hurt a patient's recovery?

The contrary seems to be true: assertive patients are those involved in their care and who want to do all they can to get better. Surgeon Bernie Siegel argues that "the most important kind of assertiveness a patient can demonstrate is in the formation of a participatory relationship with the doctor" and suggests eleven steps, which he calls "Good Patient, Bad Patient," that he encourages patients who are going to the hospital to follow. Patients have the legal right to do all of them:

1. For your hospital stay, take clothes that are practical, comfortable and individual. Plan to walk as much as possible.

2. Take room decorations of a personal and inspirational nature. . . .

3. Question authority—tests, etc. Speak up for yourself, your needs and comfort in all areas, both before and during tests.

4. Make your doctor aware of your unique needs and desires. . . .

5. Take a tape recorder and earphones. . . . Record conversations with your physician for later review and for family use.

6. Use your tape recorder in the operating room and recovery room to hear music, meditation, or messages during and after surgery. Have someone put a reminder into the doctor's orders to play the entire tape continuously.

7. . . . Instruct the surgeon and anesthesiologist to repeat positive messages to you. The simplest is that you will awaken comfortable, thirsty, and hungry.

8. Tell the surgeon to speak to you during surgery, honestly but hopefully. . . .

9. Speak to your own body, particularly the night before surgery, suggesting that the blood leave the area of surgery and that you'll heal rapidly.

10. Arrange visits and calls from those who will nurture and love you, as well as give you "carefrontation" when appropriate.

11. Get moving as soon as possible after surgery. Leave the hospital to attend group meetings, go for walks, or have meals out with friends.[43]

Not all patients will want to follow these suggestions or are the "exceptional patients" that Siegel encourages all of us to be. But the point should not be lost: you have a legal right to do these things if you so choose. And if the surgeon does not permit you to do reasonable things such as listening to music during surgery, you have the right to fire the surgeon and hire someone who will respect your wishes. Remember: "It is your body. It is your life. The final decision is yours."[44]

May a hospital lawfully prevent a patient from leaving?

No. A competent, adult patient may leave the hospital at any time, and the hospital may not prevent it. Hospitals are not prisons. If the hospital restricts your freedom to leave, you may sue the hospital for false imprisonment or for intentional confinement by threat or physical barriers against your will. No actual damages need to be proved, since the law assumes harm to you from this wrongful conduct.

This rule applies even if you have not paid the bill. In one case, for example, a patient was detained for eleven hours for not paying her bill. In concluding that she could sue the hospital for false imprisonment, the court said: "[T]he fact that the bill . . . had not been paid afforded no sort of excuse for detaining the [patient] against her will."[45] This rule also applies to detaining infants and children when their parents have not paid the bill. Courts have found hospitals liable for interfering with the parent's right to custody of the child when discharge has been refused because of failure to pay a bill.[46]

A hospital may prevent a mentally ill person from departing if the person is a danger to his or her own life or the lives and property of others, provided the hospital follows the state's laws governing involuntary commitment of the mentally ill, including a determination by a qualified psychiatrist that the person is mentally ill and a danger to himself or herself or others.

Hospitals may also request patients to sign a "discharge against medical advice form," sometimes termed discharge AMA. Patients, however, have no obligation to sign such a form as a condition of release, and hospitals can protect themselves equally well by simply having the physician or nurse document the circumstances of the patient's departure in the medical record, as well as any noncoercive attempts made to persuade the patient to stay. In rare cases, such as contagious diseases, public health authorities may have power to quarantine a patient, thus restraining the patient from leaving the premises. The state's quarantine authority is spelled out in each state's public health laws and is generally very broad—to protect the public's health from a danger posed to it by the patient.

Does a patient's attending physician retain the responsibility regarding discharge even if there is no money to pay for continuing hospitalization?

Yes. The general rule is that no patient may be discharged from a hospital except by written order of a physician familiar with the patient's condition. If the patient disagrees with the order, the patient has a right to demand a consultation with another physician before the order is carried out. In any event, however, the decision to discharge must be made on the basis of the patient's medical condition and may not take into consideration the patient's nonpayment of medical bills.

In one case, for example, a private hospital admitted an eight-year-old boy suffering from a bone infection. The bill for treatment was $1,000, but the boy's father could pay only $349. The hospital discharged the boy for failure to pay his bills and instructed the father that the boy would be safe at home under the care of a physician. In fact, the physician was not able to provide proper care at home, and the boy's condition worsened. The court found the hospital liable for negligent and wrongful discharge.[47]

A California case further illustrates the physician's responsibility. A woman, who was a member of California's Medicaid program (MediCal), complained to her physician about circulatory problems in her legs.[48] He recommended surgery, and his recommendation was approved by a before-the-fact utilization review committee that approved ten days of postoperative hospitalization for Medicaid payment. The day before she was scheduled for discharge, the physician requested an eight-day extension because of severe complications that had developed. The reviewing physician, however, authorized only a four-day extension. The patient was discharged after this four-day period without any further requests for extensions or reconsideration. Nine days later, the patient was readmitted on an emergency basis, and her right leg had to be amputated. She sued the Medicaid program, arguing that it was negligent in not granting her physician's request for the eight-day extension, and that her premature discharge directly caused the amputation of her leg. The California Court of Appeals ruled that the discharge decision was not for Medicaid to make but for her attending physician. The question of payment is distinct from the question of medical judgment about the health of the patient. The patient might be able to sue her physician, but not Medicaid, which was only trying to control costs in a reasonable manner. In the court's words, although "cost consciousness has become a permanent feature of the health care system, it is essential that cost limitation programs not be permitted to corrupt medical judgment."

The lesson from this case and others like it is clear: the attending physician's medical judgment is the most important factor regarding discharge. If patients do not think they are ready to go home or be transferred, their first recourse is to discuss the reasons for this feeling directly with the attending physician. If the discharge is medically indicated, and the patient still refuses to leave, the hospital may take steps to forcibly remove the patient as a trespasser. All steps must, however, be reasonable, and only the minimum amount of force necessary may be used. Medicare rules also require that patients have a discharge plan twenty-four hours prior to discharge.

Does a doctor ever have a duty to refer a patient to a specialist or to seek a consultation with a specialist?

The general rule is that if a doctor knows, or should know, that a patient's ailment is beyond the doctor's knowledge, technical skill, ability, or capacity to treat with a likelihood of reasonable success, the doctor is obligated to either disclose this to the patient or advise the patient of the necessity of other or different treatment.[49]

Not only must the general practitioner consult a specialist, but the specialist must also consult a specialist in another field when indicated. If a reasonably careful and skillful attending physician would have suggested consulting a specialist, a physician may be found negligent for not making such a suggestion.[50] In a circumcision case, for example, an infant's penis had to be amputated. Evidence showed that prior to the infant's discharge from the hospital, a black spot appeared on the penis, and that the spot continued to grow when he was home. On returning to the hospital the following day, both the pediatric specialist and a urology specialist were consulted. They concluded that the spot was caused by gangrene, but it was too late to do anything about it. The court found the evidence sufficient to warrant a finding by the jury that the physician who performed the circumcision should have called in a specialist prior to the child's discharge from the hospital, when something might have been done to save the child's penis.[51]

Does a hospital have a duty to ensure that doctors practicing in the hospital seek and obtain indicated consultation?

Yes, and the duty can be derived from different sources. Perhaps the best-known case dealing with this issue was decided in Illinois in 1965.[52] In that case, eighteen-year-old Dorrence Darling broke his leg while playing college football. He was treated by a general practitioner, Dr. John Alexander, in the emergency room of Charleston Community Memorial Hospital in Illinois. Alexander applied a plaster cast to the leg. Over the period of the next two weeks, Darling almost continuously complained of severe pain and pressure. His leg turned a grayish color, and the smell in his room was terrible. He was finally removed from the hospital by his parents, and his leg, having been found to be gangrenous, had to be amputated. Alexander settled out of court, and the case continued against the hospital. One of the major issues considered by the court was whether the hospital itself could be found negligent for failure "to require consultation with or examination by members of the hospital staff skilled in such treatment; or to review the treatment rendered to the plaintiff and to require consultants to be called in as needed." The court concluded the state's public-health licensing regulations, the standards of the Joint Commission, and the bylaws of the hospital provided the jury with sufficient evidence to find that the hospital had a duty to require a consultation in this case. A judgment against the hospital was accordingly affirmed.

When the need for consultation is or should be apparent because of the patient's worsening condition, both the doctor and the hospital will likely be found liable for failure to provide consultation if harm to the patient would likely have been avoided if proper consultation had been obtained.[53]

Must a doctor refer a patient to a specialist or seek a consultation on request by a patient?

The American Medical Association's (AMA) Principles of Medical Ethics require physicians to seek consultation upon patient request. Although this is an ethical, not a legal, guideline, refusal of such a patient's request "is an invitation to a malpractice suit if the attending physician turns out to be wrong [in suggesting to the patient that a consultation is not necessary]."[54]

One case in which a request for consultation was refused involved an eleven-year-old boy who was brought to a U.S. Air Force dispensary with severe abdominal pain and vomiting and referred to a naval hospital with a diagnosis of "possible appendicitis." At the emergency department of the hospital, the boy was seen by another doctor who only did a cursory physical examination. He concluded that it was not appendicitis and asked that the child be taken home. The child's mother asked that another physician be called in to look at the child, but the doctor refused. Early the following morning, the child started crying and rolling around in extreme pain. He was again taken to the emergency department and seen by an intern who gave the child pain medication and sent him home. The next day, the boy returned to the dispensary. After delays at both the dispensary and the hospital, surgery was finally performed but only *after* the boy's appendix had ruptured. As a result of the delay, peritonitis developed, and the child not only had to spend and additional three weeks in the hospital but also suffered permanent internal damage. Citing the AMA principles, the hospital's policy, the U.S. Government's Medical Department Manual, and Joint Commission standards, the court concluded that both doctors in the emergency department, and therefore the hospital that employed them, could be found negligent for failure to seek consultation.[55]

A physician who refuses your request for a consultation or referral does so at his or her own peril. If the physician is wrong in reassuring you that the treatment is proper, the physician may be found negligent for failure to respond appropriately (as a reasonably prudent physician would) to your reasonable request.

May a doctor refuse to continue to see a patient without obtaining the services of another doctor for the patient?

The general rule is that once a doctor-patient relationship is established, the doctor must continue to see the patient until one of the four following conditions is met:

- It is terminated by the consent of both doctor and patient.
- It is revoked by the patient.
- The doctor's services are no longer needed.

• The physician withdraws from the case *after* reasonable notice to the patient.[56]

Abandonment occurs when the physician unilaterally severs the doctor-patient relationship at a time when continued care is needed. If injury results to the patient because of the abandonment, the patient may sue the doctor for damages. If the treatment is in a critical stage at which abandonment might be harmful to the patient, nonpayment of bills by the patient cannot be used as a justification for refusal by the physician to extend further aid.[57]

A Virginia case illustrates how abandonment can occur. The doctor properly set a fracture and applied a cast to a child's leg. Yet when the child later complained of pain and the doctor was called, he failed to respond. The doctor then left town. When the child's parents were unable to locate the doctor, they called in another physician who cut the cast to relieve the pressure and noted evidence of an infection. When the doctor returned to town, he again refused to see the patient in the hospital and, instead, discharged the patient. At home, the pain continued, and another physician was called, who observed necrotic spots on the child's leg, which had to be amputated. In upholding a jury verdict for the patient, the court restated the general rule: "After a physician has accepted employment in a case it is his duty to continue his services as long as they are necessary. He cannot voluntarily abandon his patient, even if personal attention is no longer necessary.[58]

If a physician discharges you from the hospital, and you have a relapse and call the physician for help, the physician must also take steps to help you or face a charge of abandonment unless another physician has taken over your care.

Can a patient recover damages from a physician or a hospital for premature discharge?

As two noted medicolegal commentators have stated, "It is uniformly held by the courts that the premature discharge of a patient constitutes abandonment."[59] These commentators also note that "unfortunately, instances of premature discharge abound in the reported cases."[60]

Premature discharge can be illustrated by a particularly gruesome case from the 1920s. The physician involved had performed an unskillful operation for a strangulated hernia. After an improper incision, he closed the wound without attempting to relieve the obstructed bowel and informed the patient that she was going to die. He then ordered the patient sent home in a hearse and refused thereafter to see her at home in spite of her calls. The Rhode Island Supreme Court had no difficulty finding that the physician was liable for abandonment.[61]

What information should the patient have prior to discharge?

No patient should be discharged without a discharge plan and clear instructions regarding follow-up care, a description of problems to be on the lookout for, and contact information of a person to call if any of these problems occur. Many doctors and hospitals have standard forms they give patients that explain such basic information, and patients should this take information seriously. A social worker will often be assigned to the patient to help make arrangements for placement in a nursing home or an extended-care facility. A visiting nurse or other health aide may be assigned to see the patient at home during recuperation.

TIPS FOR ADVOCATES

- **Surgeons are likely to suggest a surgical solution.**

- **A second opinion about surgery is important,** and no competent surgeon will object to obtaining a second opinion.

- **It is the patient's body and the patient who will live with the consequences of surgery: that is why it is the patient's choice of the type of surgery and the surgeon. Make sure all your patient's questions are answered.**

- **The patient has a right to know who will actually do the surgery** (and to refuse to consent to surgery performed by a resident) and the experience (and success rate) the surgeon has had with the particular operation. The surgeon's experience is very important.

- **The patient should not take presurgery medications until the patient knows as much about the surgery as the patient wants and has signed the surgical consent form.**

- **Ask about any likely extensions of the surgery** that might only come to light during the operation, and have your patient decide what to do about them in advance of the surgery.

• **Mature and emancipated minors may usually consent to their own treatment** without telling their parents.

• **Hospitals may not treat children without parental consent except in an emergency** or after obtaining a court order.

• **Hospitals may not forbid parents from being with their children at any time** when consent for treatment or testing might be necessary; and parents should insist on staying with their children in hospitals twenty-four hours a day if they are able to spend this much time with them.

• **Hospitals may not lawfully prohibit a patient from leaving the hospital,** whether or not the bill has been paid or whether or not it is against medical advice.

NOTES

1. George Crile, Surgery, New York: Delacorte Press, 1978, xvi. *See also* Melvin Konner, Becoming a Doctor, New York: Penguin Books, 1988, 21.

2. T. B. Graboys et al., *Results of a Second-Opinion Program for Coronary Artery Bypass Graft Surgery,* 258 JAMA 1611 (1987); *and see generally* J. R. Clarke, *A Comparison of Decision Analysis and Second Opinions for Surgical Decisions,* 120 Arch. Surg. 844 (1985), and Jeanette Brown et al., *Hysterectomy and Urinary Incontinence: A Systematic Review,* 356 Lancet 535 (2000).

3. Knight Steel et al., *Iatrogenic Illness on a General Medical Service at a University Hospital,* 304 New Eng. J. Med. 638 (1981). *See also* Lori Andrews et al., *An Alternative Strategy for Studying Adverse Events in Medical Care,* 349 Lancet 309 (1997).

4. Institute of Medicine, To Err Is Human, Washington, D.C.: National Academy Press, 1999; Charles B. Inlander, L. S. Levin & E. Weiner, Medicine on Trial, New York: Prentice-Hall, 1988, 123–53.

5. N. P. Couch et al., *The High Cost of Low-Frequency Events,* 304 New Eng. J. Med. 634 (1981). On second opinions and unnecessary surgery, *see* E. G. McCarthy & G. W. Wildmer, *Effects of Screening by Consultants on Recommended Elective Surgical Procedures,* 291 New Eng. J. Med. 1331 (1974) (Specific procedures most frequently found unnecessary included hysterectomy, dilatation and curettage, breast operations, and gallbladder

removal.), and Jerome Groupman, *A Knife in the Back: Is Surgery the Best Approach to Chronic Back Pain?* New Yorker, April 8, 2002, 66.

6. *Doctor Main Variable in Mastectomy Choice,* New York Times, November 28, 2000, D10.

7. Crile, *supra* note 1, at xiii.

8. Michael L. Millenson, Demanding Medical Excellence: Doctors and Accountability in the Information Age, Chicago: Chicago U. Press, 1997.

9. Jack Wennberg, *AHCPR and the Strategy for Health Care Reform,* 64 (4) Health Affairs 68 (1992). *See also* David Kirby, *More Options and Decisions for Men with Prostate Cancer,* New York Times, October 3, 2000, D7, and Anne Barnard, *Men Seek "the Truth" on Prostate Treatment,* Boston Globe, January 18, 2003, A1.

10. *See* R. Perez-Pena, *Newly Released Data Offer Hints of Doctors' Experience,* New York Times, February 14, 2000, A20, and Arnold Epstein, *Volume and Outcome: It Is Time to Move Ahead,* 346 New Eng. J. Med. 1161 (2002).

11. Atul Gawande, *When Good Doctors Go Bad,* New Yorker, August 7, 2000, 60–69. There is also a continuing struggle between physician anesthesiologists and nurse anesthetists. *See, e.g., In This Doctor vs. Nurse Debate, Long Deep Breaths,* New York Times, October 8, 2000, B9.

12. Leonard Glantz et al., *Risky Business: Setting Public Health Policy for HIV-Infected Health Care Professionals,* 70 Milbank Q. 43 (1992).

13. In 1981, the national average for lumpectomies or wedge excisions of tumors under one centimeter was 4.8 percent, but Massachusetts and California, which had these laws, had figures of 18 percent and 10 percent, respectively. New York, which had no law, had an average of 2 percent. New York passed its own statute in 1985, and other states have continued this trend. R. L. Dabice & S. Cordes, *Informed Consent Heralds Change in Breast Treatment,* Medical News, November 11, 1985, 1, 4.

14. Jay Katz, The Silent World of Doctor and Patient, New Haven: Yale U. Press, 1984, 183–84. For current information on cancer treatment and research, call the National Cancer Institute (NCI) (800-4-CANCER).

15. The entire poem appears in John Mukand, ed., Sutured Words: Contemporary Poems about Medicine, Brookline, Mass.: Aviva Press, 1987, 124.

16. *See, e.g.,* R. J. Mayer & W. B. Patterson, *How Is Cancer Treatment Chosen?* 318 New Eng. J. Med. 636 (1988).

17. *See* Nicholas Christakis, Death Foretold: Prophecy and Prognosis in Medicine, Chicago: Chicago U. Press, 2000.

18. *Perna v. Pirozzi,* 92 N.J. 446, 457 A.2d 431 (1983).

19. *Grabowski v. Quigley,* 454 Pa. Super. 27, 684 A.2d 610 (Pa. Super. 1996).

20. *Dingle v. Belin,* 358 Md. 354, 749 A.2d 157 (Md. App. 2000).

21. Atul Gawande, *The Learning Curve,* New Yorker, January 28, 2002, 52, 61.

22. For information on surgeons who will honor a patient's request not to do blood transfusions, call 1-800-NO-BLOOD.

23. Audrey Warren, *Doctor Training on Unconscious Faces Scrutiny,* Wall Street Journal, March 12, 2003, B1.

24. Peter Ubel, Christopher Jepson & Ari Silver-Isenstadt, *Don't Ask, Don't Tell: A Change in Medical Student Attitudes after Obstetrics/Gynecology Clerkships Toward Seeking*

Consent for Pelvic Examinations on an Anesthetized Patient, 188 Am. J. Obstet. Gyn. 575 (2003); Yvette Coldicott, Catherine Pope & Clive Roberts, *The Ethics of Intimate Examinations: Teaching Tomorrow's Doctors,* 326 Brit. Med. J. 97 (2003); Peter A. Singer, *Intimate Examinations and Other Ethical Challenges in Medical Education,* 326 Brit. Med. J. 62 (2003).

25. John Dorschner, *Med Students Often Do Pelvic Exams on Women Without Consent Report Says,* Miami Herald, February 21, 2003, A1.

26. *Barnett v. Bachrach,* 34 A.2d 626 (Mun. Ct. App. D.C. 1943).

27. *Kennedy v. Parrott,* 243 N.C. 355, 362 90 S.E.2d 754, 759 (1956).

28. *Wells v. Van Nort,* 100 Ohio St. 101, 125 N.E. 910 (1919).

29. *Mohr v. Williams,* 95 Minn. 261, 104 N.W. 12 (1905).

30. Mass. Gen L. ch 112, sec. 12(F).

31. *Bishop v. Shurly,* 237 Mich. 76, 211 N.W. 75 (1926).

32. *Gulf & S.I.R. Co. v. Sullivan,* 155 Miss. 1, 119 So. 501 (1928).

33. *Younts v. St. Francis Hospital,* 205 Kan. 292, 469 P.2d 330 (1970).

34. *State v. Perricone,* 37 N.J. 463, 181 A.2d 751 (1962). When the treatment is highly invasive and may not succeed, courts are unlikely to second-guess parents. *See, e.g., Newark v. Williams,* 588 A.2d. 1108 (Del. 1991).

35. *In re Sampson,* 65 Misc. 2d 658, 317 N.W.S.2d 641 (1970), *aff'd.* 29 N.Y.2d 900, 278 N.E.2d 918 (1972).

36. *In re Seiferth,* 309 N.Y. 80, 127 N.E.2d 820 (1955). *And see generally* Jennifer L. Rosato, *The Ultimate Test of Autonomy: Should Minors Have a Right to Make Decisions Regarding Life-Sustaining Treatment?* 49 Rutgers L. Rev. 1 (1996).

37. *See* George J. Annas, *The Limits of Law at the Limits of Life: Lessons from Cannibalism, Euthanasia, Abortion, and Court-Ordered Killing of One Conjoined Twin to Save the Other,* 33 Conn. L. Rev. 1275 (2001).

38. *See* 42 Am. Jurisprudence 2d, Infants 65; *and see generally* John D. Hodson, *Infant's Liability for Medical, Dental or Hospital Services,* 53 A.L.R.4th 1249 (1987).

39. *In re Smith,* 16 Md. App. 209, 225, 295 A.2d 238, 246 (1972).

40. Paul Starr, The Social Transformation of American Medicine, New York: Basic Books, 1982, 158.

41. James Robertson, Young Children in Hospitals, New York: Basic Books, 1958; *and see* Susan Diesenhouse, *Suffering of Children Is Eased as Hospitals Change to Keep Families Near,* New York Times, December 15, 1988, B22.

42. For further information, write Barbara Popper, Children in Hospitals, 31 Wilshire Park, Needham, Mass. 02191. *See also* the excellent *A Pediatric Bill of Rights* promulgated by the Association for the Care of Children's Health, 19 Mantua Rd., Mt. Royal, N.J. 08061 (www.acch.org).

43. Bernie Siegel, Love, Medicine and Miracles, New York: Harper & Row, 1986, 173–74.

44. Crile, *supra* note 1.

45. *Gadsen General Hospital v. Hamilton,* 212 Ala. 531, 532, 103 So. 553, 554 (1925); in another case, recovery was denied because the court was not convinced that the patient's apprehension that force would be used to detain her was "reasonable" (*Hoffman v. Clinic Hospital,* 213 N.C. 669, 197 S.E. 161 [1938]).

46. *Bedard v. Notre Dame Hospital,* 89 R.I. 195, 151 A.2d 690 (1959).

47. *Meiselman v. Crown Heights Hospital,* 285 N.Y. 389, 34 N.E.2d 367 (1941). *Cf. Hicks v. U.S.,* 368 F.2d 626 (4th Cir. 1966) (Dispensary physician determined that patient had harmless instead of lethal disease without properly testing for the lethal possibility. With prompt surgery, the patient would have survived; instead, she was sent home and died from a high intestinal obstruction. In finding the dispensary physician liable, the court said: "By releasing the patient, the dispensary physician made his diagnosis final, allowing no further opportunity for revision, and this prematurely determined final diagnosis was based on an investigation not even minimally adequate." The court went on to determine that the premature discharge of the patient was the proximate cause of death.).

48. *Wickline v. California,* 192 Cal. App.3d 1630, 239 Cal. Rptr. 810 (Cal. App. 1986).

49. *Manion v. Tweedy,* 257 Minn. 59, 65, 100 N.W.2d 124, 128 (Minn. 1959). A doctor does *not,* however, become liable for the negligent acts of another physician merely by recommending the specialist, *Dill v. Scuka,* 175 F. Supp. 26 (E.D. Pa. 1959); and *Mincey v. Blando,* 655 S.W.2d 609 (Mo. App. 1983).

50. *Graham v. St. Luke's Hospital,* 46 Ill. App. 2d 147, 160, 196 N.E.2d 355, 361 (1964).

51. *Valentine v. Kaiser Foundation Hospitals,* 194 Cal. App. 2d 282, 293, 15 Cal. Rptr. 26, 32 (1961).

52. *Darling v. Charleston Community Memorial Hospital,* 33 Ill. 2d 326, 211 N.E.2d 253 (1965), *cert. denied,* 383 U.S. 946 (1966).

53. *See generally* Arthur Southwick, *The Hospital's New Responsibility,* 17 Cleve.-Mar. L. Rev. 146 (1968); Note, *Hospital Liability—A New Duty of Care,* 19 Me. L. Rev. 102 (1967); Mueller, *Expanding Duty of the Hospital to the Patient,* 47 Neb. L. Rev. 337 (1968).

54. Angela Holder, *Referral to a Specialist,* (in) AMA, Best of Law & Medicine, 1968–70 (1970), 27.

55. *Steeves v. U.S.,* 294 F. Supp. 446 (D.S.C. 1968).

56. Comment, *The Action of Abandonment in Medical Malpractice Litigation,* 36 Tul. L. Rev. 834, 835 (1962); *and see Dillon v. Silver,* 520 N.Y.S. 2d 751, 134 A.D.2d 159 (1987).

57. Comment, *supra* note 56, at 841; *E.g., Becker v. Janinski,* 15 N.Y.S. 675 (App. Div. 1891); *Ricks v. Budge,* 91 Utah 307, 64 P.2d 208 (1937). The physician may, however, properly terminate the doctor-patient relationship for refusal to pay if he or she gives the patient sufficient notice for the patient to obtain other medical attention (*Burnett v. Layman,* 133 Tenn. 323, 181 S.W. 157 [1915]). *See generally,* Maxwell J. Mehlman, *The Patient-Physician Relationship in an Era of Scarce Resources: Is There a Duty to Treat?,* 25 Conn. L. Rev. 349, 371-9 (1993).

58. *Vann v. Harden,* 187 Va. 555, 565–66, 47 S.E.2d 314, 319 (1948), *Manno v. McIntosh,* 519 N.W.2d 815, 820-22 (Iowa Ct. App. 1994).

59. Jon Waltz & Fred Inbau, Medical Jurisprudence, New York: Macmillan, 1971, 146.

60. *Id.; see also Mucci v. Houghton,* 89 Iowa 608, 57 N.W. 305 (1894); *Reed v. Laughlin,* 58 S.W. 2d 440 (Mo. 1933); *Meiselman v. Crown Heights Hospital,* 285 N.Y. 389, 34 N.E.2d 367 (1941).

61. *Morrell v. Lalonde,* 120 A. 435 (R.I. 1923).

VIII

Reproductive Health

The law has taken the lead in delineating the contours of the public debate over reproductive liberty. Most of that debate, in turn, has focused on the Supreme Court's landmark 1973 decision in *Roe v. Wade*,[1] the Court's 1992 decision in *Planned Parenthood v. Casey*,[2] and the application of both cases to so-called partial birth abortion in 2000 in *Stenberg v. Carhart*.[3] I use an overview of these critical decisions and their immediate predecessors to provide an introduction to this chapter.

The first case fully adopting the concept of reproductive liberty, *Griswold v. Connecticut,* concerned the constitutionality of a Connecticut statute that made it a crime for both married and unmarried people to use contraceptives. In striking down this statute, the Supreme Court enunciated a constitutional right to privacy suggested by "penumbras" that emanate from specific guarantees in the Bill of Rights. Defining a specific zone of privacy, Justice William Douglas, writing for the Court, focused on sexual relations in marriage:

We deal with a right of privacy older than the Bill of Rights—older than our political parties, older than our school system. Marriage is the coming together for better or for worse, hopefully enduring, and intimate to the degree of being sacred. It is an association that promotes a way of life, not causes; a harmony in living, not political faiths; a bilateral loyalty, not commercial or social projects . . . an association for as noble a purpose as any involved in prior decisions.[4]

To secure the argument, the Court also noted that the statute could not be enforced without massive and unthinkable governmental intrusion into people's lives and homes: "Would we allow the police to search the sacred precincts of marital bedrooms for telltale signs of the use of contraceptives? The very idea is repulsive to the notions of privacy surrounding the marriage relationship."

Strictly speaking, the Connecticut case applied only to married couples. But during the same term in which *Roe v. Wade* was being discussed, the Court decided another case involving a Massachusetts statute that made it a crime to sell, lend, give away, or exhibit any contraceptive device to unmarried people. In that case, the Court concluded that there was no constitutionally acceptable rationale for treating married and unmarried individuals differently with respect to contraception, and that the basis for the right to privacy was the importance of individual choice, not marriage: "The marital couple is not an independent entity with a mind and heart of its own, but *an association of two individuals,* each with a separate intellectual and emotional makeup. If the right to privacy means anything, it is the right of the *individual,* married or single, to be free from unwarranted governmental intrusion into matters so fundamentally affecting a person as the decision whether to bear or beget a child."[5] This decision presaged *Roe* by going further than the Court had to go in broadening the right to privacy to include a decision not only to "beget" a child but also to "bear" one.

ROE V. WADE

The 1973 opinion of *Roe v. Wade* is one of the most important, most controversial, and most well-known U.S. Supreme Court decisions. At issue in *Roe* was a Texas statute that made it a crime to "procure an abortion" or to attempt one, except to save the life of the mother. Justice Harry Blackmun wrote the opinion of the Court, which determined that the right of privacy existed "in the Fourteenth Amendment's concept of personal liberty." The Court concluded that this right "is broad enough to encompass a woman's decision whether or not to terminate her pregnancy. The detriment that the state would impose upon a pregnant women by denying this choice altogether is apparent. Specific and direct harm medically diagnosable even in early pregnancy may be involved. Maternity, or additional offspring, may force upon a woman a distressful life and future."

The Court also recognized, however, that the state has interests in the health of the mother and the life of the fetus that may at different times during the pregnancy be sufficiently "compelling" to permit the state to limit abortion. With regard to maternal health, the Court found this interest compelling only after the point in pregnancy at which abortion becomes more dangerous to the woman's health than carrying the fetus to term (in 1973, about the end of the first trimester). With regard to fetal life, the Court found that the state could legitimately claim a compelling interest in protecting fetal life after viability, which the Court defined as the time the fetus (as a newborn) is capable of surviving independently of its mother (then and now about the beginning of the third trimester). The Court thus concluded that states could regulate abortion procedures in ways designed to protect the pregnant woman's health after the time in pregnancy when abortion was no longer safer than childbirth, and that states could outlaw pregnancy terminations after fetal viability except when the life or health of the pregnant woman was endangered by continuing the pregnancy.[6]

Privacy, as a constitutional right, has come to be simply a one-word legal description of individual liberty (or self-determination) to make decisions that involve marriage, sterilization, contraception, and abortion. As Ronald Dworkin has aptly described, the core of self-determination in the privacy right, decisions that affect marriage and childbirth, are "so important, so intimate and personal, so crucial to the development of personality and sense of moral responsibility" that individuals must be allowed to make them "consulting their own conscience, rather than allowing society to thrust its collective decision on them."[7]

PLANNED PARENTHOOD V. CASEY

The political and legal assault on *Roe v. Wade* has continued unabated for more than thirty years, and most observers believed that the U.S. Supreme Court would overrule *Roe* in its 1992 decision in *Casey.* Surprisingly, this did not happen. In a very unusual move, three Justices, Sandra Day O'Connor, Anthony Kennedy, and David Souter, wrote a joint opinion reframing *Roe,* which (as recast by the joint opinion's authors) now stands for the proposition that pregnant women have a "personal liberty" right to choose to terminate their pregnancies prior to fetal viability that the state cannot "unduly burden."

The nature of the constitutional right to choose an abortion was seen as being derived not only from the right of privacy regarding family and personal decision making but also from cases restricting the government's power to mandate medical treatment or to bar its rejection, such as *Cruzan* (see chapter 12). The Justices concluded that the post-*Roe* medical treatment cases protecting bodily integrity "accord with *Roe's* view that a state's interest in the protection of life falls short of justifying any plenary override of individual liberty claims" and prohibit the state from forcing either continued pregnancy or abortion on a pregnant woman.

The joint opinion in *Casey* concluded its analysis by holding that a woman's constitutional "right to choose to terminate her pregnancy" continues until fetal viability. Viability was chosen because it was the most important line drawn in *Roe*, because "there is no line other than viability which is more workable," and because at viability "the independent existence of the second life can in reason and all fairness be the object of state protection [although *not* a person under the constitution] that now overrides the rights of the woman."

The joint opinion examined two provisions of the Pennsylvania antiabortion statute the Court was reviewing in detail. The first required a twenty-four-hour waiting period between consent to have an abortion and the procedure. A twenty-four-hour waiting period had been found by the lower court to be burdensome for poor, rural women who must travel long distances to a clinic. The joint opinion, however, concluded that the waiting period was part of the informed consent requirement, which "facilitates the wise exercise" of the right to choose and is not an undue burden on the exercise of that right. On the other hand, the joint opinion found a second provision, the requirement of spousal notification, could not meet the undue burden test. Because its exceptions were so narrow (not including, for example, psychological abuse and assault not reported to the police), it would "likely prevent a significant number of women from obtaining an abortion." The opinion stands for the proposition that state legislatures can write rules that hassle women seeking abortion but cannot write rules that actually prevent them from obtaining abortions.

STENBERG V. CARHART

In 2000, the U.S. Supreme Court issued its most important abortion decision since *Casey, Stenberg v. Carhart*. In a 5-4 opinion, the Court ruled that Nebraska's "partial-birth abortion" statute, which was substantially

similar to state statutes in thirty states, was unconstitutional.[8] The Nebraska statute made it a crime, punishable by twenty years in prison, for
a physician to perform a partial-birth abortion defined as "an abortion
procedure in which the person performing the abortion partially delivers
vaginally a living unborn child before killing the unborn child and completing delivery." The Court gave two reasons for finding this criminal
statute unconstitutional: the ban on this procedure did not have an exception for abortions necessary to protect the woman's health (and thus violated *Roe v. Wade*); and the procedure itself was so vaguely described and
so similar to another very common procedure (dilation and evacuation
abortion) that physicians might be afraid to offer this standard procedure
to women, thus creating an "undue burden" (under *Casey*) on their right
to choose abortion.

Stenberg reflects *Roe v. Wade*'s strong endorsement of the privacy of the
doctor-patient relationship, and the right of women and their physicians
to make the abortion decision within it. The opinion does this by focusing
much more on physicians and the medical techniques physicians employ
than on women and their lives and liberty. This was necessary because the
statute under review was aimed at restricting medical practice. *Casey*, on
the other hand, dealt with restricting women's autonomy, so that decision
was more centered on women, whose constitutional rights were directly at
stake. As *Stenberg* illustrates, the law may determine whether abortions are
permitted; but only physicians, not legislatures, may determine how they
can be safely and effectively performed in specific instances.

Ultimately, the most central question in abortion remains who makes
the decision: the state or women and their physicians together? The answer from the Supreme Court, as articulated in *Roe v. Wade* and strongly
reinforced in *Stenberg*, is the woman and her physician together. In this
respect, the Court has been remarkably consistent in its abortion cases.

These three major cases chronicle the law of abortion. The writing that
captures the human dimension of the abortion issue most effectively, however, is not a court decision but a 1985 novel, *The Cider House Rules* by
John Irving, which was well reflected in a 1999 movie of the book. The
major character of the novel is Dr. Wilbur Larch; and in about 1905,
before he decides to work in an orphanage in St. Cloud's, Maine, he confronts himself and the history of the medical profession with regard to
abortion. He reflects on the not-so-distant past when abortion was for the
most part legal, and when procedures much more complex (such as in

utero decapitation and fetal pulverization) were routinely taught to medical students:

By the time he got back to Portland, he had worked the matter out. He was an obstetrician; he delivered babies into the world. His colleagues called this "the Lord's work." And he was an abortionist; he delivered mothers, too. His colleagues called this "the Devil's work," but it was *all* the Lord's work to Wilbur Larch. As Mrs. Maxwell had observed, "The true physician's soul cannot be too broad and gentle." . . . He would deliver babies. He would deliver mothers, too.[9]

If a woman is married, is the consent of her husband ever necessary for any medical treatment?

No. The consent of a husband is never legally necessary for the treatment of a conscious, competent, married woman who consents to her own treatment. This rule has been consistently affirmed by the courts. Specific cases considered in the context of a husband suing a doctor for treating his wife without his consent have included both sterilization and pregnancy care.[10] The husband's consent was always determined unnecessary. This finding, of course, works both ways: the wife's consent is not required for any type of medical treatment of her husband.

Even before *Casey*, the U.S. Supreme Court had ruled that states may not enact legislation that permits husbands to have veto power over their wives' decisions to have an abortion, since, among other things, "it is the woman who bears the child and is more directly and immediately affected by the pregnancy."[11] An Oklahoma court ruled, consistent with other courts, that husbands also have no right to prevent their wives from undergoing sterilization. In the court's words: "We have found no authority and the plaintiff has cited none which holds that the husband has a right to a childbearing wife as an incident to their marriage. We are neither prepared to create a right in the husband to have a fertile wife nor to allow recovery for damage to such a right. We find the right of the person who is capable of competent consent to control his [or her] own body paramount."[12]

Hospitals and doctors who still use consent forms with spaces requiring the consent of the patient's husband should abolish these anachronistic relics of sexism and update their forms to reflect twenty-first-century law, medicine, and sexual equality. If you are asked to sign such a form you should simply cross out the "signature of spouse" line.

Does a patient being examined by a doctor of the opposite sex have a right to have another person of the patient's sex present in the examining room during the examination?

Yes. Although most OB/GYN (obstetrician/gynecologist) residents are women, the overwhelming majority of practicing specialists in obstetrics and gynecology are still men. Most male physicians routinely have a female assistant with them during pelvic examinations. The reason generally given is to protect themselves from a possible charge by the woman patient of improper advances. If the physician's practice is not to have another woman present, however, you have the right to demand that another woman be present during the examination if you wish.[13] Your advocate can, of course, be this person.

Feminists often advise women to "bring a friend" with them on visits to the doctor for psychological support. Such a person can act not only as a witness to what transpires but also can remind you to ask certain questions that are bothering you and make sure instructions and recommendations regarding treatment are understood. No ethical physician ever objects to this request.

Does a woman have a right to refuse to be examined by medical students, interns, or residents in a hospital setting?

Yes! All patients have a right to refuse to be examined by anyone in a hospital setting. When you are asked, "Do you mind if these other doctors look at you also?" you have every right to say, "Yes, I do mind," and refuse to permit them to examine you. Women should be especially wary when the phrase "young doctor" is used, since this almost always means medical student—usually a first- or second-year one with little or no clinical experience. In some hospitals, medical students are still referred to simply as "doctors," although this practice is unethical and fraudulent. You have a right to know both the extent of their training and the purpose of their proposed examination. You should examine their name tag if in doubt, as it should indicate the qualifications of the person, including whether or not the person is a student.[14]

Not only the medical students themselves but also the attending physician and the hospital are liable to the patient for any unauthorized examination or treatment. Consent by a patient, based on a belief that the person performing the examination is a doctor, is consent achieved by fraud or misrepresentation (if the person is not a doctor) and, as such, is not legally valid.

Does a pregnant woman have a right to be informed of the existence of genetic counseling and screening?

Yes. All pregnant women should be advised of the existence of genetic tests for serious conditions affecting the fetus and should be given the *option* of availing themselves of these tests. Physicians caring for pregnant woman have an obligation to inform them of the existence and uses of such tests as chorionic villus sampling (CVS), maternal serum alphafetoprotein screening (MSAFP), ultrasound, and amniocentesis. The American Academy of Pediatrics (AAP) and the American College of Obstetricians and Gynecologists (ACOG) Guidelines state:

Prenatal genetic counseling addresses the risk of occurrence of a genetic disorder in the family. In this process, the primary care physician, a medical geneticist, or other trained person attempts to help the individual or family

• Comprehend the medical facts, including the diagnosis, probable cause of disorder, and available management
• Appreciate the way in which heredity contributes to the disorder and the risk of occurrence or recurrence in specific relatives
• Understand the options for dealing with the risk of recurrence, including prenatal genetic diagnosis
• Choose the course of action that seems appropriate in view of the risk and the family's goals and act in accordance with that decision
• Make the best possible adjustment to the disorder in an affected family member and to the risk of recurrence in another family member

Thus, the key elements in genetic counseling are accurate diagnosis, communication, and nondirective presentation of options. The counselor's function is not to dictate a particular course of action but to provide information that will allow couples to make informed decisions.[15]

Do physicians and patients have a right to use "alternative" forms of child delivery in hospitals?

This is more a matter of moral and political right than a legal right. In fact, courts have been very reluctant to interfere with hospital delivery room policy. This issue has been most commonly addressed by "father in the delivery room" cases. Virtually all hospitals with maternity suites now permit coached childbirth (such as Lamaze or psychoprophylactic) in which the father or other supporting person is with the mother throughout the labor and delivery. Nonetheless, lawsuits to compel a change in the policies of those institutions that did not allow this were unsuccessful. This is true whether the hospital is private or public and whether the plaintiff is a pregnant woman or her obstetrician.

In the first appellate decision on this question, a Montana court found that a hospital rule that forbade the presence of fathers in the delivery room was not arbitrary or capricious, and the court refused to intrude itself "into the administration of the hospital where the hospital had acted in good faith on competent medical advice."[16] Another case involved a suit by prospective parents and their physician against a public hospital. They contended that the hospital's policy denying fathers a right to be in the delivery room violated constitutional rights, specifically, the "right of marital privacy" enunciated in the birth control and abortion decisions. The lower court dismissed their suit, and the appeals court affirmed in a 2-1 decision. I think this case would be decided differently today.[17] Almost all hospitals now actively encourage women to use their facilities for childbirth and welcome fathers in the delivery room, and a rule prohibiting the father's or other supporting person's presence would be against common practice and arbitrary. Nonetheless, couples should find a hospital and physician and make sure they understand what the couple wants and agree to it in advance.

In all cases, a pregnant woman, however, does have the right to refuse any particular medical procedure or drug offered (for example, fetal monitor, anesthesia, episiotomy, HIV screening). Control is primarily reactive, since the patient may not demand that things are done in a certain way but may only refuse interventions that are offered. With the proper hospital environment and supportive health care professionals, the childbirth experience can be satisfactory. Unlike diseases, pregnancy is usually a healthy condition, and women have time to plan, discuss, and negotiate at least some of the terms of childbirth. It must be noted, however, that women still report bullying by physicians and loss of control during hospital births.[18] If the hospital's policy or personnel are not satisfactory, the only alternative is to locate a more responsive hospital or to give birth outside of the hospital, either in a birthing center or at home.

There are two simultaneous and conflicting trends in modern obstetrics. The first is toward more relaxed and informal birthing process in the hospital. The second is toward higher cesarean section rates in the United States, now about one in four births. The first trend is the result of demands by pregnant women and increasing competition for their business. The second is much more complicated and seems to involve payment rates, possible liability concerns, the use of fetal monitors, a belief that at times a cesarean may be best for the baby, indications for cesarean sections that are unique to the United States, and even the use of elective cesareans.[19] Almost everyone agrees that large numbers of unnecessary cesarean sections are performed, but no one has found an effective way to reduce them.[20] Best-selling author Naomi Wolfe, for example, chronicled her horrible pregnancy and birth experiences, including two cesarean sections, in her book *Misconceptions*. Although her first birth was medically mismanaged, it is worth noting that her second, which was managed by a midwife, also ended with a cesarean section. Wolfe is certainly correct when she concludes that "women deserve honest brokers and true advocates who will inform them about all risks and options available, who will explore what pain can be and what it might not have to be, who will make a concerted effort to eliminate unnecessary interventions, and who will stop romanticizing either the controlled nature of high-tech mechanized labor or the culture of alternative birth."[21]

Is there a right to videotape childbirth in the hospital?

No. This is a subject to negotiate with your obstetrician. Many couples seem to want to have a videotape of the child's birth as a souvenir. Some obstetricians worry that the tape might be used in a future malpractice case, that the mother's privacy rights are being violated (although this is up to her), and that the rights of other medical and nursing personnel could be violated.[22] ACOG has issued a statement to its members that strongly discourages obstetricians from permitting videotaping and suggests that if the obstetrician does allow it, the obstetrician obtain written consent from the mother to keep a copy of the tape. The statement reads in part: "Each institution should develop policies concerning the recording of routine and emergency procedures . . . as well as the recording of deliveries. The Committee on Professional Liability strongly discourages any recording of medical and surgical procedures for patient memorabilia."[23]

If you want to videotape your delivery, check hospital policy and discuss it with your obstetrician. Videotaping should not, however, be a major factor in choosing either a hospital or an obstetrician.

Does a woman have a right to refuse a cesarean section?

Yes. Competent adults have the right to refuse any medical invasion, and women do not lose this right just because they are pregnant or in labor. No matter how highly we regard the fetus, this regard cannot justify forcing invasive and possibly dangerous surgery on its mother against her will. Forcing surgery degrades pregnant women and dehumanizes them, treating them like inert fetal containers. There has been a highly charged and emotional debate on this subject, and some "forced cesarean sections" have actually been performed in the United States under court order.[24] These courts, however, acted in emergency settings, under tremendous pressure, and in cases generally involving poor women from cultures with whom neither the physicians nor the judge could identify. The law provides no more support for these decisions than it would for one that would force a mother to "donate" a kidney or bone marrow to her child.[25]

The law must honor the rare case of a woman's refusal. This may seem callous, since some fetuses that might be salvaged may die or be born severely disabled. But it is the price society pays for protecting the rights of all competent adults and preventing forcible, physical violations of women by coercive obstetricians and judges. The rare choice between fetal health and maternal liberty *is* laced with moral and ethical dilemmas, but the force of law and the intervention of the courts and police will not make them go away.

It will be an unusual woman who can withstand the arguments of an obstetrician recommending a cesarean section when she is in active labor; but refusal is her right. The American College of Obstetricians and Gynecologists itself recognized this right in a 1987 policy statement exhorting its members to continue talking to the woman in labor, rather than to a judge, when conflicts arise. This is good advice. Judges are terrible at making emergency medical decisions, and it is inappropriate for judges to act impulsively, without benefit of reflection on past precedent and the likely future impact of their rulings. The cesarean section cases that judges have decided all suffer from lack of reflection. The delivery room is not conducive to reflection, and judges do not belong there when women are in labor.[26]

Does a dying pregnant woman have the right to refuse a cesarean section (or other surgical intervention designed to "save" the fetus) if the fetus is viable?

Yes. The fact that a pregnant woman is terminally ill or dying does not strip her of her constitutional rights; pregnant women have no obligation to undergo invasive and potentially life-threatening surgical procedures for the sake of their fetuses. Thankfully, this issue does not come up often. Nonetheless, in 1987, a young pregnant woman was forced to undergo a cesarean section in what can probably best be described as a medical and legal atrocity: the case of "Angela C." The case merits detailed discussion in this book in the hope that knowledge of it will be sufficient to prevent a similar thing from ever happening to another pregnant woman.[27] Thankfully, as of 2003, no similar case has been reported.

Angela C was a twenty-six-year-old married woman who had suffered from cancer since she was thirteen years old. About twenty-five weeks into her pregnancy, she was admitted to George Washington University Hospital, and a massive tumor was found in her lung. Physicians determined that she would die within a short time. Her husband, her mother, and her physicians agreed that keeping her comfortable while she died was what she wanted, and that her wishes should be honored. This was communicated to a hospital administrator, who called legal counsel, who in turn asked a judge to come to the hospital to decide what to do.

A District of Columbia Superior Court judge rushed to the hospital where he set up "court." After a hearing, the judge issued his opinion orally. The centerpiece was Angela C's terminal condition. In the judge's words, "The uncontroverted medical testimony is that Angela will probably die within the next 24 to 48 hours." He did "not clearly know what Angela's present views are" respecting the cesarean section but found that the fetus had a 50 to 60 percent chance to survive and less than a 20 percent chance of serious handicap. The judge concluded: "It's not an easy decision to make, but given the choices, the court is of the view the fetus should be given the opportunity to live." The court reconvened shortly thereafter when informed that Angela C, who had been unconscious, was awake and communicating. The chief of obstetrics reported that she "clearly communicated" and "very clearly mouthed words several times, 'I don't want it done. I don't want it done. I don't want it done.'" Nonetheless, without even talking to Angela C herself, the judge reaffirmed his original order. Less than an hour later, three appeals court judges heard a request for a stay over the telephone and denied it.

The cesarean section was performed, and the nonviable fetus died approximately two hours later. Angela C, now confronted with both recovery from major surgery and the knowledge of her child's death, died approximately two days later. Five months later, the appeals court issued its written opinion.[28] The opinion reads more like a Hallmark sympathy card than a judicial pronouncement. Its first paragraph, for example, ends with the following sentence: "Condolences are extended to those who lost the mother and child." The opinion is fatally flawed. The most serious error is the statement that "as a matter of law, the right of a woman to an abortion is different and distinct from her obligations to the fetus once she has decided not to timely terminate her pregnancy." This is incorrect as both a factual and a legal matter. Angela C never "decided not to timely terminate her pregnancy," and because of her fetus' affect on her health, under *Roe v. Wade* she could have authorized her pregnancy to be terminated (to protect her health) at any time prior to her death. Moreover, had the roles been reversed and an abortion was required to save Angela C's life, no legal principle would permit a judge to order the abortion against her will.

This unprincipled opinion was thankfully vacated by the full bench of the court in 1988 and thus has no legal value as precedent.[29] But it dramatically illustrates the general rule that judges should almost never go to the hospital to make emergency-treatment decisions. Rushed to an unfamiliar environment, asked to make a decision under great stress, and having no time either for reflection or for study of existing law and precedents, a judge cannot act judiciously. Facts cannot be properly developed, and the law cannot be accurately determined or fairly applied to the facts. The "emergency hearing" scenario is an invitation to arbitrariness and the exercise of raw force.

This was *not* a hard case. If there really were facts in dispute, a case conference involving the patient, family, and all attending health care personnel could have been held to assess them. Direct communication with the patient is almost always the most useful and constructive response to "problems" such as those presented by this case. Calling a judge is usually a counterproductive panic reaction. Patients and their advocates should insist that the patient's wishes, not those of hospital lawyers or uninvolved physicians, be honored.

May a pregnant woman be tested for illegal drugs without her informed consent?

No, although it took a U.S. Supreme Court decision to so decide.[30] The case involved a University of South Carolina medical program to screen selected pregnant patients for cocaine and to provide positive test results to the police. A pregnant woman who tested positive for cocaine would be given a letter from the prosecutor saying that if she successfully completed a drug-treatment program she would not be prosecuted. If she did not complete the program, however, the police would be notified and she would be arrested and charged with drug distribution and child neglect. If she tested positive at the time of delivery, she would be arrested immediately and charged with child neglect.

Under the policy, 253 women tested positive for cocaine. Thirty of them were arrested, and two were sentenced to prison. Ten of the women who were arrested sued for violation of their constitutional rights. They were represented by the American Civil Liberties Union. Nine of the ten were black. All were poor. Their lawsuit was filed in 1993. The university discontinued its policy in September 1994 in a settlement agreement with the Civil Rights Division of the Department of Health and Human Services, which was investigating whether the policy violated the Civil Rights Act. The women's lawsuit against the university, the city, and the police continued. The Fourth Amendment provides that "the right of the people to be secure in their persons, houses, papers, and effects, against unreasonable search and seizures, shall not be violated, and no Warrants shall issue, but upon probable cause, supported by Oath or affirmation, and particularly describing the place to be searched, and the person or things to be seized." The amendment prohibits unreasonable searches by the police or those working for the police without a warrant or the consent of the person searched, unless there is some special need other than law enforcement for the search that makes it reasonable. At the trial, the defendants offered two defenses for testing the urine of the pregnant women for cocaine: first, the women had in fact consented to the searches, so no warrant was necessary; and second, even without consent, the searches were justified by a "special non-law-enforcement need." The trial court rejected the second defense but put the first one to the jury, instructing the jury that it had to find in favor of the women unless it found they had consented to the search. The jury found in favor of the defendants. The women appealed.

The Fourth Circuit Court of Appeals affirmed, but for a different reason. It held that the searches were reasonable under the Fourth Amendment as a matter of law because of the "special need" to protect women and children from the complications of the maternal use of cocaine. The women appealed again. The U.S. Supreme Court, in the majority opinion written by Justice John Paul Stevens, concluded that whereas the special need in previous cases was "divorced from the State's general interest in law enforcement," in South Carolina "the central and indispensable feature of the [drug-testing] policy from its inception was the use of law enforcement to coerce the patients into substance abuse treatment."

The drug-testing policy of the Medical University of South Carolina, Stevens concluded, was "ultimately indistinguishable from the [state's] general interest in crime control." This conclusion followed from the fact that the police helped to develop the program, were involved in its day-to-day administration, determined the procedures to be followed, and coordinated the "timing and circumstances of the arrests with [university] staff," and that women were jailed. In Justice Stevens' words, "The threat of law enforcement may ultimately have been intended as the means to an end, but the direct and primary purpose of [the university's] policy was to ensure the use of those means." The case was remanded for a determination of whether the women had in fact consented to the searches, and the Court of Appeals found they had not.[31]

May a pregnant woman be charged with "fetal neglect" if she engages in behavior that injures her fetus?

A pregnant woman may be charged with fetal neglect only in South Carolina, where the state's supreme court affirmed the conviction of a woman for endangering her child by taking cocaine during the third trimester of her pregnancy.[32] The woman had pled guilty but later appealed, arguing that the child abuse statute did not apply to fetuses. The court held that the word *child* as used in the state's child abuse statute includes viable fetuses.

The problems with this approach are well illustrated by the case of Pamela Stewart, the subject of what may have been the first criminal charge ever brought against a mother for acts and omissions during pregnancy.[32] Sometime very late in her pregnancy, she was reportedly advised by her physician not to take amphetamines; to stay off her feet; to avoid sexual intercourse; and because of a placenta previa, to seek immediate medical treatment if she began to hemorrhage. According to the police, after she noticed some bleeding, she allegedly remained at home, took some amphetamines, and had intercourse with her husband. She began bleeding more heavily, and contractions began sometime during the afternoon. It was only later, perhaps "many hours" later, that she went to the hospital. Her son was born that evening. He had massive brain damage and died about six weeks thereafter.

The case against her was ultimately dismissed on the grounds that the California child support statutes did not apply to this conduct. Should the law be changed to create a new crime of fetal neglect? Does it make any sense to decree that a pregnant woman must, in effect, live for her fetus; that she must legally "stay off her feet" if walking or working might induce contractions; or that she commits a crime if she does not eat only healthy foods, smokes cigarettes or drinks alcohol, takes any drugs (legal or illegal), becomes infected with HIV, or has intercourse with her husband? Should all these "dos" and "don'ts" be cataloged in a statute, or should they be the subject of her physician's advice? And how would such a criminal law change the nature of the doctor-patient relationship?

It seems evident that the police considered the fetus, not Stewart, the doctor's patient. It also seems evident that although called "advice" and "instructions," the police believed that the physician was actually giving Stewart orders—orders that she *must* follow or face criminal penalties, including jail. This is nonsensical and dangerous: nonsensical because medical advice should remain advice—physicians are neither lawmakers nor seers—dangerous because medical advice is a vague term that can cover almost anything. Nor do after-the-fact prosecutions help individual fetuses.

If society really wants to help pregnant women and protect the health of their fetuses, the answer is not to criminalize dangerous behavior during pregnancy but to provide access to supportive prenatal care, education, and counseling. Criminalization of behavior does not merit serious discussion.[33]

Must a woman leave the hospital after giving birth within "forty-eight hours" if this is what their health plan requires?

No. The decision whether or not a patient can be safely discharged is one that can only be made by the attending physician and patient together. Nonetheless, the number of hours a woman and her newborn were permitted to stay in the hospital after childbirth was the only managed care reform issue Congress and the president have agreed on as of 2003. The legal and policy debate on this issue should not be forgotten.[34]

In the mid-1990s, health plans often restricted hospitalization benefits to twenty-four hours after a vaginal delivery and forty-eight hours after a cesarean section. The primary rationale was not to benefit mother and child but to enable the health plan to retain more insurance premium dollars. The proponents of discharging new mothers and their babies more quickly from the hospital argued that the long hospitalizations of the past were both unnecessary and potentially dangerous (because of the increased risk of nosocomial infections) for both mother and child. They pointed, quite rightly, to past excesses in length of stay and argued that increases in efficiency could be achieved without adverse affects on mother and child. The average length of hospital stay for childbirth had fallen from approximately four days in 1970 to two days in 1992 for all vaginal deliveries and from eight to four days for cesarean deliveries. Since childbirth is the most common reason for inpatient care in the United States, billions of health care dollars could potentially be saved if the average length of stay for mothers and babies were further shortened.

In 1995, Maryland became the first state to enact legislation to curtail twenty-four-hour discharge policies. The law requires insurance plans to provide coverage for maternity and newborn care, including inpatient stays, "in accordance with the medical criteria outlined in the most current version of the *Guidelines for Perinatal Care* prepared by the American Academy of Pediatrics and the American College of Obstetricians and Gynecologists." Because the AAP and ACOG recommend a forty-eight-hour stay for uncomplicated deliveries, the law had the effect of eliminating provisions for shorter lengths of stays by insurance companies and health plans.

The second state to enact legislation was New Jersey. Unlike the Maryland law, which followed medical standards as set by the AAP and ACOG, the New Jersey law specified that insurance plans must cover "a minimum of 48 hours of in-patient care following a vaginal delivery and a minimum of 96 hours of in-patient care following a cesarean section for a mother and her newly born child in a health care facility."

Shortly after New Jersey adopted its law, Senator Bill Bradley (D-N.J.), along with Senator Nancy Kassebaum (R-Kan.), proposed a federal law, arguing that uniform federal legislation that covered all American woman and children was needed. Horror stories help drive legislation. In dramatic testimony, Michelle and Steve Bauman of New Jersey told a Senate committee how their daughter had died from a streptococcus B infection two days after she was born. She and her mother had been discharged twenty-eight hours after the baby's birth. Although there is no way to know for sure, the Baumans believe that their daughter would have been properly treated had they been able to spend another twenty-four hours in the hospital. Mrs. Bauman said that "her death certificate listed the cause of death as meningitis when it should have read 'Death by the system.'"

The Newborns' and Mothers' Health Protection Act of 1996 was signed into law by President Clinton in 1996. The operative section of the law provides that unless "an attending provider in consultation with the mother" decides otherwise, no group health plan may restrict hospital benefits "for mother or newborn child, following a normal vaginal delivery, to less than 48 hours" or for cesarean section "to less than 96 hours." This federal law applies only to states that do not have the same provisions in their own laws, require that ACOG and AAP or other professional guidelines be followed, or require that the length of stay be "left to the decision of the attending provider in consultation with the mother."[35]

Studies later showed that neither early discharge nor the law prohibiting it had a marked effect on the health outcomes of newborns.[36] "Drive-through delivery" legislation is a sideshow in the debate over health care-financing reform that will have little real effect on cost, quality, or access to health care by women and their children. Length of stay is important, especially after a cesarean section, but it is not a significant surrogate measure of quality of care. It, nonetheless, took on a life of its own for the public and politicians because it could be easily understood and was a specific illustration of the general problem of premature hospital discharge. Moreover, and perhaps most importantly, action on this front permitted politicians to appear to be doing something positive to protect women and children that cost the government no money.

May a woman legally give birth at home?

Yes. There is no law in any state that requires childbirth to take place in a hospital, and no state requires women to take affirmative actions to safeguard their fetuses. All states, however, have child abuse and neglect statutes that forbid parents from abusing or neglecting their children and require them to provide their children with necessary medical attention. In the absence of known high risk to the newborn, parents may usually make a decision to have a home birth with impunity. If the parents have reason to know that complications are likely to develop that will require hospital care to save the child from death or permanent injury, however, and the child dies or is permanently injured because of home birth, the parents could be held criminally liable. The problem is neglecting care of the newborn, not the home birth itself. The charge would be child neglect in both cases and possibly manslaughter (depending on the cause of death and its predictability) if the child dies.[37] This general rule should dissuade parents from attempting to manage home births by themselves and encourage them to seek a licensed attendant at a planned home birth or to seek hospitalization when it is indicated to protect the life and health of the newborn child.

Who may provide professional care at a home birth?

In every state, physicians may attend home births. The role other attendants, such as nurse midwives and lay midwives, may play is governed by state law.[38] Statutes and qualifications vary, but in states that have specific legislation providing for the licensing of midwives, it is likely that anyone not a physician or licensed midwife who held himself or herself out as an expert on childbirth and attended a childbirth would be guilty of the crime of practicing either medicine or midwifery without a license (in a number of states, a birth attendant must have been compensated to be prosecuted).

State courts would probably follow a California Supreme Court decision that concluded the California legislature could limit, by licensure, those who could attend home births because the state had an "interest in regulating the qualifications of those who hold themselves out as childbirth attendants . . . for many women must necessarily rely on those with qualifications which they cannot personally verify."[39] The rationale is that the legislature can reasonably decide that the only way to protect the health of the public in the matter of childbirth is to ensure that those who hold themselves out as experts to the public are required to meet certain standards and be licensed. After this conclusion is reached by the enactment of a licensing statute, anyone practicing outside of its limitations would be guilty of the crime of practicing without a license.

Is it malpractice for a physician to participate in a home birth?

No. Medical malpractice (discussed in chapter 15) always involves the question of whether the physician exercised reasonable medical judgment in a particular circumstance. So long as the decision to have a home birth is made by the woman after she has been fully informed of the risks and potential complications, and so long as all generally accepted medical steps have been taken concerning screening the woman and emergency backup facilities, it is highly unlikely that any malpractice action against a physician would be successful.

In attending childbirth and counseling the pregnant woman, the physician also has a duty toward the fetus to provide it with adequate medical care both before and during the delivery.[40] This duty does not usually prevent a physician from participating in a home delivery, but it does require the physician to perform any standard screening tests to determine high-risk pregnancies and to advise pregnant women at high risk to use hospital facilities for birth.

Is there a right to procreate (to have a child)?

There is a legal right *not* to procreate, by having access to sterilization, contraception, and abortion technology through a physician, and there are strong arguments against any government interference with the decision of a married couple to have children. Nonetheless, because the welfare of children can be negatively affected, the government may limit some options involving the "new reproductive technologies." For example, the state could outlaw the sale of human embryos even if this might make it more difficult for couples to obtain embryos for use in having a child. States could also constitutionally enact a statute that designated the woman who gives birth to a child its legal mother, even if the egg used was from another woman and had been created by in vitro fertilization (IVF) and artificially implanted in her and she had previously agreed to give the child up to the "egg donor" upon birth. The rationale is that the gestational or birth mother contributes more to the child than the egg donor, takes a much greater physical risk, is more psychologically bonded with the child, is more easily identifiable than the egg donor, and will definitely be with the child at birth to protect and make treatment decisions for the child.[41] This situation, the possibility of separating the gestational from the birth mother is, of course, a product of the new reproductive technologies.

What can be done to regulate the assisted-reproduction industry?

The infertility industry has accurately been described as the "wild west" of medicine, and I believe it is time for public oversight. Other countries that have developed uniform standards for the infertility industry have appointed a committee or commission to study the issues and make legislative recommendations. The states will, of course, continue to have jurisdiction over determining motherhood, fatherhood, child custody, and related issues of family law. But national standards of commerce should be developed for assisted reproduction, as they have for organ transplantation. A national advisory committee on the new reproductive techniques should be appointed to consider uniform national rules that address the following issues: the content of informed consent in terms of the risks to parents and children; standard screening and record-keeping requirements for egg and sperm donation; the ability of children born as a result of assisted reproduction to learn the identity of their genetic and gestational parents; research on human embryos; time limits on the storage of human embryos; the use of gametes from deceased persons to produce children; and the addition of eggs and embryos (and possibly sperm as well) to the list of human tissues that cannot be purchased or sold in the United States.[42]

In late 1997, President Bill Clinton signed a bill designed to shift the emphasis in adoption practices from the rights of biological parents to the welfare of the children. The assisted-reproduction industry should move in this direction as well. As with adoption, however, it will probably take federal action to move child welfare to the center of consideration in the infertility business.

Are there any special patient bills of rights for pregnant women?

Yes. One is from the Committee of the International Childbirth Education Association and is entitled *The Pregnant Patients' Bill of Rights*.[43] Another very informative and constructive document is *The Rights of Childbearing Women from the Maternity Center Association*,[44] all but the first three items are currently recognized or probable legal rights. Both of these documents appear in appendix C.

TIPS FOR ADVOCATES

- **Women do not lose their constitutional or common law rights by becoming pregnant.**

- **Pregnant women have a constitutional right to terminate their pregnancies prior to fetal viability** (and thereafter if their life or health is in danger).

- **States may restrict abortions prior to fetal viability,** such as by imposing a twenty-four-hour waiting period, but may not enforce restrictions that actually result in women being denied the right to terminate a pregnancy.

- **The consent of the husband of a competent woman is never required for her treatment.**

- **Women have a right to have another woman present during a physical examination.**

- **Women may refuse to be examined or treated by anyone.**

- **Women have a right to have the father of the child or another advocate present during childbirth and delivery.**

- **Pregnant women have a right to refuse any medical treatment or drug,** including a cesarean section, episiotomy, anesthesia, and pain medication.

- **A woman has a right to change her mind about any decision made before or during labor or childbirth.**

- A woman and her newborn have a right to remain in a hospital up to forty-eight hours after a vaginal birth and ninety-six hours after a cesarean section (your goal, however, should be to **get mother and child out of the hospital as soon as it is safe for them to be discharged**).

Notes

1. *Roe v. Wade,* 410 U.S. 113 (1973). *See generally* Symposium Issue: *Justice Harry A. Blackmun: The Supreme Court and the Limits of Medical Privacy,* 13 Am. J. Law & Med. 153 (1987).

2. *Planned Parenthood of Southeastern Pennsylvania v. Casey,* 505 U.S. 833 (1992).

3. *Stenberg v. Carhart*, 530 U.S. 914 (2000).

4. *Griswold v. Connecticut*, 381 U.S. 479 (1965).

5. *Eisenstadt v. Baird*, 405 U.S. 438, 453 (1972) (emphasis added).

6. The U.S. Supreme Court has further defined viability as follows:

Viability is reached when, in the judgment of the attending physician on the particular facts of the case before him, there is a reasonable likelihood of the fetus' sustained survival outside the womb, with or without artificial support. Because this point may differ with each pregnancy, neither the legislature nor the courts may proclaim one of the elements entering into the ascertainment of viability—be it weeks of gestation or fetal weight or any other single factor—as the determinant of when the State has a compelling interest in the life or health of the fetus. Viability is the critical point. And we have recognized no attempt to stretch the point of viability one way or the other. (*Colautti v. Franklin*, 439 U.S. 379, 388–89 [1979])

7. Ronald Dworkin, *The Great Abortion Case*, N.Y. Review of Books, June 29, 1989, 51. *See also Lawrence v. Texas*, 123 S. Ct. 2472 (2003) (liberty protects private sexual conduct of same-sex adults).

8. It was also substantially identical to a bill that twice passed Congress and was twice vetoed by President Clinton. *See* George J. Annas, *Partial Birth Abortion, Congress, and the Constitution*, 339 New Eng. J. Med. 279 (1998), and George J. Annas, *"Partial Birth Abortion" and the Supreme Court*, 344 New Eng. J. Med. 174 (2001). A slightly revised version again passed Congress in 2003 and may set the stage for another Supreme Court decision on abortion.

9. John Irving, The Cider House Rules, New York: William Morrow, 1985, 75.

10. *E.g., Kritzer v. Citron*, 101 Cal. App. 2d 33, 224 P. 2d 808 (1950); *Rosenberg v. Feigin*, 119 Cal. App. 2d 783, 260 P.2d 143 (1953); *Rytkonen v. Lojacono*, 269 Mich. 270, 257 N.W. 703 (1934).

11. *Planned Parenthood of Central Missouri v. Danforth*, 428 U.S. 52 (1976).

12. *Murray v. Vandevander*, 522 P.2d 302, 304 (Okla. Ct. App. 1974).

13. If the doctor refuses this request in the hospital context, the doctor's method of practice is open to serious ethical question, and his or her conduct should be reported immediately to the chief of the doctor's service. The name and phone number of his chief can be obtained from one of the nurses or through the hospital administration. In a private office or clinic, the woman's remedy is probably limited to walking out, informing the local medical society and state licensing agency, and going to another doctor.

14. In one court case from the 1930s, but which remains good law today, a woman objected to being examined by a medical student just before she was about to give birth. Thereupon, an older doctor came in, performed a rectal and vaginal examination, and then had the same examination performed two or three times each by "ten or twelve young men who she took to be students." She protested repeatedly and testified, "Whenever I screamed and protested they just laughed, told me to shut up." She experienced both emotional and physical damages during the delivery. The court had no difficulty in finding this conduct "revolting" and an assault on the patient. In the court's words, "A physician or a medical student has no more right to needlessly and rudely lay hands upon a patient against her will

than has a layman." The court also determined that the hospital in which this took place could be held liable for permitting "unlicensed students to experiment on the patient and treat her without her consent" (*Inderbitzen v. Lane Hospital,* 124 Cal. App. 462, 12 P.2d 744 [1932]).

15. American Academy of Pediatrics & American College of Obstetricians and Gynecologists, Guidelines for Perinatal Care, 4th ed., Washington, D.C.: AAP, 1997, 81.

16. *Hulit v. St. Vincent's Hospital,* 164 Mont. 168, 175, 520 P.2d 99, 102 (1974).

17. *Fitzgerald v. Porter Memorial Hospital,* 523 F.2d 716 (7th Cir. 1975).

18. *See, e.g.,* Naomi Wolfe, Misconceptions: Truth, Lies and the Unexpected on the Journey to Motherhood, New York: Doubleday, 2001; Suzanne Arms, Immaculate Deception II: Myth, Magic & Birth, Berkeley, Calif.: Celestial Arts, 1994; Jessica Mitford, The American Way of Birth, London: Victor Gollancz, 1992; and Richard Johanson, Mary Newburn & Alison Macfarlane, *Has the Medicalization of Childbirth Gone Too Far?* 324 Brit. Med. J. 892 (2002).

19. *See, e.g.,* Michael Greene, *Vaginal Delivery after Cesarean Section—Is the Risk Acceptable?* 345 New Eng. J. Med. 54 (2001), and Howard Minkoff & Frank Cheevenak, *Elective Primary Cesarean Delivery,* 348 New Eng. J. Med. 10 (2003).

20. Cesarean sections did decrease steadily from 1989 to 1996 but since then have crept back up to about 22 percent of live births in 1999. *Doctors Concerned about Rise in C-Sections,* Minneapolis Star Tribune, August 29, 2000, A1. The same trend is also occurring in the United Kingdom. *Cesarean Section on the Rise,* 356 Lancet 1697 (2000).

21. Wolfe, *supra* note 18, at 203.

22. D. R. Eitel et al., *Videotaping Obstetric Procedures: Assessment of Obstetricians and Family Physicians,* 9 Arch Family Med. 89 (2000).

23. American College of Obstetricians and Gynecologists, Liability Implications of Recording Procedures or Treatments, September 1998, ACOG Opinion No. 207.

24. V. E. Kolder, J. Gallagher & M. T. Parsons, *Court-Ordered Obstetrical Interventions,* 316 New Eng. J. Med. 1192 (1987); *and see Jefferson v. Griffin Spalding Cty. Hospital Auth.,* 247 Ga. 86, 274 S.E.2d 457 (1981).

25. George J. Annas, *Protecting the Liberty of Pregnant Patients,* 316 New Eng. J. Med. 1213 (1987); *and see McFall v. Shimp,* 10 Pa. D & C.3d 90 (Allegheny Cty. 1978) (bone marrow donation cannot be compelled by law even to save a life of a relative).

26. *See, e.g., Application of the President and Directors of Georgetown College,* 331 F.2d 1000 (D.C. Cir. 1964); *and see* Sherman Elias & George J. Annas, Reproductive Genetics and the Law, St. Louis: Mosby, 1987, 256–60; and Janet Gallager, *Prenatal Invasions and Interventions: What's Wrong with Fetal Rights?* 10 Harv. Woman's L.J. 9 (1987).

27. The facts of this case are taken from the transcript. *And see* George J. Annas, *She's Going to Die: The Case of Angela C.,* 18 Hastings Center Report 23 (February 1988); letters, 18 Hastings Center Report 40 (June 1988); and Robert Burt, *Uncertainty and Medical Authority,* 16 Law, Medicine & Health Care 190 (1988).

28. *In re* A.C., 533 A.2d 611 (App. D.C. 1987).

29. *In re* A.C., 539 A.2d 203 (App. D.C. 1988).

30. *Ferguson v. City of Charleston,* 532 U.S. 67 (2001); *and see* George J. Annas, *Testing Poor Pregnant Women for Cocaine—Physicians as Police Investigators,* 344 New Eng. J. Med. 1729 (2001).

31. *Ferguson v. City of Charleston*, 308 F.3d 380 (2002).

32. *Whitner v. So. Carolina*, 328 S.C. 1, 492 S.E.2d 777 (1997). *And see* David Firestone, *Woman Is Convicted of Killing Her Fetus by Smoking Cocaine*, New York Times, May 18, 2001, A12, and Bob Herbert, *Stillborn Justice*, New York Times, May 24, 2001, A29.

33. A more detailed account is in George J. Annas, Judging Medicine, Clifton, N.J.: Humana Press, 1988, 91–96. Child neglect covers a wide variety of activities but generally involves failure to provide necessities, such as clothing, food, housing, or medical attention, to the child. Such laws *do not,* however, require parents to provide *optimal* clothing, food, housing, or medical attention to their children, and they do not even forbid parents from taking risks with their children (such as permitting them to engage in dangerous sports) or affirmatively injuring their children (such as using corporal punishment to teach them a lesson). No laws forbid mothers to smoke, to take dangerous drugs, or to consume excessive amounts of alcohol, even though these activities may have a negative effect on their children. *And see* Dawn Johnsen, *The Creation of Fetal Rights: Conflicts with Women's Constitutional Rights of Liberty, Privacy and Equal Protection,* 95 Yale L. Rev. 599 (1986).

34. For a more detailed discussion, *see* George J. Annas, Some Choice: Law, Medicine & the Market, New York: Oxford U. Press, 1998, 25–33.

35. 42 U.S.C. sec. 300gg-4 (West Supp. 1997).

36. L. L. Liu et al., *The Safety of Newborn Early Discharge: The Washington State Experience,* 287 JAMA 293 (1997) (early discharge associated with an increased risk of readmission for jaundice, dehydration, and sepsis); M. B. Edmonson et al., *Hospital Readmission With Feeding-Related Problems after Early Postpartum Discharge of Normal Newborns,* 278 JAMA 299 (1997) (early discharge following an uncomplicated postpartum hospital stay appears to have little or no independent effect on the risk of hospitalization); and Jeanne Madden et al., *Effects of a Law Against Early Postpartum Discharge on Newborn Followup, Adverse Events, and HMO Expenditures,* 347 New Eng. J. Med. 2031 (2002) (neither policy had any effect on the health outcomes of newborns). *See also* P. Braveman et al., *Early Discharge and Evidence-based Practice: Good Science and Good Judgment,* 278 JAMA 334 (1997).

37. *See* John Robertson, *Involuntary Euthanasia of Defective Newborns,* 27 Stan. L. Rev. 213 (1975).

38. *See generally* Stan Sagov et al., eds., Home Birth, Rockville, Md.: Aspen, 1984. *See also* Jenny Pang et al., *Outcomes of Planned Homebirths in Washington State: 1989–1996,* 100 Obstet. & Gyn. 253 (2002) (greater maternal and child risk than hospital births), and Martha Mendoza, *Study Sees Risks to Babies Born at Home,* Boston Globe, November 24, 2002, A18.

39. *Bowland v. Municipal Court,* 18 Cal.3d 479, 556 P.2d 1081, 134 Cal. Rptr. 630 (1976).

40. *Commonwealth v. Edelin,* 359 N.E.2d 4 (Mass. 1976).

41. *See* New York State Task Force on Life and the Law, Assisted Reproductive Technologies: Analysis and Recommendations for Public Policy, New York: NYSTFLL, 1998.

42. For more on this proposal, *see* George J. Annas, *The Shadowlands: Secrets, Lies, and Assisted Reproduction,* 339 New Eng. J. Med. 935 (1998). *See also* U.S. Congress, Office of Technology Assessment, Infertility: Medical and Social Choices, Washington, D.C.: Government Printing Office, 1988 (OTA-BA-358), and Symposium Issue: *Surrogate Mother-*

hood: Politics and Privacy, 16 Law, Medicine & Health Care 1 (1988). *See generally* Royal Commission on New Reproductive Technologies, Proceed with Care, Ottawa: Canada Communication Group, 1993.

43. ICEA Publication Center, P.O. Box 9316, Midtown Plaza, Rochester, NY 14604.

44. Maternity Center Association 281 Park Ave., So., 5th floor, New York, NY 10010.

IX

Research

The history of medical progress is to a large extent the history of medical research. There is, nonetheless, a growing awareness that the rights of subjects are often ignored in the process of medical research, and that more effective steps must be taken to protect research subjects from overzealous researchers. Many of the most blatant research abuses have occurred with especially vulnerable subjects in prisons, in mental institutions, in the military, and in residences for mentally retarded people. While all of these are important, this chapter concentrates on research in medical settings. The overall theme is that protection of the rights and welfare of research subjects must always take precedence over the goals and interests of medical researchers and their sponsors. Current mechanisms to protect research subjects are woefully inadequate.

It was once asserted that being a research subject is the price you pay for being a patient in a teaching hospital. This is nonsense. People do not automatically forfeit their rights or become transformed into laboratory animals by seeking hospital care. But it is difficult to resist the request of your physician to be a research subject in the "total institution" environment of the hospital. Nor is pressure always necessary. Often very sick people actively seek to become research subjects because they mistakenly believe a research study is treatment.

Because of the history of abuse, methods have been developed to protect the rights and welfare of research subjects. To protect the subject's *welfare*, lawful human experimentation requires a sound hypothesis based on prior work (usually on animals), reason to expect beneficial results (for society, if not for the subject), a competent researcher, and prior review by a qualified panel. To protect the subject's *rights*, lawful human experimentation requires the voluntary, competent, informed, and understanding

194

consent of the subject. This chapter explores the issues at stake when patients are asked to participate in medical research. The operative word is "asked": no patient is ever under any obligation to participate in research, and no patient is obliged to give any reason for refusing to participate in research. Today, commerce and money—pharmaceutical companies and biotech startups—are desperate to try out their products under development on humans. This is one reason why a favorite cartoon of people who study research ethics pictures a researcher at a press conference saying, "And while the drug hasn't been tested on humans, it works on mice and the stock market."

What is medical research?

No single definition captures the range of medical research or experimentation. Some physicians argue, for example, that every time any patient is treated, a "therapeutic experiment" is taking place, since that particular patient has never been treated at that particular time in that particular way. This argument is wrong because it denies that there can ever be such a thing as "standard medical treatment" and treats identically both quacks and physicians who follow accepted medical procedures. It is, however, accurate to describe the journey from medical research to accepted medical procedure as a continuum, with "innovative therapy" or "nonvalidated therapy" somewhere in between these two extremes.

Federal research regulations define research as "a systematic investigation, including research development, testing and evaluation, designed to develop or contribute to generalizable knowledge." For the purposes of this chapter, a physician-researcher is engaged in medical research on a patient-subject when the physician, using a scientific protocol as a guide, departs from standard medical practice for the purpose of obtaining new, generalizable knowledge *by testing a hypothesis.* Using a new drug or device (such as an artificial heart) that has never been tried on a human before is human experimentation (since it radically departs from standard medical care) but may not be considered research if there is no systematic attempt to obtain generalizable knowledge.

What is the difference between research and treatment?

Physicians treat patients with a treatment known to be safe and effective that the physician believes is in the patient's best interest and with the patient's informed consent. If the treatment does not work, it is abandoned and another is tried. Patients have a right to their physician's best judgment as to how to proceed. Researchers, on the other hand, follow a scientific protocol to test a hypothesis. The protocol is followed regardless of whether the experimental intervention is working or not, because the purpose of the research is to collect data to test the hypothesis. Of course, if the subject is being harmed, the research on the subject should be discontinued, but it is the research protocol, not a physician's medical judgment, that determines how a subject in a research project will be treated.

Although research and treatment have different goals and different methods, when the subject is a sick person and the researcher is a physician, both physician and patient have historically had a very difficult time distinguishing between them. Both, for example, require informed consent; the patient-subject in both settings will usually hope for a cure, and the physician-researcher in both settings will often believe that the research protocol is a reasonable "treatment" option. Motivations are often mixed, and both parties may be unable to separate wishful thinking from realistic appraisal of likely outcomes. In fact, perhaps the most common characteristic of human experimentation on sick people is what I have termed "mutual self-deception": both researcher and patient so much want the research to succeed that they deny the risks and look only at the possible—even if very unlikely—benefits. This phenomenon has been referred to as the "therapeutic illusion" or the "therapeutic misconception."

A well-known example is the case of eighteen-year-old Jesse Gelsinger of Arizona who traveled to the University of Pennsylvania in 1999 to take part in a gene transfer study related to ornithinetranscarbamylase (OTC) deficiency, lack of a liver enzyme that removes ammonia, a serious disease from which he was suffering. The study tested a cold virus to deliver the normal gene for OTC to the liver. Gelsinger was enrolled in the first phase of the study (Phase 1) in which only safety is studied not whether it will work. Gelsinger seems to have incorrectly believed that he could get some medical benefit from being a subject. Instead, the research led to his death. After he died, the medical ethicist at the University of Pennsylvania, Arthur Caplan, said that there never was any chance of benefit to Gelsinger from participating in this safety study. In his words, "If you cured anybody, you'd publish it in a religious journal. It would be a miracle. The researchers wouldn't say that. But I'm telling you. If you cured anybody from a phase one gene therapy trial, it would be a miracle. All you're saying is, 'I've got this vector, I want to see if it can deliver the gene where I want it to go without killing or hurting or having side effects.'" A multimillion dollar lawsuit against the researchers and the University of Pennsylvania by the family of Gelsinger was settled out of court within a month after its being filed, gene transfer research at the University of Pennsylvania was suspended, and the Food and Drug Administration (FDA) launched an investigation and proposed improved oversight of similar experiments.[1]

Jay Katz of Yale University, the world's leading scholar of human experimentation, has highlighted inherent problems with research in the doctor-patient relationship:

A dilemma confronts physician-investigators in the conduct of research with patient-subjects. *As physicians they are dedicated to caring for their patients, healing their pain, reducing their suffering. As investigators they are dedicated to caring for their research, advancing knowledge for the benefit of science and future patients.* These two commitments conflict whenever an individual physician-investigator comes face to face with an individual patient-subject. In today's world medical practice often encompasses both research and therapeutic aspects. The research component of any medical intervention, however, may not serve the individual therapeutic interests of patients. Instead, their well-being is subordinated to the dictates of a research protocol designed to advance knowledge for the sake of future patients.[2]

Katz is correct, although even acknowledging the differences between research and treatment is difficult for both physician-researchers and patient-subjects. As a physician, the researcher really wants to believe he or she is helping the patient—even though the research is not designed for that purpose but rather to gain new knowledge to help others. Likewise, the patient does not want to see himself or herself as a research subject or guinea pig; patient-subjects much prefer to believe that the physician is treating them for their own good, and that the research is likely to help. It is not possible to split the patient-subject into two people. On the other hand, your personal or attending physician should not have divided loyalties to you, and *you should never be a research subject without talking it over with your personal physician* and asking your personal physician to monitor you during the research as well as advise you about when to stop participating.

As I emphasize throughout this chapter, *informed consent is a necessary, but not sufficient, condition for legitimate medical research on humans.* A careful review of the science comes first. This means that the first question is whether the research should be done at all.[3] Only after this determination is made, based on such factors as prior research, risk/benefit analysis, the importance of the research to society, and the available alternatives, is it legitimate to ask a patient to be a research subject.

Should a patient's personal physician ever ask the patient to participate in the physician's own research project?

No, at least if the research involves more than minimal risk. It is bad practice that puts both the patient and the physician in untenable positions. The patient's position is compromised because the patient may feel pressured to participate for fear that the physician may not continue to provide proper care if the patient rejects the invitation to be a research subject. Likewise, the physician is compromised. In the physician-patient relationship, only the patient's best interests matter, and treatment is recommended and discussed based on the physician's view of the patient's best interests. In research, however, a protocol must be followed, regardless of the subject's best interests if the goal of obtaining generalizable knowledge is to be realized (of course, the research should be stopped if it is harming the subject). The physician may also have a financial conflict of interest, for example, by having a financial stake in the company sponsoring the research or even sponsoring the research with his or her own company.

Confusion on this point runs very deep: so deep that in 2000 the editor of the *New England Journal of Medicine* and the first director of Health and Human Services' (HHS) new Office for Human Research Protections, both active medical researchers before assuming their jobs, wrote:

Any clinical investigator will tell you that the success of a clinical trial is limited by the ability to recruit research subjects. . . . The decision [to join a trial] takes special courage, and medical science is grateful to the people who display this courage. . . . Experienced investigators know that after all the pros and cons have been considered, patients usually base their decision on whether they trust the investigator. It is, after all, the investigator who is responsible for the subject's welfare during the trial, and *it is the investigator who must always act in the subject's best interests.* The investigator must protect the subject while he or she is participating in research.[4]

This statement illustrates the power of denial among clinical investigators who persist in believing that physician-researchers can treat their subjects like patients and can consistently act in their subjects' best interests. This is simply not possible, because research by definition is not about acting in the subject's best interests; rather it is about testing a hypothesis by following a protocol (for the benefit of future patients), regardless of whether it is in the patient's best interests or not. In a randomized clinical trial, for example, whether a subject gets the experimental drug or a placebo (an inert substance, sometimes called a sugar pill) will be determined by a flip of a coin—not by what a physician thinks is "best" for the subject. It is true that researchers are responsible for the safety of their subjects; this is, however, not the same duty a physician owes a patient of acting only in the patient's best interests.[5]

You should have a physician who is only loyal to you and your health. Your physician's loyalty to you is compromised by acting as an investigator in a research protocol. Assuming they have properly gained access to your medical records (see chap. 11), other physicians can approach you to try to recruit you for research. But your personal physician should not. Instead, the appropriate role of your physician in research is to advise you about the proposed research and whether your physician thinks it is beneficial for you to be involved. If you do become a research subject, your physician should continue to advocate only for your welfare and to advise you to withdraw from the study if and when your physician thinks this is best for you (regardless of how your withdrawal might affect the research).

What is the Nuremberg Code?

The Nuremberg Code is the primary foundation of all ethical codes on human research and the most authoritative legal statement on human experimentation. This ten-point code was articulated in a 1947 court opinion following the trial of Nazi physicians for "war crimes and crimes against humanity" committed during World War II, which included experiments designed to determine which poisons killed the fastest, how long people could live submerged in ice water or when exposed to high altitudes, and if surgically severed limbs could be reattached. The court rejected the Nazi defendants' contention that their experiments with both prisoners of war and civilian concentration camp inmates were consistent with the ethics of the medical profession as evidenced by previously published unethical U.S., French, and British experiments on venereal disease, plague, and malaria, and U.S. prison experiments. The court concluded that only "certain types of medical experiments on human beings, when kept within reasonably well defined bounds, conform to the ethics of the medical profession generally."

The basis of the Nuremberg Code is a type of natural law reasoning.

In the court's words: "All agree . . . that certain basic principles must be observed in order to satisfy moral, ethical, and legal concepts." Principle 1 enunciates the primacy the law places on the consent of the subject: "The voluntary consent of the human subject is absolutely essential." The Nuremberg Code requires that the consent of the experimental subject have at least four characteristics: it must be competent, voluntary, informed, and understanding. This is to protect the subject's rights. Principle 9 permits the subject to withdraw at any time. The other eight principles deal primarily with protecting the subject's welfare: They prescribe actions that must be taken prior to and during the experiment. These include a determination that the experiment is properly designed to yield fruitful results "unprocurable by other methods"; that "anticipated results" will justify performance of the experiment; that all "unnecessary physical and mental suffering and injury" are avoided; that there is no "*a priori* reason to believe that death or disabling injury will occur"; that the project has "humanitarian importance" that outweighs the degree of risk; that "proper preparation" is taken to "protect the experimental subject against even the remote possibilities of injury, disability, or death"; that only "scientifically qualified" persons conduct the experiment; and that the experimenter is prepared to terminate the experiment if "continuation is likely to result in injury, disability, or death to the experimental subject."

The Nuremberg Code

1. The voluntary consent of the human subject is absolutely essential. This means that the person involved should have legal capacity to give consent; should be so situated as to be able to exercise free power of choice, without the intervention of any element of force, fraud, deceit, duress, overreaching, or other ulterior form of constraint or coercion; and should have sufficient knowledge and comprehension of the elements of the subject matter involved as to enable him to make an understanding and enlightened decision. This latter element requires that before the acceptance of an affirmative decision by the experimental subject there should be made known to him the nature, duration, and purpose of the experiment; the method and means by which it is to be conducted; all inconveniences and hazards reasonably to be expected; and the effects upon his health or person which may

possibly come from his participation in the experiment. The duty and responsibility for ascertaining the quality of the consent rests upon each individual who initiates, directs or engages in the experiment. It is a personal duty and responsibility which may not be delegated to another with impunity.

2. The experiment should be such as to yield fruitful results for the good of society, unprocurable by other methods or means of study, and not random and unnecessary in nature.

3. The experiment should be so designed and based on the results of animal experimentation and a knowledge of the natural history of the disease or other problem under study that the anticipated results will justify the performance of the experiment.

4. The experiment should be so conducted as to avoid all unnecessary physical and mental suffering and injury.

5. No experiment should be conducted where there is an *a priori* reason to believe that death or disabling injury will occur; except, perhaps, in those experiments where the experimental physicians also serve as subjects.

6. The degree of risk to be taken should never exceed that determined by the humanitarian importance of the problem to be solved by the experiment.

7. Proper preparations should be made and adequate facilities provided to protect the experimental subject against even remote possibilities of injury, disability, or death.

8. The experiment should be conducted only by scientifically qualified persons. The highest degree of skill and care should be required through all stages of the experiment of those who conduct or engage in the experiment.

9. During the course of the experiment the human subject should be at liberty to bring the experiment to an end if he has reached the physical or mental state where continuation of the experiment seems to him to be impossible.

10. During the course of the experiment the scientist in charge must be prepared to terminate the experiment at any stage, if he has probable cause to believe, in the exercise of the good faith, superior skill, and careful judgment required of him, that a continuation of the experiment is likely to result in injury, disability, or death to the experimental subject.[6]

The code has earned worldwide acceptance as the basis for other national and international research rules. It is a part of international common law, and I have previously argued that it can properly be viewed as both a criminal and a civil basis for liability in the United States.[7] Although the U.S. Supreme Court has endorsed the principles of the Nuremberg Code, it has held that violations of the code by the U.S. military do not provide the basis for soldiers to recover money damages from the U.S. government.[8]

Sergeant James B. Stanley had been secretly given LSD in 1958 to determine its effects. Sgt. Stanley suffered from hallucinations, periods of incoherence, and memory loss. He was discharged from the army in 1969. In 1975, the army sent him a letter asking him to cooperate in a follow-up study on the long-term effects of LSD on "volunteers who participated" in the 1958 tests. This was the first he learned of the experiment. The majority of the Supreme Court concluded that involuntary participation in human experimentation was no exception to the rule that a serviceman could not sue the United States for injuries that "arise out of or are in the course of activity incident to service."

The four dissenting judges would have provided money damages for violation of the Nuremberg Code. Justice William Brennan, writing for three of them, concluded: "The United States military developed the Code, which applies to all citizen-soldiers as well as civilians. . . . The subject of experimentation who has not volunteered is treated as an object, a sample. . . . Soldiers ought not to be asked to defend a Constitution indifferent to their essential dignity."

Even though most courts have refused to permit lawsuits for money damages on the basis of a violation of the Nuremberg Code, the code nonetheless sets a *minimal* legal standard for legal and ethical human experimentation, both in and out of the military. In 2001, for example, the highest court of Maryland adopted the Nuremberg Code as a common law standard to govern research.[9]

Have U.S. physicians and hospitals been involved in illegal and unethical medical research since World War II?

Yes. Many research scandals have occurred in the United States.[10] In a 1963 study, researchers from Sloan-Kettering Memorial Hospital injected terminally ill patients at the Jewish Chronic Disease Hospital in Brooklyn, New York, with live cancer cells to test their immune response. The patients were not informed of the type of cells injected, only that it was a "skin test."[11] In the "Tuskegee syphilis study," sponsored by the U.S. Public Health Service, which was begun with deceptive recruitment prior to World War II and continued for twenty-five years thereafter, effective treatment was withheld from a group of poor black, rural males who had syphilis so that the natural course of the disease could be studied.[12] In the "Willowbrook experiments," mentally retarded children were deliberately infected with hepatitis B so research could continue on a potential vaccine.

In the early 1960s, more than two million thalidomide tablets were distributed to twenty thousand patients in the United States by more than twelve hundred physicians as part of a research study. When told of the potentially toxic effects of the drug on fetuses, more than four hundred physicians made no effort to contact their patients directly, and many of them were unable to do so because they had kept no records of those to whom they had given the drug.[13] In 1966, Dr. Henry Beecher of Harvard Medical School reported on twenty-two unethical experiments that took place in the United States after the promulgation of the Nuremberg Code.[14] Examples included the deliberate withholding of penicillin from sufferers of streptococcal infection and the "successful" transplantation of a cancerous tumor from a daughter to her mother.

The President's Advisory Committee on Human Radiation Experiments reported in 1995 on decades of government-sponsored radiation experiments on unsuspecting Americans during the Cold War. Two of these experiments are illustrative. In the first, designed to discover the tolerable dose of uranium in humans, five terminally ill patients (four of whom were comatose) with brain tumors were injected with uranium without their consent or that of their families. In the second, the Cincinnati whole body radiation experiment, eighty-eight cancer patients were subjected to whole body radiation to determine how soldiers would likely react to a similar exposure on a nuclear battlefield. Most of the subjects were poor and black, and none is likely to have understood the reasons for this experiment, which was lethal to at least some of them and caused most of them severe nausea and vomiting.

Before the committee's *Final Report*[15] was issued, a federal judge, rightly relying in part on the Nuremberg Code, permitted a lawsuit by the families of these subjects against the researchers to proceed, stating: "The allegations in this case indicate that the government of the United States . . .

treated at least 87 of its citizens as though they were laboratory animals. If the Constitution has not clearly established a right under which these Plaintiffs may attempt to prove their case, then a gaping hole in that document has been exposed. The subject of experimentation who has not volunteered is merely an object."[16]

Some of the most publicized medical experiments in history were also done with questionable ethics. Most notable are experiments, such as the Baby Fae case, in which animal organs were transplanted into humans (xenografts).[17] Much of the experimentation involving use of the artificial heart also involved serious ethical and legal lapses in both research design and consent procedures. For example, Barney Clark, the recipient of the world's first permanent artificial heart, signed an eleven-page consent form that is notable more for its length than for its content. It was incomplete, internally inconsistent, and confusing. No provisions were made for proxy consent for additional procedures or experiments in the event Clark became incompetent, for a decision to terminate the experiment, or a plan for how Clark would die.[18] The consent form was improved for the Abiocor artificial heart experiments (2001–4), but the major improvement was the addition of a dedicated advocate for the subjects.[19]

These examples are spectacular and unusual; nonetheless, they demonstrate the point that is today made most often in gene transfer experiments: when great fame and possible fortune are at stake, ethics and law often take a back seat to even fanciful notions of "scientific advance." They also illustrate the fascination the public has with glitzy medical research and the difficulty regulators have in dealing with ambitious researchers and their biotech and pharmaceutical sponsors.

Who is likely to be asked to be a research subject?

Today, with the great increase in both commercial and government-sponsored clinical research, everyone is a potential research subject. Research sponsored by pharmaceutical companies alone has multiplied fourteen-fold in the last twenty years—from $1.5 billion in 1980 to $22.5 billion in 2000.[20] Likewise, the number of investigators participating in FDA-regulated research went from 5,500 in 1900 to almost 50,000 in 2000.[21] Similarly, federally financed research on humans has almost tripled, to approximately $20 billion annually, in the past fifteen years. Although everyone is a potential research subject, poor people continue to be used in research trials.[22]

Nonetheless, hospitalized patients who suffer from diseases that are being actively studied by researchers are probably the most likely to be recruited to be subjects in a research project. This has always been the case. As a leading medical commentator has explained:

Incapacitated and hospitalized because of illness, frightened by strange and impersonal routines, and fearful for his health and perhaps life, he is far from exercising a free power of choice when the person to whom he anchors all his hopes asks, "say, you wouldn't mind, would you, if you joined some of the other patients on this floor and helped us carry out some very important research we are doing?" When "informed consent" is obtained, it is not the student, the destitute bum, or the prisoner to whom, by virtue of his condition, the thumb screws of coercion are most relentlessly applied; it is *the most used and useful of all experimental subjects, the patient with disease.*[23]

What does an institutional review board (IRB) do?

Each hospital and medical school has an institutional review board (IRB) whose job it is to review proposed research projects *before* patients are asked to enroll in them and to approve written consent forms.[24] IRBs are *required* by federal law in all institutions that receive federal funding for research or whose sponsors submit their research results to the FDA. This prior review is critical to ensure that the risks to subjects are outweighed by the potential benefits and to determine whether the research should be done on humans.

Review of the consent form and the process for obtaining consent is also important—so that potential subjects can understand what they are being asked to do. *Consent, of course, is a process not a form,* and consent is only as good as the consent process itself. The research, together with risks, benefits, and alternatives must be fully explained and understood. It is reasonable, for example, for potential subjects to be asked questions to make sure they understand what they are getting into. On the other hand, consent cannot make an unethical experiment ethical; that is why consent is a necessary, but not sufficient, condition for ethical research.

As set forth in federal regulations, an IRB's primary responsibility is to protect human subjects by reviewing proposed research and approving it if the following requirements are met:

- Risks to subjects are minimized.
- Risks to subjects are reasonable in relation to anticipated benefits,

if any, to subjects, and the importance of the knowledge that may reasonably be expected to result.

- Selection of subjects is equitable.
- Informed consent is obtained and appropriately documented.[25]

Some studies may require special procedures to monitor data to ensure the safety of subjects and to protect the privacy of subjects and the confidentiality of records, and they may include additional provisions to safeguard subjects who are especially vulnerable to coercion or undue influence.

The IRB itself must be composed of "not less than five" members of varying backgrounds. Not all can be members of the same profession, gender diversity is encouraged, and at least one member must not be otherwise associated with the institution. In addition to professional competence in research, "the committee must be able to ascertain the acceptability of proposals in terms of institutional commitments and regulations, applicable law, and standards of professional conduct and practice." These requirements seem stringent, but they could be minimally met by having four researchers from the institution on the IRB joined by one person from the community. A quorum is defined as a majority of members but must include at least one nonscientist. This is fundamentally "peer review," review of scientists by other scientists. The National Bioethics Advisory Commission recommended in a draft report in 2000 that half of the members of IRBs should be from the community, but in their final report cut this recommendation to 25 percent of the IRB members.

IRBs were mandated as a reaction to the types of abuses in research outlined elsewhere in this chapter; mostly, however, the IRB system may have done more to protect researchers from more stringent controls that might otherwise be mandated than they have done to enhance the protection of subjects. If you have any questions about research you are asked to participate in, you should either discuss it with your own physician, or the IRB office. The principle investigator's name and phone number, as well as the phone number of the IRB office, should be on the consent form.

Of course, just because an IRB has approved a research protocol does *not* mean that you have any obligation to participate in research, or that the research is important, useful, or safe. One primary purpose of the consent process is to make sure that you understand that you have no obligation to agree to participate in any research, and that your care will not be compromised in any way if you refuse to participate. Do not defer to the IRB; make up your own mind.

Have IRBs been effective in protecting subjects?

Not very. A 1996 study by the U.S. General Accounting Office (GAO) found that in some cases at major research hospitals, "the sheer number of studies [experiments] necessitates that IRBs spend only 1 or 2 minutes of review per study."[26] This is obviously no meaningful review at all. The GAO also found little attempt by IRBs to conduct continuing reviews once the experiment had been approved and found significant conflict-of-interest problems with the members of the IRBs, most of whom were researchers from the same institution.

Likewise, a 1998 investigation by the Inspector General's Office of the Department of Health and Human Services concluded that the face of human experimentation in the United States was changing rapidly with the "expansion of managed care, the increased commercialization of research, the proliferation of multi-site trials, new types of research, the increased number of research proposals, and the rise of patient consumerism."[27] The inspector general found specifically that IRBs review "too much, too quickly, and with too little expertise," conduct minimal continuing review, have serious conflicts of interest, provide little training for either researchers or IRB members, and do not try to evaluate their own effectiveness. A two-year follow-up study in 2000 showed that little had changed.[28] And in the fall of 2000, the secretary of HHS, Donna Shalala, concluded that IRBs "are under considerable pressure" to approve research protocols quickly, and that to protect research subjects adequately they "must be strengthened."[29]

It is fair to say that as currently constituted and operated, IRBs cannot protect research subjects because they are underfunded, underappreciated, many members have intolerable conflicts of interest, they do no effective continuing review, and they conduct their business in secret with little or no input from potential research subjects or the public. In short, you and your advocate should take very little comfort in the fact that an IRB has reviewed a research proposal you are being asked to participate in. If the person asking you to consent to a research project tells you that it is all right because it has been approved by the IRB, you should be on your guard because this is a minimal *legal requirement*, not a certification that the research is appropriate for you. You can quickly move the conversation to what matters to you, risks and benefits, by asking the following questions: What will be done to me if I become a research subject that will NOT be done to me if I don't become a research subject? Why are you asking me specifically to join this research trial? What are the risks to my health or life, and what will you do to try to be sure I am not harmed?

Hospitals and research institutions have proven themselves unable to reform the IRB mechanism themselves, and the federal government remains ambivalent. Thus only patients and their advocates are likely to be effective in insisting on reform and thereby (hopefully) improving the current dismal and conflict-ridden situation. Current IRB procedures were designed to protect subjects consistent with the ability to do medical research. It is time to delete the "consistent with" phrase. The first priority should be simply to protect research subjects. If that means some research cannot be done, so be it. The protection of research subjects is an end in itself. It is not simply a means to do more research.

What are the purposes of obtaining the informed consent of research subjects?

The primary purposes of informed consent for research on humans are to promote individual autonomy and to encourage rational decision making.[30] The purpose of autonomy (also called self-determination) is to protect the individual's integrity as a person by denying anyone the right to invade the person's body without consent. People should be able to protect themselves if they receive complete information. This proposition can be approached from a variety of perspectives.

One perspective is that research on human subjects must always be a "joint enterprise" between the researcher and subject to prevent the subject from becoming an object or thing to be used, instead of a human being.[31] From this perspective, making the information necessary to obtain public consent is necessary to prevent taking advantage of subjects to the point where the types of procedures performed on them are expanded beyond what society generally would view as tolerable.[32]

Another perspective is that although the purpose of research on human beings is ultimately to benefit society through medical progress, the burdens and risks of such research will of necessity fall on only a few individuals. In this view, the subject is giving a "gift" to society—a gift that cannot rightfully be forcibly taken, and one that is devalued (and the giver debased) if the gift is based on a false assumption of the risks involved.[33]

Adequate information and free choice are essential to protect an individual's autonomy and personhood.

The objection, that respect for individual sometimes delays scientific advance, is insightfully disposed of by philosopher Hans Jonas:

Let us not forget that *progress is an optional goal,* not an unconditional commitment, and that its tempo in particular, compulsive as it may become, has nothing sacred about it. Let us also remember that a slower progress in the conquest of disease would not threaten society, grievous as it is to those who have to deplore that their particular disease be not yet conquered, but that *society would* indeed *be threatened by the erosion of those moral values whose loss,* probably *caused by too ruthless a pursuit of scientific progress, would make its most dazzling triumphs not worth having.*[34]

Rational decision making is also an extremely important goal of the informed consent doctrine, since if this goal is not achieved, the entire research enterprise is illegitimate.[35] After a candid review of risks, subjects are likely to refuse to participate in experiments that are inherently too dangerous to be ethically performed on humans, making them de facto impossible to do. And this is as it should be. As Jay Katz and Alexander Capron point out, "[W]ho other than the patient-subjects can determine whether the benefits of the procedure, conventional or experimental, outweigh the burdens that will be imposed on them?"[36] Research-physicians might also have conflicting motives, such as career advancement or monetary gain, and (as the California Supreme Court ruled in the *Moore* case)[37] these should also be disclosed to the patient. In some cases, such as when the researcher is an officer or stockholder in the company sponsoring the research, the researcher should be *disqualified* from conducting research on humans because of this conflict of interest.

What must be included in the informed consent process for research?

Federal regulations specify that potential subjects must be presented with all of the following information about the proposed research:

1. A statement that the study involves research, an explanation of its purposes and the expected duration of the subject's participation, and a description of the procedures to be followed, identifying which are experimental;

2. A description of reasonably foreseeable risks or discomforts to the subject;

3. A description of any reasonably expected benefits to the subject or to others;

4. A disclosure of appropriate alternative procedures or courses of treatment, if any, that might be advantageous to the subject;

5. A statement describing the extent, if any, to which confidentiality of records identifying the subject will be maintained;

6. For research involving more than minimal risk, an explanation about any compensation or medical treatments available if injury occurs;

7. An explanation of whom to contact for answers to questions about the research and research subject's rights, and whom to contact in the event of a research-related injury;

8. A statement that participation is voluntary and that refusal to participate will involve no penalty or loss of benefits; and that the subject may discontinue at any time without penalty or loss of benefits to which the subject is otherwise entitled.[38]

In addition, where appropriate, the consent form must include statements containing the following: the research may involve "unforeseeable risks" to the subject; the researcher may terminate the subject's participation without the subject's agreement; a listing of any additional costs the subject might be responsible for as a result of participating in the research; the consequences of withdrawal by the subject and how it can be accomplished in an "orderly manner"; provisions that any significant findings developed in the course of the research that might affect the subject's willingness to continue will be provided to the subject; and an estimate of the approximate number of subjects involved in the research.[39]

Are there special research rules for some projects?

Yes. There are also special, additional regulations designed to protect populations that are especially likely to be taken advantage of in research, such as prisoners and children. Special protections for the mentally disabled and the terminally ill have not been adopted by federal regulation, but they should be.

The FDA also has regulations that permit IRBs to approve research done in emergencies without consent under certain narrow circumstances: the research subjects must be in "a life-threatening situation, available treatments are unproven or unsatisfactory," and research is necessary to determine safety and efficacy of particular interventions. Informed consent must be found to be not feasible because the subject is incapable of consenting, legally authorized representatives are not available, and potential subjects cannot be prospectively identified.[40] The regulations have been properly criticized for their requirement, "participation in the research holds out the prospect of direct benefit to the subject." Of course, this confuses research with treatment.[41]

An IRB may waive the requirement for a signed consent form if the only record linking the subject to the research would be the consent form and this record would put the subject at risk regarding confidentiality (the subject has the choice of having a written consent form under these circumstances), and the research presents no more than minimal risk of harm and involves no procedures for which written consent is normally required outside the research context.[42]

Some categories of research, such as normal educational research, educational testing, some interview procedures, some observational research, and use of public data, are exempt from IRB review. Other categories of research, such as collection of hair and nail clippings, collection of excreta and external secretions, noninvasive clinical data recording in adults, small volume blood collection in adults, dental plaque collection, voice recordings, and moderate exercise, can be given an "expedited review."[43]

Who should obtain informed consent from a patient-subject?

A nurse or resident may provide you with information about a research project, but the Nuremberg Code makes it clear that obtaining the informed consent of the research subject is a "personal duty and responsibility" of the person in charge of the research project, the principal investigator. You should not agree to be part of a research project without talking directly with the principal investigator and then discussing it with your personal physician. Your consent should be given only to the principal investigator and only after all your questions and concerns, and those of your advocate, have been satisfactorily answered. As an advocate, it is a good idea to read the research protocol itself before discussing it with the patient and principal investigator. It is likely that the protocol will answer many of your questions.

Two critical lessons deserve repetition: informed consent is a necessary precondition to lawful human experimentation, but informed consent alone is not a sufficient precondition. Other requirements, such as the reasonableness of the experiment, review by an institutional review board, and provisions for withdrawal and compensation for harm must be met before consent is even sought.

May the next of kin or a legal guardian consent to research to be performed on an incompetent relative or ward?

Sometimes. Consent for an incompetent relative or ward is proper if the proposed research is in the "best interests" of the patient (in the sense that the likely benefits to the patient exceed the risks); *or* if the relative or ward has, while still competent, indicated that he or she would like to participate in this particular research after becoming incompetent, and the conditions anticipated by the now-incompetent patient actually exist; *or* in the unusual cases, in which there is minimal risk, but the knowledge to be gained is important to the group of patients to which the subject belongs and cannot be obtained any other way. If you are asked to provide such consent, you should always remember that there is no obligation to consent, and you should only consent if the experiment has no risk, or very little risk, to your relative or ward. Competent patients are always preferable as research subjects because they can consent on their own behalf.

To protect especially vulnerable populations, such as nursing home patients, Leonard Glantz and I have suggested that in addition to other protections, "a nursing home council, composed primarily of residents, should review and approve any protocol before the research can be conducted at the facility."[44] This is because what may seem trivial to the researcher and the IRB members in terms of risk, discomfort, disorientation, or dehumanizing effects may not seem so trivial to this vulnerable and often frightened population. Advocates must always remember that their primary role is to protect the patient. Incompetent research subjects, for example, should *never* be sedated or restrained for research, and persons consenting to research for them should be required to be with them at all times during the research so that they can exercise the subject's right to withdraw at any time on their behalf.[45]

Should compensation for injury to subjects in human research be mandatory?

Yes. But there is no legal requirement for researchers to indemnify subjects for injury. There are many compelling reasons why the researcher, the institution in which the research is conducted, the sponsor of the research, or the federal government should be required to provide research subjects with an insurance policy to compensate them for injuries suffered as subjects. This suggestion was made in early 1973 by the secretary of HHS's Commission on Medical Malpractice.[46] Others have also made it. Henry K. Beecher, for example, has argued: "Even if all reasonable precautions have been taken to protect both the subject and the investigator from physical damage as well as from unethical practices, the possibility of injury still remains. It is unreasonable to expect that society which profits actually or potentially should not share in the responsibility for what was done."[47]

A leading legal commentator, Clark Havighurst, has argued similarly that requiring research agencies to bear the financial risk of adverse or unexpected effects would be in the public interest:

The principle of societal responsibility makes not only humanitarian but economic sense, for the research industry will undertake fewer projects that are not justified by a balancing of risks (and other costs) against potential benefits if all of the potential costs are taken into account. . . . Whatever compensation system is devised must not only compensate the unlucky subject but also place the burden on those best able to evaluate and control the risks attending the experiment.[48]

Researchers are, however, required to state in the consent form whether or not they will provide compensation.[49] Unless at least medical care for injury is provided by the researcher or hospital, patients should not consent to participate in the research. Researchers should also provide compensation for pain and suffering and for loss of earnings. Lack of compensation is unfair to subjects, and by participating in research in which subjects have no compensation for research-related injuries, subjects help perpetuate the system that is unfair to all research subjects.[50]

Are terminally ill patients vulnerable to exploitation in research?

Yes. The closer we get to death, the more likely we are to view any medical intervention as a treatment that could help us, no matter how experimental or how little is known about it. There is good evidence that even terminally ill cancer patients in Phase 1 research studies (which are designed only to test various doses of a drug for harmful side effects, not to see if it will "work") think they are getting a treatment that might benefit them, when in fact they are instead simply helping researchers determine a dosage level that future subjects will get to see if the drug actually works.[51] Physicians are equally adept at denying reality and convincing themselves that they are providing therapy rather than engaging in research.

Dying patients understandably grasp at straws, but at least sometimes even the straw is an illusion. The truth is often that the patient will die no matter what experiment is tried; the only real question is how the patient will die. This is why it has been suggested (and some IRBs have adopted this suggestion) that whenever a terminally ill patient is asked to be a part of a research study, quality palliative care should always be included, and hospice care should be an alternative (discussed in chap. 13).[52] I agree with this suggestion but would go further. My own view is that the following amendments should be made to the current federal regulations that govern IRB review of research protocols to protect terminally ill patients:

1. For the purpose of these regulations a "terminally ill patient" is one whose death is reasonably expected to occur within six months even if currently accepted and available medical treatment is used.

2. In addition to all other legal and ethical requirements for the approval of a research protocol by national and local scientific and ethical review boards (including IRBs), research in which terminally ill patients serve as research subjects shall be approved only if the review board specifically finds that:

a) The research, if it carries any risk, has the intent and reasonable probability (based on scientific data) of improving the health or well-being of the subject, or of significantly increasing the subject's length of life without significantly decreasing its quality;

b) It is unlikely that the research intervention will significantly decrease the subject's quality of life because of suffering, pain, or indignity attributable to the research; and

c) Written informed consent will be required of all research participants over the age of 16 in research involving any risk, and such consent may be solicited only by a patient rights advocate who is appointed by the review committee, is independent of the researcher, and whose duty it is to fully and objectively inform the potential subject of all reasonably foreseeable risks and benefits inherent in the research protocol. The patient rights advocate will also be empowered to monitor the actual research itself.

3. The vote and basis for each of the findings in subpart (2) shall be set forth in writing by the review board and be available to all potential subjects and the public.

4. All research protocols involving terminally ill subjects shall be available to the public, and the meetings of the scientific and ethical review boards on these protocols shall be open to the public.[53]

Are there steps that could be taken to make research safer?

Yes. Moving the federal Office for Protection from Research Risks out of the National Institutes of Health in 2000, and under the secretary of HHS was a step in the right direction, but the renamed office, now called the Office for Human Research Protection or "OHRP," is still under the control of an agency primarily interested in promoting research. We need an independent federal oversight agency—a new federal human research agency—with the authority to make rules and enforce them in the area of human experimentation. The agency should have not only rule-making authority to set national standards but should also have adjudicatory authority to determine whether or not individual researchers (not just IRBs and institutions) have violated the regulations and to punish them for violations as well. Even in the absence of a new federal law, however, the following minimal steps should be taken immediately to protect research subjects:

1. Research must always be identified as research, and its purpose (to gain generalizable knowledge) always spelled out and differentiated from medical treatment designed only to benefit the patient.

2. Patients should always continue to be patients, even if they also volunteer to serve as research subjects. It is unlikely that it will ever be possible—in our death-denying and death-defying world—for patients not to indulge in self-deception by imagining that research is really treatment and that they are patients, not research subjects. We cannot separate the subject into two persons. But we can assure that the subject-patient always has a physician whose only obligation is to look out for the best interests of the patient. Thus, we can (and should) prohibit physicians from performing more than minimal risk research on their patients, and as a corollary, only permit physician-researchers to recruit patients of other physicians for their research protocols.

3. There should be strict disqualification rules for both subjects and researchers to engage in the research enterprise. At the extremes, for example, subjects who believe they have "nothing to lose" should be disqualified from participation because they are unable to give understanding consent. If you think you have nothing to lose as a research subject—you're wrong! Researchers who feel subjects have "nothing to lose" by participating should also be disqualified from doing research on them because they are not able to protect the dignity and welfare of their prospective research subjects with this attitude.

4. The term "therapeutic research" and all of its progeny, such as "experimental treatment" and "innovative treatment," should be abolished from research protocols and informed consent processes and forms. Research is research, designed to test a hypothesis and performed based on the rules of the protocol; treatment is something else, designed to benefit a patient, and subject to change whenever change is seen in the patient's best interest. Confusing research with treatment confuses both the researcher and subject and encourages self-deception by both of them.

5. The researcher should be required to disclose any and all financial incentives involved in the research to both the IRB and to the potential subjects. Those with major conflicts of interest should be disqualified as investigators. For more minor conflicts, this information should be presented to the subject in a separate written disclosure form so that the subject knows what financial incentives (i.e., conflicts of interest) may be affecting the scientific judgment or medical judgment of the researcher.

6. Institutional Review Boards should be radically overhauled and restructured, so that their role is to protect the subjects of research (not the researcher.) At a minimum, this will require democratizing the IRBs by requiring a majority of members to be community members and by opening all meetings to the public. Training and continued education should be required.[54]

What things should a patient-subject know before consenting to be a research subject?

Anyone asked to be a research subject should carefully review the following questions and make sure they can answer all of them before agreeing to participate:

- What will be done to me if I become a research subject that will NOT be done to me if I don't become a subject?
- Do I understand the research procedures and their purposes?
- What are the risks to my life, health, or bodily functions for participating in this research (including the risk to me of not getting the standard medical treatment)?
- What benefits, if any, can I reasonably expect from participating in this research?
- What is the purpose of this research? What benefits might others obtain if this research is successful? (Do I understand this is research [designed to test a hypothesis to help others] and not a treatment meant to help me?)
- If no research was being done, what would my doctor recommend be done for me?
- Has this research been approved by an IRB? (If not, do not participate!)
- Who is in charge of this research (the principal investigator)? (Make sure you talk directly with this person so the research can be properly explained to you.)
- Is the person in charge (the principal investigator) being paid by a drug company or other for-profit company to do this research? If so, how much and for what?
- Is this a randomized trial (that is, will I be assigned to the group getting the experimental intervention or to the group getting a placebo, sugar pill, or standard treatment, based on random assignment like the flip of a coin)? (If so, and if you actually want the experimental treatment, you need to find out if you can get it outside the study without the random assignment that gives you only a 50 percent chance to get it.)
- Do I have a copy of the consent form? (You are entitled to a copy by law. Make sure you get one.)
- Will I be compensated for any injuries suffered as a result of participating in this experiment? (If you will not be provided with at least free medical care for injuries sustained as a result of participation, you should *not* participate.)
- Who will have access to the results, and will the medical records with results be identifiable as my records? (If you are not satisfied that your confidentiality will be maintained, do not participate.)

• Will I get updates on the preliminary results of the research, and at what points might withdrawal from the research be a good idea?

• Who do I talk to if I have further questions about the research or my rights? (The names, titles and phone numbers of these people should be in the consent form.)

Tips for Advocates

• **Research is for the benefit of others, not for the patient.** Make sure both you and the patient understand what research is, and that it is done for the benefit of others, not for the patient's benefit, and that the patient is never under any obligation to participate in research.

• **The patient should always have his or her own physician (i.e., someone who is not the researcher)!** Make sure the patient has a physician (other than the researcher) whose only loyalty is to the patient and the patient's well-being. Ask the patient's physician whether the proposed research protocol is likely to help or hurt the patient and in what way.

• **Make sure you understand all the information in the consent form** and have access to the principal investigator if you have specific questions or concerns about the study that you think have not been adequately addressed. Get a copy of the research protocol from the principal investigator and make sure you understand the research, its purpose and its risks.

• **Make sure you know all of the risks of the study,** whom to contact if an adverse effect happens, how to contact that person, and what steps the researcher or the hospital guarantee to take to help the patient if something bad happens as a result of the research.

• If the research is being sponsored by a commercial company, make sure you know what share, if any, the patient will have in the profits from any product produced as a result of the research (this will almost always be none), and how the researcher is being paid to do the research or to recruit the patient as a subject. It is unfortunate you have to ask this, but **contemporary research is riddled with financial conflicts of interest, and you must identify them to protect the patient.** In general, the patient should not participate in any research in which the principal investigator stands to make money if the research is "successful."

• **There are special rules that protect prisoners, children, and fetuses.**

NOTES

1. *See* Paul Smaglik, *Clinical Trials End at Gene Therapy Institute,* 405 Nature 497 (2000); *Gelsinger v. U. of Pennsylvania,* Civil Complaint filed September 22, 2000 (available at www.sskrplaw.com/links/healthcare2.html); Leon Rosenberg & Alan Schecter, *Gene Therapist, Heal Thyself,* 287 Science 1751 (2000); and Eliot Marshall, *Gene Therapy on Trial,* 288 Science 951 (2000).

2. Jay Katz, *Human Experimentation and Human Rights,* 38 St. Louis L.J. 7, 7–8 (1993) (emphasis added). The inability to distinguish research from treatment is especially troubling in Phase 1 cancer studies, which have no therapeutic goals at all and yet are consistently mischaracterized in consent forms. Sam Horng et al., *Description of Benefits and Risks in Consent Forms for Phase I Oncology Trials,* 347 New Eng. J. Med. 2134 (2002).

3. John Fletcher, *The Evolution of the Ethics of Informed Consent* (in) Kare Berg & Knut Tranoy, eds., Research Ethics, New York: Alan R. Liss, 1983, 211.

4. Jeffrey M. Drazen & Greg Koski, *To Protect Those Who Serve,* 343 New Eng. J. Med. 1643 (2000).

5. Financial conflicts of interest may also make the inherent researcher-subject conflicts even worse. *Id.; and see* Bernard Lo et al., *Conflict of Interest Policies for Investigators in Clinical Trials,* 343 New Eng. J. Med. 1616 (2000); S. Van McCrary et al., *A National Survey of Policies on Disclosure of Conflicts of Interest in Biomedical Research,* 343 New Eng. J. Med. 1621 (2000); and Joseph Martin & Dennis Kasper, *In Whose Best Interest? Breaching the Academic-Industrial Wall,* 343 New Eng. J. Med. 1646 (2000). Nor do Amerocans trust the current system. Only 20 percent are very confident that people will not be recruited into clinical trials just so doctors and hospitals can make more money, and only a slightly higher percentage were very confident that study subjects were told of all the risks. Giselle Corbie-Smith, et al., *Distrust, Race and Research,* 162 Archives Int. Med. 2458 (2002).

6. Trials of War Criminals Before the Nuremberg Military Tribunals: Under Control Council Law No. 10, vols. 1 & 2, Washington, D.C.: Government Printing Office, 1949;

and see generally George J. Annas & Michael A. Grodin, eds., The Nazi Doctors and the Nuremberg Code, New York: Oxford U. Press, 1993, and Evelyn Shuster, *Fifty Years Later: The Significance of the Nuremberg Code,* 337 New Eng. J. Med. 1436 (1997). Documents from the Doctors' Trial are available at http://nuremberg.law.harvard.edu.

7. George J. Annas, Leonard H. Glantz & Barbara F. Katz, Informed Consent to Human Experimentation, Cambridge: Ballinger, 1977, 6–9.

8. *U.S. v. Stanley,* 483 U.S. 669 (1987). *See also* Philip Shenon, *C.I.A. Near Settlement of Lawsuits by Subjects of Mind Control Tests,* New York Times, October 6, 1988, A14. *And see generally* M. Cherif Bassiouni et al., *An Appraisal of Human Experimentation in International Law and Practice: The Need for International Regulation of Human Experimentation,* 72 J. of Crim. L. & Criminology 1597 (1981), and Robert J. Lifton, The Nazi Doctors: Medical Killing and the Psychology of Genocide, New York: Basic Books, 1986.

9. *Grimes v. Kennedy Krieger Institute,* 782 A.2d 807 (Md. 2001); Hazel Glenn Beh, *The Role of Institutional Review Boards in Protecting Human Subjects: Are We Really Ready to Fix a Broken System?* 26 Law & Psychology Rev. 1 (2002). Courts, however, refused to apply the Nuremberg Code to the use of an investigational drug and an investigational vaccine on U.S. troops during the Gulf War. *See* George J. Annas, *Protecting Soldiers from Friendly Fire: The Consent Requirement for Using Investigational Drugs and Vaccines in Combat,* 24 Am. J. Law & Med. 245 (1998). *See also* Robert Steinbrook, *Protecting Research Subjects: The Crisis at Johns Hopkins,* 346 New Eng. J. Med. 716 (2002).

10. *See generally* Jay Katz, Experimentation with Human Beings, New York: Russell Sage Foundation, 1972; *Ethical Aspects of Experimentation with Human Subjects,* 98 Daedalus 219 (1969). Fraud and misconduct also are recurring problems. *Pressures on Medical Researchers Create Climate Conducive to Fraud,* Wall Street Journal, February 14, 1989, B4.

11. Katz, *supra* note 2, at 10–65.

12. *See* J. Alan Brandt, *Racism, Research and the Tuskegee Syphilis Study,* 8 Hastings Center Report 21 (December 1978), and James Jones, Bad Blood, New York: Basic Books, 1976. The survivors and their heirs eventually settled a lawsuit against the federal government for $37,500 each minus attorney fees. New York Times, July 29, 1979, 26. *See also* S. Coney, The Unfortunate Experiment, Aukland, N.Z.: Penguin, 1988 (recounts a similar experiment in New Zealand regarding the natural history of cervical cancer).

13. Insight Team of the *Sunday Times* of London, Suffer the Children: The Story of Thalidomide, New York: Viking Press, 1979, 109.

14. Henry Beecher, *Ethics and Clinical Research,* 274 New Eng. J. Med. 1354 (1966). Beecher originally submitted fifty unethical studies, but the editors cut it to twenty-two "for reasons of space."

15. Advisory Committee on Human Radiation Experiments, Final Report, 1995 (also published by Oxford U. Press)

16. *In re Cincinnati Radiation Litigation,* 874 F. Supp. 796, 822 (S.D. Ohio 1995). *See also* Martha Stephens, The Treatment: The Story of Those Who Died in the Cincinnati Radiation Tests, Durham, N.C.: Duke U. Press, 2002.

17. *See* George J. Annas, *Baby Fae: The "Anything Goes" School of Human Experimentation,* 15 Hastings Center Report 15 (February 1985); Jonasson & Hardy, *The Case of Baby Fae,* 254 JAMA 3358 (1985).

18. George J. Annas, *Death and the Magic Machine: Informed Consent to the Artificial Heart*, 9 W. New Eng. L. Rev. 89 (1987). *And see* Schroeder Family, The Bill Schroeder Story, New York: William Morrow, 1987, 134, and Brauer, *The Promise That Failed*, New York Times Magazine, August 28, 1988, 46.

19. *See, e.g.*, Lawrence Altman, *For Heart Surgeons, Many Careful Steps*, New York Times, July 10, 2001, D1.

20. Pharmaceutical Research and Manufacturers of America (Pharma), Pharmaceutical Industry Profile 2000, Washington, D.C.: Pharma, 2001.

21. National Bioethics Advisory Commission, Ethical and Policy Issues in Research Involving Human Participants, Washington, D.C.: NBAC, 2001, 4. *And see* Gina Kolata & K. Eichenwald, *For the Uninsured, Drug Trials Are Health Care*, New York Times, June 22, 1999, 1.

22. In one study from the 1970s, for example, only one of three clinic patients in a study of a new drug for the induction of labor in childbirth knew they were experimental subjects. Instead of being told that an experimental drug was being used on them, they had been informed that a "new" (implying "better") drug was being used. Bradford Gray, Human Subjects in Medical Experimentation, New York: John Wiley & Sons, 1975. In a similar contemporary study, in 2000 a major Florida teaching hospital settled a case for $3.8 million in which hundreds of mostly indigent pregnant women, some of whom spoke only Spanish, were given research drugs without their informed consent. Peter Aronson, *A Medical Indignity*, National Law J., March 27, 2000, 1. The claim in this case was not that the subjects were physically harmed, but that research on them without their consent violated their human dignity. Of course, just because you have health insurance, or are white and middle class, does not mean that you won't be actively recruited to take part in medical research.

23. Franz Ingelfinger, *Informed (But Uneducated) Consent*, 287 New Eng. J. Med. 465 (1972) (emphasis added). Nor is the use of a person with a medical condition new, as Gustave Flaubert's realistic novel *Madame Bovary* (New York: New American Library, 1964, first published in 1857) illustrates. Charles Bovary decides to try to make his name as a physician by curing the local stableman's clubfoot with experimental surgery that involves screwing the foot and leg into "a kind of box, weighing about eight pounds, constructed by the carpenter and the locksmith, with a prodigal amount of iron, wood, sheet-iron, leather, nails and screws." He explains the proposal to his wife, Emma: "'What risk is there? Look!'—and he counted the 'pros' on his fingers. 'Success, practically certain. An end of suffering and disfigurement for the patient. Immediate fame for the surgeon'" (at 173). The stableman was urged to consent by the entire town, but the "decisive factor was that it wouldn't cost a cent." The experiment did not go as planned; and another physician eventually had to be called in to amputate the hideously painful and gangrenous leg (at 179–82).

24. *See generally* Robert Levine, Ethics and Regulation of Clinical Research, 2d ed., Baltimore, Md.: Urban & Schwarzenberg, 1986, and Ezekiel Emanuel et al., *What Makes Clinical Research Ethical?* 283 JAMA 2701 (2000).

25. 45 C.F.R. sec. 46.101 et.seq. (1991 rev.). On the limited value of the consent form itself, *see* George J. Annas, *Reforming Informed Consent to Genetic Research*, 286 JAMA

2326 (2001). Nor are consent forms readable by most people. Michael Paasche-Orlow, Holly Taylor & Frederick Brancati, *Readability Standards for Informed Consent Forms as Compared with Actual Readability,* 348 New Eng. Med. 721 (2003).

26. U.S. General Accounting Office, *Scientific Research: Continued Vigilance Critical to Protecting Human Subjects,* March 1996, 17.

27. Inspector General, DHHS, *Institutional Review Boards: A Time for Reform,* Washington, D.C.: Government Printing Office, June 1998.

28. Inspector General, DHHS, *Protecting Human Research Subjects: Status of Recommendations,* Washington, D.C.: Government Printing Office, April 2000.

29. Donna Shalala, *Protecting Research Subjects: What Must be Done,* 343 New Eng. J. Med. 808 (2000); Office of Inspector General, *Protecting Human Research Subjects,* Washington, D.C.: Government Printing Office, April 2000. Nor do IRBs either identify or report adverse events suffered by research subjects. In the decade 1990–2000, for example, only eight deaths were reported, whereas in a random general population, at least five thousand and as many as fifty-one thousand would have been expected. Adil Shamoo, *Adverse Event Reporting: The Tip of an Iceberg,* 8 Accountability in Research 197 (2001).

30. *See* Annas et al., *supra* note 7.

31. *See* Paul Ramsey, The Patient as Person, New Haven: Yale U. Press, 1970, 5.

32. *See, e.g.,* Margaret Mead, *Research with Human Beings,* 98 Daedalus 361 (1969).

33. Richard Tittmuss, The Gift Relationship, New York: Pantheon Books, 1971.

34. Hans Jonas, *Philosophical Reflections on Experimenting with Human Subjects,* 98 Daedalus 219 (1969) (emphasis added).

35. Jay Katz & Alexander Capron, Catastrophic Disease: Who Decides What? New York: Russell Sage Foundation, 1975, 88.

36. *Id. And see* Nancy M. P. King, *Defining and Describing Benefit Appropriately in Clinical Trials,* 28 J. Law, Med. & Ethics 332 (2000).

37. The case of John Moore is discussed briefly in chapter 6.

38. 45 C.F.R. sec. 46.116 (1991 rev.).

39. *Id.*

40. 21 C.F.R. sec. 50.24 (2000).

41. *See* Jay Katz, *Blurring the Lines: Research, Therapy, and IRBs,* Hastings Center Report, January 1997, 9–11; *and see* Raj Narayan, *Hypothermia for Traumatic Brain Injury—A Good Idea Proved Ineffective,* 344 New Eng. J. Med. 602 (2001).

42. 45 C.F.R. sec. 46.117 (1991 rev.).

43. 45 C.F.R. sec. 46.110; preliminary list published 46 Fed. Reg. 8392 (Jan. 26, 1981).

44. George J. Annas & Leonard H. Glantz, *Rules for Nursing Home Research,* 315 New Eng. J. Med. 1157 (1986). *See also* Dianne Hoffmann et al., *Regulating Research with Decisionally Impaired Individuals: Are We Making Progress?* 3 DePaul J. Health Care L. 547 (2000); Kendall An Desaulniers, Comment, *Legislations to Protect the Decisionally Incapacitated Individuals Participation in Medical Research: Safety Net or Trap Door?* 13 Regent U.L. 179 (2000–01).

45. For more on this, *see* George J. Annas, *Why We Need a National Human Experimentation Agency,* 7 Accountability in Research 293 (1999).

46. *Medical Malpractice: Report of the Secretary's Commission on Medical Malpractice* (DHEW Pub. No. OS 73-88, 1973), 79.

47. Henry Beecher, *Human Studies*, 164 Science 1256 (1969).

48. Clark Havighurst, *Compensating Persons Injured in Human Experimentation*, 169 Science 153 (1970). *See also* Guido Calabresi, *Reflections on Medical Experimentation in Humans*, 98 Daedalus 387 (1969); Irving Ladimer, ed., *Clinical Research Insurance*, 16 J. Chron. Dis. 1229 (1963); President's Commission for the Study of Ethical Problems in Medicine and Biomedical and Behavioral Research, Compensating for Research Injuries, Washington, D.C.: Government Printing Office, 1982; and Patricia Danzon, *Liability and Insurance for Medical Maloccurrences: Are Innovations Different?* (in) Mark Siegler, ed., Medical Innovations and Bad Outcomes, Ann Arbor, Mich.: Health Administration Press, 1987.

49. 45 C.F.R. 46.116(a)(6) (1991 rev.). *And see* Charles Marwick, *Compensation for Injured Research Subjects*, 279 JAMA 1854 (1998).

50. Extraordinarily difficult issues are presented by experimental cancer treatments and experimental AIDS treatments. *See, e.g.,* George J. Annas, *Questing for Grails: Duplicity, Betrayal and Self-Deception in Postmodern Medical Research* 12 J. Contemp. Health Law & Policy 297, 322 (1996). In such cases, Jerome Groopman argues, patients *must* protect themselves from the "Pygmalian complex" of biased researchers in love with their own inventions. Jerome Groopman, *Patient Protect Thyself,* Wall Street Journal, February 1, 2000, A26.

51. M. Miller, *Phase I Cancer Trials: A Collusion of Misunderstanding,* Hastings Center Report, July 2000, 34. *And see* S. Kaplan & S. Brownlee, *Dying for a Cure,* U.S. News & World Report, October 11, 1999, 34.

52. Greg Sachs, *Opportunities for Promoting Palliative Medicine in Cancer Research,* 16 Clinical Investigation 503 (1998). *See also* Daniel Callahan, *Death and the Research Imperative,* 342 New Eng. J. Med. 654 (2000). Anecdotes dominate the debate. Tom Nesi, for example, writes that of his wife, Susan, that her death from brain cancer was postponed for a few months by a research drug, but at much too high a price in terms of the quality of her (and his) life. The last two months of her life included three surgeries, five hospitalizations, and total paralysis. Tom Nesi, *False Hope in a Bottle,* New York Times, June 5, 2003, A35. In contrast, Steven Walker's wife, Jennifer, obtained a six-month remission of her colon cancer with a research drug, and "the sole side effect was a tolerable skin rash." He believes it was well worth it and that experimentation at the end of life should be encouraged. Steven Walker, *S.O.S. to the FDA,* Wall Street Journal, August 26, 2003, A12.

53. George J. Annas, *The Changing Landscape of Human Experimentation: Nuremberg, Helsinki, and Beyond,* 2 Health Matrix 119 (1992).

54. Annas, *supra* notes 45 and 50.

X

Medical Records

There are billions of visits annually in the United States to doctors' offices, clinics, HMOs (health maintenance organizations), hospitals, and other health care providers, and each visit either generates a new medical record or adds to an existing one. The variety of medical records is kaleidoscopic. In the private physician's office, medical records are generally maintained to document the patient's history, condition, and treatment; to aid in continuity of care; and to provide a record for billing. In the hospital, the Joint Commission on Accreditation of Healthcare Organizations (JCAHO) requires the medical record to contain "sufficient information to identify the patient, support the diagnosis, justify the treatment, document the course results, and promote continuity of care among health care providers."[1] Of course, medical records are also used for billing, monitoring quality of care, education, and research.

It seems reasonable to predict that an individual's medical record will eventually be accessible by both the patient and health care providers via the Internet.[2] Smart cards, which enable individuals to carry all their medical records in a credit-card-size computer-readable form or to grant access to an electronically stored record, are also being tested. The movement to electronic record has been very slow, however, and the cost of hardware and software and the extra time it takes physicians to put information into a computer has stalled its acceptance.

This chapter covers the major legal issues that surround the making, maintenance, storage, and disposal of medical records; patient access to medical records; and the growing use of genetic information and its place in the medical record. Issues of privacy and third-party access to medical records are addressed in the next chapter.

What is included in a patient's record?

Sufficient information should be included in the record to document the diagnosis and course of treatment. A physician's office records are required to conform to "accepted medical practice." Accepted practice is to maintain a record that documents the patient's history, physical findings, treatment, and course of disease. It is important for both patient and provider that complete and accurate records are maintained. If a patient accuses a physician or nurse of malpractice or incompetence, the medical record will usually be the care provider's best defense. This is because the medical record is made contemporaneously with treatment and is thus generally much more reliable than the memory of either the patient or the provider.

Requirements regarding the maintenance and content of health care facility records are usually found in state statutes and regulations that govern physician and health facility licensure. These requirements fall into three groups: (1) those that simply mandate the maintenance of records that are accurate, complete, or adequate; (2) those that set forth broad categories of information that must be included; and (3) those that provide specific requirements for information that must be included. Provisions for the signing and retention of records are often contained in state regulations as well.

Additional requirements concerning the contents of hospital records have been promulgated by the JCAHO. They include the following:

- Identification data
- Medical history, including the chief complaint; details of the present illness; relevant past, social, and family histories (appropriate to the patient's age); and an inventory by body system
- A summary of the patient's psychosocial needs, as appropriate to the patient's age
- A report of relevant physical examinations
- A statement on the conclusions or impressions drawn from the admission history and physical examination
- A statement on the course of action planned for the patient for this episode of care and of its periodic review, as appropriate
- Diagnostic and therapeutic orders
- Evidence of appropriate informed consent

- Clinical observations, including the results of therapy
- Progress notes made by the medical staff and other authorized staff
- Consultation reports
- Reports of operative and other invasive procedures, tests, and their results
- Reports of any diagnostic and therapeutic procedures, such as pathology and clinical laboratory examinations and radiology and nuclear medicine examinations or treatment
- Records of donation and receipt of transplants or implants
- Final diagnosis or diagnoses
- Conclusions at termination of hospitalization
- Clinical resumés and discharge summaries
- Discharge instructions to the patient or family; and
- When performed, results of autopsy.[3]

Is there anything that should not be included in a patient's medical record?

The debate on this question is ongoing and unresolved. On one side are those who argue that *everything* about a patient's condition and background can be relevant to proper diagnosis and treatment, and so there should be no limits on what can be put in the patient records. On the other side are those who believe that far too much sensitive and nonessential information is included in medical records, to the potential detriment of the patient.

Without attempting to resolve this basic dispute, it can be noted that, while not illegal, it is inappropriate to include personal criticisms (for example, this patient is "fat and sloppy" or "shabbily dressed again today") or offhand comments ("I love her perfume") in a patient's record. Such statements have nothing to do with diagnosis or treatment and can unfairly bias the patient's next care provider. In addition, they can lead to concealment of the record from the patient, not for any legitimate reason but simply for fear of embarrassing the person who recorded the inappropriate remarks in the record. Another reason casual comments should not be included is that the medical record may be read by many other people during its lifetime. These casual comments may be used against the patient by schools, employers, insurers, or governmental agencies. Providers are properly counseled to record *facts* about a patient (for example, "speech slurred, eyes bloodshot") rather than conclusions from these observations that may not be true (for example, "patient is an alcoholic").

Who owns a patient's medical records?

The *information* contained in the record can be properly characterized as the patient's property; therefore, the patient should be considered the owner of the medical record. Nonetheless, the owner of the paper on which the medical record is written is sometimes described as the "owner" of the record. Some states even have statutes that specify that health care facilities own the medical records in their custody. But this view puts the value of the paper over the value of the information on it and makes no sense. This view also has no applicability to electronic records, since all that exists is the information itself. The better rule is that physicians, HMOs, and medical facilities are the *custodians* of medical records, and the patient is the owner of the medical record, which others keep in their custody primarily for the patient's benefit.

What rights does the custodian of a medical record have?

Custody of the medical record is governed by many statutes (such as licensing statutes) and contracts (such as health insurance contracts), as well as by the interests of the patient in the contents of the medical record. Health care providers with custody of medical records have strong interests in them, but the patient has even stronger interests. The patient's interests are strong enough to give the patient a legal and ethical right of access to the information contained in the records, a right to a complete copy of the medical records themselves, a right to demand corrections of false information in the record, and (as discussed in the next chapter) a right to insist that the record not be shared with anyone else not involved in the patient's care or payment for care.

Why might a patient want to read the medical record?

The primary reason a patient might want to read the medical record is to better understand his or her medical condition and the treatment options available and to be better able to cooperate with the treatment chosen. Other reasons include to check the accuracy of family and personal histories, to be better informed when asked to consent to diagnostic and therapeutic procedures, to better understand the role the physician is taking in the treatment, and to appreciate more fully the state of one's health to be better able to prevent a disease or a recurrence of a disease. The medical record can be a powerful means of health education that can benefit outpatients as well as patients in the hospital and after discharge.

If you are moving out of town, out of the country, or going on a long trip, you may have a good reason to take along a copy of your medical record, or at least the discharge summary of your most recent hospital visit. There are many parts of the record (which could cover hundreds of pages), such as laboratory reports, in which you may have little or no interest. When having copies of your paper medical records made, therefore, you should try to review the entire record first and order copies only of those pages you want or need. This is not a problem with electronic records, of course, and if properly encrypted to prevent interception, they can be e-mailed to you.

Will a patient be able to understand the medical record without the help of a physician?

If the patient can decipher the handwriting in the paper record (not a problem with electronic records), knows the meaning of the abbreviations used, and has a good medical dictionary, the patient can get some important information out of the record.

As for reading the handwriting, even a physician may not be able to help. It is common practice among physicians and epidemiologists who do research with medical records to hire someone to interpret and type them before the research study is conducted. The meaning of the abbreviations used varies somewhat from hospital to hospital, and a staff member from the relevant hospital can explain what the various abbreviations mean. Abbreviations are not always what they seem. For example, SOB means shortness of breath, not son of a bitch. Even without help, you should be able to check the accuracy of the history you related, the diagnosis, test results, treatment recommended, and the drugs prescribed. Detailed record analysis, however, requires consultation with an experienced health care provider.

Do patients have the legal right to see and copy their medical records?

Yes. While some logistics problems may be encountered in exercising this right, no one seriously doubts any longer that this is a basic right of patients. The majority of states grant patients a *legal* right to see and copy their medical records by statute, regulation, or judicial decision.[4] In most other states, patients have a probable legal right to access without bringing suit. In *all* states, patients *should* routinely be provided access regardless of the law because the information in the medical record is about them; the patient has the strongest personal interest in the information; and the patient may need the information to decide on treatment, to determine whether or not to change physicians, and to discern how to plan for their future. Experts continue to decry the patchwork of state medical record statutes and to strongly recommend uniform federal legislation that both protects privacy and guarantees patient access to "their own medical records."[5] In 2003, the federal government promulgated new regulations on medical records privacy that apply to virtually all patients in the United States. The regulations include a right to access to all electronic and paper medical records and a right to request access to psychotherapy records and cover all hospitals and health plans, and any physician who does any business electronically. The new privacy regulations, also known as the HIPAA regulations, are discussed in detail in the next chapter.[6]

The new federal privacy rule sets a floor, not a ceiling, and individual states can grant patients more rights to access. Nonetheless, the new rule is helpful because state laws are so variable. For example, in some states, the statute dealing with medical records access applies only after discharge from the hospital. Some state statutes exclude access to laboratory reports, X-rays, prescriptions, and other technical information used in assessing the patient's health condition. A few state statutes require the patient to show "good cause" before the patient is permitted to read the record, but what is meant by this term is not specified in the statute. Other states have more limited statutes that either provide for access under specified circumstances or require the patient to obtain access through an attorney, physician, or relative.

State medical-licensing boards also recognize the importance of patients having access to their medical records.[7] On the federal level (for example, Veteran's Administration facilities), the Privacy Act of 1974 requires that patients be provided with direct access in most circumstances. The Privacy Protection Study Commission, established by that act, recommended, "Upon request, an individual who is the subject of a medical record maintained by a medical care provider, or another responsible person designated by that individual, be allowed access to that medical record including an opportunity to see and copy it."[8] Ninety-eight percent of Americans believe they have or should have a legal right to see their medical records.[9]

When can a physician or health care facility refuse to allow a patient access to the medical record?

The patient has a legal right to the record, and there is ultimately nothing that custodians of the medical record may legally do to prevent the patient's access. Inherent in the law, however, is the concept of reasonableness. It may be reasonable for a health care facility to suggest that the patient's physician be present while the patient inspects the record. On the other hand, it is unreasonable to require this in most circumstances. A facility or physician may also not make it financially impossible for the patient to exercise the right by imposing an exorbitant charge for copying.

Some of the statutes provide, and common sense dictates, that if the physician has good reason to believe that access to the record will be harmful to the patient, direct access by the patient may be denied. But there is no evidence to support the proposition that access to the medical record harms patients. The physician must be reasonable in this belief and should be able to document his or her belief on the basis of objective evidence. The patient should also be given the opportunity to challenge this decision and must have the right to designate another adult to receive the information on the patient's behalf.[10]

Why is it that some HMOs, health care facilities, and doctors do not want patients to see medical records?

Information can be power, and some doctors and health plans simply do not want to share decision-making power with patients. Others view patients as children and complain that patients will misunderstand the information or get upset by it. One of my favorite examples of physician distaste for patients who insist on reading their medical records while in the hospital is a study on "record reading" by four psychiatrists at a major Boston teaching hospital. The psychiatrists interviewed the 11 out of 2,500 consecutive patients at the hospital who, in a one-year period, asked to see their medical records.[11]

The authors concluded that patients who ask to see their medical records have a variety of personality defects, usually manifesting themselves in a mistrust of, and hostility toward, the hospital staff. But to locate the source of mistrust in the patient's personality, rather than in the stress of illness and hospitalization, is to forget, as psychiatrist Donald Lipsitt perceptively notes, that "doctor-patient relationship cannot be understood simply in terms of the patient's side of the equation."[12] The authors of this study of patients who ask to see their medical records fell into what Robert Burt of Yale Law School has referred to as "the conceptual trap of attempting to transform two-party relationships, in which mutual self-delineations are inherently confused and intertwined, by conceptually obliterating one party."[13] Thus, it would seem that the eleven patients at the Boston hospital who asked to read their charts "to confirm the belief that the staff harbored negative personal attitudes toward them" were correct in their belief; the psychiatrists had in fact labeled them "of the hysterical type with demanding, histrionic behavior and emotional over-involvement with the staff."

The authors of the Boston study also seem to have been unaware of the wide variety of settings in which patients have benefited from routine record access (and incorrectly asserted that there were no strikingly beneficial effects in the two studies they did cite). In one of these previous studies, for example, two patients expressed their unfounded fear that they had cancer only after their records were reviewed with them, and one pregnant patient noted an incorrect Rh typing that permitted Rho-Gam to be administered at the time of delivery.[14] In the other study, half of the patients made at least one factual correction in their records.[15]

In short, the Boston study seems to have been done primarily to try to prove that the right of access to medical records is unimportant, since it is only exercised by "mentally disturbed" people who are not improved by reading their charts. The study failed to prove this. Even if it had succeeded, we should still be unwilling to deprive patients of their right to have access to their medical records. If we believe in individual freedom and self-determination, we must give all citizens the right to make their own decisions and to have access to the same information that is available to those making decisions about them. Shared decision making is impossible without shared information.

Might access to medical records be harmful to patients?

No. The primary problems patients have with medical records involve interpreting medical abbreviations, vocabulary, and physicians' handwriting. Electronic medical records will solve the handwriting problem. In places where access has been available for years, no adverse physical or mental reactions have been reported.

In Massachusetts, for example, patient access has been mandated by statute since 1946 without a single reported adverse incident. And the Privacy Protection Study Commission, hearing from all federal agencies that had adopted access policies under the Privacy Act of 1974, found that "not one witness was able to identify an instance where access to records has had an untoward effect on a patient's medical condition."[16] Likewise, a two-year study of routine record sharing with patients at the outpatient department of Boston's Beth Israel Hospital concluded that physicians' fears about liberal patient access to records were unwarranted, and that the open access policy made the relationship between patients and professionals "more collaborative."[17]

Some physicians have suggested giving all patients copies of their records as soon as the records are made. The advantages of this system include the following:

- Increased patient information and education
- Continuity of records as patients move or change physicians
- An added criterion on which patients may base selection of physicians
- Improvement in the doctor-patient relationship by making it more open
- An added way for physicians to monitor quality of care
- Increased responsiveness to consumer needs[18]

The burden of proof is now squarely on those who would deny patients access to their records to demonstrate something other than paternalistic and self-serving reasons for this policy. And as medical records move from paper to electronic form, patients should have real-time access to their electronic medical records, accessible via computer.

Might disclosure of medical records be harmful to the physician?

This possibility is considered likely by some medical commentators, but a general policy of open access creates far fewer potential legal problems than a general policy of denying patients access to their records. Physician-commentator Michael J. Halberstam unequivocally advised against patient access, arguing, "the chart is none of the patient's business."

He further advised concealing mistakes from patients (at least those that do not seem to have caused any serious damage) and suggested that the medical record is a "time bomb lying in wait to give physicians trouble two or three years in the future."[19]

This thankfully outdated sentiment only reinforces the public's perceptions that health care providers are trying to hide something from them. Policies based on these sentiments and the secrecy it breeds lead to cynicism about the potential for peer review and increase the likelihood that a lawsuit will be filed primarily for the purposes of gaining access to medical records.

There is also evidence that a policy of open records changes the content of the records themselves. Such changes are usually improvements and include the deletion of personal comments, more detailed documentation of informed consent, and better handwriting. Patients should encourage their care providers to work with them in a partnership characterized by openness and trust, not paranoia and secrecy.

How can a patient have mistakes in the medical record corrected?

A patient should speak to the person who wrote the incorrect entry and ask that it be corrected. One of the legal lessons most health professionals have learned is to *never alter a medical record.* This is excellent advice, since a jury will often consider an altered medical record as the equivalent of admitting negligence. Nevertheless, like almost every rule, this one has some obvious exceptions: the most obvious exception is when the information in the record is incorrect. The federal privacy rules also specifically grant individuals the right to request that their medical record be amended.[20]

There have been many suggestions concerning record alteration. Perhaps the most widely recommended is to cross out the incorrect information in such a way that it is still legible, write in the correct information, and add a dated and signed note that explains why the information was changed (for example, "changed because it was later discovered to be inaccurate"). This procedure maintains the integrity of the medical record and permits the correction of false data. Electronic records can be corrected directly, so that only the accurate information appears in the record, while a record of the original information and the date and reason for the change is maintained in a separate file.[21] Each physician and health facility should have a procedure for making corrections in medical records. In the event that you ask that your medical record be corrected and your health care provider determines that no correction is warranted, you should at least be permitted to have your version of the facts added to the record.

How long will a doctor, health care facility, or HMO retain a copy of a patient's medical record?

This will vary from facility to facility and doctor to doctor, although the trend is to retain medical records forever, and electronic records will likely be kept in perpetuity. Almost all states have statutes or regulations that provide a specific minimum length of time for the retention of hospital records. These vary from two years to thirty years.

The following recommendations have been made to health care providers regarding retention of medical records:

1. In the interests of medical science and good patient care, medical records should be retained for as long as possible.

2. At a minimum, records should be retained:

    a. if the patient is a competent adult—for the longest statute of limitations which may apply, usually six years

    b. if the patient is an incompetent adult, or becomes incompetent before six years have expired—until the patient recovers plus the remaining statutory time, or another time prescribed by statute for this specific circumstance

    c. if the patient is a minor—until the patient reaches the age of majority plus the statutory period for malpractice actions, or another period specified by statute for this circumstance.

3. If the physician finds that her facilities preclude the retention of records for any longer than the recommended minimum periods, it is recommended that she notify the patient that his records will no longer be retained, and give the patient or the patient's designee the copy of the record upon payment of a reasonable fee for postage and handling.

4. Microfilm reproductions are as fully admissible in most courts as the original. However, it is advisable to retain the original records for the recommended minimum periods, since the original is more convenient to read and handle, and presence of the original minimizes the possibility of assertions that it has been altered or is incomplete.[22]

Retirement or death of a physician does not alter the confidential nature of medical records, nor does it relieve the estate of the physician of any professional liability for which the physician would otherwise be accountable. Thus, the physician or the physician's estate must continue to safeguard the confidentiality of medical records. The records, as long as they exist, are confidential, and the patient continues to have an interest in the information contained therein. Your medical records cannot, for example, be sold without your permission.[23]

What should a patient do if denied access to the medical record?

Complain. There is no valid, ethical, or legal reason to deny a competent patient access to the medical record. If you are in the hospital, you can (and should) refuse to consent to further treatment or testing until you are permitted to review your medical record. In addition, you should lodge complaints with the hospital's patient representative, hospital administrator, risk manager, ethics compliance officer, and/or the institution's ethics committee. It is almost certain that this will result in access, since denial is an old-fashioned idea that few U.S. physicians and administrators consider reasonable medical practice.

In extreme cases, the attending physician may believe that access will be harmful to your health and may not want to take personal responsibility for this potential harm. Although this explanation seems bizarre, you should be prepared to compromise by permitting the physician to give a complete copy of the record to your advocate or to another individual you designate (a friend or relative). That person can take the "responsibility" for providing you with the copy. You should also have routine access to the medical records of your children if you are consenting to their medical treatment. Guardians should also have routine access to the medical records of their wards.

Access may be more difficult to obtain after discharge from the hospital, however, for the simple reason that it is so easy for a medical records librarian to stonewall requests. Nonetheless, going directly to the office of the hospital administrator and demanding a copy of the record is usually effective. If this does not work, the help of the state attorney general, Office of Consumer Affairs, or Department of Health should be sought. You can also contact the Office of Civil Rights of the U.S. Department of Health and Human Services. If none of these public agencies will help, then the services of an attorney may have to be enlisted to gain access to the medical records. Usually, all that will be required is your signature on a form releasing the records and payment of a reasonable fee for copying them.

Remember: by requesting medical records, you not only help educate yourself about your medical condition but also help all other people who request their own medical records in the future. The more people make this request, the more routine and ordinary it becomes, and the less likely health care providers will view "record-seeking behavior" as aberrant or strange.

Do we need a "unique health identifier" for every American to make our medical records more accessible?

No. Over the past thirty years there have been a number of proposals to use the social security number as a health care identifier. The most recent proposal was by the secretary of Health and Human Services in 1998. The arguments in favor of a unique identifier for individuals are primarily that it would enhance administrative simplification and thus (perhaps) reduce administrative costs, especially for insurance companies, managed care companies, and less so for physician offices and pharmacists. At the present time, these entities use a variety of identifiers (e.g., names, names and addresses, social security numbers, and insurance numbers). Use of a single identifier would make it easier to link data with an individual and could thus facilitate ordering tests and posting results, diagnoses, and observations on the correct patient's chart. It could also help link medical records to police accident records, and workplace exposures to toxic chemicals to medical records. Each of these links could provide more efficient access to information for public health and clinical research.

The primary argument against such an identifier is that it would make it easier to link the patient's medical records with other databases, such as social security information, driving records, tax records, banking records, credit records, employment information, and other databases that contain a person's social security number. In addition, the Social Security Administration has consistently taken the position that the social security number should not become a personal identifier, and many people are against requiring Americans to have a number that uniquely identifies them and is displayed on a national identity card.[24]

It seems unlikely that the social security number will be used as a national identifier for medical records. Some other number will be developed, or records will be linked by using a set of identifiers, such as name, sex, birth date, and social security number, and mother's maiden name. Of course, it is critical that health information be placed in the proper patient's record, and that the patient's record (not someone else's) be consulted when past records are important to the patient's current care. A unique identifier should help here. Nonetheless, a unique identifier is not necessary for accurate linkage of past records or identifying them, and patients who are worried about the privacy of their medical records should not support any unique identification number that makes it easier for those who want to collect information about them.

How will the new genetics affect medical records?

It is too soon to tell for sure, since genetics has so far had much more impact on the way medicine is discussed than on how it is practiced. Nonetheless, you should know something about genetic information and how it might affect your medical care. Because of the tremendous publicity it received, most Americans have likely at least heard of the Human Genome Project, an effort to map and sequence the three billion letters that make up the genetic code of a human. In announcing that this project had (almost) been completed in the summer of 2000, President Bill Clinton said, hyperbolically,

Today we are learning the language in which God created life. We are gaining ever more awe for the complexity, the beauty, the wonder of God's most divine and sacred gift. With this profound new knowledge, humankind is on the verge of gaining immense, new power to heal. Genome science will have a real impact on all our lives—and even more on the lives of our children. It will revolutionize the diagnosis, prevention, and treatment of most, if not all, human diseases.[25]

This rosy future is unlikely.[26] Nonetheless, genetic knowledge will have an impact on all of us in many ways, including requests that we submit to various genetic tests and give permission to test our children. In the prenatal arena, there will also be hundreds, if not thousands, of new screening tests that can be performed on fetuses. The results of genetic tests may determine our risk for future illnesses, our susceptibility to a particular toxin, or our likely response to a particular drug. And DNA sequence results are likely to be included in our medical records unless we develop special rules to protect this information.

Can a person's DNA be seen as a "medical record"?

Yes. DNA can be usefully analogized to a medical record of a unique kind. DNA itself (which resides in every cell in our body that has a nucleus, analogous to the way information can be stored in a computer disk) may be considered unique and significantly more personal and private than the information currently in our medical records. A medical record itself can be analogized in privacy terms to a diary, but a DNA molecule (as distinguished from information already derived and recorded from a DNA sample) is much more sensitive. It is in a real sense a "future diary" (although a probabilistic one), and it is written in a code that we have not yet cracked.[27] But the code is being broken piece by piece, such that holders of a sample of an individual's DNA will be able to learn more and more about that individual and his or her family in the future as the code is broken. By possessing your blood sample or other source of DNA, and with the ability to decode it, an individual would have access to your probabilistic medical "future diary."[28]

Of course, DNA-based predictions will not be precise, because the expression of genetic characteristics will vary radically among individuals, from never expressed to expressed in an extreme manner, and individuals with the same genetic expression will respond differently to environmental factors. Nonetheless, this is information individuals, physicians, insurance companies, employers, and others will want and on which they will base at least some decisions affecting you. Health insurance companies, for example, may wish to deny coverage to individual applicants with genetic predispositions to serious, potentially expensive, diseases. I don't believe in genetic determinism; but I do believe genetic information can be misused and used against you, and that is a good reason why you should be able to control its creation and dissemination.

Does DNA technology create new privacy issues?

Yes. It seems reasonable to conclude that the mere existence of the technology to decode DNA will lead us to radically alter our view of informational privacy. Medical researchers, epidemiologists, and biotech companies will want access to the genetic information stored in large DNA databanks to search for genetic connections to disease. One can even envision law enforcement or child protection agencies looking for children with genetic conditions to make sure their parents are providing them with proper medical care or prevention strategies. Although it seems farfetched today, assuming that commonly possessed genes that predispose a person to skin cancer are discovered in the future and that such cancer is preventable if one stays out of the sun, one could envision searching DNA databases to identify individuals who carry these genes and then counseling them about their risks. If this is seen as reasonable, the next step could be to identify children at risk and require that their parents protect them from this genetic hazard by keeping them out of the sun and away from the beach. Similar scenarios can be constructed for virtually all common diseases that have genetic predispositions. Although one can counter that similar predictive arguments can be made for high blood pressure and high cholesterol, the identification of a genetic link will make prediction seem more scientific and prevention seem more urgent.

In the past, we have put special emphasis on information that is potentially embarrassing and sensitive (such as sexually transmitted diseases) and on information that is uniquely personal (such as a photograph of one's face). Genetic information is both potentially embarrassing and uniquely personal. The existence of such decodable information could either impel us to take privacy much more seriously in the genetic realm than we have in the medical and criminal realms or lead us to give up on maintaining personal privacy altogether. This latter response seems defeatist and unlikely, although one leading medical geneticist has already suggested that "we must prepare for others to know."[29] Is this true, or can genetic privacy be protected? The issue of genetic privacy revolves around choice in discovering and exposing personal genetic information, as well as choice in determining whether and how to treat "genetic predispositions."

The privacy issues involved in the new genetics can be illustrated by considering the genes that code for early onset Alzheimer's disease. People who carry these genes may be not only very likely to develop Alzheimer's disease but also may begin to experience symptoms in their forties. There is currently no way to prevent the disease and no effective treatment for the disease. Of course, the hope is that once the genes responsible for creating the conditions that permit or encourage Alzheimer's disease are better identified, it will be easier to find a treatment and a prevention strategy.

We would all welcome these developments. But in the meantime, of what use is the knowledge that one carries an early onset Alzheimer's gene? And even if some individuals want to know if they have such a gene, should they not have the right to keep this information from their employers, their coworkers, and others? The same questions can be asked for any gene that predisposes an individual to a disease for which there is no prevention and no cure.

What can be done to protect genetic privacy?

One way to protect genetic privacy is to codify rules for gene banks and computerized records based on genetic analysis, but this is too narrow. Although rules for gene banks are needed, it is very difficult to define what a gene bank is (and even if a bank is the right metaphor), and regulation at this level alone permits genetic analysis to be done and information to be disclosed, in circumstances that do not involve the storage of DNA samples. The law has already begun to take action on a number of levels. Regulatory approaches that have been adopted to date include an Equal Employment Opportunity Commission guideline on genetic discrimination, and many states have enacted statutes that seek to limit the use of genetic information.[30]

For the short-term, a state-by-state approach is likely. But genetic information cannot be confined by state borders, and I think we will need federal legislation to effectively protect genetic privacy. Leonard Glantz, Winnie Roche, and I believe that we not only need uniform rules for the collection, analysis, and storage of DNA samples but also that we need rules for storing and disclosing information derived from DNA samples, and that these rules must cover adults, children, incompetent persons, dead bodies, fetuses, and embryos. To codify rules for genetic privacy and make them uniform throughout the United States, we have drafted a proposed federal law, The Genetic Privacy Act.[31] This act protects "private genetic information," defined as "any information about an identifiable individual that is derived from the presence, absence, alteration, or mutation of a gene or genes, or the presence or absence of a specific DNA marker or markers, and which has been obtained: 1. from an analysis of the individual's DNA; or 2. from an analysis of the DNA of a person to whom the individual is related."

The Genetic Privacy Act provides that individuals are the owners of their own DNA and prohibits other individuals from analyzing DNA samples unless they have verified that written authorization for the analysis has been given by the individual or the individual's representative.

The individual has the right to

- Determine who may collect and analyze DNA
- Determine the purposes for which a DNA sample can be analyzed
- Know what information can reasonably be expected to be derived from the genetic analysis
- Order the destruction of DNA samples
- Delegate authority to another individual to order the destruction of the DNA sample after death
- Refuse to permit the use of the DNA sample for research or commercial activities
- Inspect and obtain copies of records containing information derived from genetic analysis of the DNA sample

A written summary of these principles must be supplied to the individual by the person who collects the DNA sample. The Genetic Privacy Act requires that the person who holds private genetic information in the ordinary course of business keep such information confidential and prohibits the disclosure of private genetic information unless the individual has authorized the disclosure in writing or the disclosure is limited to access by specified researchers.[32]

The issue of whether DNA is uniquely private or should be considered as simply one more piece of medical information can be viewed from another perspective: how well do we protect the privacy of medical information generally? That is the subject of the next chapter.

TIPS FOR ADVOCATES

- **The patient has a legal right to access to the medical record.**

Access may be temporarily blocked or discouraged, but if you insist on access, you will get it.

- In extreme cases, in which access to medical records is denied, refuse further treatment until you are provided with access and the information you need to make an informed decision about treatment.

• **The patient has a legal right to have inaccurate information in the medical record corrected.**

• **Make sure inaccurate information in the medical record is corrected.** It is the obligation of the health care providers to maintain accurate information, and they are obligated to correct false information when the true facts are brought to their attention.

• **There is no pressing need for all patients to be issued a "unique health identifier."**

• The patient's blood sample (and any cells with a nucleus) contain a medical record in the form of DNA sequences. **A DNA sample can be seen as a patient's "future diary" (although it is coded and probabilistic) and should not be decoded or read without the patient's authorization.**

• **There is a pressing need for federal legislation to protect genetic privacy.**

NOTES

1. Joint Commission on Accreditation of Healthcare Organizations, 2003 Hospital Accreditation Standards, Chicago: JCAHO, 2003, 259.

2. Laura Landro, *Tools That Can Help You Keep Your Own Accurate Medical Files,* Wall Street Journal, May 26, 2000, B1; Laura Landro, *Deal with Our Doctors,* Wall Street Journal, November 13, 2000, R23.

3. Joint Commission, *supra* note 1, at 259–60.

4. *See* Joy Pritts et al., The State of Health Privacy: An Uneven Terrain (A Comprehensive Survey of State Health Privacy Statutes), New York: Practicing Law Institute, 1999. Information on state law can be obtained from the state attorney general's office.

5. *See, e.g., The New Federal Health Privacy Regulations: How Will States Take the Lead?* 29 J. Law, Med. & Ethics 395 (2001). *And see Uneven State Medical-Record Laws Offer Pitfalls for Health Plans,* BNA Health Law Reporter, November 11, 1999, 1787.

6. Office of Civil Rights, Dept. Health and Human Services, Standards for Privacy,

Final Rule, 67 Fed. Reg. 53182 (2002), as required by the Health Insurance and Portability Act of 1996 (HIPAA). Information on the regulations can be obtained at a Web site, www.hhs.gov/ocr. There are three very narrow grounds on which physicians can refuse to make the entire medical record available to the patient under the HIPAA regulations. The patient has the right to have a refusal reviewed by another licensed health care professional (other than anyone who participated in the decision to deny access) designated by the refusing entity, and the entity must provide access to the medical record if the reviewer determines that it should do so. Access may be refused if a "licensed health care professional has determined, in the exercise of professional judgment, that the access requested is reasonably likely to endanger the life or physical safety of the individual or another person"; if "the protected health information makes reference to another person [and] the access requested is reasonably likely to cause substantial harm to such person"; or if "the request for access is made by the individual's personal representative [and access by that person] is reasonably likely to cause substantial harm to the individual or another person."

A reasonable, cost-based fee can be charged for copying, including the labor costs of copying, and postage, if applicable. Persons may also request amendments to their medical records. Physicians can require requests for amendments to be in writing and to state the reason for the requested amendment. Amendment can be denied if the person or entity to whom the request is made did not create the information or if the information is deemed to be accurate and complete. When an amendment is made, at the minimum, the amendment must be appended or linked to the record it is amending, and reasonable efforts must be made to inform others who have been provided with the original information about the amendment. If amendment is denied, the person has the right to have a statement of disagreement (to which the entity may respond as well) appended to the disputed medical record.

A person also has the right to an accounting of disclosures of protected health information made over the previous six years. There are, however, numerous exceptions to this accounting requirement, including disclosures for use in treatment, payment, and health care operations; disclosures authorized by the person or required by law; use in a facility directory or for national security or intelligence purposes; or disclosures that occurred before the compliance date for the new regulations. The accounting must include the date of disclosure, the name and address of the person or entity who received the information, and a brief description of the information disclosed and the purpose for which it was disclosed. *See* George Annas, *HIPAA Regulations: A New Era of Medical Record Privacy?* 348 New Eng. J. Med. 1486 (2003).

7. *E.g.,* the Massachusetts regulation (243 CMR 2.06 [13]), reads in part:

A licensee shall provide a patient or, upon a patient's request, another licensee or another specifically authorized person, with the following:

   i. A summary, which includes all relevant data of that portion of the patient's medical record which is in the licensee's possession, or a copy of that portion of the patient's entire medical record which is in the licensee's possession. It is within the licensee's discretion to determine whether to make available a summary or a copy of the entire medical record.

  ii. A copy of any previously completed report required for third party reimbursement.

8. Privacy Protection Study Commission, Personal Privacy in an Information Society, Washington, D.C.: Government Printing Office, 1977, 298. This recommendation is significantly broader than one made more than fifteen years ago by HHS's Medical Malpractice Commission. It recommended simply that "states enact legislation enabling patients to obtain access to the information contained in their medical records through their legal representatives, public or private, without having to file a suit." *Secretary's Report on Medical Malpractice* (HEW, DHEW Pub. No. OS 73–88, 1973), 77.

9. Equifax-Harris Survey, summarized in Privacy & American Business, January 1996, 4.

10. *E.g.,* 243 CMR 2.06 (13) (Massachusetts Board of Medicine Regulation).

11. J. H. Altman et al., *Patients Read Their Hospital Charts,* 302 New Eng. J. Med. 169 (1980).

12. Donald Lipsitt, *The Patient and the Record,* 302 New Eng. J. Med. 167 (1980). *And see* letters to the editor, 302 New Eng. J. Med. 1483 (1980); Loren Roth et al., *Patient Access to Records: Tonic or Toxin?* 137 Am. J. Psychiatry 592 (1980); V. Coleman, *Why Patients Should Keep Their Own Records,* 10 J. Med. Ethics 27 (1984); Gunther Eysenbach, *Consumer Health Informatics,* 320 Brit. Med. J. 1713 (2000); and Laura Landro, *Family Doctors Lead the Pack, Ready to Embrace E-Records,* Wall Street Journal, January 16, 2003, D4.

13. Robert Burt, Taking Care of Strangers: The Rule of Law in Doctor-Patient Relations, New York: Free Press, 1979, 113.

14. A. Golodetz, et al., *The Right to Know: Giving the Patient His Medical Record,* 57 Arch. Phys. Med. Rehab. 78 (1976).

15. D. P. Stevens et al., *What Happens When Hospitalized Patients See Their Own Records,* 86 Annals Internal Med. 474 (1977). *And see* E. J. Stein et al., *Patient Access to Medical Records on a Psychiatric Inpatient Unit,* 136 Am. J. Psychiatry 3 (1979); and M. W. Gill & D. L. Scott, *Can Patients Benefit from Reading Copies of Their Doctor's Letters about Them?* 293 Brit. Med. J. 1278 (1986).

16. Privacy Protection Study, *supra* note 8, at 297.

17. Richard Knox, *Medical Board Told Patients Should Get Access to Records,* Boston Globe, March 2, 1978, 15.

18. B. N. Shenkin & D. C. Warner, *Giving the Patient His Medical Record: A Proposal to Improve the System,* 289 New Eng. J. Med. 688 (1973). *See also* letters to the editor, 290 New Eng. J. Med. 287 (1974).

19. Michael Halberstam, *The Patient's Chart Is None of the Patient's Business,* Modern Medicine, November 1, 1976, 85.

20. 45 CFR 164.526 (December 28, 2000).

21. D. W. Chadwick et al., *Using the Internet to Access Confidential Patient Records: A Case Study,* 321 Brit. Med. J. 612 (2000). *See also* Rhonda Rundle, *Big HMO Plans to Put Medical Records Online,* Wall Street Journal, February 4, 2003, D4.

22. George J. Annas, Leonard H. Glantz & Barbara F. Katz, The Rights of Doctors, Nurses and Allied Health Professionals, Cambridge: Ballinger, 1981, 163–64.

23. *Id.*

24. *See Unique Health Identifier for Individuals: A White Paper* (available at http:// NCVHS.HHS.GOV/noiwpl/htm); *see also* Sheryl Gay Stolberg, *Health Identifier for All*

Americans Runs into Hurdles, New York Times, July 20, 1998, 1, and Judy Foreman, *Your Health History: Up for Grabs?* Boston Globe, July 20, 1998, C1.

25. Remarks of the President on Completion of the First Survey of the Human Genome Project, Transcript, 36 ASAP 1499 (June 26, 2000). *See also White House Remarks on Decoding the Genome,* New York Times, June 27, 2000, F8.

26. Neil Holtzman & Theresa Marteau, *Will Genetics Revolutionize Medicine?* 343 New Eng. J. Med. 141 (2000). *But see* Francis S. Collins et al., *A Vision for the Future of Genomics Research: A Blueprint for the Genomic Era,* 422 Nature 835 (2003).

27. George J. Annas, *Privacy Rules for DNA Databanks: Protecting Coded "Future Diaries,"* 270 JAMA 2346 (1993).

28. *See* Patricia A. Roche & George J. Annas, *Protecting Genetic Privacy,* 2 Nature Rev. Genetics 392 (2001).

29. Thomas Caskey, *Molecular Medicine: A Spinoff From the Helix,* 270 JAMA 1986 (1993).

30. George J. Annas, *The Limits of State Law to Protect Genetic Information,* 345 New Eng. J. Med. 385 (2001). *See also* Richard S. Fedder, *Legal Perspectives on Genetic Privacy and Disclosure of an Individual's Genetic Profile,* 21 J. Legal Med. 557 (2000).

31. George J. Annas, Leonard Glantz & Patricia Roche, The Genetic Privacy Act and Commentary, Boston: Boston U. School of Public Health, 1995 (available at http:// www.busph.bu.edu/Depts/HealthLaw/). *And see generally* Lori Andrews, Future Perfect: Confronting Decisions about Genetics, New York: Columbia U. Press, 2001.

32. The Genetic Privacy Act deals explicitly with three areas that are likely to breed the most controversy, and consequently the most litigation: the genetic testing of children, research using identifiable, stored DNA samples, and informing relatives of their increased risk of genetic disease based on the diagnosis of a genetically related person. Specifically, the GPA protects the privacy of children by not permitting the genetic analysis of a child under the age of sixteen unless

(1) there is an effective intervention that will prevent or delay the onset or ameliorate the severity of the disease, and

(2) the intervention must be initiated before the age of 16 to be effective, and

(3) the [minor's parent or guardian] . . . has received the disclosures required and signed the authorization. . . . Sec. 141(a).

Minors aged sixteen or seventeen must themselves consent to any analysis of their DNA and must be "accompanied by a parent or other adult family member" when they are counseled regarding the DNA analysis and its possible consequences. Research on identifiable DNA samples stored in a genetic databank or gene bank (often no more than a collection of DNA samples in a clinic) may not be conducted without specific authorization of the person if the sample can be traced back to that individual. If the sample has been stripped of all identifiers such that it is impossible to link the sample to the person, however, research may be conducted on the sample without specific authorization.

As to the issue of the geneticist's "duty to protect" other family members by informing them of a condition discovered in a patient, the Genetic Privacy Act opts for protecting privacy by prohibiting disclosures to others.

XI

Privacy and Confidentiality

The explosive growth of the Internet and its increasing use for marketing has sparked a renewed interest in privacy in the United States and around the world. Internet services have begun to post their privacy policies on their Web sites and often give users the chance to "opt out" of having their personal information collected and distributed by the Internet site visited. Nonetheless, because few Internet users have the time or inclination to read these policies, and even fewer exercise any real choice in deciding how their personal information can be used, especially for marketing purposes, many privacy advocates have called upon Congress to require explicit consent or authorization from individuals before companies can collect and share their personal information with others.

That there are no real protections for personal information on the Internet is not surprising, since this technology is relatively new.[1] But what is surprising to most people is how little overall protection there is of individual privacy in other large systems that collect and store personal records, such as credit, insurance, education, and criminal records. In all of these record-keeping systems, the privacy issue includes defining what records can be collected and stored, who has access to the records, and how the subject of the records can see, correct, and restrict access to them.

The vast majority of medical records continue to be handwritten on paper rather than typed into computers. Someday, it is likely that all medical records will be created and stored electronically, but this will require the training of all physicians and is unlikely to happen at least until computers can accurately record speech.[2] The Clinton Health Security Act proposed extensive federal rules regarding the collection and use of medical data, and although the plan itself died an ignominious death, many of its medical data provisions were revived in the 1996 Health Insurance

246

Portability and Accountability Act (HIPAA). In 2000, the secretary of Health and Human Services, Donna Shalala, issued final federal medical record privacy regulations under HIPAA that, in modified form, took effect April 2003.[3]

The new federal regulations are long and complex. Only some sections will be discussed in this chapter. In general, the regulations attempt to give patients some control over their medical records—electronic, paper, and oral—by requiring that patients be given a notice of their privacy rights, access to their own medical records, and the ability to correct mistakes in the records. Patients must be given a notice explaining that their medical records will be used by individuals directly involved in their medical treatment, payment of their bills, and health care operations. Most other uses require specific authorization. There are special protections for psychotherapy notes, but this is the only type of sensitive medical information that has its own unique rules. The rules provide boundaries on the use of medical records to ensure that they are not used for nonmedical purposes, and that when they are properly disclosed, only the minimum amount of information necessary is disclosed. The rules are national minimums: states remain free to enforce and adopt more protective privacy rules. Health care providers are required to adopt new privacy procedures and security procedures, to designate a privacy officer, and to establish grievance processes so patients can make inquiries and complaints. There is no right to bring a lawsuit for violation of the rules, but patients can complain to HHS's Office of Civil Rights.[4]

The closely related issue of medical confidentiality has been more discussed than litigated, and only a few dozen cases have reached the appellate court level. Nonetheless, the law is relatively clear on what constitutes a breach of confidentiality and what remedies a patient has when his or her medical records are improperly disclosed. This chapter continues the discussion of medical records begun in the previous chapter, focusing on the legal concepts of privacy and confidentiality, the exceptions to these doctrines, and the considerations that should go into a decision to release confidential medical information to anyone other than the patient.

What is meant by the terms *confidentiality, privacy,* and *privilege?*

Health law professor Frances Miller draws a circle on the blackboard to show the difference between privacy and confidentiality to her law school class. As she describes it, confidentiality involves relationships "inside the circle," the necessary sharing of personal information with people involved in your medical care, including your physician, nurse, and other care providers, all of whom have a duty to maintain confidentiality based on their relationship to you. Privacy, on the other hand, involves individuals "outside the circle," who are not directly involved in your care but who may want access to the private information divulged in your medical treatment to use for another purpose. These outsiders have no medical relationship with the patient.

Almost all of the law dealing with access to medical information by persons other than the patient can be categorized under the headings of confidentiality, privilege, and privacy. As commonly used, to tell someone something in confidence means that the person will not repeat the information to anyone else. *Confidentiality* presupposes that something "secret" will be told to another person (such as a doctor) who will not repeat it to someone else (such as an employer). Relationships such as attorney-client, priest-penitent, and doctor-patient are confidential relationships. In the doctor-patient context, confidentiality is understood as an expressed or implied agreement that the doctor will not disclose private information received from the patient to anyone not directly involved in the patient's care and treatment.

There are at least four senses in which the term *privacy* is used in the law in the United States. First, the term describes a constitutional right to privacy. Found in the liberty interests protected by the Fourteenth Amendment, this right to privacy is the basis for the U.S. Supreme Court opinions limiting government interference with individual decisions about such personal decisions as marriage, having children, birth control, and abortion. It specifically relates to an individual's right to make important, intimate decisions that profoundly affect one's personhood free from government interference. Second, the right to privacy has been used to characterize certain private places, such as the home and bedroom, into which citizens have a reasonable expectation that the government will not intrude. Third are private relationships, such as the spousal relationship and the doctor-patient relationship. Finally, privacy can also describe especially sensitive or "private" information, such as medical information. More generally, privacy has been defined as "the right to be let alone, to be free of prying, peeping, and snooping," and as "the right of someone to keep information about himself or his personality inaccessible to others."[5]

Privilege, sometimes called "testimonial privilege," is a legal rule of evidence, applicable only in a legal proceeding. A communication is privileged if the person to whom the information is given is forbidden by law from disclosing it in a court proceeding without the consent of the person who provided it. The privilege belongs to the client, not to the professional, although the hospital and physician may have a duty to assert it on behalf of the patient. Unlike the attorney-client privilege, the doctor-patient privilege is not recognized at common law and therefore exists only if a state statute establishes it, as most do.

Is maintaining confidentiality a legal or an ethical obligation of care providers?

It is both. Historically, the doctrine was an ethical duty applicable only to physicians. Currently, it is also a legal duty of physicians (as enunciated in case law, and some state licensing statutes), and it is becoming a legal duty of other health care practitioners as well. The Hippocratic Oath sets out the duty of confidentiality in the following words: "Whatsoever things I see or hear concerning the life of man, in any attendance on the sick or even apart therefrom, which ought not to be noised about, I will keep silent there on, counting such things to be professional secrets." This oath has been reinterpreted in section 4 of the American Medical Association's Principles of Ethics: "A physician shall respect the rights of patients, of colleagues, and of other health professionals, and shall safeguard patient confidences within the constraints of the law."

Similarly, section 2 of the American Nurses' Association Code provides, "The nurse safeguards the client's right to privacy by judiciously protecting information of a confidential nature." The interpretive statement elaborates:

When knowledge gained in confidence is relevant or essential to others involved is planning or implementing the client's care, professional judgment is used in sharing it. Only information pertinent to a client's treatment and welfare is disclosed and only to those directly concerned with the client's care. . . . The nurse-client relationship is built on trust. This relationship could be destroyed and the client's welfare and reputation jeopardized by injudicious disclosure of information provided in confidence.

The reason for these rules is that care providers must often know the most personal and possibly embarrassing details of the patient's life in order to help the patient. Patients are not likely to disclose intimate details freely unless they are certain that no one not directly involved in their care will learn of them. As one court described the patient's dilemma:

Since the layman is unfamiliar with the road to recovery, he cannot sift the circumstances of his life and habits to determine what is information pertinent to his health. As a consequence, he must disclose all information in his consultations with his doctor—even that which is embarrassing, disgraceful, or incriminating. To promote full disclosure, the medical profession extends the promise of secrecy. The candor which this promise elicits is necessary to the effective pursuit of health; there can be no reticence, no reservation, no reluctance when patients discuss their problems with their doctors.[6]

Is it realistic for hospital patients to think that medical information about them will remain secret or "confidential"?

No. The old "rule" in the hospital was that "everyone has access to the patient's medical record except the patient"; the modern rule is that everyone (including the patient) has access. This has been the reality, at least since the early 1980s. As Lawrence Altman, a physician and medical writer for the *New York Times,* has correctly noted, "It has become increasingly apparent that patients can no longer assume that intimacies about their bodies or their private lives will be held in confidence by their physicians and those who work with those physicians."[7] Altman discusses a major teaching hospital (which is far from unique) that felt it necessary to post signs in its elevators saying: "Hospital staff are reminded that patient information should not be discussed in public areas."

Information exchange in the hospital is the product of the "team" approach to medical care in that setting, as well as use of the medical record for educational, financial, research, and quality-monitoring purposes. When one of his hospitalized patients asked how many people had access to his medical record, physician and medical ethicist Mark Siegler decided to find out.[8] It was not easy. He concluded that at least seventy-five people at the hospital had a *legitimate* need to have access. These persons included the patient's six attending physicians, twelve house officers, twenty nursing personnel (on three shifts), six respiratory therapists, three nutritionists, two clinical pharmacologists, four unit secretaries, fifteen students, four hospital financial officers, and four chart reviewers (utilization review, quality assurance review, tissue review, and the insurance auditor). Information access should be limited to a "need-to-know" basis. But even on this basis, the reality is that many people will fit into the need-to-know category and thus have free access to the patient's record. Patients should know what their doctors understand by "medical confidentiality." As described in the medical codes, Siegler concluded, confidentiality is a "decrepit concept," a "myth" that we should spend no more energy perpetuating. But what Siegler has identified is the large number of people who have legitimate access to medical information: confidentiality and privacy protect against illegitimate access.

A major development accompanying computerized records is that it is easier to document who has accessed the patient's medical records by using electronic "audit trails." Unfortunately, under HIPAA patients have a right to these audit trails only if they are linked to unauthorized access to their records. The use of an audit trail is illustrated by a woman who reported in 2000 that she had been treated at a major hospital in Boston, Brigham and Women's, for a rare reproductive problem. Her records included a description of her ordeal in attempting to get pregnant, her sex life, comments on her emotional condition, and HIV testing. On discovering that her electronic medical record had been accessed more than two hundred times by hospital employees (as documented in a six-page electronic audit report) she is quoted as saying, "It feels like you're being violated over and over. It's like gang rape." The hospital defended itself by noting that her records were used for teaching residents, and that "[t]he use of patient care information for educational purposes within the institution . . . is not regarded as public disclosure or breach of confidentiality."[9] The hospital, of course, was wrong. The patient's identity need not be revealed at all to the residents (although disclosure is inevitable if the case is an especially unusual one), and the patient has the right not to have their sensitive medical information used for teaching if the patient can be readily identified from the information provided for teaching. Hospitals must draw distinctions among treatment, research, and teaching.

This reality is why many patients fear having very sensitive information about them entered in the hospital chart, such as a psychiatric diagnosis, a genetic predisposition to a disease, or even the diagnosis of HIV. They know this information will spread rapidly in the hospital and could adversely affect how they are treated by some members of the hospital staff. It could also "leak" from the hospital, affecting their housing, employment, and insurance status. Routine access by so many people makes it imperative that you *know* what is in your medical records, so you can correct mistakes that may directly affect your care and your future, and so you will be able to decide whether to authorize anyone not involved in your care to see your medical records.

There are in fact very few reported appellate cases involving breaches of confidentiality. This is likely because patients seldom learn of violations when they occur; patients do not think it is appropriate to sue for such violations (because of the cost, uncertain damages, and possible further publicity of the confidential information); and because almost all confidentiality cases are settled before they reach an appellate court.[10]

What function does the testimonial privilege serve?

The privilege not to be forced to testify is founded on the belief that certain types of relationships are so beneficial to individuals and society that they should be fostered by forbidding in-court disclosure of the communication content of the relationship. A privilege is therefore granted to encourage the employment of professionals by individuals who need their services and to promote freedom of communication in the relationship. The contrary principle is that the courtroom is a place for the discovery of truth, and no reliable source of truth should be beyond the reach of the court.

The great majority of courts currently agree that the principal reason for the privilege is to encourage a patient to freely and frankly reveal to a physician all the facts and symptoms concerning the patient's condition so that the physician will be in the best possible position to correctly diagnose and successfully treat the patient. At common law, the court's interest in the truth routinely won out, and physicians were forced to testify about what was disclosed to them by their patients. Most states have therefore adopted the privilege by statute. On the other hand, there are so many exceptions to the privilege rule that it rarely frustrates justice by withholding the truth from the court.[11]

The psychotherapist-patient privilege is the strongest privilege and generally protects all conversations between a patient and a psychiatrist, psychologist, social worker, or other psychotherapist. In 1996, the U.S. Supreme Court strongly endorsed the psychotherapist-patient privilege, finding that it was covered by the Federal Rules of Evidence (Rule 501), as applied to a police officer who fatally shot a person and later sought counseling from a licensed social worker. The Court ruled that the psychotherapist-patient privilege should be protected by the courts because

[l]ike the spousal and attorney-client privileges, the psychotherapist-patient privilege is 'rooted in the imperative need for confidence and trust.' Treatment by a physician for physical ailments can often proceed successfully on the basis of a physical examination, objective information supplied by the patient, and the results of diagnostic tests. Effective psychotherapy, by contrast, depends upon an atmosphere of confidence and trust in which the patient is willing to make a frank and complete disclosure of facts, emotions, memories and fears. Because of the sensitive nature of the problems for which individuals consult psychotherapists, disclosure of confidential communications made during counseling sessions may cause embarrassment or disgrace. For this reason, the mere possibility of disclosure may impede development of the confidential relationship necessary for successful treatment.[12]

The Court goes on to find that the privilege serves the private interests of the patient and an important public interest as well, "by facilitating the provision of appropriate treatment for individuals suffering the effects of a mental or emotional problem." The federal HIPAA regulations provide special privacy protections for psychotherapy notes for the same reason.

Where does the "right to privacy" come from?

In *Privacy and Freedom,* Alan Westin defines privacy as "the claim of individuals, groups, or institutions to determine for themselves when, how, and to what extent information about them is communicated to others."[13] He goes on to argue that, as thus defined, the concept has its roots in the territorial behavior of animals, and its importance can be seen to some extent throughout the history of civilization. Specific protections of privacy were built into the U.S. Constitution by the framers in terms that were important to their era. With the subsequent inventions of the telephone, radio, television, and computer systems, more sophisticated legal doctrines were developed in an attempt to protect the informational privacy of the individual. Many diverse acts come under the heading of privacy violations, but most involving medical records are in the area generally described as the "publication [disclosing to one or more unauthorized persons] of private matters violating ordinary decencies."

A court can conclude that the unauthorized disclosure of private medical information is actionable even without a state statute that specifically forbids it. As an Alabama court explained in a case involving disclosure of medical information by a physician to a patient's employer: "Unauthorized disclosure of intimate details of a patient's health may amount to unwarranted publication of one's private affairs with which the public has no legitimate concern, such as to cause outrage, mental suffering, shame, or humiliation to a person of ordinary sensibilities."[14]

The policy underlying the right is that because of the potential severe consequences to individuals, certain personal information about them (such as their HIV status) should not be disclosed without their permission. In the words of one legal commentator: "The basic attribute of an effective right of privacy is the individual's ability to control the flow of information concerning or describing him."[15] Most of the cases in the doctor-patient context alleging violation of the right to privacy have involved actions in which personal medical information has been published in a newspaper or magazine, and often the suit is against the publisher rather than the physician.[16] In one well-known case, however, an employer, the University of California, paid $2.2 million to settle a lawsuit brought by nine thousand employees the university had secretly tested for genetic disorders, venereal disease, and pregnancy without their consent.[17] An appeals court had written about the secret genetic testing before the settlement: "One can think of few subject areas more personal and more likely to implicate privacy interests than that of one's health or genetic makeup."[18]

Under what circumstances must a provider disclose medical information about a patient?

The doctrines of confidentiality and privacy are, on the surface, very powerful legal protections. Their effect in the day-to-day practice of medicine, however, is diluted both by the reality of hospital care and by the exceptions and defenses physicians and other care providers can raise to a charge of unauthorized disclosure of medical information. There are even times (described in the four following circumstances) when health care professionals *must* disclose confidential information, even though neither the patient nor the provider may want to:

Public Reporting Statutes

All states have statutes that require physicians to report certain listed conditions and diseases to public authorities. These generally fall into four major categories: vital statistics, contagious and dangerous diseases, child neglect and abuse, and criminally inflicted injuries. These statutes decree a public policy that takes precedence over the obligation to maintain patient confidences:

- Birth and death certificates must be filed. In the case of birth certificates, information about the parents is generally required. If death is sudden or from an accidental cause, or if foul play is suspected, the medical examiner or coroner is usually required by law to do an autopsy and file a complete report with the district attorney.
- Infectious, contagious, or communicable diseases must usually be reported. The California statute, for instance, lists cholera, plague, yellow fever, malaria, leprosy, diphtheria, scarlet fever, smallpox, typhus fever, typhoid fever, paratyphoid fever, anthrax, glanders, epidemic cerebrospinal meningitis, tuberculosis, pneumonia, dysentery, erysipelas, hookworm, trachoma, dengue, tetanus, measles, German measles, chicken pox, whooping cough, mumps, pellagra, beriberi, Rocky Mountain spotted fever, syphilis, gonorrhea, rabies, and poliomyelitis. AIDS, but not HIV status, is reportable in all states. Most public health officials agree that only a fraction of many of these diseases are reported by physicians.
- Child abuse cases must be reported. Reporting of child abuse is most common in the emergency rooms of large city hospitals. Failure to report can also subject a health professional to criminal penalties (most statutes also require nurses, social workers, teachers, and others to report).
- Specific types of injuries must be reported, such as "a bullet wound, gunshot wound, powder burn or any other injury arising from or caused by the discharge of a gun or firearm, and every case of a wound which is likely to or may result in death and is actually or apparently inflicted by a knife, icepick or other sharp instrument."[19]

Other things, such as elder abuse, must also be reported in many states.

JUDICIAL PROCESS

When a person makes his or her own physical condition an issue in a lawsuit (for example, a personal injury claim), courts reasonably permit examination of the person's physician under oath either before or during the trial.[20] Even in states that have a privilege statute, there are, as previously noted, many exceptions that permit medical information to be used in court.

STATUTES ON COST AND QUALITY CONTROL

There are a variety of state and federal statutes that permit certain monitoring agencies to have access to patient records for such purposes as peer review, utilization review, studies to protect against provider-reimbursement fraud, and licensing and accreditation surveys. The most common of these is the federal statute and regulations on Professional Review Organizations (PROs). Regulations require that the information collected under this program not be made public in any way that individual practitioners or patients can be identified.

PATIENT POSES A DANGER TO KNOWN PERSON

Until the mid-1970s, physicians were held responsible for injuries inflicted on others by their patients only when the physician was directly negligent in the treatment of the patient. For example, physicians have been held responsible for negligently failing to diagnose tuberculosis, thereby placing family members at risk, and for wrongly informing a patient's neighbor that smallpox was not contagious.[21] In addition, physicians have been responsible for wrongly informing the members of a family that typhoid fever and scarlet fever of a sibling would not infect other members of the family.[22]

The California Supreme Court has gone somewhat further, ruling that "when a therapist determines, or pursuant to the standards of his profession should determine that his patient presents a serious danger of violence to another, he incurs an obligation to use reasonable care to protect the intended [foreseeable] victim against such danger."[23] The case, *Tarasoff,* involved a patient who had threatened to kill his former girlfriend. The therapist believed him; took some initial steps to have him confined; and then, allegedly on order from his superior, dropped the case. The patient in fact killed the young woman (and was convicted of murder), and her family sued the therapist and his employer, the University of California at Berkeley. The California Supreme Court declared, in the above-quoted language, that the therapist could be found liable if he had failed to protect the intended victim by either warning her or taking other reasonable steps, such as confining his patient to a mental institution, to prevent the murder, because the therapist had a special relationship with his patient that was broad enough to include an obligation to a named intended victim. The civil case was eventually settled out of court.

The psychiatric profession argued vehemently against this ruling. Psychiatrists predicted that the decision would curtail the ability of psychiatrists to treat patients (who would not come to them because they feared being reported to the authorities). It would also, some believed, encourage psychiatrists to have potentially dangerous patients committed to mental institutions rather than take a chance of continuing to treat them on an outpatient basis.[24] Psychiatrists are correct in noting that the broader we as a society make the professional's obligation to protect others from their patient, the more psychiatrists become like police. Nevertheless, the California Supreme Court's decision that health care providers have an obligation to society as well as to their patients is correct in life-and-death situations, is reasonable, and has been followed by other courts.[25] When the life of another can be saved by breaching a confidence, the disclosure is limited, and there is no reasonable alternative for accomplishing the same objective, courts (and society in general) will properly have little difficulty mandating disclosure to someone who can prevent the harm.

When may care providers, at their own option, disclose confidential information about a patient?

Optional disclosure situations are extremely broad. The following situations indicate the vast discretion courts are likely to afford care providers who act in good faith.

For example, in the absence of a statute that forbids disclosure, the interest in protecting innocent potential victims of one's patient permits a physician to warn a *known* sexual partner of a patient infected with HIV upon diagnosis. The sex partner, of course, has his or her own duty to disclose. But unless the patient credibly agreed to disclose this information to the partner, persuaded the physician that there was no risk to the sexual partner (because they no longer were engaged in sexual relations or were practicing "safe sex"), or the obligation to protect was met by reporting the diagnosis to the state health department, the physician could disclose as well.[26]

IMPLIED CONSENT

As previously discussed, this is probably the major rationale for medical information sharing. The patient in a health facility impliedly consents to the viewing of medical record by all those directly concerned with the patient's care. This may include the nurses on all three shifts; the ward secretary; all medical students, interns, and residents; the attending physicians and consultants; and perhaps social, psychological, medical, or psychiatric researchers. As discussed later in this chapter, under HIPAA the patient must now be provided with written notice about who will have access to the medical record.

GENERAL RELEASE FORMS

Most general medical information release forms are unduly broad and so vague that the patient cannot reasonably know what they are authorizing. They therefore should no longer be used and are prohibited by HIPAA rules. The cases invalidating vague blanket surgical consent forms, which give the doctor and hospital authority to perform whatever procedures they think necessary, support this line of reasoning. A generally unsuccessful argument is that the patient's lack of bargaining power makes the signature on the form involuntary and thus ineffective (for example, a sick patient may need admission or insurance coverage and cannot afford to forgo it by refusing to sign a required form).[27]

PRIVATE INTERESTS OF THE PATIENT

Courts afford physicians generous latitude in making disclosures that physicians believe in good faith are in the best interest of their patients. This rule, for example, is used to justify many disclosures to spouses and close relatives without the patient's consent. When only the patient's individual welfare is involved, the patient should have the exclusive right to decide if and when confidential information should be released. Nevertheless, courts will probably continue to give physicians and hospitals considerable discretion in this area, so long as they can make a good faith argument that there was no reasonable alternative, and that the patient's health required the disclosure. Tell your physician explicitly not to disclose private medical information to family members if this is what you want.

What type of form should be used to authorize the release of personal medical information?

There is a long history to the answer to this question. The Privacy Protection Study Commission discovered in the early 1970s that often when an individual applies for a job, life or health insurance, credit or financial assistance, or services from the government, the individual is asked to relinquish medical information. Although this is necessary in many cases, the commission found that individuals are generally asked to sign open-ended or blanket authorizations with clauses such as one requiring the recipient to "furnish any and all information on request." The commission took the position that such blanket consent forms are unacceptable and made the following recommendations:

Whenever an individual's authorization is required before a medical care provider may disclose information it collects or maintains about him, the medical care provider should not accept as valid any authorization which is not:

(a) in writing;

(b) signed by the individual on a date specified or by someone authorized in fact to act in his behalf;

(c) clear as to the fact that the medical care provider is among those either specifically named or generally designated by the individual as being authorized to disclose information about him;

(d) specific as to the nature of the information the individual is authorizing to be disclosed;

(e) specific as to the institutions or other persons to whom the individual is authorizing information to be disclosed;

(f) specific as to the purpose(s) for which the information may be used by any of the parties named in (e) both at the time of disclosure and at any time in the future;

(g) specific as to its expiration date, which should be for a reasonable time not to exceed one year.[28]

What do federal regulations require regarding patient authorization for release of medical information?

The federal HIPAA regulations (which went into effect in 2003) require that each patient be given a notice of privacy practices for protected health information. The notice must contain, among other things, a header in capital letters that says, "This notice describes how medical information about you may be used and disclosed and how you can get access to this information. Please review it carefully."

The notice itself must describe and give an example of the uses and disclosures permitted for each of the following purposes: treatment, payment, and health care operations. The notice must contain a description of all purposes for which the provider may use protected health information without written consent or authorization, and a statement that any other uses will only be made with written authorization that may be revoked at any time. The notice must also contain a statement of the individual's rights and how to exercise them, including the right to restrict certain uses and disclosures, the right to inspect and copy protected health records, the right to amend health records, and the right to an accounting of all disclosures of protected health information. The notice must also contain a statement that the health provider is required by law to maintain privacy, as well as a statement that individuals may complain to both the provider (and the name and phone number of this person) and the secretary of Health and Human Services regarding violations of the rights set forth in the notice. The notice must also be prominently displayed at the service site.[29]

A valid authorization to disclose confidential medical information to anyone not involved in treatment, payment, or health care operations must contain the following elements, all in plain language, and a copy of the authorization must be provided to you:

- A description of the information to be used or disclosed that identifies the information in a specific and meaningful manner
- The name or identity of the person authorized to make the requested use or disclosure, and the name or identity of the person to whom the requested use or disclosure may be made
- An expiration date or event that relates to you or the purpose of the use or disclosure ("none" or "end of the research study" is sufficient for research use)
- A statement of your right to revoke the authorization in writing (and how this may be done); your right to inspect or copy the information that is the subject of the authorization, and a statement explaining the consequences of refusing to sign the authorization
- A statement that information used or disclosed pursuant to the authorization may be subject to redisclosure by the recipient and no longer protected
- Your signature and the date[30]

Even if you have signed a proper release form, the hospital, clinic, or physician might unlawfully release your medical record. In this case, you will be able to sue them for negligent release, although you will have to prove you were harmed by the release, and more people will learn about the information in your medical records. In one particularly outrageous case, a physician at Baylor University Medical Center was required to undergo treatment for his alcohol problem after an investigation was triggered by a patient who smelled alcohol on the physician's breath. At the Talbott March Center, which specialized in physicians with drug and other dependencies, the physician-patient signed an uncompleted release of medical records form to the Texas Board of Medicine, which he understood was limited to releasing records related to the treatment of his alcoholism.

When the Texas Medical Board asked for the physician's records a second time, the medical records librarian mistakenly sent them not only the alcohol treatment records but also the records of "psychosexual therapy." This caused the medical board to drastically limit the physician-patient's medical license (including supervision requirements) such that he was subsequently only able to get employment in Texas as a prison physician. The physician subsequently sued the clinic for improperly releasing his full medical records. He won a $200,000 jury verdict that was affirmed on appeal. The appeals court wrote that the clinic "breached a fiduciary duty" that it owed to its patient by failing "to obtain an informed consent" for the release of all his medical records, thus undermining "the purpose of his recovery therapy, to which he had devoted a year of his life in sincere, cooperative work."[31]

Under what circumstances do care professionals have the right to discuss the patient with other care professionals?

Care professionals who are *directly* involved in the patient's care may (and should!) discuss the patient's case among themselves. However, they may not discuss the patient with other professionals who are not directly involved with the patient's care without consent *unless* the patient's identity is protected. Hypothetical cases (based on real cases but without names or other identifiers) can be openly discussed so long as the individual patient cannot be identified.

A related question is presented when a patient's case is discussed at grand rounds at a teaching hospital. The patient is helped by the presentation, and it can be part of the patient's direct care. Nonetheless, as a matter of courtesy the patient's consent should be solicited prior to such "public" disclosure in grand rounds if the patient is easily identifiable and might reasonably object. Consent is not required if reasonable steps are taken to protect the patient's identity.

Do care professionals have the right to discuss the patient's case with the patient's family without the express consent of the patient?

Although there seems to be confusion about this, no disclosures concerning specific diagnosis or prognosis to family members should be made without the patient's express consent if the patient is competent. On the other hand, use of terms such as *stable* and *satisfactory condition* are fine. If the family is making decisions for an incompetent patient, however, the family members have a right to all the information needed to make informed treatment decisions on the patient's behalf.

When Maine passed a law forbidding all medical information disclosures not authorized by the patient in the late 1990s, public outcry led to the law being amended to permit reasonable disclosures without consent. The amended law provides that, unless specifically forbidden by the patient, a hospital may give out the patient's room number and general health status to the press or member of the public who asks about the patient by name, and it may provide the patient's religious affiliation to a member of the clergy. A previous requirement for written authorization for all disclosures was also changed to permit oral authorization "when it is not practical to obtain written authorization" and also permits surrogate authorization as well.[32] Although there were complaints that the amendments undermined confidentiality rather than protecting it, these particular changes are reasonable. They permit, for example, hospitals to tell family members calling around to locate a missing family member if the person is in the hospital, and the person's general condition.

Likewise, the HIPAA regulations permit health care entities to have directories with the following information on patients in them: name, location in the facility, general condition, religious affiliation. They permit disclosure of the religious affiliation to the clergy and disclosure of the other information to any person who inquires about the patient by name. Patients must, however, be informed of the directory and be given the opportunity to restrict or prohibit some or all of the disclosures.[33]

What recommendations did the Privacy Commission make concerning medical records?

The Privacy Protection Study Commission, established by Congress in 1974 to study privacy rights and record-keeping practices, issued its final report in 1977. This report is still the most complete and authoritative on the subject of the privacy of records. With the exception of its call for state statutes, the commission's recommendations form the core justification for the HIPAA regulations.

The commission found that medical records contain more information and are available to more users than ever before; that the control of health care providers over these records has been greatly diluted; that restoration of this control is not possible; that voluntary patient consent to disclosure is generally illusory; that patient access to their records is rare; and that steps should be taken to improve the quality of records, to enhance patient awareness of their content, and to control their disclosure. Some of the commission's major recommendations are that

- Each state enact a statute creating individual rights of access to, and correction of, medical records, and an enforceable expectation of confidentiality for medical records.
- Federal and state penal codes be amended to make it a criminal offense for any individual knowingly to request or obtain medical record information from a medical care provider under false pretenses or through deception.
- Upon request, an individual who is the subject of a medical record maintained by a medical care provider, or another responsible person designated by the individual, be allowed to have access to that medical record, including the opportunity to see and copy it; and have the opportunity to correct or amend the record.
- Each medical care provider be required to take affirmative measures to assure that the medical records it maintains are made available only to authorized recipients and on a "need-to-know" basis.
- Any disclosure of medical record information by a medical care provider be limited only to information necessary to accomplish the purpose for which the disclosure is made.
- Each medical care provider be required to notify an individual on whom it maintains a medical record of the disclosures that may be

made of information in the record without the individual's express authorization.[34]

These principles, with the exception of new state laws, have all been incorporated into the new HIPAA regulations.

May patients be photographed or videotaped by health care professionals?

Yes, but they may do so only with the patient's consent. Although most of the cases regarding photographs of patients involve the publication of the photos in newspapers or magazines, there are cases that involve physicians as well. Documentaries and television programs have also used film shot in hospitals and mental institutions. For example, in the late 1960s, filmmaker and lawyer Frederick Wiseman shot eighty thousand feet of film inside Bridgewater, a state mental institution in Massachusetts; the result was the documentary *Titicut Follies*. The Supreme Judicial Court of Massachusetts prohibited showing the film to the public in the state:

The Commissioner and Superintendent, under reasonable standards of custodial conduct, could hardly permit merely curious members of the public access to Bridgewater to view directly many activities of the type shown in the film. We think it equally inconsistent with their custodial duties to permit the general public (as opposed to members of groups with a legitimate, significant interest) to view films showing inmates naked or exhibiting painful aspects of mental disease.[35]

Elsewhere in the decision, the court used the following words to describe the invasion of privacy: "collective, indecent intrusion"; "massive, unrestrained"; and "embarrassing." The patient's right to privacy is superior to any private, and usually superior to any public, interest in obtaining information about their medical care. This means that no film, not even photographs, should be taken of patients by outsiders without their consent. This rule also applies to physicians.

This point was poignantly made in a 1976 case from Maine, which involved a patient who was dying of cancer of the larynx.[36] Both a laryngectomy and a subsequent radical neck dissection were performed. The surgeon took photographs, solely for the use in the medical record and not for publication, of the progress of the disease. On the day before the patient died, the physician entered his room, and took several final photographs. There was evidence that the patient raised a clenched fist and moved his head in an attempt to get out of the camera's range. His wife had also informed the physician she "didn't think that Henry wanted his picture taken." The trial court granted a motion for a directed verdict in favor of the physician, but the Maine Supreme Court reversed, saying that the physician's actions amounted to a violation of the patient's right to privacy:

Absent express consent . . . the touching of the patient in the manner described by the evidence in this case would constitute assault and battery if it was part of an undertaking which, in legal effect, was an invasion of plaintiff's "right to be let alone."

We are urged to declare as a matter of law that it is the physician's right to complete the photographic record by capturing on film B.'s appearance in his final dying hours, even without the patient's consent or over his objections. This we are unwilling to do.

The facial characteristics or peculiar case of one's features, whether normal or distorted, belong to the individual and may not be reproduced without his permission.[37]

Is a patient's privacy protected when using health sites on the World Wide Web?

Not generally. Privacy policies of health-related Web sites remain chaotic and diverse, and have no strong enforcement provisions. Dr. Martin Murphy, editor of the journal *The Oncologist* and a cancer survivor, believes "There should be the seal of the confessional when it comes to anonymity, and no information about the patient should even be kept [by the Web site], let alone passed along to advertisers or marketers."[38] I think he is correct, but this is not current policy, and if you want to protect your privacy and prevent Web sites from using your name and medical information to market to you, you must use a pseudonym when surfing the Web for health information, although even this may not be enough to protect your identity.

It is estimated that more than fifty million Americans have already used the Web to obtain information about medical conditions and treatments, and seeking medical information may be the number one reason people use the Internet, outranking even on-line shopping. A survey of more than six thousand Internet users conducted in 2000 found that 69 percent were "very concerned" that a Web site might sell or give away their personal information, and 81 percent said they should be able to sue if an Internet company violated its privacy policy. Almost half of all respondents who sought medical information on-line said it had improved how they cared for themselves. Sixty-three percent opposed keeping medical records on-line because they feared their medical information would become more readily available to others. The director of the study commented, "In an era when the face time a patient gets with a doctor during an average appointment has dipped below 15 minutes, many are turning to the web to get the information they crave."[39] The Internet is not, however, often used for actual communication with a person's physician: only 9 percent of respondents who used the Web to obtain health information said they had exchanged e-mail with their physician, and you should assume that e-mail communication with your physician is not confidential.

The Internet can be simultaneously a terrific place and a terrible place to find information about specific medical conditions and the treatment options available. You will want to use the Internet as a resource, however, and not to add to what other people know about you and your medical condition. Sites do not need to know who you are to provide information to you. Not-for-profit sites are much less likely than for-profit sites to collect and sell your name and medical information about yourself, and better yet, use encryption technology that prevents the Web site from knowing your identity in the first place.

What are some other examples of rights encompassed in the "right to privacy" not related to medical information?

Patients in a hospital have the following rights based on the right to privacy as enunciated in the cases discussed and referenced in this chapter. You have the right

- To refuse to see any or all visitors
- To refuse to see anyone not officially connected with the hospital
- To refuse to see persons officially connected with the hospital who are not directly involved in your care and treatment
- To refuse to see social workers and chaplains and others not directly involved in your care and to forbid them to view your records

• To wear your own bedclothes, so long as they do not interfere with your treatment[40]

• To wear religious medals

• To have a person of your sex present during a physical examination by a medical professional of the opposite sex

• Not to remain disrobed any longer than is necessary for accomplishing the medical purpose for which you are asked to disrobe

• To insist on being transferred to another room if the person sharing it with you is disturbing you unreasonably.

TIPS FOR ADVOCATES

• **Doctors and nurses have a legal and ethical duty to keep medical information confidential and not discuss it with anyone not involved in the patient's care without the patient's authorization.**

• **Read "release of medical records" forms carefully** and make necessary changes to ensure that the form is specific and limited in terms of the medical information to be disclosed, the person to whom it will be disclosed, the dates it is effective, and a guarantee that the information will not be redisclosed.

• **Ask about the hospital's policy for using the patient's medical information for teaching and research.** This use should be restricted if the patient is identifiable from the information used.

• **Do not discuss medical information, treatment, prognosis, or other information about the patient in a loud voice in the room, or in the hallway, elevators, or any common rooms in the hospital.**

• **Use privacy-protected access methods to search the Internet** for information on a specific disease or condition you do not want linked to you or the patient.

• Complain to nurses, physicians, or others who discuss the patient's condition in a context that others can overhear. They will be (or should be) embarrassed and stop it.

• Bring your own bedclothes to the hospital.

Notes

1. *See* Lawrence Lessig, Code and Other Laws of Cyberspace, New York: Basic Books, 2000. And on information today, *see generally* Simson Garfinkel, Database Nation: The Death of Privacy in the 21st Century, Sebastopol, Calif.: O'Reilly, 2000.

2. Institute for the Future, Health & Health Care 2010: The Forecast, the Challenge, San Francisco: Jorgey-Bass, 2000, 114–116.

3. Office of the Secretary, Department of Health and Human Services, Standards for Privacy of Individually Identifiable Health Information, 45 C.F.R. 160 through 164 (December 20, 2000); Final Rules 67 Fed. Reg. 53182 (2002). *See generally* the Web site www.hhs.gov/ocr/hipaa/ for guidance and updated information from the Office of Civil Rights of the Department of Health and Human Services.

4. There are civil penalties of $100 per incident up to $25,000 per year per person. There are also criminal penalties for "knowingly and improperly disclosing" medical information or obtaining medical information under false pretenses of up to $50,000 and one year in prison for obtaining or disclosing protected health information; up to $100,000 and up to five years in prison for obtaining protected health information under "false pretenses," and up to $250,000 and up to ten years in prison for "obtaining or disclosing protected health information with the intent to sell, transfer, or use it for commercial advantage, personal gain or malicious harm." 42 USC 1320d-6. *And see generally* George J. Annas, *HIPAA Regulations: A New Era of Medical Record Privacy?* 348 New Eng. J. Med. 1486 (2003), and www.healthprivacy.org.

5. Sam Ervin, *Civilized Man's Most Valued Right*, 2 Prism 15 (June 1974); *cf.* Alan Westin & M. Baher, Data Banks in A Free Society, New York: Quadrangle, 1973, 17–20; Arthur Miller, The Assault on Privacy, New York: New American Library, 1972, 184–220. *And see generally* ABA Forum Committee on Health Law, A Practical Guide to Access, Disclosure and Legal Requirement to Hospital, Patient, Medical Staff and Employment Records, Chicago: American Bar Association, 1987; Amitai Etzion, The Limits of Privacy, New York: Basic Books, 1999; and Patricia Carter, *Health Information Privacy: Can Congress Protect Confidential Medical Information in the "Information Age"?* 25 Wm. Mitchell Law Rev. 223 (1999).

6. *Hammonds v. Aetna Cas. & Sur. Co.,* 243 F. Supp. 793, 801 (N.D. Ohio 1965); *and see Hicks v. Talbott Recovery System,* 196 F.3d 1226 (11 Cir. 1999).

7. Lawrence Altman, *Physician-Patient Confidentiality Slips Away,* New York Times, September 27, 1983, C1.

8. Mark Siegler, *Confidentiality in Medicine—A Decrepit Concept,* 307 New Eng. J. Med. 1519 (1982).

9. Raja Mishra, *Confidential Medical Records Are Not Always Private,* Boston Globe, August 1, 2000, D1.

10. In *Curry v. Corn,* 277 N.Y.S.2d 470 (1966), for example, the physician disclosed information to his patient's husband, who was contemplating divorce action. In *Schaffer v. Spicer,* 215 N.W.2d 134 (S.D. 1974), the patient's psychiatrist disclosed information to her husband's attorney to aid him in a child-custody case. And in *Berger v. Sonneland,* 26 P.3d 257 (Wash. 2001), the physician disclosed confidential information to the patient's

ex-husband. Representative of the insurance cases are *Hague v. Williams,* 37 N.J. 328, 181 A.2d 345 (1962), in which the pediatrician of an infant informed a life insurance company of a congenital heart defect that he had not informed the child's parents of; and *Hammonds v. Aetna* (*supra* note 2), in which the physician revealed information to an insurance company when the insurance company falsely represented to him that his patient was suing him for malpractice. Cases involving reporting to employers include *Beatty v. Baston,* 13 Ohio L. Abs. 481 (Ohio App. 1932), in which the physician revealed to a patient's employer during a workman's compensation action that the patient had venereal disease; *Clark v. Geraci,* 208 N.Y.S.2d 564 (Sup. Ct. 1960), in which a civilian employee of the U.S. Air Force asked his doctor to make an incomplete disclosure to his employer to explain absences, but the doctor made a complete disclosure including the patient's alcoholism; *Horne v. Patton,* 291 Ala. 701, 287 So. 2d 824 (1973), which involved the disclosure of a long-standing nervous condition; and *Alberts v. Devine,* 395 Mass. 59, 479 N.E.2d 113 (1985), *cert. denied,* 474 U.S. 1013 (1985), which involved disclosure of psychiatric information to a minister's clerical superiors that resulted in his not being reappointed.

11. The most important exceptions are the following:

• Communications made to a doctor when no doctor-patient relationship exists
• Communications made to a doctor that are not for the purposes of diagnosis and treatment or are not necessary to the purposes of diagnosis and treatment (for example, who inflicted the gunshot wound and why)
• In actions involving commitment proceedings, wills, and insurance policies
• In actions in which the patient brings his physical or mental condition into question (for example, a personal injury suit for damages, raising an insanity defense, malpractice action against a doctor or hospital)
• Reports required by state statutes (for example, gunshot wounds, acute poisoning, child abuse, motor vehicle accidents, and, in some states, venereal disease)
• Information given to the doctor in the present of another not related professionally to the doctor or known by the patient.

And see generally Katherine Benesch & Theresa Homisak, *The Physician-Patient Relationship: Privileges and Confidentiality* (in) Miles Zaremski & Louis Goldstein, eds., Medical Hospital Malpractice Liability, New York: Callaghan & Co., 1987, and Kelly Korell, *Testimonial Privilege for Confidential Commnications between Relatives other than Husband and Wife—State Cases,* 62 A.L.R. 5th 629 (1998).

12. *Jaffee v. Redmond,* 518 U.S. 1 (1996). *See* Lynda Womack Kennedy, *Role of Jaffee v. Redmond's 'Course of Diagnosis or Treatment' Condition in Preventing Abuse of the Psychotherapist-Patient Privilege,* 35 Ga. L. Rev. 345 (2000).

13. Alan Westin, Privacy and Freedom, New York: Atheneum, 1967, 7.

14. *Horne v. Patton, supra* note 10, 287 So. 2d at 830.

15. Arthur Miller, *Personal Privacy in the Computer Age,* 67 Mich. L. Rev. 1091 (1968).

16. In 1939, for example, *Time* magazine published a story in its "Medicine" section with a photograph of the patient, a young woman who was receiving treatment for uncontrollable gluttony apparently induced by a condition of the pancreas (*Barber v. Time, Inc.,* 348 Mo. 1199, 159 S.W.2d 291 [1942]). Other cases, such as *Horne v. Patton* (*supra*

note 10), however, indicate that publication is not necessary to sustain an invasion-of-privacy action, for example, having unauthorized persons in a delivery room (*DeMay v. Roberts,* 46 Mich. 160, 9 N.W. 146 [1881]). Permitting unauthorized persons to view confidential medical records may also be an invasion of privacy.

17. *Genetic Testing: University of California Settles Lawsuit Alleging Testing of Workers Without Consent,* 9 BNA's Health Law Reporter 1245 (2000).

18. *Norman-Bloodsaw v. Lawrence Berkeley Lab.,* 135 F.3d 1260 (9th Cir. 1998).

19. *See, e.g.,* Cal. Health & Safety Code sec. 2554; *Landeros v. Flood,* 17 Cal. 3d 399, 131 Cal. Rptr. 69, 551 P.2d 389 (1976) (physician could be liable to child for injury suffered from child abuse after physician's failure to report earlier incident of child abuse); *and see generally Denver Pub. Co. v. Dreyfus,* 184 Colo. 288, 520 P.2d 104 (1974) (autopsy reports open to public under Open Records Act). No statute is needed to authorize release of confidential medical information when a danger to the public exists. The leading case enunciating this exception, *Simonsen v. Swenson,* 104 Neb. 224, 177 N.W. 831, was decided by the Supreme Court of Nebraska in 1920. In that case, a man who was visiting a small town was seen by a physician who was also the physician for the hotel in which he was staying. The physician diagnosed syphilis and advised the patient to "get out of town," or he would tell the hotel's owner. When the patient remained in town, the doctor notified the landlady, who disinfected his room and placed his belongings in the hallway. The court decided that the doctor had the right to reveal only as much information concerning a contagious disease as was necessary for others to take proper precautions against becoming infected, and that his actions under the circumstances were justified.

20. *E.g., Dennie v. University of Pittsburgh School of Medicine,* 638 F. Supp. 1005 (W.D. Pa. 1986); and *Commonwealth v. Petrino,* 480 A.2d 1160 (Pa. 1984), *cert. denied.* 471 U.S. 1069 (1985); *and see* F. Turkington, *Legal Protection for the Confidentiality of Health Care Information in Pennsylvania,* 32 Vill. L. Rev. 259 (1987).

21. *Hofmann v. Blackmon,* 241 So. 2d 752 (Fla. App. 1970); *and see Wojcik v. Aluminum Co. of America,* 183 N.Y.S.2d 351, 357–58 (1959); and *Jones v. Stanko,* 118 Ohio St. 147, 160 N.E. 456 (1928).

22. *Davis v. Rodman,* 147 Ark. 385, 227 S.W. 612 (1921) (typhoid); and *Skillings v. Allen,* 143 Minn. 323, 173 N.W. 663 (1919) (scarlet fever).

23. *Tarasoff v. Regents of U. of California,* 131 Cal. Rptr. 14, 20, 551 P.2d 334, 340 (1976) (emphasis added).

24. Alan Stone, *The Tarasoff Decisions: Suing Psychotherapists to Safeguard Society,* 90 Harv. L. Rev. 358 (1976); *and see* Note, *Where the Public Peril Begins: A Survey of Psychotherapists to Determine the Effects of Tarasoff,* 31 Stan. L. Rev. 165 (1978).

25. *See, e.g., McIntosh v. Milano,* 168 N.J. Super. 466, 403 A.2d 500 (1979); *Bradley Center v. Wessner,* 287 S.E.2d 716 (Ga. Ct. App. 1982); *Williams v. U.S.,* 450 F. Supp. 1040 (D.S.D. 1978); *Bardoni v. Kim,* 390 N.W.2d 218 (Mich. 1986); *Davis v. Lhim,* 335 N.W.2d 481 (Mich. 1983); *Lipari v. Sears & Roebuck,* 497 F. Supp. 185 (Neb. 1980); *duty to warn not found: Furr v. Spring Grove State Hospital,* 454 A.2d 414 (Md. App. 1983); *Cooke v. Berlin,* 735 P.2d 830 (Ariz. 1987); *Hinkelman v. Borgess Medical Center,* 403 N.W.2d 547 (Mich. 1987). *See generally* Note, *Psychiatrist's Liability to Third Parties for Harmful Acts Committed by Dangerous Patients,* 64 N.C.L. Rev. 1534 (1986).

26. Lawrence Altman, *Sex, Privacy and Tracking HIV Infections,* New York Times,

November 4, 1997, F1; Lynda Richardson, *Wave of Laws Aimed at People with HIV,* New York Times, September 25, 1998, A1; and Lynda Richardson, *Progress on AIDS Brings Movement for Less Privacy,* New York Times, August 21, 1997, A1.

27. *See* discussion of "blanket consent forms" in chapter 6. *See also* Jon Merz, Pamela Sankar & Simon Yoo, *Hospital Consent for Disclosure of Medical Records,* 26 J. Law, Med. & Ethics 241 (1998).

28. Privacy Protection Study Commission, Personal Privacy in an Information Society, Washington, D.C.: Government Printing Office, 1977, 314. For example, most life insurance companies require all who apply for insurance to agree to release their medical records to the Medical Information Bureau (MIB), an information exchange agency operated by approximately seven hundred life insurance companies in the United States and Canada (information on an individual's file can be obtained by writing MIB at Box 105, Essex Station, Boston, Mass. 02112).

29. 45 C.F.R. 164.520.

30. 45 C.F.R. 164.508.

31. *Hicks v. Talbott Recovery* System, 196 F.3d 1226 (11 Cir. 1999); *see also* American Psychiatric Association, Confidentiality and Third Parties, Washington, D.C.: APA, 1975, 13.

32. *Legislature Approves Substantial Rewrite of Last Year's Patient Confidentiality Law,* 8 BNA's Health Law Reporter 1000 (1999).

33. 45 C.F.R. 164.510. Members of the media have expressed frustration with the new rules. Laura Meckler, *Hospitals to Guard Patient's Privacy,* Boston Globe, February 15, 2003, A3.

34. Privacy Protection Study Commission, *supra* note 28, at 293–314.

35. *Commonwealth v. Wiseman,* 356 Mass. 251, 259, 249 N.E.2d 610, 616 (1969).

36. *Berthiaume v. Pratt,* 365 A.2d 792 (Me. 1976).

37. *Id.,* at 796–97. *See also Knight v. Penobscot Bay Medical Center,* 420 A.2d 915 (Me. 1980) (A jury verdict in favor of the hospital in which the husband of a staff nurse had viewed a birth was affirmed. The jury had been instructed to find in favor of the plaintiff only if it found the intrusion was *intentional* and "would be highly offensive to a reasonable person."), and *Doe v. Mills,* 212 Mich. App. 73, 536 N.W.2d 824 (1995) (finding a cause of action for invasion of privacy and intentional infliction of emotional distress for displaying plaintiff's name on a sign outside an abortion clinic with the words: "Please Don't Kill Your Baby.").

38. Laura Landro, *Cancer Support Sites Are Raising Questions about Medical Privacy,* Wall Street Journal, April 28, 2000, B1. Some health sites are working on a code of ethics, but it has no enforcement provision. In general, there is agreement that health sites should "disclose their financial backers, should clearly date their content, all sources should be named, there should be a clear separation between advertising and editorial content, and an easy method for users to submit comments or complaints." Laura Landro, *Web Health Groups Ponder How to Set Universal Standards,* Wall Street Journal, November 3, 2000, B1. *See also* William Safire, *Stalking the Internet,* New York Times, May 29, 2000, A19 (arguing that "[t]he only genuine online privacy protection is *informed, written consent*" [emphasis in original]).

39. *Web Health Sites Get Heavy Use, Study Says,* Boston Globe, November 27, 2000,

A4; and *Web Users Search for Medical Advice Most Often*, Wall Street Journal, November 27, 2000, B14 (reporting results of a study conducted by the Pew Internet and American Life Project, March to August 2000).

40. The hospital gown, also known as a johnnie, is aptly described by Stephen Hall: "In the long history of human apparel, the most pathetic garment ever created is undoubtedly the contemporary, standard-issue hospital gown. Halfheartedly floral, flimsy, and limp with serial launderings of God knows how many emergent bodily fluids, it is a kind of off-the-rack shroud that perfectly, if inadvertently, accentuates human frailty; to illness's conventional cosmetic torments of pallor and lassitude, it adds a final dollop of indignity." Stephen S. Hall, Merchants of Immortality: Chasing the Dream of Human Life Extension, New York: Houghton Mifflin, 2003, 338.

XII

Care of the Dying

Americans are skilled, even gifted, at denying death. Nonetheless, our culture also produces constant reminders of our mortality. Mitch Albom's *Tuesdays with Morrie,* which was at or near the top of the *New York Times* best-seller list for more than four years, is one example. The book is built on weekly conversations between Albom and his dying college professor, Morrie Schwartz, who has amyotrophic lateral sclerosis (ALS), Lou Gehrig's disease. Albom's reflections on his life and coming death are universal and account for the book's popularity. At one point, Albom says, for example, that he wants to die "serenely, peacefully." He continues, "I don't want to leave the world in a state of fright. I want to know what's happening, accept it, get to a peaceful place, and let go."[1]

When pressed, virtually all Americans agree: we want to die peacefully, comfortably, at home, surrounded by our loved ones. Yet few of us do. Albom manages it in the end, but for most of us, death will come painfully, in a hospital filled with strangers. This reality is reflected in a popular 1999 play that won the Pulitzer Prize: Margaret Edson's *W;t.* The main character is also a retired college professor, Vivian Bearing. Vivian is dying of cancer, and all of the play's action takes place in a hospital. Vivian is dehumanized and treated like just another entry in a research log. Ultimately, she dies a violent death. Although she has asked not to be resuscitated should her heart stop, she dies with a resuscitation team yelling, administering electrical shocks, and pounding on her chest, while the nurse tries to stop them saying, "She's NO CODE! Order was given—*(she dives for the chart and holds it up as she cries out)* Look! Look at this! DO NOT RESUSCITATE." The code team ultimately stops, and as the lights in the theater fade to black, we hear the resuscitation team saying, "It's a doctor fuckup. What is he, a resident? Got us up here on a DNR. Called a code on a no-code."[2]

Dying the way we want to die may be an unattainable fantasy. We can, however, certainly do much better than we do now in planning for our own deaths and respecting the wishes of dying patients.[3] The pervasive fear of loss of control at the end of life has made the "right to die" the most discussed patient right. Of course, if we don't protect and promote the right of patients during their lives, we cannot expect patient rights to be honored near death, when the right to refuse treatment is more important than the right to treatment. This chapter focuses on rights most pertinent to the dying patient and on the problems faced by families and professionals charged with their care, with the goal of making dying a better experience for everyone involved, but especially for the patient.

Does a patient have a right to know that his or her physician considers the patient's condition terminal?

Yes. There is no justification for withholding this information from a patient. Surveys from the 1950s and early 1960s indicated that although 90 percent of all patients wanted to know their diagnosis, even if terminal, 60 to 90 percent of physicians preferred to withhold a terminal diagnosis.[4] By the late 1970s, surveys revealed a dramatic shift, with 97 percent of physicians indicating that their general policy is to disclose a terminal diagnosis.[5] Much of this shift can be attributed to more public discussions of death. It also reflects a more realistic assessment of who is dying, who must make plans for death, and thus who has a right to know this information.

Some physicians, nonetheless, still rationalize their preference for withholding a terminal diagnosis on the basis that such a decision can only be made on a case-by-case basis, and that it is seldom possible to know for certain that a patient is dying. Such a stance, unfortunately, can be easily translated into a policy of almost never telling, especially if the patient has a family with which the physician can share the diagnosis. And it fails to appreciate that what is ultimately at issue is truthfulness about uncertainty. A second rationale advanced is that "the patient knows anyway." If this is true, not telling only forces both the patient and those around the patient to live the lie, increasing the patient's conflict and anxiety. A final argument is that the patient should not be forced to abandon hope. Hope may be essential, but hoping for immortality is irrational. A cancer patient may begin treatment hoping he will be cured, for example, then hoping he will live to see his daughter graduate from college, and finally hoping that dying will not be too painful. Honesty about a terminal diagnosis is not the same thing as denying the patient realistic hope for a good life that remains and a peaceful death. To help the patient accept and deal with the diagnosis of a terminal illness, the physician must continue to talk with the patient openly and to assure the patient that everything necessary will be done to keep the patient comfortable.

Rights carry duties but also options. If a patient clearly expresses a desire not to be told a diagnosis or prognosis, it is proper for the physician to ask who else the patient would like to be informed (e.g., the advocate) and to inform that person instead. This should be rare, however. Death is inevitable, and planning for it is a personal responsibility we should not shirk off on our relatives and loved ones.

Does a dying patient have a right to demand that no one in the patient's family be told of the diagnosis of a terminal illness?

Yes. Even physicians who generally prefer not to tell dying patients about a terminal diagnoses often feei compelled to tell someone, usually the family. When this is done, the patient is deprived not only of the right to know the truth but also of the rights of confidentiality and privacy. The patient has the right to make this demand and to expect physicians and nurses to respect it and not breach confidentiality.

One possible explanation for physicians telling families in addition to or instead of patients is that once the patient is labeled terminal, the physician ceases to treat the individual alone and begins to treat the family unit as "the patient." Reluctance to candidly discuss terminal diagnosis with the patient makes concentration on the family almost inevitable. The tragedy is the resulting isolation of the patient from truth and family. Both patient and family try to pretend all is well, although each knows better. Visits are uncomfortable for family members, who talk of trivialities, such as the weather or sports, and almost unbearable for the patient whose impending death is transformed into a mockery.

When patients are denied the opportunity to discuss their own deaths, they are simultaneously stripped of their dignity as adults and are treated like children. Leo Tolstoy describes the dehumanizing effect of deception in *The Death of Ivan Ilyich:*

What tormented Ivan Ilyich most was the deception, the lie, which for some reason they all accepted, that he was not dying but was simply ill, and that he only need keep quiet and undergo a treatment and then something very good would result. . . . This deception tortured him—their not wishing him to admit what they all knew and what he knew. . . . Those lies—lies enacted over him on the eve of his death and destined to degrade this awful, solemn act to the level of their visiting, their curtains, their sturgeon for dinner—were a terrible agony for Ivan Ilyich.[6]

The "survivor knows best" attitude is illustrated by the words of a woman who described the death of her uncle as beautiful: "John died happy, never even realizing he was seriously ill."

Can a terminally ill patient give informed consent to risky treatment if the patient does not know that the doctor considers the patient's condition terminal?

No. If the patient lacks this vital piece of information, the patient's probable motive for consenting to any medical procedure, the belief that it will help restore health, is based on misinformation. Consent given without the knowledge of one's terminal diagnosis is based on incomplete information and is therefore not valid consent.

The legacy of withholding information from patients is that some patients no longer believe anything health professionals tell them. The financial conflicts of interest inherent in some managed care plans have increased patient suspicion that relevant information may be withheld to save the health plan money. Some oncologists, for example, report that the hardest task they have is persuading patients that they do not have cancer. It is important for all of us that these attitudes, and the practices that breed them, be challenged and changed. Only routine openness and honesty can accomplish a change in patient attitudes.

Does a patient have a right to know his or her prognosis?

Yes, but as discussed in the chapter on informed consent, prognosis is often difficult information to obtain. I had this point reinforced to me by a Japanese researcher who found, while doing a study of U.S. physicians, that although U.S. physicians are much more likely to share serious diagnoses with their patients than are Japanese physicians, they are just as reluctant to share a terminal prognosis as their Japanese counterparts.[7] A study reported in 2000 confirmed this. In this study of 258 physicians caring for 326 cancer patients at five Chicago hospitals, nearly all the physicians were willing to estimate how long the patient was likely to live. Nonetheless, even if the patient insisted on knowing how long the physician thought they had to live, only one in three of the physicians said they would give a truthful answer. One in four physicians said they would refuse to respond to such a request, saying instead something like, "Only God knows," and another two in five said they would lie. Of this group, three out of four said they would tell patients they had longer to live than they really believed they had. The reasons for lying about prognosis turned out to be similar to reasons physicians used to lie about diagnosis: fear that the truth might harm patients by making them give up hope and thus shortening their lives. But as one of the coauthors of the study, Dr. Nicholas Christakis, noted, many patients die in pain, institutionalized, and broke: "I firmly believe that a lot of these deficits could be partially addressed if people had access to more reliable prognostic information. . . . Part of the reason we die badly is because we don't see death coming and we don't plan accordingly."[8] Christakis is exactly right, and patients (and their advocates) should insist on truthful prognosis information. On the other hand, patients and their advocates also need to know that medical prognosis is not an exact science, and that physicians usually overestimate how long terminally ill patients have to live.[9]

May a competent adult patient refuse treatment even if he or she will die without it?

Yes. It is almost incredible that anyone ever thought that it was acceptable to force unwanted treatment on a patient. Competent adults may refuse *any treatment,* including lifesaving and life-sustaining treatment and artificial nutrition and hydration. Procedures do not have rights; people do. And a patient has the right not to have his or her body invaded by *any* medical procedure. The decision to undergo treatment is not a medical decision. It is a personal decision that can be legitimately made only by the patient who will be directly affected. Contemporary courts agree that for competent patients the finding of a "good prognosis" is insufficient to justify the state to forcibly treat these individuals. Whether a prognosis is "good" is not a medical issue and not an issue that can be resolved by an objective test. A prognosis is good or bad based on a subjective evaluation of the situation by the patient. If a person is empowered by law to decide to undergo medical treatment, it follows that the person also has the right to decline such treatment. If a person cannot decline treatment, the right to decide whether or not to undergo a treatment becomes a sham, equivalent to a "right to agree with your doctor."

It is never proper for the state to force its view of a "good" life on a competent patient. The right to refuse medical treatment is not conditioned on the state's (or doctor's) finding, or not finding, that the proposed treatment is "good." Rather, it is based on the right of each citizen to make important personal decisions. The tragedy of modern American medicine is that it still encourages people to endure invasive and expensive treatment they may not want while simultaneously denying others treatment they desperately want and need.

A corollary to the rule is that there is no legal or ethical distinction between a patient's right to refuse to begin treatment (such as ventilator support) and a patient's right to have an ongoing treatment stopped. The legal right to order both are the same and are based on the same legal principle of autonomy. Moreover, if treatment once begun could not be stopped, trials of therapy (to see if an intervention might help) could not be done, and this irrational result could lead to needless deaths.

What does it mean to be competent to choose or refuse treatment?

In the context of medical care, a person is competent if the person can understand the nature and consequences of the illness or condition and the nature and consequences of the proposed medical procedure. This is a factual question, requiring a discussion with the patient. If a patient understands the information needed to give informed consent, then the patient is competent to either give or refuse consent.[10] An unconscious patient is obviously incompetent, as are very young children. With these exceptions, no simple categories of incompetent people exist.

In a leading case, for example, Rosaria Candura, a seventy-seven-year-old woman, suffered from gangrene in her foot and refused to undergo a recommended amputation. The court found that she was combative and defensive at times, that she was sometimes confused, that her mind wandered, and that her concept of time was distorted. Nonetheless, she demonstrated a high degree of awareness and acuity "when responding to questions concerning the proposed operation." The patient made clear that she did not want to have the operation, even though she knew her decision probably would shortly lead to her death. The court concluded that she understood the nature and consequences of her decision and had made her choice "with full appreciation of the consequence." As a result of this, she was competent.[11]

The *Candura* case also illustrates another important fact: a patient's competence is usually not questioned as long as the patient agrees to undergo recommended medical procedures. As the court pointed out, the physicians had previously accepted her consent to have a toe amputation and later to have part of her right foot removed. They were also prepared to accept her consent to this operation. "Until she changed her original decision and withdrew her consent to the amputation, her competence was not questioned. But the irrationality of her decision does not justify a conclusion that Mrs. Candura is incompetent in the legal sense. The law protects her right to make her own decision to accept or reject treatment, whether that decision is wise or unwise."[12] If a patient is competent to consent to an operation, the patient is competent to refuse consent as well.

All adults are presumed competent until proven otherwise. Therefore, anyone who wishes to treat a person without consent on the basis of that person's incompetency must demonstrate that because of some mental or physical disease or disability the patient cannot understand the nature and consequences of the proposed procedure and the consequences of refusing to undergo the procedure. The refusal to undergo the procedure, however "irrational" that decision may appear, is never sufficient alone to prove incompetence. Since the ability to understand (sometimes called "capacity") is a *factual* question, anyone who can determine the relevant facts (i.e., what information is needed for informed consent and whether the patient understands this information) can determine capacity. This includes the patient's family and the patient's advocate. However, only a court can determine that a person is legally incompetent and appoint a legal guardian to act on behalf of an incompetent patient.

Are there legal limits on the right of a competent patient to refuse treatment?

Other than some limits that apply to institutionalized mental patients and prisoners, there really are none. Nevertheless, courts have said that the individual's right to refuse treatment must be balanced against a variety of state interests if the state challenges the patient's decision. State interests include (1) preservation of life, (2) protection of innocent third parties, (3) prevention of suicide, and (4) maintenance of the ethical integrity of the medical profession.

Preservation of life. The clearest statement on the state's interest in preserving human life is by the Massachusetts Supreme Judicial Court: "The constitutional right of privacy . . . is an expression of the sanctity of individual free choice and self-determination as fundamental constituents of life. The value of life as so perceived is lessened not by a decision to refuse treatment, but by the failure to allow a competent human being the right of choice."[13] In other words, life without liberty is not the type of life the state should compel.

Protection of innocent third parties. This is probably the strongest state interest that has been expressed by the courts, but ultimately this interest cannot justify forcing treatment on a competent adult, who has no obligation to undergo treatment for the benefit of another person.[14]

Prevention of suicide. Like murder, suicide (or self-murder) requires a specific intent to cause death and an action putting the death-producing agent in motion. In cases of refusing treatment, it is not that the patient wants to die but rather that the patient does not want to undergo a certain treatment and is willing to accept death as a consequence of that decision. Additionally, the patient does not set the death-producing agent in motion, since patients seldom cause the illnesses or condition they will die from.[15]

Maintenance of the ethical integrity of the medical profession. Medical ethics do not require the forcible treatment of competent patients; therefore, courts have not ordered treatment on this basis. Courts have almost never ordered competent individuals to undergo any treatment more invasive than a blood transfusion and are unlikely to do so in the future. The spectacle of a competent patient being strapped down, chemically restrained, and forced to undergo a medical procedure he or she does not want is so abhorrent to a free society that medical professionals (and lawyers and judges) most often work to ensure it never occurs. As one judge has pointed out, "The notion that an individual exists for the good of the state is, of course, quite antithetical to our fundamental thesis that the role of the state is to ensure a maximum of individual freedom of choice and conduct."[16]

Who has the right to refuse lifesaving treatment on behalf of an incompetent patient?

This is one of the most controversial areas of medical jurisprudence. Courts now realize that neither good medical practice nor the law requires that incompetent patients be continuously treated with all the resources that medical science and technology have to offer. Judges have concluded that competent individuals have the right to refuse treatment, and incompetent persons should not be deprived of this right simply because they are incapable of expressing their wishes. Accordingly, a way must be found to enable incompetent individuals to have a similar right exercised on their behalf.

The most famous case, that of Karen Ann Quinlan, was decided by the New Jersey Supreme Court in 1976.[17] At the time the case was brought to court, Quinlan was twenty-one years old and in a "chronic vegetative state." She required constant medical attention, and it was thought that she would die if the ventilator was removed. All the physicians who examined her concluded that she suffered from incurable brain damage and would never awaken from her comatose condition. Her parents wanted the ventilator removed, but the physicians refused. Her father petitioned the court for appointment as her guardian with the explicit power to order the removal of the ventilator. The trial court rejected his request.

On appeal, the New Jersey Supreme Court decided that the constitutional right to privacy was broad enough to include the right to refuse treatment in such a dire situation, and that this right could be exercised on the patient's behalf by the guardian. The court also found that physicians were leery of terminating treatment in such cases because of their fear of possible civil and criminal liability. To relieve this fear, the court set up a procedure to try to make physicians more comfortable. Specifically, the court decided that if all of the following conditions applied—the family requested discontinuance of treatment; the patient's physician concluded that there was "no reasonable possibility" of the patient's returning to a "cognitive, sapient state;" the "guardian and family" of the patient concurred; and a hospital "ethics committee" agreed with this conclusion —then the participants in the decision would be immune from civil and criminal liability.

The Massachusetts Supreme Judicial Court almost immediately thereafter came to the same conclusion but ruled that if the parties wanted immunity from civil and criminal liability, they would have to apply to a court (not merely an ethics committee).[18] It should be emphasized, however, that neither court required recourse to either courts or ethics committees. These bodies must be consulted only if prospective immunity from lawsuits is seen as necessary by the physician or hospital. Since no health care provider has even stood trial for terminating treatment on such seriously ill individuals with family consent, the need for immunity ranges from nonexistent to highly questionable.

What criteria have courts established to determine when treatment of an incompetent patient can be stopped or withheld?

Both the *Quinlan* and *Saikewicz* courts adopted the *substituted judgment* doctrine, a legal term for what the person would decide if the person could decide. The goal is, as the *Saikewicz* court put it, "to determine with as much accuracy as possible the wants and needs of the individual involved." The *Quinlan* court similarly stated that "the only practical way to prevent destruction of the right [to refuse treatment] is to permit the guardian and family of Karen to render their best judgment . . . as to whether she would exercise it in the circumstances."

The goal is to treat the incompetent person as the person would choose to be treated if the person were competent. In a case such as *Quinlan,* this was possible, since Karen Quinlan was competent for many years, and it is likely that her family, with whom she had a long and loving relationship, could reasonably determine what she would likely want done. But in *Saikewicz* (the case of a never-competent adult) and in the case of a seriously ill newborn, this doctrine is impossible to apply because there is no way to determine what the patient would want. This is because the patient has never made *any* important decisions, and so there is no basis on which to determine the patient's subjective preferences for treatment because there is no basis to conclude that the patient has a unique value system.

When substituted judgment cannot be used, it is necessary to determine what is in the patient's best interest. This is usually done by judging the benefits and burdens of treatment. The *best interests* test is objective, rather than subjective, and is based on what a reasonable person would think is best for the patient. In the case of Karen Quinlan, for example, trying to determine what Quinlan would tell us she wanted done if she had a "lucid moment" during which she could converse with us is an example of trying to apply substituted judgment. Taking a survey to see what treatment most people think would best for Quinlan is an example of a best interests approach. It is important to stress that the proper question is not would the patient be "better off dead," but rather whether continuing a specific medical treatment would provide a benefit to the patient.

What has the U.S. Supreme Court said about the rights of competent and incompetent patients to refuse medical treatment?

Other than the physician-assisted suicide cases discussed in the next chapter, the primary opinion of the U.S. Supreme Court on the right to refuse medical treatment is the case of Nancy Cruzan, decided in 1990. That case involved a young woman in a persistent vegetative state, exactly the same condition as Karen Ann Quinlan. Unlike Quinlan, however, Cruzan could breathe on her own and only needed fluids and nutrition (delivered by tubes) to survive. The question before the U.S. Supreme Court involved Cruzan's constitutional rights, as well as the authority of the state of Missouri to make rules about how her rights could be exercised.[19] Cruzan's parents wanted the feeding tubes removed. The state of Missouri took the position that the decision to refuse treatment by refusing further tube feeding was a personal one that only Cruzan herself could make. If she had been competent, Cruzan could refuse further use of feeding tubes or any other treatment. Since she was not competent, however, Missouri's rule (as enunciated by its highest court)[20] was that her parents or guardians had to present "clear and convincing evidence" of her intent to refuse fluids and nutrition, such as a written document specifying that if she was ever like Quinlan she would not want any treatment, including fluids and nutrition, even though she knew she would die without such treatment.

Chief Justice William Rehnquist, writing for a 5-4 majority of the Court, found that because this was a personal, life and death decision, Missouri could constitutionally require clear and convincing evidence of Cruzan's refusal of fluids and nutrition before permitting the tubes to be removed. Justice William Brennan wrote a strong dissent, arguing that this high a level of proof did more to frustrate Cruzan's wishes than honor her autonomy. Justice Sandra Day O'Connor, who provided the majority with its fifth vote, wrote that in her view had Cruzan simply said if she was ever unable to make medical decisions for herself, she'd want her mother to make them for her, that would have been a constitutionally protected delegation of her authority, and the state of Missouri would have to honor her mother's decisions as her own.

Although the case went against Cruzan and her family, it nonetheless helped establish that *there is a constitutional right to refuse treatment* (five Justices, the four dissenters and Justice O'Connor explicitly acknowledged this right); *there is no constitutional difference between artificially delivered fluids and nutrition and any other medical treatment* (six Justices explicitly found no distinction, and none of the other three found a constitutionally relevant distinction); and delegation of your decision-making authority to another (who can be called a health care agent) to make medical decisions for you when you are unable to make them yourself is constitutionally protected. (This is Justice O'Connor's point, but the four dissenters, and likely Justice Rehnquist as well, seem to agree with it.) There are no holdings for any of these conclusions; nonetheless, by 2004 all of them have been widely if not unanimously accepted. When Cruzan's case returned to the trial court, oral testimony of a friend that Nancy Cruzan herself would not want further artificial fluids and nutrition was accepted as sufficient to provide clear and convincing evidence of her wishes on this subject, and tube feeding was accordingly discontinued.

A few states, such as New York, nonetheless require that fluids and nutrition be explicitly refused in written form before a health care agent and physician are given good-faith immunity under the state's advance directive law.[21] State law cannot, however, affect constitutional rights, and the patient's wishes, if known, are determinative. Courts in a few states have found it difficult to order treatment terminations on severely brain-damaged but conscious patients who have not left clear and convincing evidence of their wishes.[22] Unfortunately, these courts have missed the point: almost no one wants to live in such a condition, and the "default" position should be to honor autonomy by permitting refusals based on the next of kin's best judgment of what the patient would want.

What is a living will?

The term *living will* (one form of an "advance directive") was coined by Luis Kutner in 1969; it describes a document in which a competent adult sets forth his or her wishes concerning medical treatment in the event he or she becomes incompetent in the future.[23] In this sense, it is like a will, but since it takes effect prior to death, it is termed a "living" will. Because of the absence of specific judicial sanction and the lack of clear rules regarding their execution and use, many individuals and organizations have long advocated that states pass specific statutes supporting the living will, and by 2000 every state had passed some form of living will or health care proxy law.

Most states, however, have limitations on the individuals covered by living will statutes, generally applying only to "terminally ill." This removes from their protection the very categories of patients who are likely to need this protection the most, chronically ill patients such as Earle Spring (kidney dialysis), William Bartling (mechanical ventilator), and Claire Conroy (tube feeding). As the President's Commission for the

Study of Ethical Problems in Medicine also noted, "[S]uch a limitation greatly reduces an act's potential."[24] All state laws include specific instructions that must be followed in the execution of an advance directive, and some permit the declarant to refuse only specified procedures.[25]

The only certain thing is that when we become comatose or incompetent, others will make treatment decisions for us. If these decision makers know what decisions we would make, we can hope and trust that they will act consistently with our directions. The law supports them if they do. But to follow our directions, they must know what they are. It is therefore critical that each of us tell our relatives and friends how we want to be cared for in the event of incompetence.

Many people have said simply, "I don't want to be like Karen Quinlan," meaning that they do not want to be kept alive on a mechanical ventilator if they are permanently unconscious. This type of statement is extremely helpful to physicians and families. But thankfully, most of us will not end up like Karen Quinlan. The best strategy is to designate one or more persons to act on our behalf to make treatment decisions when we are unable to make them ourselves. This should be done in writing, using a form called a health care proxy form. In addition, it is a good idea to tell this person (and your family) how you want to be treated in various situations. This can be done verbally, but it is best to write down directions in a form that can be understood by others (such as a letter or a living will).

What is a health care proxy?

A health care proxy is a written document wherein you give someone else the authority to make medical decisions for you, consistent with your directions. The person given authority to act for you in a health care proxy document is your health care agent (who can also act as your advocate). You are called the principal. The health care proxy becomes effective (or "springs" into effect) only when the principal becomes incompetent.[26]

Almost all states have health care proxy laws, and most states have enacted durable power-of-attorney statutes that pertain specifically to health care decisions. There is nothing in the durable power-of-attorney statutes to prevent you from using this document to designate an individual to make health care decisions for you, and this document has been widely recommended for this purpose.[27]

I used to believe that it made the most sense for an individual to execute a document that contains the elements of both a health care proxy and a living will: a document that delegates decision-making authority for treatment decisions to a specified person, that also contains explicit decisions to a specified person, and that also contains explicit instructions as to what types of decisions an individual wants made. Nonetheless, because of the inherent difficulties of both predicting how you will likely die and what interventions physicians might use to keep you alive, *I now recommend that you use the durable power of attorney or health care proxy form to name a person to make decisions for you.* You can write a personal letter to your health care agent, stating in as much detail as you can, what you want and do not want. Your agent can use this letter if helpful, but if your predictions are wrong, the agent need not disclose it, since it will confuse rather than clarify your intentions. Of course, your major intention must be to delegate all medical decision-making authority to your agent.

The durable power of attorney can be revoked at any time so long as the principal is competent. If a guardian is appointed for the principal (after incompetence), the guardian can revoke the health care agent's power, just as the principal could. Accordingly, it is prudent for the individual to nominate the person designated as the health care proxy to be the individual's guardian as well. Except in extraordinary circumstances, courts will honor the principal's choice for guardian.[28]

May parents refuse life-sustaining treatment for their children?

They usually may not, even for religious reasons. As the U.S. Supreme Court stated in another context, "Parents may be free to become martyrs themselves. But it does not follow they are free . . . to make martyrs of their children."[29] Parents have a legal obligation to provide their children with "necessary medical care." When alternative modes of treatment are available, and each alternative is consistent with generally accepted medical practice, parents may choose among them. But when the only alternative is nontreatment, parents may lawfully choose this option only if it is consistent with the "best interests" of the child. To deny the child life-saving treatment is usually considered child neglect, and the state has an obligation to exercise its *parens patriae* power to protect children from neglect.

Society's view of the sanctity of human life is so important that when a duty to treat exists and treatment is withheld, both the parents and the physician could be charged with homicide.[30] Few such cases have ever been brought in the United States, however. One involved a charge of attempted homicide for the initial failure to treat conjoined twins born in Danville, Illinois, but it was dropped for lack of evidence.[31] The children were eventually successfully separated, and at last report, they were doing "moderately well." The other homicide charge was brought against three members of a cult for failure to properly feed and provide medical treatment for a child.[32]

What are the "Baby Doe" regulations?

A baby with Down syndrome, known only as Baby Doe, died in Bloomington, Indiana, on April 15, 1982, at the age of six days, following a court-approved decision that routine lifesaving surgery be withheld. The infant had a tracheoesophageal fistula (a connection between the trachea and esophagus that makes eating impossible) that was not repaired; instead the child was medicated with phenobarbital and morphine and allowed to starve to death. The court believed that if there was a dispute among physicians regarding treatment, the parents should be able to withhold treatment. Given existing legal principles, however, that require treatment if it is in the child's best interests, it seems that legally and ethically Baby Doe should have been treated.[33] The public, accordingly, was properly outraged that he was not.

On the strength of the Baby Doe case, the Department of Health and Human Services (HHS) wrote a letter to approximately seven thousand hospitals, on May 18, 1982, putting them on notice that it was unlawful (under section 504, of the Rehabilitation Act of 1973) for a recipient of federal financial assistance to withhold from a handicapped infant nutritional sustenance or medical or surgical treatment required to correct a life-threatening condition if (1) the withholding is based on the fact that the infant is handicapped, and (2) the handicap does not render treatment or nutritional sustenance contraindicated.

In emergency regulations published in March 1983, HHS required the conspicuous display of a sign containing the substance of the May 1982 letter in each delivery ward, maternity ward, pediatric ward, nursery, and intensive care nursery. Included in the notice was a toll-free, twenty-four-hour "hotline" number that individuals with knowledge of any handicapped infant being discriminated against by being denied food or customary medical care were encouraged to call. The HHS officials were given authority to take "immediate remedial action" to protect the infant, and hospitals were required to provide access to their premises and medical records to agency investigators. These regulations, and their successors, were ultimately invalidated by the U.S. Supreme Court,[34] but they served to focus public debate on the appropriate treatment of disabled newborns and the respective roles of the state and federal governments in protecting children.

When is refusing treatment for an infant considered child neglect?

The federal Child Abuse Amendments of 1984, among other things, explicitly brand the withholding and withdrawal of medically indicated treatment and nutrition from disabled infants as a type of child abuse. The law requires individual states, as a condition for continued federal funding of their child abuse programs, to establish special procedures to deal with this form of child abuse.

On April 15, 1985, HHS issued final regulations (that apply to states, not physicians or hospitals) to implement the new law. Treatment may be withheld if

1. The infant is chronically and *irreversibly comatose;*

2. The provision of such *treatment would merely prolong dying;* not be effective in ameliorating or correcting all of the infant's life-threatening conditions; *or otherwise be futile* in terms of survival of infant; or

3. The provision of such *treatment would be virtually futile* in terms of survival of the infant and the treatment itself under such circumstances would be *inhumane.*[35]

The "virtually futile" exception provides latitude for physicians to make reasonable medical judgments regarding most treatments. Medical judgment is given central authority and specifically includes the withholding of "other than appropriate nutrition, hydration, or medication" to an infant when any of the exceptions listed above apply. Whether or not one of the exceptions applies is determined solely on the basis of "reasonable medical judgment," which the regulation defines as a "medical judgment that would be made by a rationally prudent physician, knowledgeable about the case and the treatment possibilities with respect to the medical conditions involved." Nutrition and hydration can be withheld from an infant when they are not "appropriate" in the attending physician's "reasonable medical judgment."

The Baby Doe episode and the Child Abuse Amendments of 1984 have heightened awareness of the rights of disabled newborns. But the law now is almost precisely the same as it had been for the prior two decades: withholding necessary medical treatment can be child neglect if treatment would be in the child's best interests. Enforcement of this law is and should be the responsibility of the states, not the federal government.[36]

May a child's "quality of life" be taken into account in making a decision not to treat?

The answer to this question depends to a large extent on what is meant by the ambiguous term *quality of life*. A trial court case in Maine, for example, involved a newborn who was blind, had no left ear, some abnormal vertebrae, and "some brain damage." The child also had a tracheoesophageal fistula, and the parents and physicians decided that this defect should not be corrected because the child would have a life "not worth preserving." The court concluded that "the doctor's qualitative evaluation of the value of life to be preserved is not legally within the scope of his expertise." Since the repair of the fistula was in no sense "heroic," and the treatment did not involve serious risk, the court said that the procedure must be performed.[37]

Courts will not permit nontreatment decisions to be made solely on the basis of the incompetent person's future mental or physical disability. In an extreme case, however, when the child will not live long and will only experience pain or suffering, or when the child is permanently unconscious, it will often not be in the child's best interests to be given specific treatments. Another way to say this is that from the child's own perspective, further medical treatment does not provide a benefit for the child.

Children often suffer terribly from pain when they are terminally ill, even more so than adults, because they are seldom referred for either palliative care or hospice care.[38] Parents and caregivers must work together to ensure that all dying children get the proper care and that their pain is effectively alleviated.

What is CPR (cardiopulmonary resuscitation) for?

The National Conference on CPR and ECC (electrocardiac conversion), cosponsored by the American Heart Association and the National

Academy of Science, stated clearly: "The purpose of CPR is the prevention of sudden, unexpected death. CPR is not indicated in certain situations such as in cases of terminal irreversible illness where death is not unexpected."[39]

CPR is contraindicated when it will do no good; that is, the patient will die soon anyway, and nothing can be done to stop the course of the disease. When the patient's condition is hopeless, no medical intervention is ethically or legally required because all medical interventions are useless. In cases in which CPR is known not to work, the decision can and should be made by the attending physician.

Determining that a medical intervention cannot achieve a specific goal, such as revival of consciousness, is an issue peculiarly within the competence of the medical profession. And if CPR cannot reverse cardiac arrest, then obviously CPR is not indicated. Indeed, if CPR is known to be ineffective for the goal sought by the patient, and given that CPR is intrusive and unproductive, there is no justification to inflict it on a patient regardless of the wishes of the family.

May a patient refuse CPR?

A patient may refuse any medical intervention, including CPR. CPR seems to have been treated differently from other medical procedures because it is administered under emergency conditions and, if successful, can be lifesaving. Physicians have a legal privilege to treat unconscious or otherwise incompetent patients in emergencies without consent, because time is of the essence and obtaining informed consent under such circumstances is impossible. Nonetheless, if the emergency can be anticipated, and if the patient refuses to consent to an intervention, such as CPR or the administration of a blood transfusion, in advance, the intervention may not be either legally or ethically imposed on the patient.

Senior physicians say that when blood transfusions were first introduced, no one could die in a hospital without getting a blood transfusion. Although CPR is almost a half century old, the general rule today often seems to be that no one can die in a hospital without CPR. This is medical practice in many institutions, but it is not the law. Patients have the legal right to refuse to be resuscitated, and physicians have an obligation to discuss CPR with them if there is a reasonable possibility that it may be used on them during their hospital stay. CPR when done in a hospital is an extremely invasive procedure, involving the possibility of placing a tube in the trachea for artificial respiration, electrocardial shock, intravenous lines, cardiac medications, and possibly the placement of a temporary pacemaker. If a patient refuses it, the physician should enter a "do not attempt resuscitation" (DNAR) order in the patient's chart. This means that resuscitation should not be attempted in the event the patient's heart stops beating, and the patient will die. Patients and families must realize, however, that CPR is not magic. Unless the cardiac arrest is sudden and unexpected, even if the patient is resuscitated, he or she will likely die soon. The probability of CPR's success in the hospital depends largely on the patient's medical condition.[40]

May a patient demand CPR even if it is not medically indicated?

No. Patients do have a right to refuse any treatment but do not have a right to demand that their physicians mistreat them by invading their bodies in ways that are contrary to good medical practice. For example, if CPR is *never* successful in hospitalized patients with metastatic cancer, it is useless and futile in this category of patients; therefore physicians should not do CPR, and patients have no right to demand that they do.[41] Likewise, patients have no right to demand a kidney, heart, or liver transplant if such a transplant is not "medically indicated" and would be futile.

Depriving patients of futile treatments does not implicate autonomy. As a philosopher and a philosopher-physician have properly noted:

Patients or families who demand CPR when it will almost certainly be futile almost always do so because of denial of the prospect of death, magical thinking about miracles of modern medicine, or benign television images of CPR. The physician who offers CPR under these conditions only supports these natural defense mechanisms and suggests, moreover—regardless of what he or she might say to the contrary—that CPR does offer something of value. Under these conditions, the patient's choice of CPR will be based on a misunderstanding of its benefits, and therefore will frustrate the pursuit of autonomy rather than serve it.[42]

It should be noted, however, that the state of New York has a law that mandates the use of CPR unless the patient or the patient's proxy has refused it.[43] This law improperly treats CPR as a unique treatment that patients will be subjected to without consent and seems to say that physicians must use it even when it is futile. But useless treatment is by definition no treatment at all and so should not be offered or performed. Every hospital accredited by the Joint Commission on Accreditation of Health-care Organizations (JCAHO) must have a DNAR policy, and patients have a right to know the hospital's DNAR policy and, of course, to refuse CPR in advance.

Are dying patients especially vulnerable to experimental and nonconventional treatments?

Dying patients are especially vulnerable to requests to try experimental and nonconventional treatments because of their own desire to prolong life and because of the typical physician's view that death is a defeat. Jay Katz has noted that in fighting against disease, "when medical knowledge and skills prove impotent against the claims of nature," physicians often resort to "disguised magical thinking." He continues, "At such times, all kinds of senseless interventions are tried in an unconscious effort to cure the incurable magically through a 'wonder drug,' a novel surgical proce-dure, or a penetrating psychological interpretation . . . doctors' heroic at-tempts to try anything may not necessarily be responsive to patients' needs but may turn out to be a projection of their own needs onto patients."[44]

Doctors often use the excuse that a dying patient has "nothing to lose" from taking part in an experiment. This is not true from the patient's perspective, since the patient may have the dying process prolonged, may experience more pain, or may even be rendered permanently incompetent or comatose. The most public experiments in the history of the world, those dealing with the artificial heart, have made it clear to everyone that there are fates worse than death, and that there are prices that are too high to pay even for added months of life.[45] Nor can experiments on dying children, such as transplanting a baboon heart into Baby Fae or doing multiple organ transplants, be justified solely on the basis that the child would die without the surgical intervention.[46] The scientific truth in each of these cases was that the child would die in any event; the experimental intervention only dictated the manner of death. The issue of research on terminally ill patients is dealt with in more detail in chapter 9. The ques-tions of euthanasia and suicide are addressed in the next chapter.

TIPS FOR ADVOCATES

- **Physicians are more likely to discuss diagnosis and treatment options than prognosis.** Make sure you know what the physician thinks the patient's prognosis is, meaning how long the physician thinks the patient has to live and the likely course of the disease.

• A physician's estimate of **how long a patient is likely to live is often inaccurate,** and the inherent uncertainty in such an estimate must be appreciated.

• **It is important that patients know that they are dying** so they can complete whatever tasks they want, prepare spiritually for death, and make treatment decisions fully informed of their prognosis.

• **A competent adult patient may refuse any treatment,** including life-prolonging and life-sustaining treatment and fluids and nutrition, and may order that any ongoing treatments be stopped.

• **Fluids and nutrition artificially delivered are legally no different than any other medical treatment** and can be refused like any other medical treatment, even if refusal will likely lead to the patient's death.

• **Capacity is functionally defined in the medical context as the ability to understand the information needed to make an informed decision.** If a patient is competent, the patient may both agree to and refuse any medical intervention. Only a judge may declare a person incompetent and appoint a legal guardian.

• **Patients have a constitutionally protected right to name a health care agent** to make health care decisions for them when they become incompetent.

• **Make sure your patient signs a "health care proxy" form designating you, their advocate, as their health care agent.** A patient's health care agent, or proxy, has the same legal authority the patient would have, if competent, to consent to treatment or refuse treatment, including artificially delivered fluids and nutrition.

• **Ask your patient to write down as clearly and completely as possible how the patient wants to be treated or not treated in specific**

cases (for example, cardiac resuscitation should their heart stop). Use this writing (which can be in letter form) to aid you when making decisions on behalf of the patient if and when the patient becomes incompetent.

 • **Parents and guardians may refuse medical care for children if the medical care provides no benefit to the child or the benefit is outweighed by the risks or invasiveness of the treatment.**

NOTES

1. Mitch Albom, Tuesdays with Morrie, New York: Doubleday, 1997, 106–7.

2. Margaret Edson, W;t, New York: Faber & Faber, 1998, 84–85.

3. *See, e.g.,* John Cloud, *A Kinder, Gentler Death,* Time, September 18, 2000, 60–74, and Bill Moyers, *On Our Own Terms,* a four-part PBS television series aired in September 2000 (pbs.org/onourownterms).

4. William Kelly & Stanley Kelly, *Do Cancer Patients Want to Be Told?* 27 Surgery 825 (1950); Robert Samp & Anthony Currieri, *Questionnaire Survey on Public Cancer Education Obtained from Cancer Patients and Their Families,* 10 Cancer 382 (1957); Donald Oken, *What to Tell Cancer Patients?* 175 JAMA 1120 (1961); *see generally* Robert Veatch, Death, Dying and the Biological Revolution, New Haven: Yale U. Press, 1976, 204–48.

5. *E.g.,* D. H. Novack et al., *Changes in Physician Attitudes Toward Telling the Cancer Patient,* 241 JAMA 897 (1979). For an excellent discussion of telling the truth to terminally ill patients, *see* S. Bok, Lying, New York: Pantheon, 1978, 220–41; *and see* Timothy Quill, *Initiating End-of-Life Discussions with Seriously Ill Patients: Addressing the Elephant in the Room,* 284 JAMA 2502 (2000).

6. Leo Tolstoy, The Death of Ivan Ilych and Other Stories, New York: New American Library, 1960, 137. *See also* Susan Block, *Psychological Considerations, Growth, and Transcendence at the End of Life,* 285 JAMA 2898 (2001), and Charles F. von Gunten, Frank Ferris & Linda Emanuel, *Ensuring Competency in End-of-Life Care: Communication and Relational Skills,* 284 JAMA 3051 (2000).

7. Naoko Miyaji, *The Power of Compassion: Truth Telling among American Doctors in the Care of Dying Patients,* 36 Social Sci. & Med. 249 (1993).

8. Daniel Haney, *Dying Patients Often Misled, Study Finds,* Boston Globe, May 21, 2000. *See also* Marjorie Kagawa-Singer & Leslie Blackhall, *Negotiating Cross-Cultural Issues at the End-of-Life,* 286 JAMA 2993 (2001), and Bernard Lo et al., *Discussing Religious and Spiritual Issues at the End of Life: A Practical Guide for Physicians,* 287 JAMA 749 (2002).

9. *See, e.g.,* Nicholas Christakis & Elizabeth Lamont, *Extent and Determinants of*

Error in Doctors' Prognosis in Terminally Ill Patients: Prospective Cohort Study, 320 British Med. J. 469 (2000).

10. *See generally* George J. Annas & Joan Densberger, *Competence to Refuse Medical Treatment: Autonomy vs. Paternalism,* 15 Toledo L. Rev. 561 (1984).

11. *Lane v. Candura,* 6 Mass App 377, 376 N.E.2d 1232 (1978); *and see In re Yetter,* Northampton Co. Orphans Ct., No. 1973-533 (Pa. 1973) (Williams, J.) (Yetter, for example, was a sixty-year-old woman who had been involuntarily committed to a mental hospital with a diagnosis of schizophrenia. When a lump in her breast was discovered, she refused to consent to a biopsy, which would be followed by removal of her breast should cancer be found. The refusal was based on the fact that her aunt had died after a similar procedure, and she was afraid of the operation. At the court hearing, Yetter testified that she did not want to undergo the procedure because "it could interfere with her genital system, affecting her ability to have babies, and would prohibit a movie career." The court found that even though she was getting more delusional, she had consistently opposed the surgery during her lucid periods and therefore was competent to refuse the surgery.).

12. *Lane v. Candura, supra* note 11, at 1235–36. *See also* President's Commission for the Study of Ethical Problems in Medicine, Deciding to Forego Life Sustaining Treatment, Washington, D.C.: Government Printing Office, 1983, and President's Commission for the Study of Ethical Problems in Medicine and Biomedical and Behavioral Research, Making Health Care Decisions, Washington, D.C.: Government Printing Office, 1982.

13. *Superintendent of Belchertown v. Saikewicz,* 373 Mass. 728, 370 N.E.2d 417 (1977).

14. *See Norwood Hospital v. Munoz,* 409 Mass. 116, 564 N.E.2d 1017 (1991), and George J. Annas, Leonard H. Glantz & Barbara F. Katz, The Rights of Doctors, Nurses and Allied Health Professionals, Cambridge: Ballinger, 1981, 84.

15. *See* discussion of the legal aspects of suicide in the next chapter.

16. *In re Osborne,* 294 A.2d 372, 375, n. 5 (D.C. Ct. App. 1972).

17. *In re Quinlan,* 70 N.J. 10, 355 A.2d 647 (1976).

18. *Saikewicz, supra* note 13. For a more detailed discussion of these two cases, *see* George J. Annas, *Reconciling Quinlan and Saikewicz: Decisionmaking for the Terminally Ill Incompetent,* 4 Am. J. Law & Med. 367 (1979). The *Quinlan* and *Salikewicz* cases have been followed on these points by most other state supreme courts, and none has required routine court approval for such decisions.

19. *Cruzan v. Director, Missouri Dept. of Health,* 497 U.S. 261 (1990). For more, *see* George J. Annas, *The Insane Root Takes Reason Prisoner: The Supreme Court and the Right to Die* (in) Standard of Care: The Law of American Bioethics, New York: Oxford U. Press, 1993, 85–115.

20. *Cruzan v. Harmon,* 760 S.W.2d 408 (Mo. 1988).

21. For a more complete discussion of the fluids and nutrition issue, *see* Norman Cantor, *The Permanently Unconscious Patient, Non-feeding and Euthanasia,* 15 Am. J. Law & Med. 381 (1989). *See also* Alan Meisel et al., *Seven Legal Barriers to End-of-Life Care: Myths Realities, and Grains of Truth,* 284 JAMA 2495 (2000).

22. *See, e.g., Conservatorship of Wendland,* 26 Cal. 4th 519, 28 P.3d 151 (2001), and Bernard Lo et al., *The Wendland Case: Withdrawing Life Support from Incompetent Patients Who Are Not Terminally Ill,* 346 New Eng. J. Med. 1489 (2002).

23. Luis Kutner, *Due Process of Euthanasia: The Living Will, a Proposal,* 44 Ind. L. Rev. 539 (1969). *See also* B. D. Colen, The Essential Guide to the Living Will, New York: Pharos Books, 1987.

24. President's Commission, *Deciding to Forego, supra* note 12.

25. Almost all living will statutes suffer from the following shortcomings:

• They are restricted to terminally ill patients and thus exclude from their protection the vast majority of elderly individuals; the term *terminally ill* is so vague that it is subject to arbitrary interpretation and application.

• They limit the types of treatment a person can refuse to those that are "artificial" or "extraordinary," thus excluding many burdensome treatments; and these vague terms lead to arbitrary interpretations.

• They do not permit an individual to designate another person to act on the individual's behalf (like a durable power of attorney) and do not set forth criteria under which the person so designated is to exercise this authority, thus greatly restricting the usefulness of the document in cases not precisely predicted by the individual.

• They do not require health care providers to follow the patient's wishes as set forth in the declaration; thus, the rights of the patients are not treated as superior to those of the health care providers.

• They do not explicitly require health care providers to continue palliative care (comfort and pain relief) to a patient who refuses other medical interventions.

Because of these shortcomings, living will statutes cannot resolve the many complex issues discussed in this chapter. What these statutes primarily do is say that if a patient is terminally ill, and if the physician can do nothing to sustain the patient's life, and if the patient does not want life sustained, and the doctor agrees with the patient's decision, then the doctor *may* (but does not have to) follow the patient's desire and be assured criminal and civil immunity. One proposal to remedy these shortcomings is the Right to Refuse Treatment Act, a "second-generation" living will act developed by the Legal Advisers Committee of Choice in Dying. The act enunciates a competent adult's right to refuse treatment and provides a mechanism by which competent people can both state how they wish to be treated in the event of incompetence and name another person to enforce those wishes. In terms of its treatment of such central issues as the capacity to consent and the standard by which a proxy decision maker is to act, the Right to Refuse Treatment Act is carefully crafted and in conformity with the conclusions of the Presidential Commission's for the Study of Ethical Problems Legal Advisers, *The Right to Refuse Treatment Act,* 73 Am. J. Public Health 918 (1983); and President's Commission, *Deciding to Forego, supra* note 12, at 428.

26. *See* New York State Task Force on Life and the Law, Life-Sustaining Treatment: Making Decisions and Appointing a Health Care Agent, New York: Task Force, 1987.

27. *Id.,* and President's Commission, *Deciding to Forego, supra* note 12. *And see Matter of Mary O'Connor,* 72 N.Y.2d 517, 531 N.E.2d 607 (1988), and *Cruzan supra* note 19. *And see* Shelley Lee, First Aide: Why Medical Powers of Attorney Are Getting More Attention These Days (and No, a Living Will Is Not Enough), Wall Street Jounal, March 24, 2003, R6.

28. For an excellent discussion of how to try to make better living wills instead, *see* Norman Cantor, *Making Advance Directives Meaningful,* 4 Psychology, Public Policy & Law 629 (1998); *and see also* Norman Cantor, *Twenty-Five Years after Quinlan: A Review of the Jurisprudence of Death and Dying,* 29 J. Law, Med. & Ethics 182 (2001).

29. *Prince v. Massachusetts,* 321 U.S. 158, 170 (1944).

30. John Robertson, *Involuntary Euthanasia of Defective Newborns: A Legal Analysis,* 27 Stan. L. Rev. 213 (1975).

31. John Robertson, *Dilemma at Danville,* 11 Hastings Center Report 5 (November 1981).

32. Ralph Ranalli, *Legal Opinions Vary on Sect Case: Severity of Charges Raises a Question,* Boston Globe, November 19, 2000, B1. *See generally, Pennsylvania v. Nixon,* 563 Pa. 425, 761 A.2d 1151 (2000), and *Commonwealth v. Twitchell,* 416 Mass, 114, 617 N.E.2d 609 (1993).

33. *See* Sherman Elias & George J. Annas, Reproductive Genetics and the Law, Chicago: Year Book, 1987, 170.

34. *Bowen v. American Hospital Association,* 476 U.S. 610 (1986).

35. *Child Abuse and Neglect Prevention and Treatment Program: Final Rule,* 50 Fed. Reg. 14877 (Apr. 15, 1985) (emphasis added).

36. Elias & Annas, *supra* note 33, at 168–85.

37. *Maine Medical Center v. Houle,* Maine Superior Ct., Civil Action No. 74-149 (1974); *and see* P. Stinson & R. Stinson, The Long Dying of Baby Andrew, Boston: Little Brown, 1983.

38. Joan Stephenson, *Palliative and Hospice Care Needed for Children with Life Threatening Conditions,* 284 JAMA 2437 (2000). *And see* Mickey Eisenberg & Terry Mengert, *Cardiac Resuscitation,* 344 New Eng. J. Med. 1304 (2001).

39. *Standards and Guidelines for Cardiopulmonary Resuscitation (CPR) and Emergency Cardiac Care (ECC),* 244 JAMA 453 (1980).

40. *See* Leslie Blackhall, *Must We Always Use CPR?* 317 New Eng. J. Med. 1281 (1987); *and see* J. E. Ruark & T. A. Raffin, *Initiating and Withdrawing Life Support: Principals and Practices in Adult Medicine,* 318 New Eng. J. Med. 25 (1988); G. E. Taffet et al., *In-Hospital Cardiopulmonary Resuscitation,* 260 JAMA 2069 (1988); and D. J. Murphy, *Do-Not-Resuscitate Orders,* 260 JAMA 2098 (1988).

41. Blackhall, *supra* note 40.

42. T. Tomlinson & H. Brody, 318 New Eng. J. Med. 1758 (1988); *and see* T. Tomlinson & H. Brody, *Ethics and Communication in Do-Not-Resuscitate Orders,* 318 New Eng. J. Med. 43 (1988). *See also* Paul Helft et al., *The Rise and Fall of the Futility Movement,* 343 New Eng. J. Med. 293 (2000).

43. 1987 N.Y. Laws 818; N.Y. Public Health Law art. 29(B).

44. Jay Katz, The Silent World of Doctor and Patient, New Haven: Yale U. Press, 1984, 151.

45. *See, e.g.,* George J. Annas, *Death and the Magic Machine: Informed Consent to the Artificial Heart,* 9 W. New Eng. L. Rev. 89 (1987).

46. George J. Annas, Judging Medicine, Clifton, N.J.: Humana Press, 1987, 284–90.

XIII

Suffering, Pain, and Suicide

The experience of suffering and pain are often feared more than death itself. Many, perhaps most, dying people are inadequately medicated for pain, and few physicians seem to know how to properly treat pain. A 2001 study of the Institute of Medicine, for example, concluded:

Improvements in the development and delivery of symptom control and other aspects of palliative care needed in the late stages of cancer (and other chronic diseases) have not kept pace with the medical advances that have allowed people to live longer. For at least half of those dying from cancer, death entails a spectrum of symptoms, including pain, labored breathing, distress, nausea, confusion, and other physical and psychological conditions that go untreated or undertreated and vastly diminish the quality of their remaining days.[1]

Physician-writer Lewis Thomas has tellingly observed that doctors "are as frightened and bewildered by the act of death as everyone else. Death is shocking, dismaying, even terrifying." Thomas continued, "A dying patient is a kind of freak . . . an offense against nature itself."[2] It is not surprising that physicians have difficulty talking candidly with dying patients and caring for them, issues dealt with in the previous chapter. But dying patients are also often undermedicated for pain; referred to hospice late, if at all; and provided with inadequate palliative care. Americans know this, and although death is a culture-wide enemy, and death-denial a cultural trait, many Americans also fear the process of dying slowly in an impersonal modern hospital. Proposals for physician-assisted suicide, publication of self-help suicide books, and the media's fascination with suicide machines and methods are all symptoms of the problems modern medicine has with dying patients rather than solutions.

There is strong public support for palliative care (active total care of patients when cure is no longer the goal), and virtually all Americans agree with palliative-care specialists that comprehensive palliative care is mandatory, not optional. The Institute of Medicine report found that "much of the suffering" it documented "could be alleviated if currently available symptom control means were used more widely."[3] Palliative-care specialists also argue persuasively that pain should be seen as the "fifth vital sign," and that physicians should always check not just a patient's temperature, blood pressure, pulse, and respiration but also ask if the patient is in pain, assess that pain on a scale of mild to severe, and prescribe the proper medication to deal with the pain. This chapter deals explicitly with suffering, pain, and the related issue of suicide.

Do patients have a right to demand that their physician give them sufficient pain medication to relieve their pain?

Yes. Physicians have a duty to alleviate pain. It is not acceptable medical practice to fail to properly treat pain.[4] Physicians have no right to require patients to suffer needlessly nor to withhold needed and medically appropriate pain medications. Nonetheless, it is almost universally agreed among physicians that 50 to 90 percent of terminally ill patients do not receive proper pain management.[5] This is a major medical scandal. Patients want pain relief and need it for decent quality of life and quality of death. Physicians have a duty to properly treat their patients. There is no law that prohibits physicians from giving patients all the pain medication needed to make them comfortable, even if such medication might shorten the patient's life or increase the risk of a cardiac or respiratory arrest. As will be discussed in more detail later in this chapter, all nine justices on the U.S. Supreme Court agree with this. Patients have no legal or ethical obligation to endure pain, and physicians *do* have a legal and ethical obligation to alleviate their patients' pain.[6]

Do hospitals have an obligation to assess and manage pain?

Yes. The Joint Commission on Accreditation of Healthcare Organizations (JCAHO) issued standards that went into effect in 2001 that require hospitals and nursing homes to make sure physicians and nurses take pain seriously. Their new basic pain standard states simply: "Patients have the right to appropriate assessment and management of pain."[7] The JCAHO explains the intent of this new standard as follows: "Pain can be a common part of the patient experience; unrelieved pain has adverse physical and psychological effects. The patient's right to pain management is respected and supported. The health care organization plans, supports, and coordinates activities and resources to assure the pain of all patients is recognized and addressed appropriately."

Doctors have no way of scientifically measuring the amount of pain a patient is suffering; there is no test or instrument to measure pain. As a result, patients must be very explicit with their physicians about their pain and insist that it be taken seriously and treated appropriately. If you are medicated for pain but are still in pain, you must tell your doctor or nurse! Physicians often classify pain by duration, cause, location, pattern, and severity. It is also very important for patients to be explicit about how the pain is affecting their overall well-being and ability to function.[8] And as the president of the American Pain Society, Christine Miaskowski, has cautioned, "Patients are going to have to demand better care. Unrelieved pain has negative effects. Just like they need an antibiotic to treat infection, they need analgesics to treat their pain."[9] It is your advocate's job to make sure you get the pain medication you need. The pain of dying children is particularly poorly managed, and parents should insist that their dying children be kept pain-free.[10]

In addition to the right to have pain properly managed in the hospital setting, hospice and palliative-care programs have also become much more available to patients in their homes.

Do dying patients have a right to use narcotics for pain relief?

Yes, if they are needed to relieve pain. State and federal laws on controlled substances have been rightly criticized as sometimes inhibiting physicians from prescribing opioids at all or in high enough doses.[11] But this is an outdated excuse, not a valid reason. Contemporary physicians have much more to fear from civil liability suits brought against them for undermedication.[12]

Experience demonstrates that to be effective in pain relief, doses of narcotics need not be so high as to distort reality. The objection of some people that narcotics should be denied to terminally ill patients because they might become addicted or their chromosomes might be damaged is ridiculous on its face. When he was dying of cancer thirty years ago, columnist Stewart Alsop wrote eloquently of the experience and suggested that the patients be allowed "to decide for themselves how much pain-killing drug they will take—it is, after all, they, not the doctors, who are suffering the agonies."[13]

Do dying patients have a right to use marijuana?

No. A number of states, including California, have laws that permit physicians to discuss marijuana use with their patients who could benefit from it, especially patients experiencing pain or nausea from cancer chemotherapy, and permit patients to use the physician's statements on the benefits of marijuana as a defense to the charge of violating the state's law prohibiting the possession and cultivation of marijuana.[14] Statutes like this have broad public support, since virtually no one thinks it is reasonable to initiate criminal prosecution of patients with cancer or AIDS who use marijuana on the advice of their physicians to help them through conventional medical treatment for their disease. Anecdotal evidence of the effectiveness of smoked marijuana abounds.[15] Perhaps the most convincing is the account of the late Harvard professor and author Stephen Jay Gould, one of the world's first survivors of abdominal mesothelioma. Gould wrote about his experiences when he started intraveneous chemotherapy:

Absolutely nothing in the available arsenal of anti-emetics worked at all. I was miserable and came to dread the frequent treatments with an almost perverse intensity. I had heard that marijuana often worked well against nausea. I was reluctant to try it because I have never smoked any substance habitually (and didn't even know how to inhale). Moreover, I had tried marijuana twice [in the sixties] . . . and hated it. . . . [M]arijuana worked like a charm. . . . [T]he sheer bliss of not experiencing nausea—and not having to fear it for all the days intervening between treatments—was the greatest boost I received in all my year of treatment, and surely had a most important effect upon my eventual cure.[16]

Similarly, in patients with AIDS, marijuana has been credited with counteracting such side effects of treatment as severe nausea, vomiting, loss of appetite, and fatigue, as well as stimulating the appetite to help prevent weight loss.

Nevertheless, the federal government and its Drug Enforcement Agency (DEA) has vigorously opposed such laws and has threatened to target physicians who recommend marijuana to their patients for prosecution. The DEA also closed down a facility in California that sold marijuana to sick people, and the legality of this action was affirmed by the U.S. Supreme Court.[17]

State law cannot, of course, change federal law, and as long as the federal government outlaws the use of marijuana, patients for whom it would be helpful will have to rely on illegal or legally questionable means to obtain it. This is insanity: seriously ill patients (not just terminally ill patients) and their physicians should have access to whatever they need to fight for their lives or to die without intolerable pain and suffering. Federal drug laws, or DEA enforcement policies must, however, be changed to make this happen.

What is a hospice program?

The National Hospice Foundation defines *hospice care* as "the model for quality, compassionate care at the end of life," which involves a "team-oriented approach to expert medical care, pain management, and emotional and spiritual support expressly tailored to the patient's needs and wishes." The core of hospice care is the belief that all of us have the "right to die pain free and with dignity, and that our families will receive the necessary support to allow us to do so."[18]

The focus of hospice is on caring, not curing, and in most cases patients will be able to be cared for at home and die at home. The ability to die at home, however, often depends on whether one or more family members is willing and able to act as the primary caregiver, backed up by a hospice team, which includes nurses, a physician, home health aides, social workers, and clergy.

Hospice is funded by Medicare, private health insurance, and Medicaid (in most states), and it generally requires a prognosis of death within six months. A major problem is getting physicians to refer patients to hospice in a timely manner so the patient can benefit from it. Many physicians believe that good hospice care requires three months in a program.[19] The average length of hospice stay fell from seventy-four days in 1992 to fifty-nine days in 1998, the median from twenty-six to nineteen days. Congressman Charles Grassley of Iowa has properly observed that "short lengths of stay hurt patients and their families because they struggle too long without the support hospice offers."[20] A Government Accounting Office report issued in 2000 found several factors influence utilization of hospice, including physician referral practices, awareness of the benefit, and unwillingness of patients and their families and providers to talk about death.[21]

What is palliative care?

The Center to Advance Palliative Care defines *palliative care* as "the comprehensive management of the patient's physical, psychological, social, spiritual and existential needs." It is primarily concerned with terminal care but can be part of any serious or life-threatening condition for which pain and symptom control are critical. Its basic precepts are respecting patient goals and choices, comprehensive care, interdisciplinary care, support of the family, and building support systems for excellent care at the end of life. As leading authority and pioneer of palliative care, Dr. Kathleen Foley, has put it, "Death is inevitable, but severe suffering is not."[22]

Palliative care "affirms life and regards dying as a natural process that is a profoundly personal experience for the individual and the family. Palliative care neither hastens nor postpones death, but rather seeks to relieve suffering, control symptoms and restore functional capacity while remaining sensitive to personal, cultural and religious values, beliefs and practices. . . . [H]ospice is one form of palliative care."[23] Perhaps the key difference between palliative care and most of the rest of medical care is that palliative-care practitioners acknowledge directly and openly that dying is a normal part of life for all of us and our families.

What are the "Five Wishes" and the "Seven Promises"?

These are both well-publicized attempts to make the dying process better for both patients and their caregivers. The "five wishes," a form promulgated by Aging with Dignity, gives people five areas to document their "wishes" and is a type of combination health care proxy and living will:

1. The person I want to make care decisions for me when I can't.
2. The kind of medical treatment I want or don't want.
3. How comfortable I want to be.
4. How I want people to treat me.
5. What I want my loved ones to know.[24]

The first two issues are dealt with in chapter 12 in the material on advance directives and health care proxies. Number 3 has special relevance to pain, and the form usefully asks you to cross out any of the following you *don't* agree with (few patients would disagree with any of them):

- I do not want to be in pain. I want my doctor to give me enough medicine to relieve my pain, even if that means that I will be drowsy or sleep more than I would otherwise.
- If I show signs of depression, nausea, shortness of breath, or hallucinations, I want my caregivers to do whatever they can to help me.
- I want my lips and mouth kept moist to stop dryness.

I think the five wishes is a reasonable way to discuss and document your directions. My primary objection is the word "wishes," which should be labeled "directives." This is not "never, never land" and we are not characters in *Peter Pan*. Real-life patients have legal rights, including the legal right to *insist* on all of the things in the "five wishes" form as rights, not just to wish for them. Of course, your advocate will have to make sure your directions are carried out, since you will not be able to insist on your rights at all times when you are dying.

The seven promises of the National Coalition on Health Care properly put the obligation on physicians to make the following seven promises to a dying patient:

- You will have the best of medical treatment, aiming to prevent exacerbation, improve function and survival, and ensure comfort.
- You will never have to endure overwhelming pain, shortness of breath, or other symptoms.
- Your care will be continuous, comprehensive, and coordinated.
- You and your family will be prepared for everything that is likely to happen in the course of your illness.
- Your wishes will be sought and respected, and followed whenever possible.
- We will help you consider your personal and financial resources and we will respect your choices about their use.
- We will do all we can to see that you and your family will have the opportunity to make the best of every day.[25]

Every patient should expect this type of care, and your advocate can help make sure these promises are kept.

Is physician-assisted suicide legal?

It is legal only in Oregon, and in November 2001, the U.S. attorney general acted to try to prevent physicians from prescribing any overdoses to suicidal patients as well.[26] As of 2003, the case is still in the courts, and the Oregon law remains in effect. California, Washington, Michigan, Maine, and Oregon have all held public initiatives that would permit physicians to prescribe overdoses of drugs to their terminally ill, suicidal patients, but only the initiative in Oregon passed.[27] Since it went into effect in 1997, about one to two patients a month (of more than two thousand Oregonians who die each month) have used the Oregon suicide scheme to end their lives. Here's how it works.[28]

Oregon's Death with Dignity Act permits physicians to comply with the request of a terminally ill competent adult patient, who has less than six months to live, for a prescription of lethal drugs: "An adult who is capable, is a resident of Oregon, and has been determined by the attending physician and consulting physician to be suffering from a terminal disease, and who has voluntarily expressed his or her wish to die, may make a written request for medication for the purpose of ending his or her life in a humane and dignified manner in accordance with this act."

The law requires that the request for a drug prescription be in writing and signed in the presence of at least two witnesses who agree that the patient is competent and acting voluntarily. Required contents of the form are also specified. Residents of long-term-care facilities must have at least one witness with qualifications specified by the state's department of human resources. At least two physicians must agree that the patient will likely die from a terminal illness within six months, the patient must be referred for counseling if a psychiatric or psychological disorder is suspected, and the attending physician must ask (but cannot require) the patient to notify his or her next of kin about the request. Records must be maintained, and a sample of records must be reviewed annually by the state's health division.

Two waiting periods are built into the law. Two oral requests are required, the second no less than fifteen days after the patient's original oral request, before the required written request can be accepted, and the prescription itself cannot be provided less than forty-eight hours after the written request. No physician is required to write a prescription upon request, but physicians are provided with immunity from "civil or criminal liability or professional disciplinary action" for "good faith compliance" with the act. This immunity specifically extends to "being present when a qualified patient takes the prescribed medication to end his or her life in a humane and dignified manner."

The Oregon law seems to have been written in response to the generally favorable public reaction to the case of Dr. Timothy Quill, who prescribed lethal drugs to his terminally ill cancer patient Diane, and to avoid the much more negative public reaction to Jack Kevorkian, who usually used carbon monoxide poisoning to assist suicides. The writers of the law implicitly repudiated Kevorkian and his methods and exclusively endorsed the Quill prescription method. A drug overdose is also consistent with Hemlock Society ideology, which teaches that a suicide by drugs is "peaceful, bloodless dying."

I have never much liked Oregon's law because I think it is unnecessary and dangerous—unnecessary because physicians already had the legal right (and obligation) to adequately treat their patients' pain. Dangerous because it could easily extend to patient killing (euthanasia) and takes attention away from the real pain and suffering of patients and places it exclusively on physicians and their extraordinarily exaggerated fear of prosecution.

Is there a constitutional right to physician-assisted suicide?

No. The U.S. Supreme Court ruled in *Washington v. Glucksberg* in 1997 that there is no such right.[29] The Court's "established method" of defining a new fundamental constitutional right has two parts: the right must be "deeply rooted in this nation's history and tradition" or fundamental to ordered liberty, and it must have a "careful description." The Court easily concluded there is no historic tradition of treating suicide as a fundamental right, observing that to find such a right the Court would instead "have to reverse centuries of legal doctrine and practice, and strike down the considered policy choice of almost every state."

The Court characterized the case of Nancy Cruzan (a young woman in a persistent vegetative state) whose parents wanted artificial feeding discontinued as a case that involved the constitutional right to refuse medical treatment. As discussed in the previous chapter, this right is supported in common law battery and informed consent doctrine and by "the long legal tradition protecting the decision to refuse unwanted medical treatment." In contrast, suicide "has never enjoyed similar legal protection," and the "two acts are widely and reasonably regarded as quite distinct." In *Cruzan*, the Court said, "we certainly gave no intimation" that the right to refuse treatment could be "somehow transmuted into a right to assistance in committing suicide."

Because the Court concluded that no fundamental constitutional right to suicide could be found in our nation's history or in the concept of ordered liberty, the state of Washington had only to demonstrate that its assisted-suicide law was "rationally related to legitimate government interests" for its law to be constitutional. The Court found that "this requirement is unquestionably met here." The Court listed the following legitimate governmental interests that could support the Washington law: (1) preserving human life; (2) preventing suicide; (3) protecting the integrity and ethics of the medical profession; (4) protecting vulnerable groups from abuse, neglect and mistakes; and (5) preventing a start "down the path to voluntary and perhaps even involuntary euthanasia."

Is a treatment refusal that leads to death the same as committing suicide?

No. The U.S. Supreme Court examined this question in *Vacco v. Quill*,[30] the 1997 companion case to *Washington v. Glucksberg*. The lower court had concluded that since ending or refusing life-sustaining medical treatment is "nothing more nor less than assisting suicide," the anti-assisted-suicide law prohibiting those terminally ill people who are not dependent on medical technologies from ending their lives with assistance denies them equal protection of laws. The Supreme Court emphatically disagreed, specifically upholding as rational the distinction between withholding or withdrawing life-sustaining treatment and assisting suicide, "a distinction widely recognized and endorsed in the medical profession and in our legal traditions." The Court also noted that by permitting one to everyone and prohibiting the other to everyone, all citizens are treated the same: "Everyone, regardless of physical condition, is entitled, if competent, to refuse unwanted lifesaving medical treatment; no one is permitted to assist a suicide."

The Court agreed with previous courts that "when a patient refuses life-sustaining medical treatment, the patient dies from an underlying fatal disease or pathology; but if a patient ingests lethal medication prescribed by a physician he is killed by that medication." The Court noted that when a physician provides palliative care, "in some cases, pain killing drugs may hasten a patient's death, but the physician's purpose and intent is, or may be, only to ease his patient's pain." On the other hand, a doctor who assists a suicide necessarily intends that the patient dies. Similarly, a patient who commits suicide with a doctor's aid "necessarily has the specific intent to end his or her own life, while a patient who refuses or discontinues treatment might not." The Court pointed out that the law has historically distinguished between actions done "because of" a given end and actions done "in spite of" their unintended but foreseen consequences. Intent matters.

Is there a right not to suffer?

The two U.S. Supreme Court opinions just discussed support this right (although the cases did not explicitly find it), and five justices used specific language that could be used to find such a right in the future.

Justice Sandra Day O'Connor's opinion in *Glucksberg,* the only concurring opinion that any other justice agreed with, suggests that there might be a right to avoid "great" suffering near death. She made three points: (1) there is no legal barrier preventing "a patient who is experiencing great pain" from "obtaining medication, from qualified physicians, to alleviate that suffering, even to the point of causing unconsciousness and hastening death"; (2) the state's interests therefore justify prohibiting physician assisted suicide; and (3) state legislatures are the proper forum for an "extensive and serious evaluation of physician-assisted suicide and other related issues."

Justice Ruth Bader Ginsburg concurred with Justice O'Connor. Justice Stephen Breyer was concerned about dying patients who get insufficient pain medication. Breyer concluded that if a state ever did prohibit physicians from providing sufficient palliative care—"including the administration of drugs as needed to avoid pain at the end of life"—the Court would be presented with a different case, "and might have to revisit its conclusions in these cases."

Justices John Paul Stevens and David Souter each wrote longer concurring opinions. Justice Stevens concluded that it is possible that some other particular case (which he does not describe) might impose "an intolerable intrusion on the patient's freedom" by outlawing "the only possible means of preserving a dying patient's dignity and alleviating her intolerable suffering." Justice Souter seems to favor something like a right to end one's life with dignity that would apply not only to a person dying in pain but also in unacceptable "dependency and helplessness."

Why isn't there a constitutional right to physician-assisted suicide?

In retrospect, it is easy to see how the right to physician-assisted suicide failed to gain constitutional recognition in the Supreme Court. First, to find such a constitutional right, the Court would have had to find a constitutional right to suicide itself, and there is no historical or legal support for this. Second, the analogies the proponents relied on, abortion and the right to refuse treatment, were easily distinguishable. The right to refuse treatment is deeply rooted in American law, and so are the principles of intent and causation in the criminal law—principles that distinguish suicide from treatment refusal and assisted suicide from withdrawing or withholding treatment. Third, to agree with the assisted-suicide proponents the Court would have had to limit any constitutional right it found to a small group of citizens (competent, suffering, terminally ill people near death) and a particular method of suicide (e.g., overdosing on prescription drugs), limitations that have no constitutional precedent.

The Court only had to find the state interests in outlawing assisted suicide "rationally-related to a legitimate state interest" to uphold these statutes. Nonetheless, it seems reasonable to conclude that a majority of the Court would have permitted the states to continue to outlaw physician-assisted suicide even if the justices thought it was a fundamental constitutional right, because at least some of these interests, especially avoiding the slippery slope to active euthanasia, are compelling.[31] It is worth noting, however, that there is no law against suicide and no law that prohibits people from hoarding drugs that might be used to commit suicide.

What is the law on physicians prescribing drugs for terminally ill patients who might use them to end their lives?

The U.S. Supreme Court explicitly endorsed the principle of the double effect, and the logic of the *Washington v. Glucksberg* opinion implicitly supports the conclusion that physicians can continue to write prescriptions for medically indicated drugs even with the knowledge that the patient *might* use the drugs to commit suicide, as long as the physician's *intent* is to prolong the patient's life or relieve pain (a legitimate medical purpose). A physician who writes a drug prescription under these circumstances is not engaged in physician-assisted suicides by legal definition.

The opinions are also consistent with the views of the New York Task Force on Life and the Law, whose report, *When Death Is Sought,* is cited as the authority at numerous points by the justices.[32] The task force has been especially critical of autonomy assertions to justify physician-assisted suicide. Two other points that the task force makes are worth emphasizing. The first relates to legal causation, which is used by courts to determine legal accountability, not simply to describe facts. In the context of a physician treating a dying patient, many causes may contribute to death. But, as the task force properly observes: "When a variety of factual causes are necessary, but not individually sufficient, to bring about a particular result, the determination of which among them are properly cited as causative for legal purposes becomes a policy judgment, reflecting underlying assumptions about rights, duties, and moral blame."[33] The judges' views of "rights, duties, and moral blame" help explain why we do not hold physicians accountable as causal agents for deaths that occur after life-sustaining treatments have been removed at the patient's insistence, or when a patient undergoing surgery dies on the operating table. Courts have always recognized that death under medical care does not take place in a moral vacuum.

The second point is one emphasized in all of the concurring opinions: "The effort to characterize morphine drips as a form of covert euthanasia is extremely misguided."[34] This effort is a mistake for two reasons. The first is a factual one: morphine use is often necessary for proper medical care, and it is never necessary to accompany it with "winks and nods." Death is neither necessarily hastened nor intended by use of a morphine drip. "Properly titrated" morphine usually does not hasten death at all because of "the rapid development of tolerance to the respiratory depressant effects."[35] The second is that even in those cases in which increasing the morphine dosage "may accelerate" the patient's death, this fact "does not make their use equivalent to assisted suicide or euthanasia." The question is, Is the risk of death "justified in light of the paucity and undesirability of other options?" This point, and the centrality of the principle of the double effect, is well recognized in medical practice: "[M]edical treatment sometimes requires significant trade-offs, and acceptance of negative consequences for legitimate medical purposes is not equivalent to causing those consequences for their own sake."[36]

The quest for a constitutional right to physician-assisted suicide failed in the Supreme Court because it has no coherent basis in constitutional law. The right to refuse treatment, on the other hand, is a long-recognized right. It is not discretionary with physicians, who are legally and ethically required to honor it; patients have a right to insist that their bodies not be invaded without their consent.

TIPS FOR ADVOCATES

- **Patients have a right not to suffer and to be kept pain-free.**

- **Physicians have a legal and ethical obligation to keep their patients pain-free to the extent possible.**

- **All patients should have their pain regularly assessed and effectively treated.**

- **Most physicians do not know how to manage pain:** insist that the physician gets a proper consult if the pain is not adequately addressed.

- **Palliative care is a human right.** Dying is one of the most personal activities of life; there is a right to be supported in it and (if possible) to die at home, without pain, and with loved ones.

- Hospice care requires a prognosis of six months or less to live for eligibility; but if the patient does not die within six months, **hospice care can continue as long as the patient is expected to die within the next six months.**

- **There is no right to physician assistance in suicide** (i.e., a prescription for a drug overdose to die); but **there is a right to be kept pain-free and a right to refuse any and all medical treatments, including fluids and nutrition, even if these actions hasten death.**

- **There is no law against "hoarding" drugs that patients can use to kill themselves.**

- **There is no law against physicians discussing anything medical with their patients,** including methods to commit suicide, or using illegal drugs such as marijuana. What physicians cannot do is encourage their patients to violate the law.

Notes

1. Institute of Medicine, Improving Palliative Care for Cancer, Washington, D.C.: National Academy of Sciences, 2001, 3. *See also* Institute of Medicine, When Children Die: Improving Palliative and End-of-Life Care for Children and Their Families, Washington, D.C.: National Academy Press, 2002.

2. Lewis Thomas, *Dying as Failure,* Annals Am. Acad. Pol. Soc. Sci. 1 (1980).

3. Institute of Medicine, *supra* note 1, at 5.

4. *See, e.g.,* Symposium, *Relieving Unnecessary Treatable Pain for the Sake of Human Dignity* (Sandra Johnson, ed.), 29 J. Law, Med. & Ethics 11 (2001).

5. Institute of Medicine, Approaching Death: Improving Care at the End of Life, Washington, D.C.: National Academy of Sciences, 1997; SUPPORT, *A Controlled Trial to Improve Care of Seriously Ill Hospitalized Patients: The Study to Understand Prognoses and Preferences for Outcomes and Risks of Treatment (SUPPORT),* 274 JAMA 1591 (1995); R. Bernabei et al., *Management of Pain in Elderly Patients with Cancer,* 279 JAMA 1877 (1998). Physicians who improperly or inadequately treat pain should be reported to the state's medical licensing board and may be disciplined. *See* Sheryl Gay Stolberg, *Amid New Calls for Pain Relief, New Calls for Caution,* New York Times, October 19, 1998, D3; and Federation of State Medical Boards, *Model Guidelines for the Use of Controlled Substances for Treatment of Pain,* 1998.

6. Symposium, *supra* note 4.

7. Joint Commission on Accreditation of Healthcare Organizations, 2000 Hospital Accreditation Standards, Chicago: JCAHO, 2000, 79 (Standard RI.1.2.8); *and see* Donald M. Phillips, *JCAHO Pain Management Standards Are Unveiled,* 284 JAMA 428 (2000). JCAHO does not, however, require that pain be assessed or recorded as "the fifth vital sign." Carole Patterson, *Unravel Pain Standards for Higher Compliance,* 33(3) Nursing Management 20 (2002).

8. Joanne Lynn & Joan Harrold, Handbook for Mortals: Guidance for People Facing Serious Illness, New York: Oxford U. Press, 1999, 72–76. The questions your physician will ask about your pain include the following: Where is the pain? What does it feel like? On a scale of 0 to 10, with 0 being no pain and 10 being overwhelming pain, how bad is your pain now? When do you get this pain? What makes the pain better? What makes the pain worse? How is the pain affecting your life? Are you taking any medications for the pain? (*Id.,* at 75). *And see* their Web sites for more information (www.painandthelaw.org; www.partnershipforcaring.org).

9. *New Hospital Rules Order Measurements of Pain, Its Relief,* Wall Street Journal, December 26, 2000, B10. *See also* Laurie Tarkan, *New Efforts Against an Old Foe: Pain,* New York Times, December 26, 200, D1. This standard is likely to be especially important in nursing homes. Judy Zerzan et al., *Access to Palliative Care and Hospice in Nursing Homes,* 284 JAMA 2489 (2000).

10. Abigail Trafford, *Children of Denial: Recent Advances in End of Life Care Haven't Reached the Youngest Patients,* Washington Post, June 20, 2001, A1. *See, e.g.,* G. Perilongo et al., *Palliative and Terminal Care for Dying Children,* 37 Med. Pediatric Oncology 59

(2001); S. Chaffee, *Pediatric Oncology Care,* 28 Primary Care 365 (2001); and D. E. McCallum, P. Byrne & E. Bruera, *How Children Die in Hospitals,* 20 J. Pain Symptom Management 417 (2001).

11. Ann Alpers, *Criminal Act or Palliative Care? Prosecutions Involving the Care of the Dying,* 26 J. of Law, Medicine & Ethics 308 (1998); J. H. Von Roenn et al., *Physician Attitudes and Practice in Cancer Pain Management: A Survey from the Eastern Cooperative Oncology Group,* 119(2) Annals Internal Med. 121 (1993); C. S. Hill, *The Negative Influence of Licensing and Disciplinary Boards and Drug Enforcement Agencies on Pain Treatment with Opioid Analgesics,* J. Pharmaceutical Care in Pain & Symptom Control 43 (1993). *And see,* regarding needed changes in financing pain management, Timothy S. Jost, *Medicare and Medicaid Financing of Pain Management,* 1 J. Pain 183 (2000).

12. *See, e.g.,* Barry Furrow, *Pain Management and Provider Liability: No More Excuses,* 29 J. Law, Med. & Ethics 28 (2001).

13. Stewart Alsop, *The Right to Die with Dignity,* Good Housekeeping, August 1974, 69.

14. *See, e.g.,* George J. Annas, *Outlawed Choices* (in) Some Choice: Law, Medicine and the Market, New York: Oxford U. Press, 1998, 88–96. *And see Conant v. Walters,* 309 F.3d 629 (9th Cir. 2002).

15. Lester Grinspoon & James Bakalar, Marijuana: The Forbidden Medicine, revised ed., New Haven: Yale U. Press, 1997.

16. Stephen Jay Gould, *It Worked Like a Charm,* Times, May 4, 1993. Gould originally wrote of his experiences with marijuana at the request of Lester Grinspoon, Grinspoon & Bakalar, *supra* note 15, 39–40.

17. United States v. Oakland Cannabis Buyer's Co-op, 532 U.S. 483 (2001).

18. For this, and much more information about hospice, see the Web site of the National Hospice Foundation (www.hospiceinfo.org).

19. Nicholas Christakis & Elizabeth Lamont, *Extent and Determinants of Error in Doctor's Prognosis in Terminally Ill Patients: A Prospective Cohort Study,* 320 Brit. Med. J. 469 (2000); Jim Ritter, *Study Examines Stay at Hospices,* Chicago Sun Times, February 18, 2000, 12.

20. Average length of stay has declined from seventy-four to fifty-nine days and half of hospice patients died within nineteen days in 1998. Larry Lipman, *Panel on Aging Finds Shorter Hospice Stays,* Atlanta Journal & Constitution, September 19, 2000, 7A.

21. U.S. Congress, Government Accounting Office, Medicare: More Beneficiaries Use Hospice but for Fewer Days of Care, (GAO/ HEHS-00-182), September, 2000 (available at www.gao.gov). *See also* Medicare Payment Advisory Commission, Medicare Beneficiaries' Access to Hospice: Report to the Congress, Washington, D.C., MEDPAC, 2002 (in 2000, 23 percent of all Medicare decedents and 60 percent of those who died of cancer used hospice services).

22. Anastasia Toufexis, *Pioneer in the Battle to Avert Needless Pain and Suffering,* New York Times, November 6, 2001, D5. *See also* Charles von Gunten, *Secondary and Tertiary Palliative Care in US Hospitals,* 287 JAMA 875 (2002) ("Palliative care consultation services and specialty units are a response to the shortcomings of the curative health model for patients for whom no cure exists.").

23. For this, and much more information about palliative care, see the Web site of the

Center to Advance Palliative Care in Hospitals and Health Systems at New York's Mount Sinai School of Medicine (www.capcmssm.org). *See also* Thómas A. Preston, Final Victory: Taking Charge of the Last Stages of Life, Roseville, CA: Forum, 2000.

24. Aging with Dignity, PO Box 1661, Tallahassee, FL 32302, (850) 681-2010 (www.agingwithdignity.com). Also featured by the AMA (Damon K. Marquis) in its Advance Care Planning: A Practical Guide for Physicians, Chicago: AMA Press, 2001, 25–35.

25. National Coalition on Health Care, Promises to Keep: Changing the Way We Provide Care at the End of Life, 2000. *See* Mike Mitka, *Suggestions for Help When the End Is Near,* 284 JAMA 2441 (2000), and Paul Bascom & Susan Tolle, *Responding to Requests for Physician-Assisted Suicide,* 288 JAMA 91 (2002).

26. Sam Howe Verhovek, *U.S. Acts to Stop Assisted Suicides,* New York Times, November 7, 2001, 1; *and see* Robert Steinbrook, *Physician-Assisted Suicide in Oregon: An Uncertain Future,* 346 New Eng. J. Med., 460 (2002).

27. For much more on the Oregon law, *see* George J. Annas, *Oregon's Bloodless Choice* (in) Some Choice: Law, Medicine & the Market, New York: Oxford U. Press, 1998, 216–23; Linda Ganzini et al., *Physicians Experiences with the Oregon Death and Dignity Act,* 342 New Eng. J. Med. 557 (2000); and Sherwin Nuland, *Physician-Assisted Suicide and Euthanasia in Practice,* 342 New Eng. J. Med. 583 (2000).

28. The number increased to three a month in 2002 from two a month in the two previous years. Katrina Hedberg et al., *Letter to the Editor: Five Years of Legal Physician-Assisted Suicide in Oregon,* 348 New Eng. J. Med. 961 (2003).

29. *Washington v. Glucksberg,* 521 U.S. 702 (1997).

30. *Vacco v. Quill,* 521 U.S. 793 (1997).

31. For much more on these cases, *see* George J. Annas, *The Bell Tolls,* (in) Some Choice: Law, Medicine & the Market, New York: Oxford U. Press, 1998, 224–245. Robert Burt argues persuasively, in the context of these cases, that self-determination regarding suicide is an illusion. Robert Burt, Death Is That Man Taking Names, Berkeley: U. California Press, 2002, 106–22.

32. New York Task Force on Life and Law, When Death Is Sought: Assisted Suicide and Euthanasia in the Medical Context, New York: State Task Force on Life and the Law, 1994; and *Supplement to the Report,* April 1997.

33. *Id., Supplement,* citing H. L. Hart and T. Honore, Causation and the Law, 2d ed., Oxford: Oxford U. Press, 1985.

34. Kathleen Foley, *Controversies in Cancer Pain: Medical Perspectives,* 63 Cancer 2257 (1989).

35. *Id.,* and W. C. Wilson, M. G. Smedira, & C. Fink, *Ordering and Administering of Sedatives and Analgesics During the Withholding and Withdrawal of Life Support from Critically Ill Patents,* 267 JAMA 949 (1992).

36. My colleagues Leonard Glantz and Wendy Mariner and I made this point in some detail in a footnote in the brief of the bioethics professors in these cases:

It should be noted that no case has ever held that a physician who prescribes drugs a patient later uses to commit suicide is guilty of assisting suicide. No physician has ever been charged with such an offense. It is surprising that the Ninth Circuit Court of Appeals could simultaneously find that the doctors in Washington run a "severe risk of prosecution," 79 F.3d at 795, and that there is "no reported American case of criminal punishment being meted out to a doctor for helping a patient hasten his own death." 79 F.3d at 811. In its footnote 54, it describes two cases where physicians were charged with directly administering lethal injections to patients. While the court refers to these as assisted suicide cases, they were in fact homicide cases. Both physicians were acquitted.

It is unlikely that the mere prescription of drugs for a patient constitutes assisted suicide. The named plaintiff in the Second Circuit Court of Appeals case, Dr. Timothy Quill, admitted in an article published in a prestigious medical journal that he has prescribed a lethal dose of sleeping pills for a patient so she could decide at some future time whether or not to commit suicide with these pills. Timothy Quill, *Death and Dignity: A Case of Individualized Decision Making,* 434 New Eng. J. Med. 691 (1991). Based on this admission, a grand jury investigated the case and refused to indict. Furthermore, the New York Board for Professional Medical Conduct conducted an investigation to determine if Dr. Quill should be disciplined for his actions. The panel found Dr. Quill acted lawfully and appropriately. It noted that he could not determine with certainty what use the patient might make of the drugs he prescribed. Even if Dr. Quill prescribed the drugs believing they might be used by the patient to commit suicide, he did not participate in the taking of her life. The panel did not wish to interfere with the good medical practice of physicians who prescribe drugs to relieve a terminally patient's anxiety, insomnia or pain because the physician suspects the patient may later use the medication to terminate his or her life. *See* John Alesandro, Comment, *Physician Assisted Suicide and New York Law,* 57 Alb. L. Rev. 820 (1994). Thus, in the only case ever investigated that resembles the activities the plaintiffs claim are illegal in New York, the authorities ruled that the actions were lawful.

It must be kept in mind that the activity in question is the *prescription* of drugs by physicians. Once the prescription is written the patient must decide whether to fill it, and then must decide whether to use the drugs for the lawful purpose for which a prescription is written, such a relief of insomnia, or to take these drugs to commit suicide. These decisions all occur over a lengthy period of time. Thus, there is a long and tenuous chain of events between the writing of the prescription and its use for suicidal purposes.

This is quite different from prosecuted assisted suicide cases, where there is a close link between the assistance and the act of suicide. In one case a defendant helped her sister to commit suicide by attaching a vacuum cleaner hose to the end of an exhaust pipe of a car, gave her sister the other end of the hose, said good-bye and closed the garage door as she left. In another case a husband helped his cancer ridden wife commit suicide by preparing an overdose of sedatives, sitting with her while she ate it, and helping her put a plastic bag over her head. Catherine Shaffer, Note, *Criminal Liability for Assisting Suicide,* 86 Colum. L. Rev. 348 (1996). In these cases, and others cited in the article, the "assistance" that was found to be unlawful was much more direct than writing prescriptions, much closer in time to the commission of the suicide, and led directly to the suicide. At least three of the six patient-petitioners in these two appeals were not suicidal at the time they signed their declarations, but rather wanted exemptions from the drug laws so that they could have their physicians write them prescriptions for lethal drugs that they *might* use at some time in the future to commit suicide *if* their suffering became intolerable. 79 F.3d 794–5; 80 F.3d 720–21. It is notable, given the relief sought in this case by the plaintiffs, that no court has actually concluded that writing a prescription constitutes assisting suicide.

XIV

Death, Organ Donation, and Autopsy

Teenager Jesica Santillán suffered from a heart condition that physicians in her hometown in rural Mexico did not understand. Her, parents, despairing of Mexican medicine, had themselves and her smuggled into the United States in search of better care. They wound up at Duke University Medical Center where Jesica was placed on the waiting list for a heart-lung transplant. The transplant went tragically wrong as, unknown to the surgeon until midway through the procedure, the donated organs, which were blood-type A, did not match Jesica, who was type O. Although this catastrophic mistake is almost always fatal, surgeons searched for a second donor and performed a second heart-lung transplant on Jesica. Jesica, however, almost immediately developed bleeding into her brain, and shortly thereafter her brain functions ceased. Her parents, nonetheless, asked that she not be removed from the ventilator that was permitting her body to take in oxygen. Jesica's mother told the press that she believed the doctors were "taking her off the medicine, little by little, in order to kill her. They want to rid themselves of this problem."[1] Told later that their daughter was dead, the parents asked for a second opinion. The hospital reportedly declined, saying they had confirmed death on the basis of brain criteria. Shortly thereafter, physicians removed her from the ventilator. They also asked the family if they wanted to donate any of Jesica's organs or tissues. The family declined, although later it was said that because of the language barrier they may not have understood the request.[2] Shortly thereafter, the *New York Times* reported that lawyers for the family said, "they would pore over her medical records and request more tests after the autopsy."[3]

There are many aspects to this case, which became a national news event, including its role in the debate regarding a cap on "pain and suffer-

316

ing" damages in medical malpractice suits, and the continuing debate on ways to avoid medical errors. Both of these issues are dealt with in the following chapter. Three other aspects of the Santillán tragedy form the focus of this chapter: the determination of death, organ donation, and autopsy.

Death is the end for the patient, but many decisions must still be made by the patient's family and care providers. If death occurs under circumstances that permit the deceased patient to be an organ donor (usually a sudden, accidental death), the family will likely be asked to consider donating the deceased's organs. Tissue donation will be an option in many more cases. Under some circumstances, an autopsy may be requested. In unusual circumstances, the medical examiner or coroner may order an autopsy to determine the cause of death. And ultimately, the patient's family must be given custody of the body to cremate or bury.

All states have a version of the 1968 Uniform Anatomical Gift Act, and many states amended their act after revisions were proposed in 1987. By following the provisions of your state's act, you can help your family make decisions about organ donation by specifying what you would like done when you die. For the benefit of both your family and sick people on waiting lists for organs, you should make your wishes regarding organ donation known to your family, and you should complete an organ donor card.

Who has the legal authority to declare a person "dead"?

Physicians have the legal authority and responsibility to determine if a person is dead and to declare or pronounce a person dead. Death has historically been a medical determination, based on medical and legal criteria. Reliance on physicians to determine death is part of our culture as well as our law. In the classic American film *The Wizard of Oz*, for example, Munchkin City's judge will not let the mayor proclaim that the Wicked Witch is dead until her death is verified "legally" and calls on the coroner to see "if she is morally, ethically, spiritually, physically, positively, absolutely, undeniably and reliably dead." The coroner, who presents her death certificate, says that he has examined her and has concluded that "she's not only merely dead, she's really most sincerely dead." Traditionally, physicians have determined death using the criterion of irreversible cessation of the respiration and heartbeat. Since the early 1960s, however, a heart that had ceased beating could sometimes be restarted with cardiopulmonary resuscitation (CPR). But when CPR is either unsuccessful or untried and the person's heart stops beating, the person is dead because the heartbeat (and thus circulation) has irreversibly ceased.

The heart does not require the brain to function to continue to beat spontaneously, but the lungs need instructions from the brain stem to breathe. With the introduction of mechanical ventilators that breathe for the patient, it became possible to artificially sustain respiration and heartbeat after they would otherwise have ceased because the brain had been totally destroyed, and thus the brain stem could not instruct the lungs to breathe. To prevent the waste of medical resources in intensive care units and to enable the legal recovery of the organs without committing battery or homicide, a new criterion to determine death was proposed and is now universally accepted in the United States: brain death.

What is "brain death"?

Brain death, more properly, death based on brain criteria, is a term used to describe a method of determining death. Bodies attached to mechanical ventilators whose brains have been totally and irreversibly destroyed, and who therefore can *never* breathe on their own, meet brain death criteria. The original definition was proposed in 1968 by the Harvard Ad Hoc Committee on the Definition of Death.[4] After more than a decade of public discussion and debate, the American Medical Association, the American Bar Association, the National Conference of Commissioners on Uniform State Laws, and the President's Commission for the Study of Ethical Problems in Medicine and Biomedical and Behavioral Research, endorsed the following language for the determination of death: "An individual who has sustained either 1) irreversible cessation of circulatory and respiratory functions, or 2) irreversible cessation of all function of the entire brain, including the brain stem, is dead. A determination of death must be made in accordance with accepted medical standards."[5]

This definition is also used in the Uniform Determination of Death Act that has been formally adopted by most states. It is worth noting that part two, the brain death part, is triply redundant to underscore that the definition refers to *all* function of the *entire* brain (including the brain stem), not just to the higher, or cognitive, functions of the brain. Thus, for example, individuals such as Karen Ann Quinlan and Nancy Cruzan, who are permanently unconscious (a condition referred to as a permanent vegetative state) are not dead. This is because, among other things, they are capable of breathing without mechanical assistance, which demonstrates that their brain stem still functions and provides signals to the lungs. It should also be emphasized that both heart- and brain-based criteria are accepted medical and legal criteria to determine death. A person who fulfills either criterion is dead. "Brain dead" is an unfortunate descriptive term that suggests that the person is not "really dead." But this is wrong: a person who meets brain death criteria is dead and should be described simply as "dead."[6] Confusion over brain death certainly played a role in the Jesica Santillán case described at the beginning of this chapter.

The definition is biologically based and accepted by the medical profession. Because of CPR, cessation of heartbeat does not necessarily mean irreversible destruction of the brain, but total brain destruction is death. Most states have laws that specifically adopt brain death; nonetheless, brain death criteria is primarily a medical, not a legal, construct. The courts in all states have deferred to the medical profession in determination of death questions. Thus, physicians in *all* states have the legal authority to pronounce death on the basis of brain death criteria, so long as they do so in accordance with accepted medical standards.[7]

Does a patient's family have any say in the determination of death?

No. No family member can bring the dead back to life. Determination of death is a medical determination made by applying accepted medical standards. If, however, the family has reason to doubt that a determination of death has been made in accordance with accepted medical standards, the family may properly insist that a qualified medical specialist (a neurosurgeon or neurologist) is called in to confirm the determination of death before the ventilator is disconnected and organ harvesting begins. The family may also want to be present when it is determined that brain death criteria are met, and there should be no objection to their presence.[8] Once the determination of death has been confirmed, however, the family has no right to insist that any treatment be continued, as the parents of Jesica Santillán learned.[9] All treatment should cease upon pronouncement of death (since a corpse cannot benefit from medical treatment), and the body should be released to the family for burial (unless organ donation or autopsy is planned). In order to avoid conflicts of interest, the physician who declares a person dead may not, under the Uniform Anatomical Gift

---

UNIFORM DONOR CARD

of _____
                              (name of donor)

In the hope that I may help others, I hereby make this anatomical gift, if medically acceptable, to take effect upon my death. The words and marks below indicate my desires. I give:

      (a) ❑   any needed organs or tissue
      (b) ❑   only the following organs or tissue

_____
      (Specify the organ[s] or tissue[s])

for the purposes of ❑ transplantation, ❑ therapy, ❑ medical research or ❑ education:

      (c) ❑   my body for anatomical study if needed.

Limitations or special wishes, if any:

_____

_____

Act, participate in any tissue or organ harvesting or transplant any tissue or organ obtained from the deceased.

Does brain death apply to children?

Yes, but because of the nature of the brain of a young child, it is medically more difficult to determine the irreversible absence of brain function. Special guidelines have therefore been suggested for children in the following age categories: seven days to two months; two months to one year; and one to five years of age.[10] In children under one week of age, an accurate determination of death based on brain criteria is even more difficult because of brain physiology at that age.

It has been suggested that children born with no upper brain function, called anencephalic infants, should be considered legally dead so that their organs can be harvested for use by other newborns who could survive with them. This would require a new definition of death, however, since as long as an anencephalic infant can breathe on its own, the infant is not dead (since a functioning brain stem is necessary for the anencephalic infant to breathe). Anencephalic infants who can breath on their own are living children, by definition, and therefore cannot be used as organ donors until they stop breathing and are declared dead.[11]

How can a person donate organs or tissues to others so that they may have them upon the individual's death?

Under the Uniform Anatomical Gift Act (1987 revision), a version of which is law in every state, any person eighteen years or older and of sound mind may make a gift, effective upon the person's death, of all or any part(s) of his body to the following recipients for the following purposes:

- Any hospital, physician, surgeon, or procurement organization for transplantation, therapy, medical or dental education, research advancement of medical or dental science
- Any accredited medical or dental school, college or university for education, research, advancement of medical or dental science, or therapy
- Any specified individual for transplantation or therapy needed by that individual

The gift can be made by signing an organ donor card (see figure) in the presence of two witnesses who also sign it.

The person who signs the card usually carries it in his or her wallet. In most states, the gift can be revoked either by destroying the card or by an oral revocation in the presence of two witnesses. A "no commercial, for-profit use of my organs or tissues" clause does not currently appear under the limitations of the act, but as discussed later in this chapter, it should, and you can add it yourself to the form you sign.

May an individual place conditions on the organ and tissue donation?

Yes. As the uniform donor card indicates, an individual may specify which organs and tissues are to be donated, the person or institution to whom they are to be donated, and for what purpose the donated tissue and organs are to be used. A donor may also specify how the body is to be buried following its medical use. The donee may accept or reject the gift. If accepted, and if only part of the body is donated, that part must be removed without unnecessary mutilation, and the remainder of the body must thereafter be turned over to the surviving spouse or other person responsible for burial.

May a deceased's next of kin consent to donate organs if the deceased has not filled out a donor card?

Yes. Every state statute so provides, and each statute also lists the order of priority of those (based on family relationship) who can consent if there is no known objection by the deceased donor or a person in a higher priority class. Most states give first priority to the spouse, then to parents, and then to siblings. Only a few states permit the patient's health care proxy to donate organs. I think these states are wrong to give the proxy this authority. The legal authority of a health care agent ends with the death of the patient, and to add this postmortem authority to an agent who otherwise only has authority during the patient's life (and is thus only concerned with the patient's quality of dying), creates unnecessary confusion and can create a conflict of interest.[12]

Everyone in the United States should be aware that even if a person signs a donor card, virtually no physician, hospital, or organ procurement organization will take organs from the person's dead body without the consent of the next of kin.[13] This is *not* because to do so would be illegal (it is not) or unethical (it is not). It is primarily because it does not seem "right" to most physicians. Hospitals and organ procurement organizations must also deal with the surviving family members, and it is clumsy public relations to take organs from a deceased patient without obtaining the next of kin's agreement regardless of what the law says.

The next of kin have significant legal authority in organ and tissue donation, but this authority is not unlimited. Neither you, nor your family, for example, can require that organs only be given to a member of the same race or religion as you.

How many Americans have signed organ donor cards?

Despite intense public promotion for more than two decades, fewer than 20 percent of all Americans have signed organ donor cards.[14] One reason is that we simply do not like to think about our own deaths. Another is that Americans remain unable to deal with death, and therefore to seriously consider organ donation. For example, 90 percent of the public say they "strongly approve of organ donation"; nonetheless, only about half that number have even discussed organ donation with their families or would be willing to give permission to donate a family member's organ. Almost all neurosurgeons would donate a family member's organ, but only half of them have ever talked to their own families about their own wishes regarding organ donation.[15] There are also fears and misconceptions that inhibit signing organ donor cards. In a Gallup poll used by the National Task Force on Organ Transplantation, for example, the following reasons were given for not signing such cards, in order of importance:

1. They might do something to me before I am really dead.
2. Doctors might hasten my death.
3. I don't like to think about dying.
4. Family might object.
5. Too complicated to give permission.[16]

What is "required request" and "routine inquiry"?

These are mechanisms designed to increase the number of organ donors in the United States. In the late 1980s, the federal government and more than forty states enacted "required request" legislation to require someone designated by the hospital or organ procurement organization to ask the next of kin of every potential organ or tissue donor whether or not they want to donate.[17] There are no effective penalties for noncompliance, and many of these laws are not being followed.

An alternative mechanism is "routine inquiry" in which every patient is asked, upon admission to the hospital, if the person wants to be an organ donor. The goal is to increase organ donation; but it seems more likely to actually decrease it both because such routine inquiry might unduly upset hospital patients, especially those who had come for minor, elective procedures who might then say no prematurely, and because once this "no" is noted in a patient's chart, it could preclude future donation if the person has decided differently but does not put it in writing.

These suggestions are well meaning. But the law cannot force people to talk about a subject they do not want to talk about. Education concerning the need for organs, the use to which they will be put, and sensitive treatment of patients and their families are the most constructive ways to increase organ donation.[18]

May a hospital refuse to release a body to the relatives if the relatives refuse to agree to organ donation?

No. Neither the patient nor the patient's relatives are under any obligation to donate organs or tissues. This is a voluntary act, and coercion has no place in organ procurement or harvesting.

One unusual case illustrates the problems with coercion. A twenty-year-old who committed suicide by shooting himself in the head was rushed to the hospital and placed on a ventilator. Within an hour, the emergency room physician had informed his parents that their son was "brain dead" and asked them to consider donating his organs for transplant. Three hours later, a neurologist confirmed death and again sought the parents' permission to use their son's organs. The parents asked to think it over until the morning, at which time they said no and asked for their son's body. The physicians refused to remove the ventilator and asked that they think more about organ donation. This charade went on for another two days before the hospital and physicians finally released the body to the parents, but only after they had agreed to sign a hurriedly drafted and totally unnecessary release form that read:

We have been advised by the attending physicians of our son, Jeffrey Strachan, that he has been declared "brain dead." It is therefore requested that all life support-life-support-death [*sic*] devices be discontinued as soon as possible.

In making this request we are fully aware of our legal responsibilities and further hold harmless John F. Kennedy Memorial Hospital and the attending physicians with regard to discontinuance of life support devices.

The New Jersey Supreme Court affirmed a jury decision that the hospital had wrongfully withheld the son's body from his parents. In the court's words: "Although plaintiffs were told that their son was brain dead and nothing further could be done for him, for three days after requesting that their son be disconnected from the respirator plaintiffs continued to see him lying in bed, with tubes in his body, his eyes taped shut, and foam in his mouth. His body remained warm to the touch . . . a scene fraught with grief and heartache."[19]

The actions of the doctors and hospital in this case were disgraceful and caused real suffering to real people. Family members should not be asked to consent to organ or tissue donation until after a determination of death has been made; if they refuse, mechanical ventilation must be immediately discontinued and the body released to them for burial.

Must corpses be medically screened before their organs or tissues are used in transplant?

Yes. Donors must be carefully screened to assure that their organs and tissues are suitable for transplant, and that they harbor no infectious agents, such as HIV. Both the physicians who harvest the tissues and the hospital in which the transplant is performed may be held liable for damages if deficient screening procedures result in injury to the recipient.

In one case, for example, two different patients received corneal transplants from the same donor. The transplanted corneas infected both eyes in both recipients, resulting in total blindness. The patients sued. The eyes had been removed by a first-year ophthalmology resident, who had reviewed an incomplete chart of the deceased patient and had secured permission of the deceased's wife for the removal of his corneas. The hospital had no checklist that could be used as a guide, and the resident based his decision solely on what he had learned orally from senior residents.

At the trial, it was found that published criteria existed and were fairly uniform around the country. These standards contraindicated the use of any cadaver that had a history of certain medical conditions. The donor was a "60 year old white male, heavy alcoholic with cirrhosis of the liver proven at autopsy" and had suffered from several other serious diseases. The court concluded that "whoever may have had the responsibility of determining the suitability of the corneas for transplant would have been required, in the exercise of due care, to review carefully and exhaustively the medical history of the proposed donor." The jury could also have found the hospital itself was negligent "in failing to set up a procedure which would assure that the party responsible for determining the suitability of the cornea for transplant would have access to all of the relevant medical records of the proposed donor."[20]

Recipients of organ and tissue transplants have a right to rely on those who select the donor to properly screen for conditions that contraindicate use. This principle is applicable to all types of donations, from hearts and kidneys to sperm and blood.

Can a hospital be successfully sued for removing organs or tissues without the family's consent?

A successful suit can be brought only in extreme cases in which it can be demonstrated that the hospital acted "dishonestly, maliciously, fraudulently, or unconscionably." This is because health care facilities are protected by the Uniform Anatomical Gift Act for actions taken under it so long as they act in "good faith." A Minnesota court determined the meaning of good faith in a 1998 case in which a young man was killed by a self-inflicted gunshot to the head and was declared brain dead at the Mayo Clinic.[21] His mother then filled out an organ donor form, and checked the "yes" box next to the phrase, "Permission is granted for organ or tissue donation for transplantation, research, or education purposes." Later she informed a representative from the organ procurement agency that she did not want her son's organs used for medical research or education. The representative wrote "no research" on the organ donor form but did not write "no educational purposes" on it.

Because of the manner of death, an autopsy was ordered by the coroner over the mother's objections. As a standard part of the autopsy, the son's pelvic block (consisting of his prostate, seminal vesicles, bladder, and rectum) was removed. The pathologist, who had read a copy of the revised organ donor form, decided to keep the pelvic block for educational purposes and had it mounted in plexiglass for use in medical school. This action was later discovered by the mother, and she sued the Mayo Clinic. The trial court dismissed her case, and an appeals court affirmed on the basis that Minnesota's version of the Uniform Anatomical Gift Act protected all involved from any liability because they acted in good faith. The appeals court agreed that the procurement agency representative should have accurately written the mother's "no educational purposes" instruction down, but it concluded that "in the absence of fraud or design to seek an unconscionable advantage" this negligent failure did not remove its good faith immunity protection.

The lesson from this case is that both courts and legislatures highly value the organ procurement process, and will protect it. Thus, it is incumbent upon family members who do not want their loved ones' organs used in specific ways, such as for research or education, or for commercial purposes, to not only say so clearly but to make sure those involved know about it. The best way is to make the changes you want on the organ procurement authorization form yourself.

May human organs and tissues be sold?

They may not be sold for transplantation or therapy. Under the Uniform Anatomical Gift Act, for example, a person may not purchase or sell body parts for transplantation or therapy. Violation is a felony punishable by a fine not exceeding $50,000 or imprisonment not to exceed five years, or both. Federal law also prohibits the purchase and sale of organs and tissue for use in human transplantation.[22] These laws did not prevent a person from offering his kidney for sale on eBay, the on-line auctioneer, in 1999, probably as a hoax. The bids went to $5.7 million before the macabre kidney auction was pulled, and eBay clarified its policy of not offering illegal items for sale.[23] Because of the great demand for human organs, many proposals have been put forth over the years to change the law to allow for sales by live donors. These proposals have all been soundly rejected because they would undermine altruism and equality and permit the rich to literally live off the bodies and blood of the poor.[24]

Reasonable payments to hospitals and physicians are permissible under federal and state law for the costs associated with the removal, transportation, implantation, processing, preservation, quality control, and storage, or, in the case of a living donor, for the expenses of travel, housing, and lost wages incurred by the donor. In 1997, an Arkansas court determined that payment of $101,500 for a bone marrow "donation" was not a lawful, reasonable payment but an illegal sale of an anatomical part.[25] The parties themselves actually filed the lawsuit to seek court enforcement of their agreement. The court concluded that the agreement was illegal and "offensive," and that society is committed to the principle that body parts should only be given as a gift.

Are donated organs and tissues ever used for commercial purposes?

Yes. Even though persons, organizations, and corporations alike are all prohibited by law from selling or purchasing body parts, once donated, these parts may be processed and developed into profitable products.[26] Many people are unaware of the numerous potential products that exist and are continually being developed by for-profit companies utilizing human body parts. These commercial products are often used as medical therapy or medically needed implants. Nonetheless, the for-profit use of tissue donated to nonprofit organ procurement agencies threatens to infect the entire organ procurement system. The quickly growing for-profit use of donated tissue was made public in 2000 by investigative reporters of the *Orange County Register* in California.[27] Although there has been no success in increasing the number of organ donors, tissue donation has increased 172 percent in the past five years. And nonprofit tissue banks often act as intermediaries for for-profit companies they have established or do business with.

According to the *Orange County Register*, a typical donor may provide tissue, including skin, tendons, heart valves, veins, corneas, and bone (bone is replaced with PVC pipe to keep the body's shape for open-casket funerals), which a nonprofit tissue bank can sell for $14,000 to $34,000, and which will be processed and sold by a for-profit firm for up to $220,000.[28] Sales of tissues by the nonprofit tissue banks have enabled some of them to pay extremely high salaries and perks to their executives and this in turn corrupts their nonprofit mission and may also be an illegal diversion of charitable funds. Former Food and Drug Administration commissioner David Kessler has observed, "[L]ots of guys just view this as a commodity. . . . [I]f [they] weren't in this business, they'd be in concrete."[29] It is likely that most people who donate their loved ones' organs and tissues would *not* do so if they knew the tissues were being processed not only to be sold for therapeutic uses but also for cosmetic surgery.

The nation's sixty-three tissue banks and fifty-nine organ procurement agencies have been described as trying to find a way to accurately describe their relationship with for-profit companies to potential donors and their families. The answer is obvious: tell the truth and give donors a clear and easy way to restrict their gift of tissue to the nonprofit sector of the health care industry. When dealing with any organ or tissue procurement agency you should ask about their commercial, for-profit ties. If the agency is not forthcoming, it does not respect you or your loved one and does not deserve to be a recipient of your gift.[30]

Why are autopsies performed?

An autopsy is a comprehensive study of a dead body performed by a trained physician with a specialty in pathology, who employs recognized dissection procedures and techniques. The most common purpose of autopsies is to determine the cause of death, but autopsies also serve valuable educational functions. Nevertheless, autopsy rates in U.S. hospitals have fallen from about 50 percent in the 1940s, to 35 to 15 percent in the 1980s, and to below 10 percent today. This dramatic decline is attributable to a variety of causes, including lack of payment, better techniques to determine the cause of death, and the elimination of autopsy requirements by the Joint Commission on Accreditation of Healthcare Organizations.[31] Physicians also seem to believe that autopsies could lead to malpractice suits against them. According to the noted pathologist Cyril Wecht, however, "most medicolegal experts believe that thorough postmortem examinations much more often than not serve to provide factual, objective information to the decedent['s]" family that negates their suspicions and obviates their desire to pursue a medical malpractice lawsuit.[32] Usually, only the thoracic, abdominal, and cranial (chest, stomach, and head) cavities are opened during an autopsy, and neither the face nor the hands are cut or disfigured in any way.

If the cause of death is potentially a genetically related condition or infectious disease, exact determination may help other family members. Also, if the cause of death might have been related to medical malpractice, autopsy findings may help to prove or disprove this. The family may also simply wish to know the exact cause of death or may agree to an autopsy to contribute to medical education or research. If a hospital doctor requests the autopsy from the family, the cost of the autopsy is almost universally absorbed by the hospital and does not appear as a separate item on the patient's bill.

Who has the legal authority to consent to an autopsy?

Under the statutes of most states, the next of kin (the surviving spouse, if there is one, then other survivors in order of family relationship) has the authority to consent to an autopsy. It has been ruled by courts on numerous occasions that there is no property interest in a dead body. Nonetheless, the next of kin does have a strong interest in seeing that the deceased is properly buried, and this interest is strong enough to give the next of kin the right to possession of the body in the same condition it was in at death.[33] It is "the personal feelings of the survivors that are being protected" by the law.[34] Some courts also recognize that the right of possession, control over organ and tissue donation, and the right to bury can together be properly characterized as a property interest in the body.[35] Only an autopsy ordered by a state official can override the family's interests, and even in this case, the decision must be made in good faith or the autopsy is illegal.

A hospital can be held liable for performing an autopsy without permission.[36] In one case, the hospital was held liable for payment of damages for mental suffering when an autopsy was performed without consent, even though the widow did not detect the autopsy at the funeral. She found out about it only when she read the death certificate ten days later. The consent form had been signed by the doctor and two nurses as witnesses before being presented to the widow. She refused to sign it, but it was placed in the record anyway, and the doctor who performed the autopsy thought that permission had been granted because of the form.[37]

The extent of damages awarded for an unauthorized autopsy is not measured by the extent of the mutilation of the body but by the effect of the procedure on the "feelings and emotions of the [surviving relatives] who have the duty of burial."[38] The rights of individuals to control their own body tissues and the rights of survivors to protect the bodies of their loved ones from exploitation would be stronger if a property interest in one's own body was recognized by the law.

Laws in about half of the states also specifically give the patient the right to consent to an autopsy. Also, since under the provisions of the Uniform Anatomical Gift Act, a person may give all or a limited part of his or her body for education, research, and the advancement of medical science, the person may give his or her body to a hospital for the sole purpose of performing an autopsy. The probable reason doctors almost never ask patients to consent in advance to autopsies is that it seems callous. Moreover, few hospitals would permit the autopsy, even with this authorization, over family objection.

May a hospital retain any portion of the body after autopsy?

No. The hospital may not retain any tissues or organs without the permission of the person who consented to the autopsy, except in those states that permit removal of corneas and/or pituitary glands in the absence of a known objection.[39] Standard forms for permission generally include permission to retain samples, and the rule against retention does not cover limited small portions of organs taken for further study. The person consenting to the autopsy, however, has the right to place whatever limitations on the consent he or she wishes. The reasonable expectation of the public is that larger portions of the body will not be retained, even for research, without consent.[40]

A hospital could also be liable if it misplaces an entire body. In a Florida case, a jury awarded $150,000 in damages to a couple when a hospital lost the corpse of their premature baby. The mother testified, "I still have my doubts that Paul ever died."[41] This case was, however, overturned on appeal. The court ruled that recovery required proof of "wantonness, willfulness or malice" on the part of the hospital.[42]

Do health care professionals or students have a right to practice their skills on a corpse?

No. After death, the relatives, who have the right to bury the body, have the exclusive right to consent to use of the corpse for medical education.

Any unauthorized use or mutilation of the body after death is illegal and unethical. Before death, only the patient has the right to consent to training or nonbeneficial research on his or her body.

It is disturbing that a 1998 study of house officers (recent medical graduates in training programs) found that almost one-third of them thought it was acceptable to practice placing femoral-vein (a major leg vein) catheters on live patients during CPR, and 16 percent of the house officers surveyed had actually attempted to perform such a procedure for practice.[43] The authors of the study were quite properly appalled by what they found and noted that this practice is "inconsistent with current standards of medical ethics" and uses patients simply "as means" to the end of medical education. They suggested use of animals and mannequins instead, as well as the use of fresh cadavers. Patient advocates must be on the alert to make sure patients are not used simply for practice without their consent.

Fresh cadavers are frequently used to practice such things as vaginal exams and intubations.[44] Even though it is certainly better for patients that dead bodies rather than live patients are used for such practice, consent must be obtained in each instance. Without consent, the main lesson students are learning is a false one: that it is acceptable to use deception to further their education.[45]

Tips for Advocates

- **Except in very unusual cases involving EMTs and hospice nurses, only a physician may declare death,** and the determination of death can be made either on the basis of irreversible heart function or irreversible brain function (so-called brain death).

- **When a person is declared "brain dead," the person is dead.**

- **Your authority to make decisions for your patient under a health care proxy ends with the patient's death;** nonetheless, you can still be an important source of information about what your patient would want done concerning organ and tissue donation and autopsy.

- Your patient's wishes concerning organ and tissue donation should be set forth in an **organ donor card** signed by the patient; if possible, try to see that the patient's wishes are followed by the hospital. Discuss this with your patient, if possible, and help the patient make out an organ donor card that accurately sets out the patient's wishes.

• **If the patient did not want organs or tissues removed, make sure everyone knows about it and have this decision written in the medical record.**

• **Organ and tissue donation is entirely voluntary.** Neither the hospital nor physicians may discriminate against you or your family in any way for not donating.

• **If you are asked to donate the organs or tissues of a next of kin, make sure you ask if any commercial or for-profit use will be made of any tissue if you care about this. You may refuse or restrict such use.**

• The patient's next of kin must consent to **an autopsy** unless the medical examiner (or coroner) orders an autopsy in the case of suspected homicide, suicide, or accidental death.

NOTES

1. Jerry Adler, *A Tragic Error,* Time, March 3, 2003, 21.

2. Ed Bradley, *Anatomy of a Mistake,* 60 Minutes, March 16, 2003 (transcript), 4.

3. Randl Archibold, *Focus Shifts to Decisions Made at End of Girl's Life,* New York Times, February 24, 2003, A11. *And see* Lawrence Altman, *Even the Elite Aren't Immune to Errors,* New York Times, February 23, 2003, 16, and David Resnick, *The Jesica Santillán Tragedy: Lesson Learned,* 33 Hastings Center Report 15 (July 2003).

4. Ad Hoc Committee of the Harvard Medical School to Examine the Definition of Brain Death, *A Definition of Irreversible Coma,* 206 JAMA 337 (1968).

5. President's Commission for the Study of Ethical Problems in Medicine and Biomedical and Behavioral Research, Defining Death, Washington, D.C.: Government Printing Office, 1981.

6. Alexandra K. Glazier, *"The Brain Dead Patient Was Kept Alive" and Other Disturbing Misconceptions: A Call for Amendments to the Uniform Anatomical Gift Act,* 9 Kansas J. Law & Public Policy 640 (2000). *See also* Alexander Morgan Capron, *Brain Death—Well*

Settled Yet Still Unresolved, 344 New Eng. J. Med. 1244 (2001); Eelco Wijdicks, *The Diagnosis of Brain Death,* 344 New Eng. J. Med. 1215 (2001).

7. *See* George J. Annas, Judging Medicine, Clifton, N.J.: Humana Press, 1988, 365–69.

8. The only study I know of related to the presence of family members during brain-death testing was done in the United Kingdom. It showed that although two-thirds of physicians and nurses believed that families benefited by being present during testing, only a minority of physicians actually invited families to be present. Janet Pugh et al., *Presence of Relatives During Testing for Brain Stem Death: Questionnaire Study,* 321 Brit. Med. J. 1505 (2000).

9. The Santillán case is described at the beginning of this chapter. New York State and New Jersey health regulations seem to provide the patient or family some voice in choosing the basis on which death will be determined. These provisions are irrational political compromises that can only breed confusion (*see, e.g.,* N.Y. Public Health Law, art. 29(B) [1987]). *See* Michael Grodin, *Religions Exemptions: Brain Death and Jewish Law,* 36 J. Church & State 401 (1994).

10. Task Force for the Determination of Brain Death in Children, *Guidelines for the Determination of Brain Death in Children,* 21 Annals of Neurology 616 (1987).

11. *In re T.A.C.P.,* 609 So.2d 588 (Fla. 1992). *See also* George J. Annas, *From Canada with Love: Anencephalic Newborns as Organ Donors?* 17 Hastings Center Report 36 (December 1987); Alexander Capron, *Anencephalic Donors: Separate the Dead from the Dying,* 17 Hastings Center Report 5 (February 1987); and Alan Shermon et al., *The Use of Anencephalic Infants as Organ Sources,* 261 JAMA 1773 (1989).

12. *See generally* George J. Annas, *The Health Care Proxy and the Living Will,* 324 New Eng. J. Med. 1210 (1991).

13. Task Force on Organ Transplantation, Organ Transplantation, Washington, D.C.: Health and Human Services, 1986. The selling of organs for transplant is also outlawed in the United States. *See* Annas, *supra* note 7, 378–83, and *infra* note 22. *See also* Donald Joralemon, *Shifting Ethics: Debating the Incentive Question in Organ Transplantation,* 27 J. Med. Ethics 3035 (2001); Michael Friedlaender, *The Right to Sell or Buy a Kidney: Are We Failing Our Patients?* 359 Lancet 971 (2002); and Hans Schlitt, *Paid Non-Related Living Organ Donation: Horn of Plenty or Pandora's Box,* 359 Lancet 906 (2002).

14. Task Force, *supra* note 13, and *Hearings on Organ Transplants: Hearings Before the Subcomm. on Investigations and Oversight of the House Committee on Science and Technology,* 98th Cong., 1st Sess. (April 13, 14, 27, 1983).

15. Jeffrey Prottas, *Health Professionals and Hospital Administrators in Organ Procurement: Attitudes, Reservations and their Resolutions,* 78 Am. J. Public Health 642 (1988).

16. Task Force, *supra* note 13, at 38.

17. George J. Annas, *Paradoxes of Organ Transplantation,* 78 Am. J. Public Health 621 (1988).

18. I also think that aggressive programs to use non-heart-beating donors and to encourage organ donation of nonvital organs (almost always kidneys) by living nonrelatives create many more problems than they solve. *See, e.g.,* Renee C. Fox, *"An Ignoble Form of Cannibalism": Reflections on the Pittsburgh Protocol for Procuring Organs from Non-Heart-Beating Cadavers* (in) Robert M. Arnold, et al., eds., Procuring Organs for Transplant: The Debate Over Non-Heart-Beating Cadaver Protocols, Baltimore: Johns Hopkins U. Press,

1995, 155–164, and Yves Vanrenterghem, *Cautious Approach to Use of Nonheart-beating Donors*, 356 Lancet 528 (2000). *See also* Live Organ Donor Consensus Group, *Consensus Statement on Live Organ Donor*, 284 JAMA 2919 (2000).

19. *Strachan v. John F. Kennedy Memorial Hospital*, 109 N.J. 523, 538 A.2d 346, 351 (1988).

20. *Ravenis v. Detroit General Hospital*, 63 Mich. App. 79, 84, 234 N.W.2d 411, 414 (1975).

21. *Rahman v. Mayo Clinic*, 578 N.W.2d 802 (Minn. App. 1998). *See also Hicks v. U.S.* 631 F.Supp. 1207 (So.D. Ohio, 1986) and *Ramirez v. Health Partners of So. Arizona*, 972 P.2d 658 (Ariz. Ct. App. 1998).

22. 42 USC sec. 274e (1984).

23. Leo Strandora, *Ebay Halts Kidney Auction*, New York Daily News, September 3, 1999, 3. *See also* Norman Levinsky, *Organ Donations by Unrelated Donors*, 343 New Eng. J. Med. 430 (2000) (ethical issues involved in donating a kidney to a stranger), and Live Organ Donor Consensus Group, *supra* note 18.

24. *See, e.g.,* Gloria J. Banks, *Legal & Ethical Safeguards: Protection of Society's Most Vulnerable Participants in a Commercialized Organ Transplantation System*, 21 Am. J. Law & Med. 45 (1995). Pennsylvania has proposed to pay up to $300 of hotel and meal expenses of families who donate organs. This strikes me as simply silly: it is unlikely that any family will donate organs they would otherwise not donate for a "night on the town." *See Organ Donation Debate*, USA Today, June 2, 1999, A14. On commercial practices in other countries, *see* Michael Finkel, *This Little Kidney Went to Market*, New York Times Magazine, May 27, 2001, 26, and Craig Smith, *On Death Row, China's Source of Transplants*, New York Times, October 18, 2001, A10.

25. *Wilson v. Adkins*, 57 Ark. App. 43, 941 S.W.2d 440 (1997). The debate on selling organs continues. *See, e.g.,* Jennifer Saranow, *What is Your Body Worth?*, Wall Street Journal, May 6, 2003, D1.

26. For a good discussion of the legal and ethical issues involved in the commercial use of human tissues and cells, *see* Lori Andrews & Dorothy Nelkin, Body Bazaar: The Market for Human Tissue in the Biotechnology Age, New York: Crown, 2001. *See also* U.S. Congress, Office of Technology Assessment, New Developments in Biotechnology: Ownership of Human Tissues and Cells, Washington, D.C.: Government Printing Office, 1987, and George J. Annas, *Outrageous Fortune* (in) Standard of Care, New York: Oxford U. Press, 1992, 167–77.

27. *See* Mark Katches, William Heisel & Ronald Campbell, *Donors Don't Realize They Are Fueling a Lucrative Business*, Orange County Register, April 16, 2000, 1. *See also* Peter Monaghan, *Scholarly Watchdogs for an Ethical Netherworld*, Chronicle of Higher Education, October 6, 2000, A23 (on worldwide problem of organ sales), and *supra* note 24.

28. *Id. And see* William Heisel, *Tissue-Bank Group Steps Closer to Full Disclosure*, Orange County Register, September 13, 2000, 1.

29. Stephen Hedges & William Gaines, *Donor Bodies Milled into Growing Profits*, Chicago Tribune, May 21, 2000, 1C.

30. You can see what commercial ties your local tissue bank has on the Orange County Register's Web site (www.ocregister.com/health/body/organweb00625cci.shtml).

31. C. S. Landefeld, et al., *Diagnostic Yield of the Autopsy in a University Hospital and a Community Hospital,* 318 New Eng. J. Med. 1249 (1988); George Lundberg, *Low Tech Autopsies in the Era of High-Tech Medicine: Continued Value for Quality Assurance and Patient Safety,* 280 JAMA 1273 (1998).

32. Cyril Wecht, Letter, 281 JAMA 2184 (1999), quoting R. J. Zarbo, P. H. Baker, & P. J. Howanitz, *The Autopsy as a Performance Measurement Tool: Diagnostic Discrepancies and Unresolved Clinical Questions,* 123 Arch. Pathol. Lab. Med. 191 (1999).

33. *Infield v. Cope,* 58 N.M. 308, 270 P.2d 716 (1954); *Gahn v. Leary,* 318 Mass. 425, 61 N.E.2d 844 (1945).

34. *Strachan, supra* note 19, and *Kohn v. U.S.,* 591 F.Supp. 568 (E.D.N.Y., 1984).

35. *Brotherton v. Cleveland,* 923 F.2d 477 (6th Cir. 1991), and *Whaley v. Tuscola,* 58 F.3d 1111 (6th Cir. 1995).

36. A hospital can also be held liable in a civil law suit for refusing to deliver a body and, instead, inducing a coroner to perform an autopsy. *E.g., Darcy v. Presbyterian Hospital,* 202 N.Y. 259, 95 N.E. 695 (1911).

37. *French v. Ochsner Clinic,* 200 So. 2d 371 (La. App. 1967).

38. *Id.,* at 373, and *Strachan, supra* note 19; *and see* George J. Annas, *The Cases of the Live Buried Mother and the Dead Unburied Baby: Negligence or Outrageous Conduct?* 5 Orthopaedic Rev. 71 (March 1976).

39. States that permit corneas and/or pituitary glands to be harvested under "presumed consent" include Arkansas, California, Connecticut, Delaware, Florida, Kentucky, Maryland, Michigan, Missouri, Ohio, Oklahoma, Tennessee, Texas, and West Virginia. *See* Banks, *supra* note 24, at 68.

40. For example, over a three-year period, an associate medical examiner in Milwaukee removed and stored the testicles from about seventy males on whom she had performed autopsies. The incident received much publicity. She defended the practice in the name of medical research (although she had not commenced any research on the testicles she had collected): "In view of the fact that testicles are removed during an autopsy, I don't see why it is a crime, as has been implied, to put them in a jar instead of back in the body." The answer, of course, is that it is the individual and the next of kin who have the right to decide how the body will be disposed of, not the medical examiner. Neil Rosenberg, *Examiner Says She Will Stop Stealing Testicles from Dead,* Milwaukee Journal, June 26, 1979, 1. *And see, Doctor Admits He Sold Corpses' Parts,* New York Times, September 4, 1988, 50.

41. Reported in Boston Globe, November 28, 1973, 2.

42. *Brooks v. South Broward Hospital District,* 325 So. 2d 479 (Fla. Dist. Ct. App. 1975), and Wilson, *supra* note 25. A related issue is the use of tissue from dead fetuses following elective abortion. The laws of most states permit the use of fetal tissue for research and transplantation but only with the consent of the mother. Sale of fetal tissue is prohibited by federal law. *See supra* note 22; *and see generally* John Robertson, *Fetal Tissue Transplants,* 66 Wash. U.L.Q. 443 (1988).

43. Lauris Kaldjian et al., *Insertion of Femoral-Vein Catheters for Practice by Medical House Officers during Cardiopulmonary Resuscitation,* 341 New Eng. J. Med 2088 (1999). *See also* R. M. McNamara et al., *Requesting Consent for an Invasive Procedure in Newly Deceased Adults,* 273 JAMA 310 (1995).

44. J. P. Orlowski et al., *The Ethics of Using Newly Dead Patients for Teaching and Practicing Intubation Techniques,* 319 New Eng. J. Med. 439 (1988) (the authors advocate the use of dead bodies "in the absence of expressed dissent"); *and see* Paul Glader, *Doctors Question Use of Dead or Dying Patients for Training,* Wall Street Journal, November 12, 2002, B1.

45. Alice Fleury Kerns, *Better to Lay It out on the Table Rather than Do It Behind the Curtain: Hospitals Need to Obtain Consent Before Using Newly Deceased Patients to Teach Resuscitation Procedures,* 13 J. Contemporary Health Law and Policy 581 (1997); Mark Wicclair, *Informed Consent and Research Involving the Newly Dead,* 12 Kennedy Institute Ethics J. 351 (2002); and Rebecca Pentz et al., *Revisiting Ethical Guidelines for Research with Terminal Wean and Brain-Dead Participants,* 33 Hastings Center Report 20 (January 2003), and Lila Guterman, *Crossing the Line? Medical Research on Brain-Dead People Raises Ethical Questions,* Chronicle of Higher Education, August 1, 2003, A13.

XV

Patient Safety and Medical Malpractice

T he first goal of all patient advocates (and all health care professionals) should be patient safety: to try to prevent injury to the patient. The ancient Hippocratic principle for physicians is the same: "first, do no harm." Prevention is always better than cure. Unfortunately, our patient safety tools are primitive. As the Institute of Medicine noted in its highly acclaimed 2000 report on medical errors, *To Err Is Human: Building a Safer Health System,* between forty-four thousand and ninety-eight thousand Americans are killed each year as a result of medical errors.[1] Even using the lower estimate, this makes medical errors the eighth-leading cause of death in the United States, with more patients dying from medical errors than from motor vehicle accidents (44,458), breast cancer (42,297), or AIDS (16,516).[2] Moreover, many more errors result in pain, loss of function, disfigurement, and injury.[3] Obviously, action must be taken to make the health care system safer.

The Institute of Medicine opened its report with several cases, including that of Willie King, who had the wrong leg amputated, and eight-year-old Ben Kolb, who died during minor surgery in a drug mix-up. The first example the report referred to was that of the experienced and knowledgeable health reporter for the *Boston Globe,* Betsy Lehman, who is described as dying "from a drug overdose during chemotherapy." But more should be said about Lehman, and thanks to the insightful and persistent reporting of her fellow health journalist at the *Boston Globe,* Richard Knox, we know a lot about what happened to her.[4]

Lehman was thirty-seven years old, and the mother of two young daughters, when she was diagnosed with breast cancer. Following surgery and six months of chemotherapy, a biopsy revealed malignant cells in her lungs. She opted for an experimental approach to try to eradicate the

337

cancer: high-dose chemotherapy followed by an autologous stem cell transplant to reconstitute her immune system, which would give her about a 25 percent chance of a cure. She entered one of the country's leading cancer hospitals, Dana Farber, in November 1994. A young physician, working as a research fellow, misread the experimental protocol, and instead of ordering the prescribed daily dose of the cancer drug Cytoxan (grams multiplied by her body surface, which would have been 1.6 grams a day for four days), he ordered a dosage four times as large (multiplying by four instead of one and getting a daily dose of 6.5 grams instead of 1.6). At least five other physicians and nurses followed this mistaken order, including a senior physician.

Lehman received 26 grams of the highly toxic drug over four days; the just-barely safe dosage for four days is about 7 grams. She also received a four-fold overdose of another drug (an ulcer drug thought to boost the effectiveness of Cytoxan), during the same time period. Within days, Lehman was desperately ill, much sicker than she had ever been on high dose chemotherapy, and tried to get the staff to understand that something unusual and bad was happening. Sometime after 11:00 A.M., she called a friend and left a message on her answering machine that something was "wrong," saying, "I don't know what's wrong, but something's wrong." When the friend called back before noon she got no answer. At 12:15 P.M., a member of the treatment team found Lehman in bed with no pulse or respiration; her skin was blue. It had been forty-five minutes since anyone had looked in on her. Resuscitation efforts were fruitless, and she was pronounced dead. She was thirty-nine years old.

There are many lessons from this case, which differs from the other forty-four thousand to ninety-eight thousand medical deaths caused annually from medical errors primarily in that the victim was a medical reporter whose newspaper investigated her death. First, it is essential that every hospitalized patient, especially those undergoing extreme medical interventions, have his or her own advocate, and that the advocate (preferably advocates working in shifts) be with the patient twenty-four hours a day. Lehman had knowledgeable and supportive friends and family, but they did not question the drugs used or their dosages. Even if any of them had been there when she tried to call for help, the overdose was so high that nothing may have helped her. Second, physicians and nurses working with very sick people must listen to patients. Providers often distance themselves from patients and see pain and suffering as just part of the treatment or disease. Another cancer patient at the same hospital wrote in a note to herself while in the hospital, "I feel as if I'm a non-person when I'm inside the walls of Dana Farber." Lehman's husband, a scientist who works at the hospital, described his wife in the following terms: "She was dealing with horrendous symptoms. The whole lining of her gut from one end to the other was shedding. She was vomiting sheets of tissue. They said this was the worst they'd seen. But the doctors said this was all normal with stem cell transplant." Nurses noted that almost all stem cell transplant patients suffer bad reactions. As one nurse put it, "[Y]ou can get awfully cavalier." Reporter Richard Knox concluded, "A sobering aspect of the case is the ultimate powerlessness of even the savviest medical care consumer to guard against slipshod care." Third, it often takes many mistakes to translate a medical error into harm to a patient. Dealing effectively with patient safety requires more than simply assigning blame: it will often require changes in the hospital systems, including things such as computerized drug ordering and checking systems and redundant order confirmations.

The hospital settled a medical malpractice case with Lehman's husband for an undisclosed amount of money. More importantly, the publicity from the case prompted the hospital and others to take preventive actions, most of which did involve systems changes. These actions include installing a computer system that automatically blocks excessive drug dosages; eliminating the one-page "schema," or summary of complex experimental protocols; supervising junior physicians more tightly; and instituting a system (including a daily rating of side effects and their severity) for paying closer attention to patients' symptoms and reports of pain and distress. Safety experts and the Joint Commission on the Accreditation of Health Care Organizations have called for action to address the pervasive problem of patient safety, but most proposals have been stalled with the primary excuse that identifying error-prone physicians could subject them to malpractice suits.[5] This response should be unacceptable to the medical public: there is a critical problem of patient safety, and using secrecy and cover-ups to protect physicians rather than using transparency and accountability to protect patients is unprofessional and dangerous for patients.

Among the specific recommendations made by the Joint Commission to improve patient safety are improving the accuracy of patient identification (so, for example, the patient gets the proper test or surgical procedure and the right type of blood); improving communication among caregivers (including notations of telephone orders and use of abbreviations); eliminating wrong-site and wrong-patient surgery; and improving the effectiveness of the clinical alarm systems.[6] All of these make sense, but they are only a start.

Prevention of injury must be the focus of patient safety measures. Medical malpractice litigation comes only after the harm is done, and it is expensive, slow, and disruptive. Nonetheless, litigation is often the only method injured patients have to seek compensation for their injuries when physicians, hospitals, and health plans injure them through negligence. In short, patient safety is the goal, and litigation is one method of trying to achieve it.

Does a patient have a right to be told that a physician has injured him or her?

Patients do have a right to this information because the harm was suffered by the patient, and the patient cannot give informed consent to further treatment (e.g., to alleviate the harm) or give their informed consent to have additional procedures done by a particular physician without this knowledge. Subsequent treatment performed after the injury by a physician who withheld information from the patient could reasonably be considered a battery. Although it is unlikely that a patient would file a lawsuit on this basis alone (the lawsuit would more likely be for the negligent injury itself), cover-ups add harm to the patient and make it much more likely the patient will file a lawsuit when he or she finds out about it.[7] Moreover, fraudulent concealment of injury can, as discussed below, toll the statute of limitations for filing a lawsuit.

Physicians have argued that they would be "digging their own graves" by informing patients about harm they have caused, and there is no doubt that presenting patients with this information is difficult. Nonetheless, it is critical to both patient trust and patient safety that this information be disclosed. Disclosure is part and parcel of the physician's fiduciary duty to the patient. Patients do not expect or demand perfection—what they expect, and should demand, is truthfulness. The Joint Commission agrees and has added new patient rights standards that require that "[p]atients and, when appropriate, their families are informed about the outcomes of care, including unanticipated outcomes." This standard specifically includes the worst mistakes, those the Joint Commission calls "reviewable sentinel events," such as medication error that results in death, wrong-patient or wrong-site surgery, maternal death, and transfusions of the wrong blood type.[8]

What is a medical malpractice lawsuit?

Medical malpractice is a type of lawsuit brought by a patient against a care provider (usually a physician) for injuries suffered as a result of the provider's negligence (failure to live up to the profession's standard of care). Medical malpractice is a fault-based liability system, which means that the person at fault is responsible to pay for the harm inflicted on an injured person. Whether the provider is at fault is determined in an adversary proceeding, usually a trial, in which the provider and the patient are each represented by legal counsel. The trier of fact, usually a jury, must decide if the provider is responsible for the patient's injury because the provider failed to meet the standard of care: the care a "reasonably prudent provider in the same or similar circumstances" would have provided.

Primarily because they are usually decided by lay juries in public, physicians have deplored malpractice lawsuits for over a century and a half. In 1845, for example, physicians indicated alarm at the increase in malpractice lawsuits and suggested alternatives to jury trials, such as committees made up of physicians, to judge such claims.[9] In 1872, the American Medical Association (AMA) recommended that physicians be appointed independent arbiters by the court to judge their peers.[10] Physicians have also historically hated the term *malpractice* itself, a term that denotes "evil" or "bad" practice. As physician-attorney William Sage has noted, "Much of the medical profession's resistance to regulatory accountability can be traced to the sense of betrayal and persecution most physicians feel when accused of malpractice."[11] Most physicians tend to think the law is arbitrary and alien, and that lawyers are out to get them if they don't watch out (and maybe even if they do). Medicolegal expert Marshall Kapp, who surveyed physicians on this subject, sums it up this way, "Physicians' view of the universe as a scary and dangerous place for them and their patients has become such a commonplace and automatic assumption that I half expect tomorrow's newspapers to trumpet the discovery of an 'anti-lawyer' gene that predisposes carriers to pursue medical careers." Kapp continues: "Repeatedly and vigorously, physicians indicate that their primary anxiety about legal system entanglement is fear of the traumatic experience of being civilly sued for malpractice, an event which they interpret as a deeply personal and intimate, yet simultaneously an embarrassingly public affront against their very integrity and worth as professionals and people."[12]

Most physicians do not distinguish between being sued and successfully defending a suit, seeing the very act of being named a defendant as horrific. Physicians also tend to overestimate the probability that they will be sued, and if sued, assume the system is stacked against them.[13] All of this helps explain why physicians try to avoid lawsuits and tend to treat perceived legal threats as much more important than medical ethics: "do the right thing" is often replaced by "do the thing that will keep me out of legal trouble." The most destructive result is the continued excuse for not telling patients (and the public) about medical errors: I might be punished by a lawsuit. The fact is, however, that patients want their physicians to admit mistakes to them, and most experts seem to agree that such physician candor with patients makes it less likely that the patient will sue.[14]

More than 80 percent of all malpractice suits are brought on the basis of an incident that occurred in a hospital. About 15 percent involve doctors' offices, and the rest occur in nursing homes, HMOs, surgical centers, and other settings. Our society permits injured patients to bring malpractice suits for three basic reasons: to control quality by holding health care providers accountable for their actions, to compensate patients for injury, and to provide emotional vindication by giving patients an opportunity to express dissatisfaction with the care they have received.[15]

What must a patient prove to win a malpractice claim?

For a patient to win a malpractice claim against a physician or other provider, the burden of proof is on the patient to demonstrate four elements: duty, breach, harm, and causation. Each element must be proven by a preponderance of the evidence (that it is more likely than not true). *Duty* to a patient requires the establishment of a provider-patient relationship and is defined by the relevant standard of care. The standard by which a provider's actions are measured is that of a reasonably prudent provider under the same or similar circumstances.[16] *Breach* of duty is specific conduct on the part of the provider, action or inaction, and is also measured by the applicable standard of care. The next element is the actual injury or *harm* suffered by the patient, and this is measured in monetary terms.[17] If the patient wins, the patient will be compensated for the harm caused in the form of money, sometimes called "damages." Finally, *proximate cause* denotes a causal connection between the provider's conduct and the harm alleged by the patient; that is, the provider's breach of duty must be the cause of the patient's harm. The plaintiff cannot usually recover any money damages for improper conduct on the part of the defendant if the breach of duty itself produced no harm or injury.

Do physicians guarantee that patients will get better?

Generally, they do not. Usually the contract or agreement between the physician and the patient does not include a guarantee of a good result.[18] But a physician could change the terms of the contract by specifically including a guarantee. For example, in one case, a doctor treating a patient for ear trouble suggested that he should undergo some specific operations. The doctor allegedly advised the patient that even though his condition might not be improved by the operations, his hearing would not be worsened as a result. After three operations, the patient's hearing was much worse. The patient based his lawsuit on the breach of an express contract, the statement by the doctor that his hearing would not get worse. The trial court concluded that the facts alleged were sufficient to find that there was an enforceable contract, and the Supreme Court of Kansas, on appeal, agreed.[19]

May patients hold all physicians to the same standard of care regardless of where they practice?

Yes, although this was not always the rule. Historically, the "locality rule" was applied so that the standard of care required of a nonspecialist physician was that commonly practiced by other physicians in the same community or similar communities.[20] Some courts even restricted the locality rule to the same community. The reason given for the locality rule was that there were significant differences between the facilities and opportunities for consultation in different places, particularly between large cities and those in rural areas.[21]

With better and more uniform medical education, rapid exchange of medical knowledge, and the growth and availability of medical centers and the ability to refer patients to them, the rationale for the locality rule no longer exists. Through the years, the rule has been altered; in some states, it has been modified, and in others, it has been completely abandoned.[22]

The local standard of practice may be considered by the jury as one factor but is seldom the sole determinant of the standard of care. Expert witnesses can usually be used from any part of the United States (and from other countries, such as England and Canada, as well) to testify on the standard of care.[23]

What is the standard of care for a specialist?

The law imposes a higher duty on a specialist than on the general practitioner. By definition, a specialist is a physician who devotes special attention to a particular organ or area of the body, to the treatment of a particular disease, or to a particular category of patients. The specialist is required to possess that degree of knowledge and ability, and to exercise that amount of care and skill, ordinarily possessed and exercised by other physicians practicing in the same specialty, regardless of geographic location.[24] This rule is substantially identical in all states and applies to all specialties.[25]

How can an injured patient prove that a physician failed to meet the recognized standard of medical care?

Usually, the injured patient must present the testimony of *an expert medical witness* (a licensed physician) to establish that the defendant failed to fulfill a duty, and that as a result, the patient was injured. The standard of care is that of the reasonably prudent physician in the same or similar circumstances, and in most cases only another physician has sufficient "expert" knowledge to establish that standard. The expert witness explains to the jury what the medical community recognizes as the standard of care in a particular situation and further gives an opinion as to whether or not the physician's conduct met that standard of care. A jury of lay people is not competent to know the standard of care in a medical matter or whether the defendant complied with it. Therefore, as a matter of law, the plaintiff's case will usually be dismissed unless the necessary expert testimony is presented.[26]

When the case involves a specialist, usually the expert witness is from the same specialty. As long as the subject matter of the case is common to both specialties, a specialist in one area may be permitted to testify against a specialist in another.[27] Similarly, a specialist may testify to the standard of care of a general practitioner as long as the specialist is familiar with the applicable standard of care.[28]

The general rule that requires expert testimony in malpractice cases does not apply in situations in which the negligence is so obvious that a jury of lay people can determine it without the help of expert witnesses. This rule, called *res ipsa loquitur,* "the thing speaks for itself," is applicable when all three of the following conditions are met:

- An injury has occurred of a type that does not ordinarily occur in the absence of negligence.
- The instrumentality or conduct that caused the injury was, at the time of the injury, in the exclusive control of the defendant.
- The plaintiff was not guilty of contributory negligence.[29]

The *res ipsa loquitur* doctrine has been used mainly in cases involving foreign objects (such as sponges) left in the patient after surgery, burns from heating equipment during treatment, and injury to a part of the patient's body outside the treated area.[30] For example, the Minnesota Supreme Court ruled that *res ipsa loquitur* applied when a surgeon, who was in exclusive control of a scalpel that broke during an operation, left part of the scalpel in the patient.[31] Many states have passed statutes modifying the doctrine in medical malpractice actions to restrict its application to specific situations, such as foreign objects, explosions, and burns.

When is it too late to bring a malpractice suit?

A statute of limitations sets the time period within which a person must commence a lawsuit. This time limit is to ensure that a trial takes place soon after the occurrence of the alleged negligence, so that witnesses and other evidence are most likely to be available, and so that people do not have to go through life with the threat of lawsuits being brought against them for things done long ago.

Many states have a statute of limitations specifically applicable to medical malpractice actions. If not, the statute applicable to tort claims will usually govern. A lawsuit not initiated within the specified time period is barred and will be dismissed on a motion by the defendant. State laws differ on the length of time provided for starting a lawsuit and on when the time period begins to run, but most have a one- to three-year statute of limitations on medical malpractice suits, and two years is common.

The time period begins to run when the elements of a lawsuit occur:

when the negligent act or omission allegedly occurs; when the doctor-patient relationship or continuous series of treatments ends; or when the harm to the patient is, or reasonably should have been, discovered (the *discovery rule*). The modern trend is to apply the discovery rule. It is a rule of common sense. How could the injured patient be expected to bring a lawsuit when the patient neither knew nor reasonably could have known about the injury? Some states limit application of the discovery rule to cases involving allegations of foreign objects left in patients following surgery. In other states, it has been held inapplicable in cases involving misdiagnosis,[32] drug treatment,[33] and the incorrect administration of a blood test.[34] Some states extend the discovery rule to all cases of medical malpractice.[35]

A statute of limitations may be tolled, or prevented from running, for a variety of reasons. The most common ones are that the injured patient is a minor,[36] incompetent,[37] or in the armed services; the defendant is absent from the state;[38] or the defendant has fraudulently concealed the basis for the suit.[39]

How do injured patients pay their attorneys?

Most lawyers take medical malpractice cases on a contingency fee basis. Under this fee system, a lawyer is not paid for the lawyer's time worked, but paid only for out-of-pocket expenses if the suit is lost. If the lawsuit is won, the lawyer takes a percentage, usually about 25 to 33 percent of the final damage award, as well as payment for expenses incurred in bringing the suit. The exact percentage must be set in a contract with the client, usually as soon as a lawyer is hired. The rules for reasonable fees are governed by state law and legal codes of ethics. This payment system, called the *contingency fee system,* is often blamed for contributing to the number of malpractice claims in the United States. It is argued that contingency fees encourage lawyers to pursue claims of doubtful merit or to sue for unjustifiably large amounts for legitimate claims in the hope of achieving recovery through settlement or awards from sympathetic juries.

Legislation has been enacted in many states to regulate plaintiffs' attorney fees. These have taken various forms. Some states require that the court review an attorney's proposed fees and approve what it considers "reasonable fees." Several states set fixed percentage ceilings for contingency fees in malpractice actions. Others adopt a sliding scale, most often expressed in terms of a percentage of the final award. Under this arrangement, as the amount recovered increases, the lawyer's percentage decreases. In attempting to establish reasonable guidelines for the amount that a plaintiff's attorney can receive from the injured patient's award, these statutory provisions perform a needed service. To the extent that they reduce the number of claims brought by diminishing the willingness of attorneys to handle meritorious claims that have low expected damage payments, they are a disservice to those injured patients who cannot otherwise afford legal counsel.

The contingency fee structure compels lawyers to screen out claims that are spurious, or for which recovery appears less than probable, and to refuse to take malpractice cases for which damages would not amount to enough to cover their expenses. Since the attorney, rather than the patient-plaintiff, bears the financial risk of losing the suit, the attorney has no incentive to invest any time or money in a claim for which recovery appears doubtful. In addition, with the average unregulated fee rate approximately one-third of recovery, many lawyers decline malpractice cases that will probably achieve settlements or awards of less than $100,000, because the expected compensation for the amount of time expended by the attorney is not worthwhile. The threshold expected value for the acceptance of cases for which recovery is less than probable is, on the average, higher, perhaps as much as $500,000.

What is a medical malpractice pretrial screening panel?

A pretrial screening panel is an informal procedure designed to screen out nonmeritorious claims quickly and inexpensively and to encourage the settlement of other cases amicably. More than thirty states have established review plans by law. Additionally, there are a small number of voluntary, nonstatutory mediation plans sponsored by state or local medical societies and bar associations. The typical pretrial review applies to any malpractice action brought against a physician, regardless of the size of the claimed damages. The panel consists of three to seven members, including at least one attorney, one physician, and frequently one consumer member. The hearing itself is almost always informal. The parties have the choice of accepting the panel's decision, negotiating their own settlement, or rejecting the decision of the panel and proceeding to court.

When court action is undertaken, and the panel's decision is in favor of the patient, the panel is often obligated to help the patient obtain the necessary expert medical testimony for trial. On the other hand, the party that loses the panel decision may face various "penalty" provisions for deciding to disregard the panel decisions and go to court. For example, some states provide that the findings of the panel are admissible at a later trial of the case. Some statutes require the party rejecting the panel decision to post a cost bond to cover court costs, which is payable if the opposing party prevails at trial.

What is alternative dispute resolution for medical malpractice claims?

In an effort to resolve cases that would otherwise crowd court dockets and cost both plaintiffs and defendants large amounts of money, both courts and private parties have increasingly used various alternative (to the court system) dispute resolution methods, including mediation, arbitration, and neutral third-party case evaluation. Statutes and court rules provide the courts with the authority to encourage utilization of these procedures, and the decisions made by them may be enforced by courts.

More specifically, arbitration and mediation are private, nongovernment procedures between two parties, in this case an injured patient and a physician, health provider, and/or hospital or health plan. Parties to the dispute agree to submit their case to the judgment of an impartial person or panel, appointed by agreement, by statute, or by a judge. Imposed arbitration or mediation is generally applied to disputes under a certain maximum monetary amount, with a jury trial preserved for more major cases.

Many states have passed legislation specifically providing for binding arbitration of medical malpractice claims by written agreement of the parties, and malpractice claims can be arbitrated in at least thirty states under the general arbitration statute. Arbitration is sometimes offered in group plans, such as HMOs and other prepaid health plans, in which the agreement to submit malpractice claims to binding arbitration is part of the subscriber's contract. Because an individual is not required to become a member of such a group plan, the acceptance of the obligation to arbitrate is considered voluntary.

Are there major problems with the current medical malpractice system?

It has been persuasively argued that the current medical malpractice system "provides poorly for the needs of negligently injured patients, encourages costly, contentious, and wasteful litigation, and is predisposed to both groundless lawsuits and excessive awards."[40] Many of these conclusions, including those of the 1999 report of the Institute of Medicine mentioned at the beginning of this chapter, rely heavily on a Harvard University–New York State study, which attempted to measure the incidence of medical malpractice in New York hospitals in 1984 by an extensive review of medical records.[41] This study concluded that about 4 percent of all hospital patients suffer an adverse event, and one-fourth of these, or 1 percent of all hospital patients, are victims of medical malpractice resulting in injury, with 25 percent ending in death. The researchers also estimated that only one malpractice claim was filed for every eight instances of medical negligence (using a different method of data analysis, they noted that the actual number could be as low as one claim for every fifty instances of negligence). The study also indicated that only about half of the injured patients who actually file a claim are eventually compensated for their injuries.[42] If the New York figures are extrapolated to the United States, as many as ninety-eight thousand patients are killed a year in the United States by medical malpractice (the high end figure used by the Institute of Medicine). Likewise, in a 2000 survey, one in three physicians and four in ten Americans reported that either they or a family member had been a victim of a preventable medical error.[43]

The fact that so many deaths and injuries are related to negligence puts the system's ability to prevent injury in serious question, and the fact that so few people who are negligently injured actually get any money makes it a very poor method to compensate for injury.[44] The "system" also suffered a series of high medical malpractice insurance premium increases in the mid-1970s, mid-1980s, and again in 2002–3 that have led many states to change their legal system to make it more difficult for injured patients to seek compensation from physicians and hospitals. On the other hand, as William Sage has pointed out, "tort reform is not an intuitive solution to rampant medical error. Why should the medical profession, which historically criticized lawyers for inventing medical errors where none existed, receive even greater protection from lawyers now that we know errors to be widespread?"[45]

Historically, physicians have responded to increases in their medical malpractice insurance premiums by suggesting changes in the tort system. Most consistently, they have argued for caps in "pain and suffering" awards and for changes in the contingency fee system to a sliding scale.

On the other hand, physicians have recognized the power of malpractice litigation to influence reform and have been at the forefront of the fight in Congress to give patients the right to sue their health plans for restrictive policies that injure patients.

Lawyers have generally argued that changing the tort system is misplaced, recommending instead that physicians set up much tougher methods of policing themselves to eliminate incompetent and impaired physicians and thereby protect the public, and noting that changes in the legal system were tried in the 1970s and 1980s and failed as a method to prevent insurance premiums from rising, and that this demonstrates that the real problem is not with the legal system.

Consumer groups, such as Ralph Nader's Public Citizen, continue to view the professional debate between doctors and lawyers as a sideshow, and they are correct. Changes in malpractice insurance premiums are more related to the business cycle and poor planning by insurance companies than to either the number of malpractice suits or the size of damage awards.[46] The real question is how to protect patients from harm and how to provide care and support to those patients who are harmed. Alternative approaches and modifications in malpractice insurance and litigation deserve fair hearings but should be judged against the three primary goals of the current tort system: compensation for injury, quality control, and responsiveness to consumers. Only changes that enhance one or more of the goals, without diminishing others, deserve serious consideration.

How is medical malpractice litigation related to informed consent?

Although physician anxiety about lawsuits is not new, the public's perception of what is possible in medicine, and medicine's power over disease, has changed dramatically and in some cases naively. This perception is shared by both patients and their physicians and has been spawned by the arrival of the "new technological age" of medicine. Technology has given us, as novelist Don Delillo puts it, "an appetite for immortality."[47] We believe that diseases *can* be controlled, and that physicians *should* be able to do something for us when we fall ill. We want to believe that we can have it all: live our lives without regard to physical or mental dangers and then go to the "repair shop" (the hospital) when we suffer a physical or mental "breakdown" and have it fixed. We have adopted the image of ourselves that commentators on industrialization have feared for decades: we see ourselves as machines, and physicians as mechanics. If physicians cannot repair us, it must be because they lack the skill, do not know the latest techniques, or make a mistake.

The major problem with medical malpractice is medical malpractice itself and the associated problem of cover-ups. But unrealistic expectations on the part of patients, and ritualistic silence and demands for blind faith on the part of physicians, exacerbate the broader medical malpractice situation greatly. Enhancing the doctor-patient partnership by taking informed consent and shared decision making seriously could go a long way toward "solving" the medical malpractice problem. This will require acknowledging uncertainty in medical diagnosis and treatment by both patients and physicians. This acknowledgment alone should radically decrease the felt need for "defensive medicine," doing things not for the benefit of the patient but to make the physician look better in the event of a malpractice suit.

How can state licensing boards be strengthened to help protect patients from incompetent and impaired physicians and nurses?

All physicians and nurses must obtain a state license before they can "practice medicine" or "practice nursing." The general requirements for licensure are the possession of a specified academic degree (such as an MD or OD), successful completion of a written examination, and "good moral character." Once the licensing agency (usually known as the Board of Registration in Medicine for physicians and the Board of Registration in Nursing for nurses) grants the license, it almost never takes it away, and it usually has no formal method for monitoring actual practice. The inability of these state agencies to protect the public from impaired professionals has been a source of much public criticism. This should not be surprising in an era when even professional associations agree that 5 to 10 percent of all physicians and nurses are seriously impaired by drugs, alcohol, or psychological problems. The public has historically (and accurately) viewed state licensing agencies, which are dominated by members of the profession rather than by members of the public, as existing primarily to protect doctors and nurses rather than to protect the public.

It is unusual for a patient to even think about complaining to a state licensing agency about an allegedly incompetent or impaired physician or nurse. This is unfortunate, because although an injured patient must prove four elements to win a malpractice suit (duty, breach, damages, and causation), the licensing board need only prove the first two (duty and breach, that is, that the individual failed to exercise the same reasonable prudence that a qualified professional would have in the same or similar circumstances) to take disciplinary action against a professional, at least if such negligence is a pattern.

The effectiveness of state licensing boards could be greatly improved if the public was given all or at least a majority of the positions on the board; if the boards were adequately staffed and funded to deal with complaints; if the boards effectively informed the public how to bring complaints; and if the boards demonstrated to the public that complaints would be handled fairly and expeditiously, and the process and results would be made public. In addition, licensing boards should be given the authority (if they do not already have it) to order physical and psychiatric examinations of allegedly impaired physicians and drug- and alcohol-screening tests on physicians when there is reason to believe that their behavior is endangering patients. Positive tests should be followed up by mandatory treatment programs and supervised practice for a period of time after treatment, if the practitioner desires to keep his or her license to practice.

A licensing board can censure a practitioner, suspend a practitioner's license for a period of time, or revoke a license to practice altogether. Some licensing boards also have the authority to impose fines. Boards can also act creatively by conditioning continued licensure on fulfilling requirements to do specific things, such as retraining in a specialty, continuing to obtain psychiatric or substance-abuse help, or doing community service.

Since licenses are granted for life, theoretically a professional need not open a book or medical journal after licensure. Thus, a physician who graduated from medical school in 1960 may still be practicing and using 1960 knowledge, which is the equivalent today of what using leeches would have been in 1960. To help prevent this, most licensing boards require physicians and nurses to take continuing education courses to keep up on new developments. But since no tests are given, there is no way to evaluate the effectiveness of continuing education.

How does a patient file a complaint against a care provider?

Patients can file a complaint in writing with the state Board of Medicine (for physicians), Board of Nursing (for nurses), or Board of Dentistry (for dentists). The names and addresses of these agencies can be obtained from the office of the state attorney general or the state office of consumer affairs. Although patients will not receive any money should the complaint be found meritorious and the provider disciplined, patients are helping to prevent the provider from hurting other patients. This is an important role of citizens, and if you believe your physician or nurse might injure others, you should file a complaint with the licensing board. The complaint should set forth the facts as you know them, together with all documentation you have. In addition, you should be prepared to release relevant medical records to the board (they will be kept confidential). You may also file a complaint against a hospital with the agency that licenses hospitals—usually the department of public health. You need a lawyer to file a lawsuit. You do not need a lawyer to file a complaint with a licensing agency.[48]

How does an injured patient find a lawyer to bring a malpractice suit?

It is not easy. Finding a good lawyer is at least as hard as finding a good doctor. When looking for a lawyer who specializes in medical malpractice and personal injury law, perhaps the two most important qualities are experience and compassion. Ask friends about lawyers they have worked with, and if you have a family lawyer, ask this person as well. Do not rely on advertisements in the yellow pages, newspapers, or TV. You can also get names from the local bar association (some states have specialty bar groups for health law issues), and the local office of the American Civil Liberties Union. It is important to feel comfortable with your lawyer, because medical injury is such a personal and traumatic experience and the lawsuit itself may take years to resolve. You should interview at least three lawyers before deciding on which one is right for you. Experience is extremely important, but as important is compassion—and confidence on your part that the lawyer will treat your case as a priority and be available to discuss it with you as it moves along. You have a right to demand competence, zealous representation, and open communication from your lawyer. The lawyer gets paid only if the case is won or settled and then will get a percentage of the settlement. This percentage (usually 25 to 50 percent), and all other details should be made explicit and put in writing at the time you retain the lawyer.

What can patients do to protect themselves from malpractice?

The most important thing you and your advocate can do is to *question everything,* and when you're not satisfied, get a second opinion.

The Institute of Medicine properly called the patient "a major unused resource in most hospitals" to prevent injuries.[49] Physicians, nurses, and hospitals, of course, should protect patients. Nonetheless, the Institute of Medicine is correct to note, regarding medication (and other treatments): "Not only do patients have a right to know the medications they are receiving, they should also know what the pills or injections look like and how often they are to receive them." The Institute of Medicine urges physicians and hospitals to make patients part of the treatment team and to use patients as "a final 'fail-safe' step" to make sure incidents such as the overdose death of Betsy Lehman and even the mismatched organs of Jesica Santillán are prevented.[50] Specifically, the institute, following the recommendations of the National Patient Safety Partnership, urges patients to ask the following questions before accepting a newly prescribed medication:

- Is this the drug my doctor ordered? What are the trade and generic names of the medication?
- What is the drug for? What is it supposed to do?
- How and when am I supposed to take it and for how long?
- Is this new medication safe to take with other over-the-counter or prescription medication or with dietary supplements that I am already taking? What food, drink, activities, dietary supplements, or other medication should be avoided while taking this medication?[51]

Getting the wrong medication or the wrong dose of the right medication may be the most frequent medical error in hospitals, but sometimes the wrong patient gets a surgical procedure, or the right patient gets the wrong operation. These mistakes are always preventable. In one case that became famous because it was published in the medical literature, a sixty-seven-year-old woman mistakenly underwent cardiac electrophysiology, a potentially dangerous and invasive heart test (instead of the cerebral angiography she had been admitted for) that was scheduled to be performed on another patient, a seventy-seven-year-old woman with a similar name. When she protested to the nurse that came to take her to the test, the nurse, who was at the end of her shift, told her she could refuse the test when she got to the electrophysiology laboratory. At the laboratory, a physician (who had seen the other woman the night before) was paged and spoke to the patient, who he assumed was the other woman, and assured her it was fine to proceed with the test. All in all, seventeen different mistakes were made that enabled the patient to get the wrong procedure.[52] Of course, a patient advocate would have prevented the patient from being taken from her room in the first place. But as the coauthor of the case study Dr. Mark Chassin noted, while a family member or a patient advocate would have prevented the mix-up, it was the hospital's responsibility. In Chassin's words, "Why should we have to rely on patients to protect themselves? Hospitals ought to be the safest places in the world."[53]

Surgeons are also taking the lead in trying to prevent operations on the wrong patient and the wrong site. Their "Statement on Ensuring Correct Patient, Correct Site, and Correct Procedure Surgery," published in late 2002, includes making sure "the correct patient is being taken to the operating room" and that the correct procedure is performed. This should be done with the patient personally (or the patient's representative), and "in the case of a bilateral organ, limb, or anatomic site (for example, hernia), the surgeon and the patient should agree and the operating surgeon should mark the site prior to giving the patient narcotics, sedation, or anesthesia."[54] Patients and their advocates should, of course, make sure that these safety procedures are followed, especially that the site of the surgery is correctly identified with the patient and marked on the patient's body. It is especially important to recall the general rule that "the patient is always right," sometimes rephrased, "the patient is presumed right, at least until proven wrong." Specifically, it is critical that physicians and nurses learn to listen to their patients and their advocates, since this is the beginning of taking patient safety seriously.

Although quality of care is the new mantra of medicine, little is actually known about quality, and the resources patients and their advocates have to assess quality are limited. The federal government has established a national practitioners databank that lists all physicians and the legal actions that have been taken against them, including both malpractice suits and the loss or suspension of hospital privileges. This information is currently *not* available to the public, but it should be.[55] Physicians have a terrible record of disciplining each other, and there is no evidence that it is improving. The public needs this information to protect themselves.[56] With the rapid growth of the Internet and the medical resources available on-line, patient access to relevant information is improving. The information varies in quality, but as discussed in appendix A, use of the Internet is almost indispensable for information about diseases or conditions, and the alternative treatments available for them.

Overall the medical malpractice system illustrates most of the major themes of this book: providing patients with complete and accurate information is good, while secrecy and cover-ups are destructive; prevention is always better than trying to cure a disease or compensate for injury; patients cannot protect themselves from harm alone—all patients need advocates to help and protect them when they are sick; only the patient (and the patient's family) must live with the results of treatment and mistreatment—that's why all important decisions should be made by the patient; patients have rights, but none are self-executing, and it requires both knowledge and skill to exercise their rights.

My hope is that this book provides you with the knowledge you and your advocate need to make it more likely you will get the treatment that is appropriate for your condition, and less likely that you will be the victim of medical negligence or indifference. It's your life; it's your body; it's your right to make the important decisions about your life and your body yourself.

TIPS FOR ADVOCATES

- Patient safety should be everyone's first priority.
- Hospitals are dangerous places, and the patient safety movement is new.
- The patient is always right about his or her own body (at least until proven wrong).
- You and your patient should demand all the information you need to make a decision.
- Know the drugs and doses your patient is taking, as well as their side effects (confirm that the proper drugs are being administered each time).
- Know the surgical procedure your patient is having and discuss it with the surgeon (if it is a bilateral site, make sure the site is properly marked by the surgeon).
- Your patient has the right to be told of any unforeseen complications, including those caused by negligence.
- Preventing harm is much better than filing a malpractice suit to try to obtain compensation for harm.

- **Communication is difficult in the hospital and is often compromised between shifts.**

NOTES

1. Institute of Medicine, To Err Is Human: Building a Safer Health System, Washington, D.C.: National Academy of Sciences, 2000.
2. A 2001 study challenged these numbers as too high. Rodney Hayward & Timothy Hofer, *Estimating Hospital Deaths Due to Medical Errors,* 286 JAMA 415 (2001). That study, however, discounted deaths of patients with less than three months to live and relied on an extremely small sample size. Ken Shine & William Richardson, *Statement Regarding Medical Errors,* August 3, 2001 (Institute of Medicine Announcement).
3. Shine & Richardson, *supra* note 2, at 2.
4. All of the material on the Lehman cases is from articles by Richard Knox in the *Boston Globe,* March 1995 through April 1997. Knox is now with National Public Radio.
5. *See* Troyen Brennan, *The Institute of Medicine Report on Medical Errors—Could It Do Harm?* 342 New Eng. J. Med. 1123 (2000); Lucian Leape & Donald Berwick, *Safe Health Care: Are We Up to It?* 320 Brit. Med. J. 725 (2000); Larry Palmer, *Patient Safety, Risk Reduction and the Law,* 36 Houston L. Rev. 1609 (1999), Wendy Mariner & Frances Miller, Medical Error Reporting: Professional Tensions Between Confidentiality and Liability, Boston: Massachusetts Health Policy Forum, 2001. (available at http://www.sihp. brandeis.edu/mhpf/prof_liability_Issue_Brief.pdf).
6. Joint Commission on Accreditation of Healthcare Organizations, 2003 Hospital Accreditation Standards, Chicago: Joint Commission Resources, 2003, 208–11; and *2003 National Patient Safety Goals* (outlined at www.jcaho.org/accredited+organizations/ patient+safety/npsg/npsg_03.htm).
7. Charles Vincent, *Understanding and Responding to Adverse Events,* 348 New Eng. J. Med. 1051 (2003); *see also* Thomas Gallagher et al., *Patients' and Physicians' Attitudes Regarding the Disclosure of Medical Errors,* 289 JAMA 1001 (2003) ("Patients were unanimous in their desire to be told about any error that caused harm," at 1003), and Rae Lamb et al., *Hospital Disclosure Practices: Results of a National Survey,* 22(2) Health Affairs 73 (2003) (hospitals much less likely to disclose preventable harms than nonpreventable harms).
8. Joint Commission, *supra* note 6, at 79–80, and 53–65.
9. Chester Burns, *Malpractice Suits in American Medicine Before the Civil War,* 43 Bull. Hist. Med. 41 (1969). *See also* James Mohr, *American Medical Malpractice Litigation in Historical Perspective,* 283 JAMA 1731 (2000).
10. Donald Konold, A History of American Medical Ethics: 1847–1912, Madison: State Historical Society of Wisconsin, 1962, 50–51.
11. William Sage, *Principles, Pragmatism, and Medical Injury,* 286 JAMA 226 (2001).
12. Marshall B. Kapp, Our Hands Are Tied: Legal Tensions and Medical Ethics, Westport, CT: Auburn House, 1988, 1–2. This is not a new problem. *See, e.g.,* George J.

Annas, *Law and Medicine: Myths and Realities in the Medical School Classroom,* 1 Am. J. Law & Med. 195 (1978).

13. Kapp, *supra* note 12; *and see* Michael Saks, *Do We Really Know Anything about the Behavior of the Tort Litigation System—and Why Not?* 140 U. Penn L. Rev. 1147 (1992).

14. A. B. Witman et al., *How Do Patients Want Physicians to Handle Mistakes? A Survey of Internal Medicine Patients in an Academic Setting,* 156 Archives of Internal Med. 2565 (1996). *And see supra* note 7.

15. Frances Miller, *Medical Malpractice Litigation: Do the British have a Better Remedy?* 11 Am. J. Law & Med. 433 (1986). *See also* George J. Annas & Frances Miller, *The Empire of Death: How Culture and Economics Affect Informed Consent in the U.S., the U.K., and Japan,* 20 Am. J. Law & Med. 357 (1994).

16. In extremely rare cases, in which the entire medical profession or specialty has failed to keep up with medical advances, the courts themselves will define "reasonable prudence." *See, e.g., Helling v. Carey,* 519 P.2d 981 (Wash. 1974) (failure to do routine glaucoma test is negligent as a matter of law), and the informed consent cases discussed in chapter 6.

17. *E.g., Lab v. Hall,* 200 So. 2d 556 (Dist. Ct. App. 1967).

18. *E.g., Hill v. Boughton,* 146 Fla. 505, 1 So. 2d 610 (1942).

19. *Noel v. Proud,* 189 Kan. 6, 367 P.2d 61 (Kan. 1961).

20. *E.g., Williams v. Chamberlain,* 316 S.W.2d 505 (Mo. 1958).

21. *Michael v. Roberts,* 91 N.H. 499, 23 A.2d 361 (1941).

22. *E.g., Brune v. Belinkoff,* 354 Mass. 102, 235 N.E.2d 793 (1968); *Murphy v. Little,* 112 Ga. App. 517, 145 S.E.2d 760 (1965); *Dougals v. Bussabarger,* 73 Wash. 2d 476, 438 P.2d 829 (1968); *Blair v. Eblen,* 461 S.W.2d 370 (Ky. 1970). *See also Tallbull v. Whitney,* 172 Mont. 326, 564 P.2d 162 (1977).

23. Tin Cramm et al., *Ascertaining Customary Care in Malpractice Cases: Asking Those Who Know,* 37 Wake Forest L. Rev. 699 (2002) (expert witnesses can be from any part of the United States, as well as Canada or England); John Ely, *Determining the Standard of Care in Medical Malpractice: The Physician's Perspective,* 37 Wake Forest L. Rev. 861 (2002); and Arthur Hartz et al., *Physician Surveys to Assess Customary Care in the Medical Malpractice Cases,* 17 Gen. Int. Med. 546 (2002).

24. *E.g., Francisco v. Parchment Med. Clinic,* 407 Mich. 325, 285 N.W.2d 39 (1979) *Robbins v. Footer,* 553 F.2d 123 (D.C. Cir. 1977). *And see* Cramm, *supra* note 23.

25. *E.g., Barnes v. Bovenmyer,* 255 Iowa 220, 122 N.W.2d 312 (1963); *Lewis v. Read,* 80 N.J. Super. 148, 193 A.2d 255 (1963); *Belk v. Schweizer,* 268 N.C. 50, 149 S.E.2d 565 (1966); *Siirila v. Barrios,* 58 Mich. App. 72, 228 N.W.2d 801 (1975), *aff'd,* 398 Mich. 576, 248 N.W.2d 171 (1976).

26. *Sims v. Helms,* 345 So. 2d 721 (Fla. 1977); *see also Buckroyd v. Bunten,* 237 N.W.2d 808 (Iowa 1976); *Marshall v. Tomaselli,* 118 R.I. 190, 372 A.2d 1280 (1977). For an excellent nonfiction account of the role of expert witnesses in medical malpractice litigations, *see* Barry Werth, Damages: One Family's Legal Struggles in the World of Medicine, New York: Simon & Schuster, 1998.

27. *Radman v. Harold,* 279 Md. 167, 367 A.2d 472 (1977). But *see Callahan v. William Beaumont Hosp.,* 400 Mich. 177, 254 N.W.2d 31 (1977).

28. *Siirila v. Barrios,* 398 Mich. 576, 248 N.W.2d 171 (Mich. 1976).

29. *E.g., Mondot v. Vallejo Gen. Hosp.*, 152 Cal. App. 2d 588, 313 P.2d 78 (1957); *Irick v. Andrew*, 545 S.W.2d 557 (Tex. Ct. Civil App. 1976).

30. *E.g., Seneris v. Haas*, 45 Cal. 2d 811, 291 P.2d 915 (1955).

31. *Young v. Caspers*, 311 Minn. 391, 249 N.W.2d 713 (1977). A study published in 2003 concluded that "leaving behind of foreign bodies in the patient after surgery is an uncommon but dangerous error" most frequently associated with emergency procedures, unplanned changes in surgery, and overweight patients. More than fifteen hundred cases of instruments left in the body occur annually in the United States. Atul Gawande et al., *Risk Factors for Retained Instruments and Sponges after Surgery*, 348 New Eng. J. Med. 1229 (2003).

32. *Robinson v. Weaver*, 550 S.W.2d 18 (Tex. 1977).

33. *Proewig v. Zaino*, 394 N.Y.S.2d 446, 57 A.D. 892 (1977).

34. *Simmons v. Riverside Methodist Hosp.*, 44 Ohio App. 2d 146, 336 N.E.2d 460 (1975).

35. *Sanchez v. South Hoover Hosp.*, 132 Cal. Rptr. 657, 553 P.2d 1129 (1976); *Moran v. Napolitano*, 71 N.J. 133, 363 A.2d 346 (1976).

36. *Graham v. Sisco*, 248 Ark. 6, 449 S.W.2d 949 (1970); *Chaffin v. NiCosia*, 261 Ind. 698, 310 N.E.2d 867 (1974).

37. *Miller v. Dickert*, 190 S.E.2d 459 (S.C. 1972).

38. *Swope v. Printz*, 259 S.C. 1, 468 S.W.2d 34 (1971).

39. *Nardone v. Reynolds*, 538 F.2d 1131 (5th Cir. 1976).

40. William M. Sage, *Enterprise Liability and the Emerging Managed Health Care System*, 60 Law & Contemp. Problems 159 (1997).

41. Harvard Medical Practice Study, Patients, Doctors and Lawyers: Studies of Medical Injury, Malpractice Litigation and Patient Compensation in New York, Boston: Harvard Medical Practice Study, 1990; Troyen A. Brennan et al., *Incidence of Adverse Events and Negligence in Hospitalized Patients: Results of the Harvard Medical Practice Study I*, 324 New Eng. J. Med. 370 (1991); Howard H. Hiatt et al., *A Study of Medical Injury and Medical Malpractice: An Overview*, 321 New Eng. J. Med. 480 (1989); Lucian L. Leape et al., *The Nature of Adverse Events in Hospitalized Patients: Results of the Harvard Medical Practice Study II*, 324 New Eng. J. Med. 377 (1991); David Hyman, *Medical Malpractice and the Tort System*, 80 Texas L. Rev. 1639 (2002).

42. Id., and A. Russell Localio et al., *Relation Between Malpractice Claims and Adverse Events Due to Negligence: Results of the Harvard Medical Practice Study III*, 325 New Eng. J. Med. 245 (1991).

43. Robert Blandon et al., *Views of Practicing Physicians and the Public on Medical Errors*, 347 New Eng. J. Med. 1933 (2002).

44. George J. Annas, Barbara Katz & Robert Trakimas, *Medical Malpractice Litigation under National Health Insurance: Essential or Expendable?* 1975 Duke L.J. 1335 (1976); *and see* Dietz, Baird & Bero, *The Medical Malpractice Legal System* (in) U.S. Dept. of Health, Education, and Welfare, Report of the Secretary's Commission on Medical Malpractice, Appendix, Washington, D.C.: HEW, 1973, 87, 199.

45. William Sage, *Medical Liability and Patient Safety*, 22 Health Affairs 26, 30 (July 2003). The best book on the crisis of the mid-1970s is Sylvia Law & Stephen Polan, Pain and Profit: The Politics of Malpractice, New York: Harper & Row, 1978. On the 1980s,

see Patricia Danzon, *The Effects of Tort Reforms on the Frequency and Severity of Medical Malpractice Claims,* 48 Ohio St. L.J. 413 (1987); Note, *The Constitutionality of Medical Malpractice Legislative Reform: A National Survey,* 18 Loyola U. Chicago L. J. 1053 (1987); and Note, *1986 Tort Reform Legislation: A Systematic Evaluation,* 73 Cornell L. Rev. 628 (1988). *See also* Patricia Danzon, Medical Malpractice, Cambridge: Harvard U. Press, 1985. The book on the 2002–3 insurance crisis has yet to be written, although law professor Maxwell Mehlman has usefully summarized ten fairness objections to the current system that would seem to make it ultimately untenable in his *Resolving the Medical Malpractice Crisis: Fairness Considerations* (2003):

(1) it only purports to compensate victims of negligence; (2) the punishment objective conflicts with the deterrence objective; (3) it lacks validity, reliability, and predictability; (4) compensation is inconsistent and only somewhat proportional; (5) financing mechanisms are unfair and undependable; (6) it may leave some patients without adequate access to necessary health care services; (7) deterrent signals are erratic; (8) it operates by rules that providers feel are unfair; (9) some injured patients cannot obtain adequate representation; and (10) parties often are not treated with dignity and respect. Available at http://medliabilitypa.org/research/mehlman0603/MehlmanReport.pdf. *See also* Michelle Mello et al., *The New Medical Malpractice Crisis,* 348 New Eng. J. Med. 2281 (2003).

46. *See generally* Joan Claybrook, *Medical Errors, Not Lawsuits Are Real Cause of Rising Malpractice Insurance Premiums,* January 9, 2003 (available at www.citizen.org/pressroom/print release.cfm?ID=1297). *See also* Rachel Zimmermann & Cristopher Oster, *Insurers' Missteps Helped Provoke Malpractice "Crisis,"* Wall Street Journal, June 24, 2002, A1; Josh Goldstein, *Collapse Spreads Misery,* Philadelphia Inquirer, March 2, 2003, E1; and Joseph Trester, *Malpractice Insurance: No Clear or Easy Answers,* New York Times, March 5, 2003, C1.

47. Don Delillo, White Noise, New York: Penguin, 1986, 285. *And see* Kapp, *supra* note 12, at 161–62.

48. Medicare patients and their families can also complain about the quality of care, and their complaint will be investigated by a peer review organization. The process is described in written material that must be provided to all Medicare patients. Results of Medicare investigations will also now be routinely disclosed to patients. Although federal law provides that the results of the investigation will be provided to the patient, until 2001, the results were only provided if the physician consented to disclosure. This policy was challenged in 1999 by Alan Levine, whose mother died of a stroke within six days of being treated for an asthma attack. He wanted to know what happened, but the Florida peer review organization refused to give him the results of their investigation. He sued with the help of the Public Citizen Litigation Group and won. The conclusion of the peer review was that the treatment of his mother "did not meet professionally recognized standards of quality. Specifically, she received medications to which there was a documented possible allergy." Robert Pear, *Medicare Shift: Doctors' Errors to be Disclosed,* New York Times, January 2, 2001, A1. *And see* Tanya Albert, *PROs Must Tell Patients of Injury Result,* Am. Med. News, August 6, 2001, 5.

49. Institute of Medicine, *supra* note 1, 169.

50. The Federal Drug Administration has also proposed making drug labeling easier for physicians to read and understand, as well as using bar-codes to identify drugs.

51. Institute of Medicine, *supra* note 1, *and see* David Bates et al., *Effect of Computerized Physician Order Entry and the Team Intervention on Prevention of Serious Medication Errors,* 280 JAMA 1311 (1998) (a computerized prescription system can decrease medication errors by 50 percent).

52. Mark Chassin & Elise Becher, *The Wrong Patient,* 136 Arch. Int. Med. 826 (2002). *See also* William Sage, *Putting the Patient in Patient Safety,* 287 JAMA 3003 (2002).

53. Denise Grady, *Oops, Wrong Patient: Journal Takes on Medical Mistakes,* New York Times, June 18, 2002, D1.

54. American College of Surgeons, *Statement on Correct Patient, Correct Site, and Correct Procedure Surgery,* 87 Bulletin Am. College of Surgeons, December 2002. Residents have suggested other ways to reduce medical errors, including reducing unnecessary pages, improving transfer of information about patients between shifts, open discussion of errors, and better training in performing procedures. Kevin Volpp & David Grande, *Residents' Suggestions for Reducing Errors in Teaching Hospitals,* 348 New Eng. J. Med. 851 (2003).

55. *See* General Accounting Office, *National Practitioner Data Bank: Major Improvements Are Needed to Enhance Data Bank's Reliability,* (GAO-01-130) (2000); Laura-Mae Baldwin, *Hospital Peer Review and the National Practitioner Data Bank,* 282 JAMA 349 (1999); George D. Lundberg, Severed Trust: Why American Medicine Hasn't Been Fixed, New York: Basic Books, 2000, 166–68; Susan Landers, *Data Bank Overseer Cautions Against Making It Public,* Am. Med. News, April 3, 2000, 8; and Linda Prager, *Mandatory Reports Cloud Error Plan,* Am. Med. News, March 13, 2000, 1. Massachusetts has a Web site that contains much of this information about Massachusetts physicians.

56. In an extreme and horrifying example, James Stewart, author of Blind Eye: How the Medical Establishment Let a Doctor Get Away with Murder, New York: Simon & Schuster, 1999, chronicles how medical school officials, hospital officials, residency program supervisors, and state medical boards permitted Michael J. Swango, now a convicted serial killer, to move from state to state and hospital to hospital and continue to kill unsuspecting patients by lethal injections along the way. Nicknamed "Double O Swango" by his fellow medical students, he may have killed dozens of patients, although in 2000 he pleaded guilty to killing only three. *See* Michael Cooper, *Ex-Doctor Charged in 3 Patient Deaths,* New York Times, July 12, 2000, A23, and Charles LeDuff, *Ex-Doctor to Admit to Murdering Three Patients on Long Island,* New York Times, September 6, 2000, A29. *And see generally* Herbert Kinnell, *Serial Homicide by Doctors: Shipman in Perspective,* 321 Brit. Med. J. 1594 (2000) (an inquiry later found British physician Harold Shipman had killed at least 215 of his patients; Warren Hoge, *British Inquiry Finds Doctor Killed 215 of His Patients,* New York Times, July 20, 2002, A4); and George J. Annas, *Medicine, Death and the Criminal Law,* 333 New Eng. J. Med 527 (1995).

APPENDIX A
Internet Resources

APPENDIX B
Convention on Human Rights and Biomedicine

APPENDIX C
Childbearing Patient Bills of Rights

INDEX

APPENDIX A

Internet Resources

A cartoon in a recent issue of the *British Medical Journal* pictures a woman patient in the office of a harried physician with the results of an Internet (sometimes referred to as the World Wide Web, or simply, the Web) search in her hands. She is saying, "I'm sorry Doctor, but again I have to disagree." The Internet has empowered some patients by providing them with a new and accessible source of information. As health care expert Jeff Goldsmith has put it, medical knowledge tends to decay and become outmoded extremely rapidly, with thirty-one thousand new medical citations appearing each month. "Into this expanding knowledge vacuum charges the cyber-assisted patient."[1] It is not surprising that physicians, who have been ordered or encouraged to cut down average patient visits to seven to ten minutes, often resent patients who show up with articles from the Internet, because the physician often does not have time to read the articles, let alone evaluate them. Moreover, much of the information on the Internet is inaccurate or misleading.

One study, for example, analyzed 371 Web sites on Ewing sarcoma, an uncommon bone cancer. The search revealed mistakes the researchers described as "shocking," mainly in the non-peer-reviewed sites. The researchers also found that using the disease name in a search engine was not always fruitful. In their words, "Attempts to access medical information from the Internet may be very cumbersome and time-consuming. Patients may spend hours in fruitless, frustrating searches, finding a few helpful sites but sifting through many dead ends."[2]

Physicians have, nonetheless, been advised to take the opportunity to discuss Internet information with their patients by keeping an open mind, understanding that the patient wants more information, suggesting other Web sites if the information is questionable, and telling the patient not to act on Web information without consulting the physician first.[3]

Although some have suggested that there should be certification or seals of approval on health Web sites, Tony Delamothe, the Web editor of the *British Medical Journal,* has argued rather persuasively that no one has any real idea about how to do this, that no current method has been tested for reliability or validity, and that "for other more familiar sources of information—newspapers, magazines, books, and radio and television programs—we cope unassisted by kitemarks [seals of approval]."[4]

Using the Internet to find medical information can be rewarding, but it can also be extremely frustrating. Although more than one hundred million Americans sought health information on the Internet in 2000, up from seventy million in 1999, their experience was uneven. Only 56 percent (compared with 73 percent in 1999) said the Internet helped them to gain an understanding of their health problems; and only 41 percent said it helped them to manage their personal health care. The chair of the Harris Poll, which took the survey, said, "The bloom is off the rose. . . . Even though more people than ever are on the Web looking for health information, the level of satisfaction has dropped sharply."[5]

What can you do to make it more likely that you will profit from using the Internet to obtain health information? Columnist Tara Parker-Pope of the *Wall Street Journal* suggests you first start with a medical dictionary and your medical records, looking up the words you don't know and using them in your search. Second, she suggests you locate an advocacy group by searching for one using the name of your illness. These groups will often have already done the searches you want to do. Third, she suggests you go to a medical library (your local library may do as well). The research librarian there will often help you use the Internet to locate medical articles on your condition, and the libraries often have computers you can use on site. To locate the library nearest you, contact the National Library of Medicine at 1-888-FIND-NLM or at www.nlm.nih.gov. (You can also use their sites to find medical publications: www.medlineplus.gov, www.nih.gov, and www.healthfinder.gov.) Finally, Parker-Pope suggests locating a specialist in your disease, either by contacting the authors of relevant medical articles or by hiring a doctor-search firm, such as Best Doctors (www.bestdoctors.com, or 1-888-DOCTORS).[6]

In addition to possible misinformation, the other major problem with Internet health sites is privacy. Every health site should have its privacy policy posted on its home page; should clearly state what uses, if any, it will make of your information; and should provide you with a way to disable any "persistent cookies" that it could use to track your use of its site.[7] To protect yourself from having your personal information used for marketing and other purposes, it has been recommended that when you visit a medical site, you (1) find out the site's privacy policy; (2) look for experts on the site's medical advisory board; (3) scrutinize the sponsorship and advertising on the site and make sure it is clearly marked and separated from editorial content; and (4) avoid "spam" by not signing up, for example, to receive messages from the site by e-mail.[8] Many hospitals have Internet sites that are primarily marketing tools to encourage patients to come there for care. There are also organizations that will provide second opinions or do research on clinical trials for your disease for you.[9] Some of the most useful sites are www.Webmed.com (health and medical news); www.webmed.com (general medical resources), and www.healthscout.com (personal and family health news, interactive checkups). The National Cancer Institute's site (www.cancer.gov) is excellent. There are also sites that tell you how to evaluate health information found on the Internet, such as the Internet Health Coalition's site (www.ihealthcoalition. org/content/tips.html).

On the whole, while I believe information can be power, in the U.S. health care system information alone is no guarantee of anything. That is why I continue to believe that increasing and enforcing patient rights is a much more effective way to empower patients than simply giving them access to more information. There are sites you can visit to learn more about your legal rights as a patient. These include the Health Law Department of the Boston University School of Public Health (www.patient-rights.org); the People's Medical Society (www. peoplesmed.org); the National Health Law Program (www.NHELP.org); the American Civil Liberties Union (www.aclu.org); Families USA (www.familiesusa. org); the American Association of Retired Persons (www.aarp.org); and the National Association for Home Care (www.nahc.org). Internet sites relating to advance directives, palliative care, and hospice are contained in the notes to chapters 12 and 13. There are also patient safety sites that you may find useful. The best ones include the Leapfrog Group (www.leapfroggroup.org) and the National Patient Safety Foundation (www.npsf.org).[10]

Finally, if you need a lawyer and cannot find one through your family and friends, contact your local librarian or a specialty bar association or advocacy group (such as the women's bar association, GLAD, battered women shelters, hotlines, etc.). Here are two Web sites that can be helpful: Martindale-Hubbell (www. lawyers.com) and Findlaw (www.findlaw.com).

NOTES

1. Jeff Goldsmith, *How Will the Internet Change our Health System?* 19 Health Affairs 148 (2000).

2. Jane E. Brody, *The Health Hazards of Point-and-Click Medicine,* New York Times, August 31, 1999, D1.

3. Tyler Chin, *Site Reading,* American Medical News, October 23/30, 2000, 22. *See also* Sasha Shepperd *et al., Helping Patients Access High Quality Health Information,* 319 British Med. J. 764 (1999), and Alejandro Jadad, *Promoting Partnerships: Challenges for the Internet Age,* 319 British Med. J. 761 (1999).

4. Tony Delamothe, *Quality of Websites: Kitemarking the West Wind,* 321 British Medical J. 843 (2000).

5. Laura Landro, *More People Are Using Internet Health Sites, But Fewer Are Satisfied,* Wall Street Journal, December 29, 2000, A9.

6. Tara Parker-Pope, *Six Steps to Help You Start Your Own Search for Medical Answers,* Wall Street Journal, August 11, 2000, B1. *See also* Joan Stephenson, *National Library of Medicine to Help Consumers Use Online Health Data,* 282 JAMA 1675 (2000).

7. Margaret Winker *et al., Guidelines for Medical and Health Information Sites on the Internet: Principles Governing AMA Web Sites,* 283 JAMA 1600 (2000). *And see* e-Health Code of Ethics of the Internet Healthcare Coalition at www.ihealthcoalition.org.

8. Rebecca Winters, *Your Vital Signs OnLine,* Time, February 28, 2000, G4. *See also* Faith McLellan, *"Like Hunger, Like Thirst": Patients, Journals, and the Internet,* 352 Lancet SII39 (1998).

9. *See* Tara Parker-Pope, *Virtual Second Opinions: When the Web Can Be Better Than Seeing a Local Doc,* Wall Street Journal, August 12, 2003, D1, Tara Parker-Pope, *Research for Hire: Firms Help Patients Find Latest Cures for Chronic Illnesses,* Wall Street Journal, November 26, 2002, D1. *See also* Laura Landro, *HHS Makes It Easier to Find Official Health Data Online,* Wall Street Journal, November 7, 2002, D4 (www.HHS.gov), and Laura Landro, *Going Online to Make Life-and-Death Decisions,* Wall Street Journal, October 10, 2002, D1 (e.g., Mayo Clinic, www.mayo-clinic.com).

10. There are many others, and my not mentioning them does not mean they won't be helpful. *See, e.g.,* the website of P.U.L.S.E. (Persons United Limiting Substandards and Errors in Healthcare), www.pulseamerica.org, an organization dedicated to improving patient safety.

APPENDIX B

*Convention on Human Rights
and Biomedicine*

CHAPTER I—GENERAL PROVISIONS

Article 1—Purpose and object

Parties to this Convention shall protect the dignity and identity of all human beings and guarantee everyone, without discrimination, respect for their integrity and other rights and fundamental freedoms with regard to the application of biology and medicine.

Each Party shall take in its internal law the necessary measures to give effect to the provisions of this Convention.

Article 2—Primacy of the human being

The interests and welfare of the human being shall prevail over the sole interest of society or science.

Article 3—Equitable access to health care

Parties, taking into account health needs and available resources, shall take appropriate measures with a view to providing, within their jurisdiction, equitable access to health care of appropriate quality.

Article 4—Professional standards

Any intervention in the health field, including research, must be carried out in accordance with relevant professional obligations and standards.

CHAPTER II—CONSENT

Article 5—General rule

Any intervention in the health field may only be carried out after the person concerned has given free and informed consent to it.

This person shall beforehand be given appropriate information as to the purpose and nature of the intervention as well as on its consequences and risks.

The person concerned may freely withdraw consent at any time.

Article 6—Protection of persons not able to consent

1. Subject to Articles 17 and 20 below, an intervention may only be carried out on a person who does not have the capacity to consent, for his or her direct benefit.

2. Where, according to law, a minor does not have the capacity to consent to an intervention, the intervention may only be carried out with the authorisation of his or her representative or an authority or a person or body provided by law.

The opinion of the minor shall be taken into consideration as an increasingly determining factor in proportion to his or her age and degree of maturity.

3. Where, according to law, an adult does not have the capacity to consent to an intervention because of a mental disability, a disease or for similar reasons, the intervention may only be carried out with the authorisation of his or her representative or an authority or a person or body provided for by law.

The individual concerned shall as far as possible take part in the authorisation procedure.

4. The representative, the authority, the person or the body mentioned in paragraphs 2 and 3 above shall be given, under the same conditions, the information referred to in Article 5.

5. The authorisation referred to in paragraphs 2 and 3 above may be withdrawn at any time in the best interests of the person concerned.

Article 7—Protection of persons who have mental disorder

Subject to protective conditions by law, including supervisory, control and appeal procedures, a person who has a mental disorder of a serious nature may be subjected, without his or her consent, to an intervention aimed at treating his or her mental disorder only where, without such treatment, serious harm is likely to result to his or her health.

Article 8—Emergency situation

When because of an emergency situation the appropriate consent cannot be obtained, any medically necessary intervention may be carried out immediately for the benefit of the health of the individual concerned.

Article 9—Previously expressed wishes

The previously expressed wishes relating to a medical intervention by a patient who is not, at the time of the intervention, in a state to express his or her wishes shall be taken into account.

Chapter III—Private life and right to information

Article 10—Private life and right to information

1. Everyone has the right to respect for private life in relation to information about his or her health.

2. Everyone is entitled to know any information collected about his or her health. However, the wishes of individuals not to be so informed shall be observed.

3. In exceptional cases, restrictions may be placed by law on the exercise of the rights contained in paragraph 2 in the interests of the patient.

Chapter IV—Human genome

Article 11—Non-discrimination

Any form of discrimination against a person on grounds of his or her genetic heritage is prohibited.

Article 12—Predictive genetic tests

Tests which are predictive of genetic diseases or which serve either to identify the subject as a carrier of a gene responsible for a disease or to detect a genetic predisposition or susceptibility to a disease may be performed only for health purposes or for scientific research linked to health purposes, and subject to appropriate genetic counseling.

Article 13—Interventions on the human genome

An intervention seeking to modify the human genome may only be undertaken for preventive, diagnostic or therapeutic purposes and only if its aim is not to introduce any modification in the genome of any descendants.

Article 14—Non-selection of sex

The use of techniques of medically assisted procreation shall not be allowed for the purpose of choosing a future child's sex, except where serious hereditary sex-related disease is to be avoided.

Chapter V—Scientific Research

Article 15—General rule

Scientific research in the field of biology and medicine shall be carried out freely, subject to the provisions of this Convention and the other legal provisions ensuring the protection of the human being.

Article 16—Protection of persons undergoing research

Research on a person may only be undertaken if all of the following conditions are met:

i. there is no alternative of comparable effectiveness to research on humans,

ii. the risks which may be incurred by that person are not disproportionate to the potential benefits of the research,

iii. the research project has been approved by the competent body after independent examination of its scientific merit, including assessment of the importance of the aim of the research, and multidisciplinary review of its ethical acceptability,

iv. the persons undergoing research have been informed of their rights and the safeguards prescribed by law for their protection,

v. the necessary consent as provided for under Article 5 has been given expressly, specifically and is documented. Such consent may be freely withdrawn at any time.

Article 17—Protection of persons not able to consent to research

1. Research on a person without the capacity to consent as stipulated in Article 5 may be undertaken only if all the following conditions are met:

i. the conditions laid down in Article 16, sub-paragraphs i to iv, are fulfilled;

ii. the results of the research have the potential to produce real and direct benefit to his or her health;

iii. research of comparable effectiveness cannot be carried out on individuals capable of giving consent;

iv. the necessary authorisation provided for under Article 6 has been given specifically and in writing, and

v. the person concerned does not object.

2. Exceptionally and under the protective conditions prescribed by law, where the research has not the potential to produce results of direct benefit to the health of the person concerned, such research may be authorised subject to the conditions laid down in paragraph 1, sub-paragraphs i, iii, iv, and v above, and to the following additional conditions:

i. the research has the aim of contributing, through significant improvement in the scientific understanding of the individual's condition, disease or disorder, to the ultimate attainment of results capable of conferring benefit to the person concerned or to other persons in the same age category or afflicted with the same disease or disorder or having the same condition.

ii. the research entails only minimal risk and minimal burden for the individual concerned.

Article 18—Research on embryos in vitro

1. Where the law allows research on embryos *in vitro*, it shall ensure adequate protection of the embryo.

2. The creation of human embryos for research purposes is prohibited.

CHAPTER VI—ORGAN AND TISSUE REMOVAL FROM
LIVING DONORS FOR TRANSPLANTATION PURPOSES

Article 19—General rule

1. Removal of organs or tissue from a living person for transplantation purposes may be carried out solely for the therapeutic benefit of the recipient and

where there is no suitable organ or tissue available from a deceased person and no other alternative therapeutic method of comparable effectiveness.

2. The necessary consent as provided for under Article 5 must have been given expressly and specifically either in written form or before an official body.

Article 20—Protection of persons not able to consent to organ removal

1. No organ or tissue removal may be carried out on a person who does not have the capacity to consent under Article 5.

2. Exceptionally and under the protective conditions prescribed by law, the removal of regenerative tissue from a person who does not have the capacity to consent may be authorised provided the following conditions are met:

    i. there is no compatible donor available who has the capacity to consent,

    ii. the recipient is a brother or sister of the donor,

    iii. the donation must have the potential to be life-saving for the recipient,

    iv. the authorisation provided for under paragraphs 2 and 3 of Article 6 has been given specifically and in writing, in accordance with the law and with the approval of the competent body,

    v. the potential donor concerned does not object.

CHAPTER VII—PROHIBITION OF FINANCIAL GAIN AND DISPOSAL OF A PART OF THE HUMAN BODY

Article 21—Prohibition of financial gain

The human body and its parts shall not, as such, give rise to financial gain.

Article 22—Disposal of a removed part of the human body

When in the course of an intervention any part of a human body is removed, it may be stored and used for a purpose other than that for which it was removed, only if this is done in conformity with appropriate information and consent procedures.

CHAPTER VIII—INFRINGEMENTS OF THE PROVISIONS OF THE CONVENTION

Article 23—Infringements of the rights or principles

The Parties shall provide appropriate judicial protection to prevent or to put a stop to an unlawful infringement of the rights and principles set forth in this Convention at short notice.

Article 24—Compensation for undue damage

The person who has suffered undue damage resulting from an intervention is entitled to fair compensation according to the conditions and procedures prescribed by law.

Article 25—Sanctions

Parties shall provide for appropriate sanctions to be applied in the event of infringement of the provisions contained in this Convention.

Chapter IX—Relation between this Convention and other provisions

Article 26—Restrictions on the exercise of the rights

1. No restrictions shall be placed on the exercise of the rights and protective provisions contained in this Convention other than such as are prescribed by law and are necessary in a democratic society in the interest of public safety, for the prevention of crime, for the protection of public health or for the protection of the rights and freedoms of others.

2. The restrictions contemplated in the preceding paragraph may not be placed on Articles 11, 13, 14, 16, 17, 19, 20 and 21.

Article 27—Wider protection

None of the provisions of this Convention shall be interpreted as limiting or otherwise affecting the possibility for a Party to grant a wider measure of protection with regard to the application of biology and medicine than is stipulated in this Convention.

APPENDIX C

Childbearing Patient Bills of Rights

THE PREGNANT PATIENT'S BILL OF RIGHTS

1. *The Pregnant Patient has the right,* prior to the administration of any drug or procedure, to be informed by the health professional caring for her of any potential direct or indirect effects, risks or hazards to herself or her unborn or newborn infant which may result from the use of a drug or procedure prescribed for or administered to her during pregnancy, labor, birth, or lactation.

2. *The Pregnant Patient has the right,* prior to proposed therapy, to be informed, not only of the benefits, risks and hazards of the proposed therapy but also of known alternative therapies, such as available childbirth education classes which could help to prepare the Pregnant Patient physically and mentally to cope with the discomfort or stress of pregnancy and the experience of childbirth, thereby reducing or eliminating her need for drugs and obstetric intervention. She should be offered such information early in her pregnancy in order that she may make a reasoned decision.

3. *The Pregnant Patient has the right,* prior to the administration of any drug, to be informed by the health professional who is prescribing or administering the drug to her that any drug which she received during pregnancy, labor and birth, no matter how or when the drug is taken or administered, may adversely affect her unborn baby, directly or indirectly, and that there is no drug or chemical which has been proven safe for the unborn child.

4. *The Pregnant Patient has the right* if cesarean birth is anticipated, to be informed prior to the administration of any drug, and preferably prior to her hospitalization, that minimizing her and, in turn, her baby's intake of nonessential pre-operative medicine will benefit her baby.

5. *The Pregnant Patient has the right,* prior to the administration of a drug or procedure, to be informed of the areas of uncertainty if there is NO properly controlled follow-up research which has established the safety of the drug or procedure with regard to its direct and/or indirect effects on the physiological, mental and neurological development of the child exposed, via the mother, to the drug

375

or procedure during pregnancy, labor birth or lactation- (this would apply to virtually all drugs and the vast majority of obstetric procedures).

6. *The Pregnant Patient has the right,* prior to the administration of any drug, to be informed of the brand name and generic name of the drug in order that she may advise the health professional of any past adverse reaction to the drug.

7. *The Pregnant Patient has the right* to determine for herself, without pressure from her attendant, whether she will accept the risks inherent in the proposed therapy or refuse a drug or procedure.

8. *The Pregnant Patient has the right* to know the name and qualifications of the individual administering a medication or procedure to her during labor or birth.

9. *The Pregnant Patient has the right* to be informed, prior to the administration of any procedure, whether that procedure is being administered to her for her or her baby's benefit (medically indicated) or as an elective procedure (for convenience, teaching purposes or research).

10. *The Pregnant Patient has the right* to be accompanied during the stress of labor and birth by someone she cares for, and to whom she looks for emotional comfort and encouragement.

11. *The Pregnant Patient has the right* after appropriate medical consultation to choose a position for labor and for birth which is least stressful to her baby and to herself.

12. *The Obstetric Patient has the right* to have her baby cared for at her bedside if her baby is normal and to feed her baby according to her baby's needs rather than according to the hospital regimen.

13. *The Obstetric Patient has the right* to be informed in writing of the name of the person who actually delivered her baby and the professional qualifications of that person. This information should also be on the birth certificate.

14. *The Obstetric Patient has the right* to be informed if there is any known or indicated aspect of her or her baby's care or condition which may cause her or her baby later difficulty or problems.

15. *The Obstetric Patient has the right* to have her baby's hospital medical records complete, accurate and legible and to have their records, including Nurses' Notes, retained by the hospital until the child reaches at least the age of majority, or, alternatively, to have the records offered to her before they are destroyed.

16. *The Obstetric Patient,* both during and after her hospital stay, has the right to have access to her complete hospital medical records, including Nurses' Notes, and to receive a copy upon payment of a reasonable fee and without incurring the expense of retaining an attorney.

The Bill of Rights, from the International Childbirth Educational Association, concludes by appropriately noting, "It is the obstetric patient and her baby, not the health professional, who must sustain any trauma or injury resulting from the use of a drug or obstetric procedure. The observation of the rights listed above will not only permit the obstetric patient to participate in the decisions involving her and her baby's health care, but will help to protect the health professional and the hospital against litigation arising from resentment or misunderstanding on the part of the mother." Although this document can be viewed primarily as a political one aimed at helping to encourage change in obstetric practices and at empowering pregnant women, almost all of its provisions have at least some support in the law. Items 1, 7, 8, 9, 11, 13, and 14 can properly be labeled "legal rights," and most of the remainder, including 15 and 16, can be labeled "probable legal rights."[1]

THE RIGHTS OF CHILDBEARING WOMEN

1. Every woman has the right to health care before, during, and after pregnancy and childbirth.

2. Every woman and infant has the right to receive care that is consistent with current scientific evidence about benefits and risks. Practices that have been found to be safe and beneficial should be used when indicated. Harmful, ineffective, or unnecessary practices should be used only in the context of research to evaluate their effects.

3. Every woman has the right to choose a midwife or a physician as her maternity care provider. Both caregivers skilled in normal childbearing and caregivers skilled in complications are needed to ensure quality care for all.

4. Every woman has the right to choose her birth setting from the full range of safe options available in her community, on the basis of complete, objective information about benefits, risks and costs of these options.

5. Every woman has the right to receive all or most of her maternity care from a single caregiver or a small group of caregivers, with whom she can establish a relationship. Every woman has the right to leave her maternity caregiver and select another if she becomes dissatisfied with her care.

6. Every woman has the right to information about the professional identity and qualifications of those involved with her care, and to know when those involved are trainees.

7. Every woman has the right to communicate with caregivers and receive all care in privacy, which may involve excluding nonessential personnel. She also has the right to have all personal information treated according to standards of confidentiality.

8. Every woman has the right to receive maternity care that identifies and addresses social and behavioral factors that affect her health and that of her baby.

She should receive information to help her take the best care of herself and her baby and have access to social services and behavioral change programs that could contribute to their health.

9. Every woman has the right to full and clear information about benefits, risks, and costs of the procedures, drugs, tests and treatments offered to her, and of all other reasonable options, including no intervention. She should receive this information about all interventions that are likely to be offered during labor and birth well before the onset of labor.

10. Every woman has the right to accept or refuse procedures, drugs, tests and treatments, and to have her choices honored. She has the right to change her mind.

11. Every woman has the right to be informed if her caregivers wish to enroll her or her infant in a research study. She should receive full information about all known and possible benefits and risks of participation, and she has the right to decide whether to participate, free from coercion and without negative consequences.

12. Every woman has the right to unrestricted access to all available records about her pregnancy, her labor, and her infant; to obtain a full copy of these records; and to receive help in understanding them, if necessary.

13. Every woman has the right to receive maternity care that is appropriate to her cultural and religious background, and to receive information in a language in which she can communicate.

14. Every woman has the right to have family members and friends of her choice present during all aspects of her maternity care.

15. Every woman has the right to receive continuous social, emotional, and physical support during labor and birth from a caregiver who has been trained in labor support.

16. Every woman has the right to receive full advance information about risks and benefits of all reasonably available methods for relieving pain during labor and birth, including methods that do not require the use of drugs. She has the right to choose which methods will be used and to change her mind at any time.

17. Every woman has the right to freedom of movement during labor, unencumbered by tubes, wires, or other apparatus. She also has the right to give birth in the position of her choice.

18. Every woman has the right to virtually uninterrupted contact with her newborn from the moment of birth, as long as she and her baby are healthy and do not need care that requires separation.

19. Every woman has the right to receive complete information about the benefits of breastfeeding well in advance of labor, to refuse supplemental bottles

and other actions that interfere with breastfeeding, and to have access to skilled lactation support for as long as she chooses to breastfeed.

20. Every woman has the right to decide collaboratively with caregivers when she and her baby will leave the birth site for home, based on their condition and circumstances.

All but the first three items of this bill of rights, from the Maternity Center Association, are currently recognized as probable legal rights.[2]

Notes

1. ICEA Publications Center, P.O. Box 9316, Midtown Plaza, Rochester, NY 14604.
2. Maternity Center Association, 281 Park Ave. So., 5th floor, New York, NY 10010.

INDEX